AFTER JESUS

THE TRIUMPH OF CHRISTIANITY

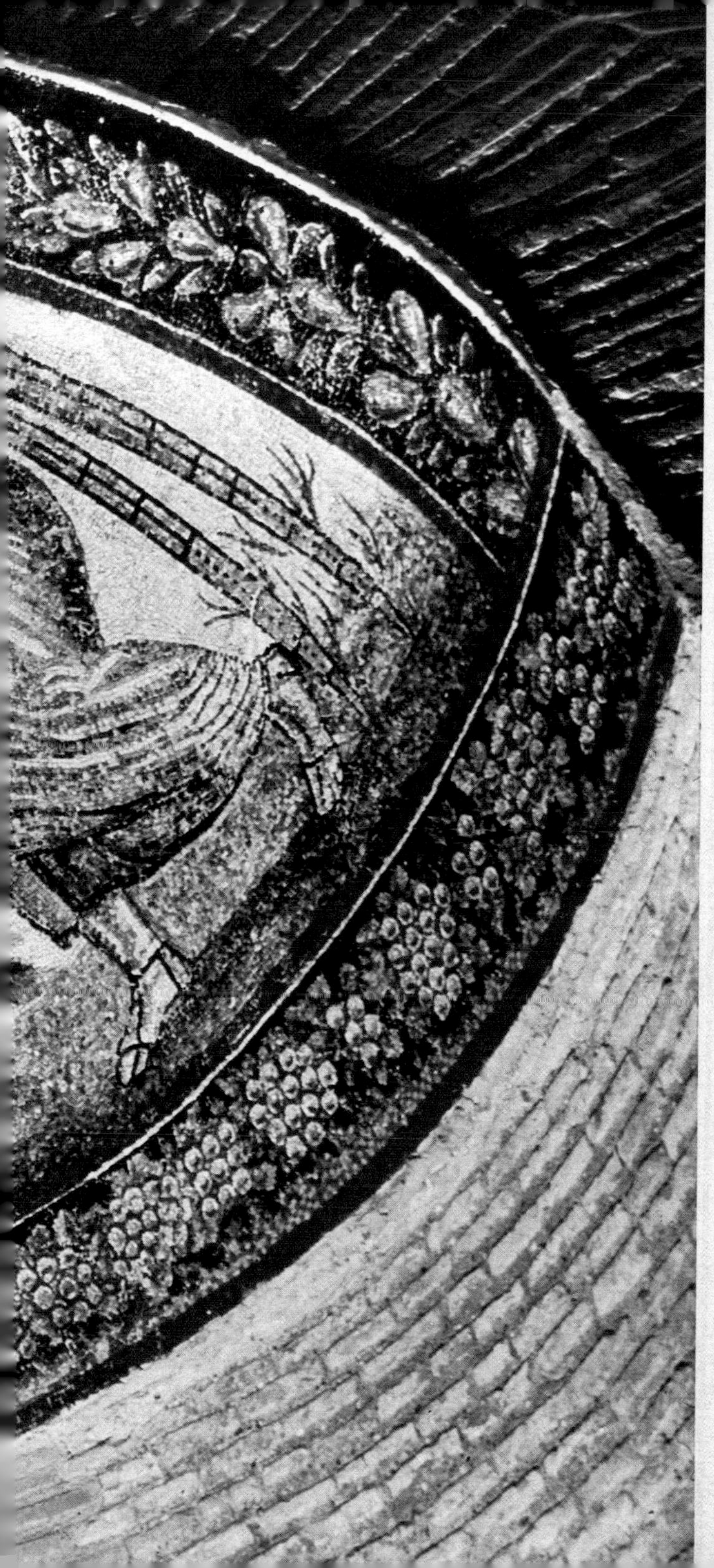

AFTER JESUS

THE TRIUMPH OF CHRISTIANITY

The Reader's Digest Association, Inc.
Pleasantville, New York   Montreal

COVER: *It was a moment of triumph in the summer of* A.D. *452, when Pope Leo I persuaded Attila the Hun not to attack Rome. Leo is shown here being greeted by excited crowds on his return from meeting with the barbarian leader, as he rides past the original basilica of St. Peter's on Vatican Hill.*

TITLE PAGE: ***(Left)*** *A fourth-century mosaic from Rome's Santa Costanza Church shows Christ bestowing the keys of authority upon Peter (Matthew 16:19).* ***(Right)*** *This anchor symbol from a Christian tombstone in Rome's catacombs dates from the third century, when Christians were still persecuted. The anchor represents the security provided by church membership. The two fishes stand for church members.*

AFTER JESUS

STAFF

Editor: Gayla Visalli
Art Editor: Evelyn Bauer
Senior Editor: David Rattray
Senior Associate Editor: Barbara C. Loos
Senior Research Editor: Hildegard B. Anderson
Research Associate: Barbara A. Guarino
Art Associate: Martha Grossman
Editorial Assistant: Jeffrey L. Akellian

CONTRIBUTORS

Art Associate: Ann Terrell
Art Production Associate: Sandra Berinstein
Writers: Jane R. Baun, Rita G. Christopher, Donald R. Cutler, Marleen B. Flory, Charles Flowers, Robert Kiener, Robert Thurston, Edward Wakin, Peter Young
Researchers: Mary Hart, Tim Guzley, Raïssa Silverman, Sara Solberg
Picture Researcher: Sybille Millard
Copy Editor: Susan Converse Winslow
Indexer: Sydney Wolfe Cohen

PRINCIPAL ADVISERS AND CONSULTANTS

Jaroslav Pelikan, *Sterling Professor of History, Yale University*
Thomas L. Robinson, *Quondam Professor of Biblical Studies, Union Theological Seminary*

EDITORIAL CONSULTANTS

Robert B. Eno, S.S., *Professor of Church History, The Catholic University of America*
Cyril Mango, *Bywater and Sotheby Professor of Byzantine and Modern Greek Language and Literature, Oxford University*

READER'S DIGEST GENERAL BOOKS

Editor in Chief: John A. Pope, Jr.
Managing Editor: Jane Polley
Executive Editor: Susan J. Wernert
Art Director: David Trooper
Group Editors: Will Bradbury, Norman B. Mack, Kaari Ward
Group Art Editors: Evelyn Bauer, Robert M. Grant, Joel Musler
Chief of Research: Laurel A. Gilbride
Copy Chief: Edward W. Atkinson
Picture Editor: Richard Pasqual
Rights and Permissions: Pat Colomban
Head Librarian: Jo Manning

The acknowledgments and credits that appear on pages 337–340 are hereby made a part of this copyright page.

Library of Congress Cataloging in Publication Data

After Jesus : the triumph of Christianity.
p. cm.
Includes bibliographical references and index.
ISBN 0-89577-392-9
1. Church history—Primitive and early church, ca. 30–600.
BR162.2.A34 1992
270.1—dc20 91-8873

Printed in the United States of America

CONTENTS

Introduction

THE EXPECTED MESSIAH

Early Christians liked to picture Jesus as the Good Shepherd, a perfect embodiment of the protective, caring community.

People everywhere sensed that an era was ending and a messianic king might be arriving any day. Jesus was one of the many candidates, but his death seemed to doom the movement that had grown up around him. News of his Resurrection changed everything.

The death of Jesus was not an end but a beginning. A band of Jews, believers in a Messiah who would ultimately be rejected even by their own nation, a group scorned as a superstitious rabble by cultured Greeks and Romans, began to spread a strange and distinctive message. Almost reflexively, the immense power of the Roman Empire set itself against the growing sect, and within a short time just to be a Christian had become a capital offense. Erratic but often ferocious persecutions buffeted the movement, forcing its members to defend themselves both in their way of life and in their literature. As Christianity expanded, it survived slander, hatred, and internal dissensions to gain power and respectability, and after some 300 years it even won control of its onetime enemy, the Roman Empire.

The triumph of Christianity brought with it an awareness that a new, or modern, world distinct from the ancient world had come into being. The very term *modern* comes from the writings of the sixth-century Christian statesman Cassiodorus. Christianity was to represent not only a break with the past but a means of transmitting the Greco-Roman heritage to later generations. The preservation of pagan civilization can also be counted as a Christian triumph.

The mystery remains: Why did the curtain rise on this drama just as Jesus met his end on a cross in Jerusalem? Historians debate the exact course of events in the crucial weeks after his death, but there is no doubt that as the story "After Jesus" begins, his disciples have been changed by their experiences—changed miraculously, they believe—and are ready to carry on Jesus' mission. One might imagine that since Jesus had provoked so much opposition and had been crucified, his disciples might have left his person in the background and put the emphasis only on his teachings. On the contrary, they stressed Jesus himself as the long-prophesied Messiah.

Most Jews thought about the coming Messiah in glorious terms. He would be a great king like his ancestor David. He would overthrow oppression, destroy idolatry, establish justice, and bring peace. In place of such great expectations the disciples proclaimed that a small-town carpenter, crucified by the Roman governor, was the Messiah.

To speak of the Messiah and crucifixion in the same breath seemed a contradiction—scandalous, foolish. It is often hard for present-day people, after the cross has been glorified for so many centuries, to imagine the disgrace linked with crucifixion during Roman times. For the ancients, the word itself carried not a single positive connotation. It implied that the crucified person was one who had so offended the much admired laws of Rome as to deserve the most severe and demeaning punishment. Such a person could hardly be a savior.

Early Christians met these objections by asserting that God had shown Jesus to be the Messiah (or, in New Testament terms, the Christ) by the very act of raising him from the dead. Indeed, the idea of a crucified Messiah was such an astonishing reality that it overturned many of the religious doctrines and expectations they had formerly held. Centuries were to pass, however, before Christians felt at ease representing Jesus on the cross pictorially. In the early days they embraced more positive images of him, such as the Good Shepherd bearing a lamb on his shoulders.

A kaleidoscope of images

Jesus left behind not a single word of his own writing. He was known only through traditions based on the disciples' memories. Yet the faith he elicited in those disciples set off an explosion of creative reflection about God's purposes and Jesus' role within them. That explosion rumbled through the centuries discussed in this book and indeed reverberates today.

The image of Jesus passes through kaleidoscopic transformations as one follows the developments of Christian thought through the ages. Controversies, schisms, even violent confrontations, have raged over the nature of Christ. Given the crucial importance placed on the person of the Christ and the indirect character of all knowledge of him, it is difficult to see how things could have been different. Generation after generation of believers looked back to the great figure of Jesus and saw him through the lens of the particular concerns of their time.

The New Testament shows that divergent understandings of Jesus go back to the time of his own ministry. Jesus asked his disciples, "Who do men say that I am?" They responded with seemingly wild speculation that he might be Elijah or John the Baptist risen from the dead. As recorded in Mark 8:31, Simon Peter spoke for the disciples in saying to Jesus, "You are the Christ." But Jesus himself went immediately beyond that confession by foretelling his impending sufferings and death.

During the first decades after Jesus' ministry, the memories of his teachings, healings, and way of life had to be integrated into the knowledge of his death and Resurrection. Those who followed "in Jesus' footsteps" remembered his life, interpreted those memories in the light of the Scriptures, and applied the result to their own lives. All were confident that Christ had opened a new way of salvation, but some drew more radical conclusions than others. Men such as Stephen, described in Acts as "full of grace and power," stirred up anger by proclaiming that Jesus had made the Temple in Jerusalem and all of its sacrifices obsolete. Stephen's interpretation of Jesus was explosive because it profoundly challenged the Law of Moses and thereby set the theme for the first great controversy about the meaning of Jesus. Stephen's declarations also led to his own martyrdom and to the persecution of his like-minded brethren.

Was Jesus the Messiah who confirmed Mosaic Law and empowered his disciples to fulfill those ancient commandments, or did he offer forgiveness and salvation apart from the Law, Temple sacrifices, and circumcision, offering them to Jews and non-Jews alike? Profoundly different futures opened before the new faith, depending on the answers to those questions.

Ironically it was a strict Pharisee named Paul who became the advocate for Stephen's vision, as the new faith spread from Jerusalem to such great cities as Rome and Antioch. Paul powerfully portrayed the image of Christ on the cross as God's own sacrifice for sin, a sacrifice to benefit all humanity, apart from the Law of Moses. Remembering Christ's death in the joyful and serious celebration of the Lord's Supper became the centerpiece of Christian worship.

Paul's letters show, however, that throughout his life equally fervent Christians presented the opposing vision of a Christ who brings salvation to the Gentiles by teaching them to observe the Law of Moses, including its commandment of circumcision. His letters also reflect that some Christians found his stress on the Crucifixion uninspiring at best. They advocated a vision of Jesus that emphasized not his disgraceful execution but his miraculous powers, powers that they claimed to continue manifesting. Yet other early Christians stressed not so much Jesus' miracles or his Crucifixion as his prophetic teaching and challenge to live a self-sacrificing way of life.

Integrating the images

Many in the following generation of "heirs of Jesus Christ" sought to integrate these diverse images of Jesus. Each of the four Gospels is an in-depth presentation of the treasured traditions. Some questions that confounded the preceding generation have been settled. Others, such as the growing break between Christianity and Judaism, are reflected in all of the Gospels. All the Gospels also treat the Passion in greater detail than any other part of his story. And yet, despite their common elements, each Gospel offers a unique vision of Jesus. Each evangelist has told the story in a way that interprets it for the needs of his particular community of believers. No one of the Gospels can be substituted for another.

As the church early in the second century stepped farther out onto the world stage and began "defending the faith" before a wider audience, new images of Jesus came into use. The apologist Justin Martyr tried to link the gospel to the philosophical movements of his time by speaking of Christ as a preexistent Logos ("Word," or "Reason") that had spoken at times through such philosophers as Socrates but had become incarnate only in Jesus. In this light, Christianity was the only truly rational belief.

Other teachers pushed far beyond the bounds of traditional belief. The reformer Marcion saw in Jesus the emissary of a previously unknown God, wholly different from the God of the Old Testament. Gnostic teachers developed elaborate mythologies in which Jesus was the final emanation of a distant, unreachable Divinity and the revealer of mystic knowledge. A new image of Christ, manifested in newly created secret gospels, was for them the vehicle to express a profound sense of alienation from the world that many felt in the second and third centuries. More traditional Christian authors defended the four canonical Gospels and the Christian belief in the God of the Old Testament as the Father of Jesus Christ.

As the church grew to be a major force in the empire, Christians strove to clarify their image of Christ. Some saw him as a man adopted by God as his son. Others saw him as a manifestation of God himself. Followers of an influential theologian named Arius believed that Jesus was the first and noblest creature of God, supreme above all creations but a creature nonetheless. Against this view, Bishop Athanasius and his followers insisted on the seemingly impossible paradox that Christ was fully God and fully man. The variations on these images seemed endless.

The evolving structure of the church raised the stakes and intensity of the debate. The church had survived persecution, heresy, and schism by developing internal discipline and a hierarchy of authority that mirrored the empire's. But such a structure tended to demand unity of thought and belief, especially as the church began to move from the shadow of illegality into the sunlight of official patronage. On the basis of Scripture and tradition, honest people could and did disagree about theological issues, but imperial policy promoted a united church under the authority of the emperor. Dissent thus became treason. Dissident clergy were exiled, imprisoned, sometimes even killed.

From the vantage point of the present day, when religious pluralism is tolerated in numerous countries where beliefs are considered matters of individual conscience rather than state policy, the account of these battles over theology may seem bewildering. But the combatants themselves understood viscerally that what was at stake was not just a correct interpretation of Scripture or a philosophical debating point or even ecclesiastical power and control. The debates defined the basic images through which many people perceived their world and their place in it. A clear understanding of basic issues may have seemed the only possible alternative to chaos.

One may certainly regret that warring armies ever engaged in mutual slaughter in the name of Christ, but one cannot deny that the image of Christ—as an ascetic, as a warrior, as a cosmic ruler, as a focus of mystic contemplation, as a man elevated by God, as God descending to man, or as God and man existing simultaneously—has held the minds of the people of many ages with an unshakable power. When we see today the light of Jesus in the eyes of a child hearing the Christmas story, in the labors of a theologian who is struggling to penetrate the mysteries of faith, or in the voice and touch of a Mother Teresa ministering to the outcasts of Calcutta, we know the story continues and lives as powerfully as ever—and all from such hopeless beginnings. Who could have imagined!

These mosaics of sixth-century Ravenna show favorite conceptions of Jesus current in late antiquity and the early Middle Ages. At left, Christ as a youthful warrior tramples the lion and the serpent of temptation in the wilderness of this world. The open book reads, "I am the way, the truth, and the life" (John 14:6). At right, Christ as the merciful judge sits enthroned in heaven amid blue-haloed angels, his right hand raised in benediction.

CHRONOLOGY

600 Years at a Glance

During the period covered in this book, classical antiquity came to an end, paganism gradually died out, and a civilization based on Christianity began to take shape. A brief overview of the process is given in the following chart.

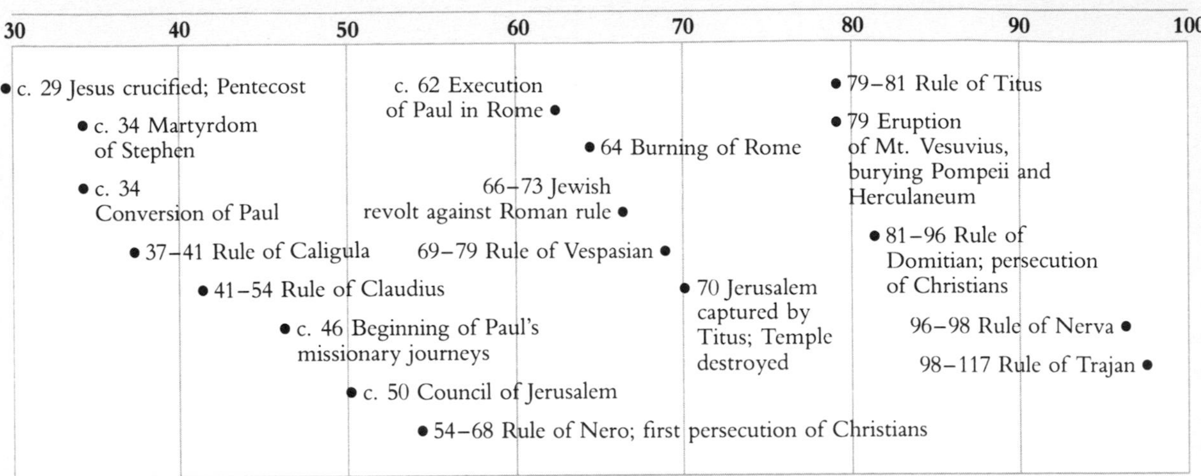

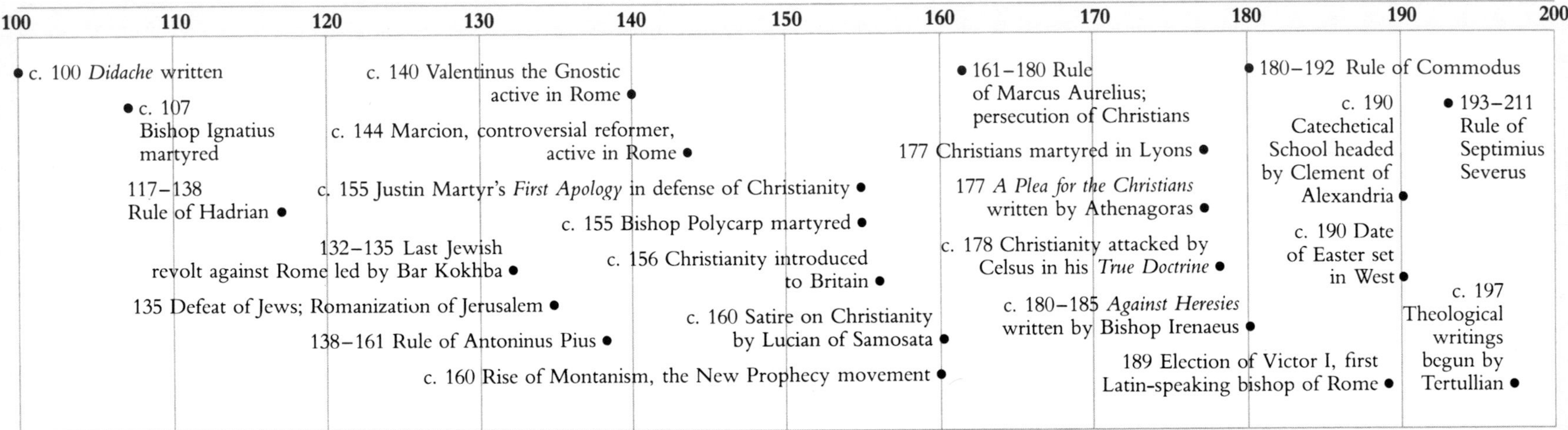

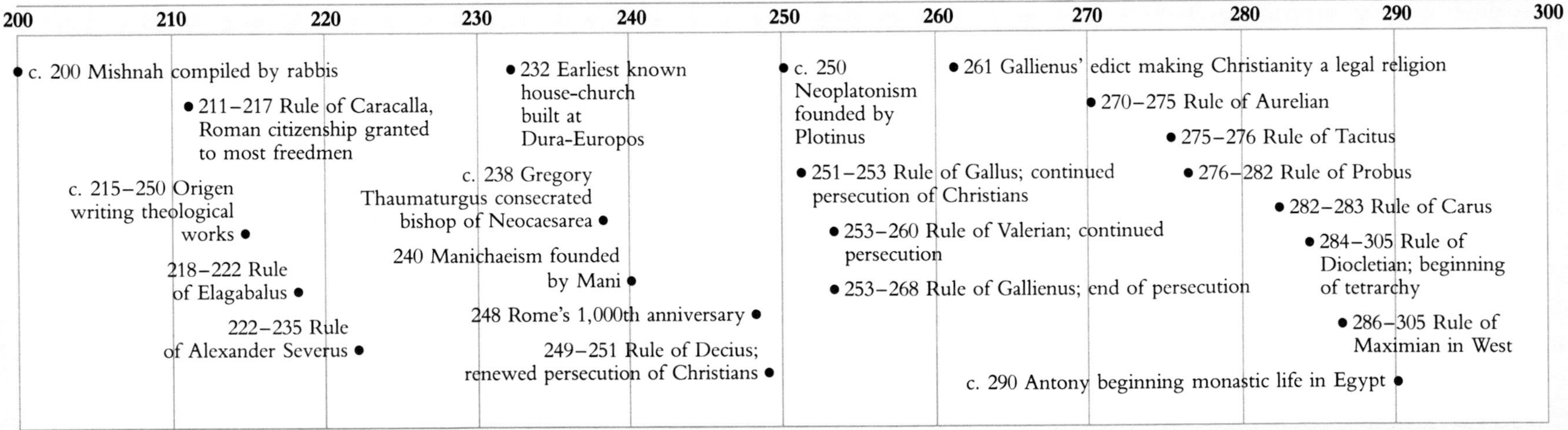

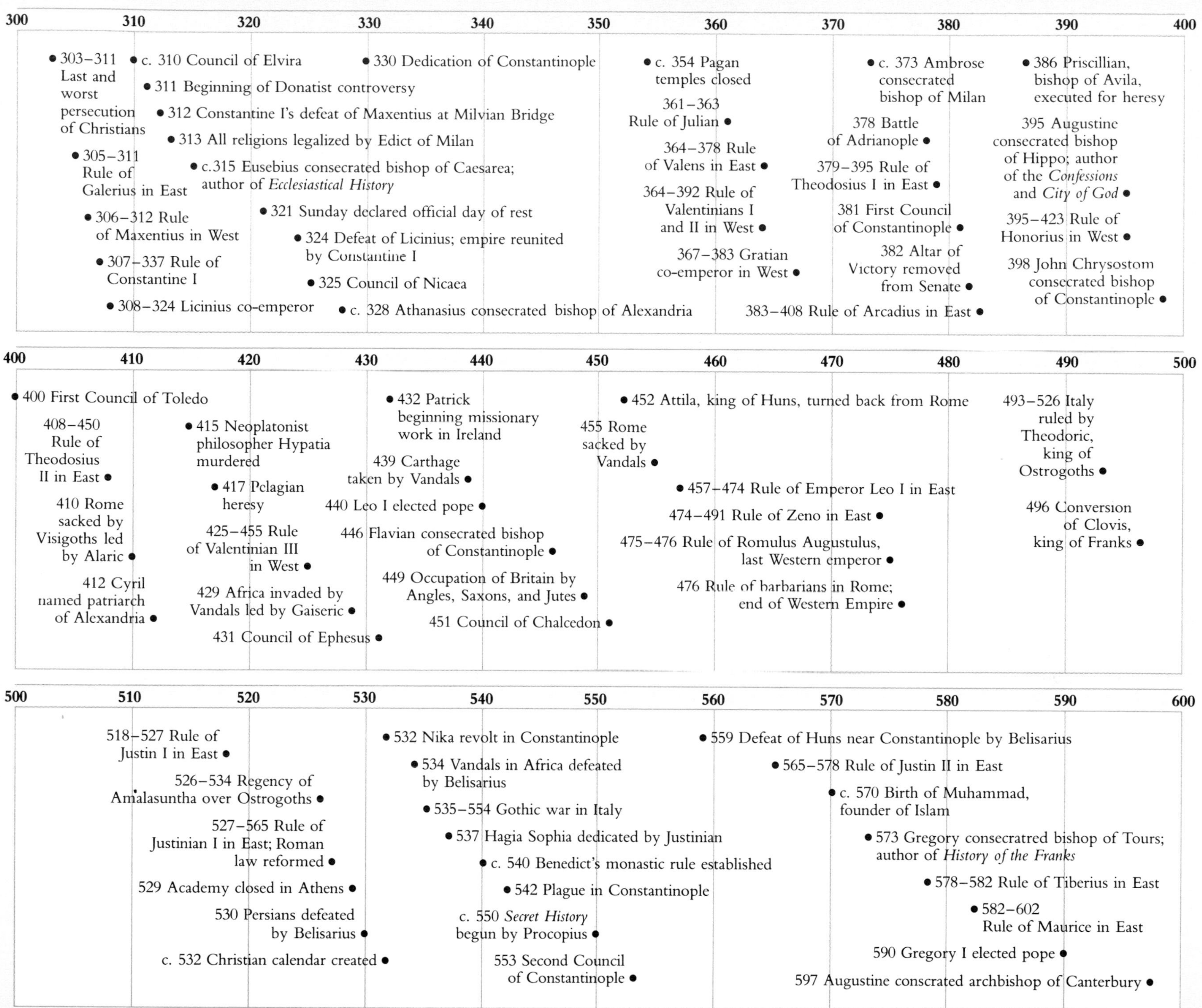

300
310
320
330
340
350
360
370
380
390
400
303–311 Last and worst persecution of Christians
c. 310 Council of Elvira
330 Dedication of Constantinople
c. 354 Pagan temples closed
c. 373 Ambrose consecrated bishop of Milan
386 Priscillian, bishop of Avila, executed for heresy
311 Beginning of Donatist controversy
361–363 Rule of Julian
312 Constantine I's defeat of Maxentius at Milvian Bridge
378 Battle of Adrianople
395 Augustine consecrated bishop of Hippo; author of the *Confessions* and *City of God*
313 All religions legalized by Edict of Milan
364–378 Rule of Valens in East
305–311 Rule of Galerius in East
c.315 Eusebius consecrated bishop of Caesarea; author of *Ecclesiastical History*
379–395 Rule of Theodosius I in East
364–392 Rule of Valentinians I and II in West
321 Sunday declared official day of rest
381 First Council of Constantinople
395–423 Rule of Honorius in West
306–312 Rule of Maxentius in West
324 Defeat of Licinius; empire reunited by Constantine I
367–383 Gratian co-emperor in West
382 Altar of Victory removed from Senate
307–337 Rule of Constantine I
398 John Chrysostom consecrated bishop of Constantinople
325 Council of Nicaea
308–324 Licinius co-emperor
c. 328 Athanasius consecrated bishop of Alexandria
383–408 Rule of Arcadius in East
400
410
420
430
440
450
460
470
480
490
500
400 First Council of Toledo
432 Patrick beginning missionary work in Ireland
452 Attila, king of Huns, turned back from Rome
493–526 Italy ruled by Theodoric, king of Ostrogoths
408–450 Rule of Theodosius II in East
415 Neoplatonist philosopher Hypatia murdered
455 Rome sacked by Vandals
439 Carthage taken by Vandals
417 Pelagian heresy
457–474 Rule of Emperor Leo I in East
410 Rome sacked by Visigoths led by Alaric
440 Leo I elected pope
496 Conversion of Clovis, king of Franks
474–491 Rule of Zeno in East
425–455 Rule of Valentinian III in West
446 Flavian consecrated bishop of Constantinople
475–476 Rule of Romulus Augustulus, last Western emperor
449 Occupation of Britain by Angles, Saxons, and Jutes
412 Cyril named patriarch of Alexandria
429 Africa invaded by Vandals led by Gaiseric
476 Rule of barbarians in Rome; end of Western Empire
451 Council of Chalcedon
431 Council of Ephesus
500
510
520
530
540
550
560
570
580
590
600
518–527 Rule of Justin I in East
532 Nika revolt in Constantinople
559 Defeat of Huns near Constantinople by Belisarius
534 Vandals in Africa defeated by Belisarius
565–578 Rule of Justin II in East
526–534 Regency of Amalasuntha over Ostrogoths
c. 570 Birth of Muhammad, founder of Islam
535–554 Gothic war in Italy
527–565 Rule of Justinian I in East; Roman law reformed
537 Hagia Sophia dedicated by Justinian
573 Gregory consecratred bishop of Tours; author of *History of the Franks*
c. 540 Benedict's monastic rule established
529 Academy closed in Athens
542 Plague in Constantinople
578–582 Rule of Tiberius in East
530 Persians defeated by Belisarius
c. 550 *Secret History* begun by Procopius
582–602 Rule of Maurice in East
590 Gregory I elected pope
c. 532 Christian calendar created
553 Second Council of Constantinople
597 Augustine conscrated archbishop of Canterbury

Chapter One

IN JESUS' FOOTSTEPS

Jesus told his disciples to go forth and preach in his name to all nations as soon as they were "clothed with power from on high." The dramatic coming of the Holy Spirit to guide believers along the way transformed his anxious followers into a joyous and dynamic fellowship.

On a fateful summer morning, in about the year A.D. 29, some 120 followers of a Jewish teacher named Jesus gathered in Jerusalem. The atmosphere of their meeting was charged with the excitement of the feast day—Pentecost—a wheat-harvest festival celebrated 50 days after Passover. Suddenly something arrived among them: it had the sound of a wind, like a mighty storm sweeping out of heaven and filling the house. And they saw something: it looked like tongues of fire that divided and seemed to sit burning on each of them. But most important, they experienced power, as God's Holy Spirit filled them. When this force, which they had never felt before, surged within them, the company of disciples knew that their lives had been permanently changed. They went forth into a burgeoning throng of curious pilgrims, who had heard the noise as they were heading for the Temple. The disciples began to speak as they had never spoken before, and those who heard them understood as if each were being spoken to in the tongue of his homeland.

On the day of Pentecost, after Jesus' death, his disciples were suddenly filled with the Holy Spirit and began to speak excitedly about the works of God. Strangely, their ecstatic words were heard not as a Galilean dialect of Aramaic (their native language) but as all the languages spoken by the pilgrims visiting Jerusalem.

Who were these disciples and what had brought them together? As described near the beginning of the New Testament book The Acts of the Apostles, this group was centered around the 11 who remained of Jesus' 12 closest disciples. Jesus had designated these men as his special Apostles, or emissaries, and now they were led by one of their number, Simon Peter. The missing Apostle, Judas Iscariot, who had betrayed Jesus to his enemies, was dead. While the Gospel of Matthew says he hanged himself in remorse, Acts states that he died in a headlong fall. The place of his demise, a site outside Jerusalem, is known as the Field of Blood, for it was supposedly bought with the blood money, or 30 pieces of silver, that Judas had received for his betrayal of Jesus.

The fact that Jesus had chosen Twelve Apostles was significant, since the number possibly symbolized the 12 tribes of Israel. The Apostles determined to restore their complement by casting lots to choose a replacement for Judas, believing that God would then manifest his will. The lot fell to Matthias, a disciple who had followed Jesus throughout his ministry and could bear witness to his Resurrection.

The company also included scores of other disciples who joined the Apostles in continual prayer. Most are unknown, but among those mentioned by name in the New Testament were Jesus' mother, Mary, and the young men who were believed by many to be his brothers, perhaps all four—James, Joseph, Simon, and Judas. In his Gospel, Luke also makes note of women who had followed and supported Jesus while he was still in Galilee and had accompanied him to Jerusalem. These included Mary from Magdala in Galilee (known to us as Mary Magdalene); Joanna, the aristocratic wife of Chuza, who was the steward of Herod Antipas; and also the mother of James and John, two of the Twelve. She had evidently joined her sons in following Jesus from Galilee to Jerusalem.

When the disciples gathered on the morning of Pentecost, they were united by a common sense of expectation and a shared awareness of events just past. Their teacher, Jesus, had been executed by the Roman governor of Judea seven weeks earlier, and the despair they felt then had made them think of disbanding. But something had happened. Through a series of gripping encounters and remarkable visions, many of the followers, if not all, had come to the firm conviction that they had seen Jesus alive again. They realized that his work was not finished and that they themselves were to continue it.

The group had pulsed with expectation since Jesus' last appearance 10 days earlier, when he had promised his Apostles that they would be witnesses for him "in Jerusalem and in all Judea and Samaria and to the end of the earth." They had been filled with wonder at his words, no doubt, but in their wildest dreams they could hardly have imagined the glory and pain, drama and history, that would flow from that commission. They were a band of disciples whose testimony was destined to change the world.

Together they had spent the last 10 days in seclusion, as the narrow streets and the great plazas of Jerusalem were coming alive, filling with the clamor of thousands visiting the city for Pentecost. Although not every male Jew could, as the law commanded, journey to the Temple each year for the festival, many pilgrims assembled from every part of Palestine and the huge Diaspora, or Dispersion, of Jews who lived in communities from Rome to Babylon. The costumes and languages of diverse lands filled the city as the celebrants brought offerings of new grain and loaves of bread and lambs to present to God in the Temple.

Recollections of Jesus

We will never know just what those disciples were thinking or expecting that morning as they came to this moment of personal and historic transformation, though for some, at least, we have a few hints. Acts names the Twelve Apostles: "Peter and John and James and Andrew, Philip and Thomas, Bartholomew and Matthew, James the son of Alphaeus and Simon the Zealot and Judas the son of James" and then finally Matthias. Several of these Apostles are hardly more than names. Still, through the New Testament some remarkable recollections about the group have come down to us, enough to allow us several glimpses of the memories that might have flowed through their minds as they reflected on how their lives had been changed.

In the forefront was Simon Peter (who was also called Cephas), about whom more is known than any of the others. Only a few years earlier his name had been just Simon, and he, with his brother Andrew, was settled into the steady, small-town life of a fisherman on the Sea of Galilee. His daily concerns had been the condition of their nets and boat, how the carp and tilapia were running in the lake, what prices they could get in the markets of Capernaum, and whether or not they could pay their taxes to Herod Antipas and the Roman overlords.

Several stories are told of Simon's early encounters with Jesus. Perhaps he remembered the day when his brother Andrew, who had gone to hear the prophet John the Baptist, had hurried back to him with the news that the Messiah, God's anointed deliverer, had been discovered. Andrew then had taken Simon to meet a carpenter named Joshua, or Jesus, from the little town of Nazareth. Or he might have reflected on the moment when he and Andrew were casting a net as they stood in the shallows along the shore, and Jesus had walked by. Jesus said simply, "Follow me and I will make you become fishers of men." They did not understand what he meant, but his presence, the authority with which he spoke, seemed to compel them to follow.

Simon had become Jesus' closest companion, fiercely loyal to him, though often perplexed by his ministry. On one occasion when Simon was traveling with Jesus and other disciples near the northern sources of the Jordan River, they had been talking of the rumors and reports that had spread about Jesus. Some said he was Elijah or Jeremiah or some other prophet come to life. Jesus had turned to them and asked pointedly, "But who do you say that I am?" At that moment Simon must have felt the words come rushing from him, "You are the Christ."

Perhaps by the day of Pentecost more painful memories had faded—that he had rebuked Jesus when first told of his coming suffering, or that he had boasted of his loyalty and then, when Jesus was on trial for his life, denied, more than once, that he knew him. The moment had come for Simon to step forth and proclaim a message never heard before.

Many believed that the place where the disciples waited for the descent of the Holy Spirit at Pentecost was the same "upper room" where the Last Supper was celebrated. Though no one knows the site of those events, this room in the Church of St. Mary of Zion in Jerusalem was built to commemorate them. The silver coins below are like those given to Judas Iscariot for betraying Jesus after the Last Supper.

As a tax collector, the Apostle Matthew would have received coins like the one above bearing the image of Tiberius. Taxes had to be paid in coinage that carried the likeness and name of a Roman emperor.

The fishermen John and James, sons of Zebedee, who had also abandoned their nets to join Jesus' innermost circle, might have been thinking about why he had called them "sons of thunder." Once, when a Samaritan village had refused entrance to Jesus, the hotheaded brothers had asked him to command a fire from heaven to consume the village. Jesus, of course, had declined. Another time, according to the Gospel of Mark, they had asked their master if they could sit beside him in heaven, and Jesus had said, "You do not know what you are asking."

Others in the company had their own recollections of Jesus as one who had redirected their lives and brought them to this Pentecost. Matthew, for example, could recall his former life as a collector of taxes and tolls under Herod Antipas in Capernaum. It was a living, but he and everyone else knew that Herod was Rome's puppet and that by collecting taxes Matthew was strengthening Rome's oppressive hold on the people. That made him a despised outsider to nearly everybody except others like himself. He certainly never expected a teacher like Jesus to have anything for him but rebukes. But to his surprise Jesus had come to him at his toll station and called him to be a follower. Not only that, Jesus had dined with him and his tax-collector friends and others ostracized from the community. "I came not to call the righteous," Jesus had said, "but sinners." Since then, Matthew had never looked back.

Tax collectors were generally despised for their role in exacting tribute for Rome and were not allowed to hold public or religious office. However, their job provided opportunities to acquire considerable wealth.

On the morning of Pentecost Matthew might have looked across the room and seen the Simon who was known as a Zealot, or in Aramaic, a Cananaean. He was a man evidently linked to one of the rag-tag guerrilla groups that out of zeal for God's law tried to keep up active opposition to every aspect of Roman rule over God's people. Before Jesus had called them both, Simon had despised everything that Matthew stood for, and the feeling was surely mutual. But now they were together, experiencing the same spirit, fellow witnesses to a teacher who had bridged chasms of politics and society.

The Apostle Thomas possibly reflected on his own doubts and faith. An ardent follower of Jesus, he had been ready to risk anything for him. Once when it appeared that Jesus was going into a dangerous situation, where he might have been killed by stoning, Thomas had urged his fellow disciples, "Let us also go, that we may die with him." But later, when Jesus had died alone, Thomas evidently thought that everything was over. When others told him, "We have seen the Lord," he could not risk faith. "Unless I see in his hands the print of the nails, and place my finger in the mark of the nails, and place my hand in his side," he had vowed, "I will not believe." For eight days he lived with his doubts and fears, unable to bring himself to share the faith and sense of peace that had been restored to the other disciples. But then, as the Gospel of John recounts, Jesus himself came and showed Thomas his wounds and urged him, "Do not be faithless, but believing."

Among the group also was Philip, from the same town in Galilee as Peter and Andrew, and probably his friend Nathanael. (Since the early Middle Ages some scholars have argued that Nathanael may actually be the same person as Bartholomew, one of the Twelve, but there is no way to be sure.) Philip would have remembered with wonder the day when Jesus had come to him and said, "Follow me." Later Philip had told Nathanael, "We have found him of whom Moses in the law and also the prophets wrote, Jesus of Nazareth, the son of Joseph." Nathanael had tartly retorted, "Can anything good come out of Nazareth?" Philip simply invited him, "Come and see."

If ever there was an opposite to cautious Thomas, it was Nathanael. The first time Jesus saw him, he characterized the man as "an Israelite indeed, in whom is no guile!" and indicated that he had seen him before (in a vision). That was enough for Nathanael. "Rabbi," he exclaimed, "you are the Son of God! You are the King of Israel!"

The Last Supper

Besides their personal recollections of incidents preceding Pentecost, the Apostles waiting expectantly that day had memories of events they had shared. These became part of the heritage they passed on to later believers. One incident in particular had puzzled them at the time it occurred; this was the Last Supper, a feast of fellowship in which Jesus and the Twelve Apostles had participated the evening before his death. As they sat around the table, Jesus had shocked the gathering by predicting that he would be arrested soon because of treachery by someone at the table.

As the Gospel of John recalled the event, Jesus announced: "Truly, truly, I say to you, one of you will betray me." When asked, "Lord, who is it?" Jesus answered, "It is he to whom I shall give this morsel." He then gave the morsel to Judas Iscariot.

There were other astonishing events at the Last Supper. The Apostles might even have reminisced about them: Jesus quite unexpectedly washing the feet of his disciples to give them an image of the kind of service they should be ready to offer one another and others; Jesus giving each of them bread and wine, saying, "Take; this is my body. . . . This is my blood . . . , which is poured out for many"; and Jesus bidding his disciples to cleave to the belief that he would soon return and that eventually the Holy Spirit would sustain and guide them.

After supper, Jesus went to pray in the Garden of Gethsemane, where, as Judas knew, he was in the habit of meeting with the disciples. It was there that Judas singled him out for arrest. The soldiers brought Jesus before the high priest and the Sanhedrin, the 71-man council of Jerusalem's Jews. At this tribunal, the council accused Jesus of claiming to be the Christ, the Son of God, a blasphemy that in their eyes deserved the death sentence. They condemned him forthwith and turned him over to Pontius Pilate, the Roman prefect, or governor, of Judea.

When Pilate asked him if he was King of the Jews, Jesus replied, "You have said so." Pilate then examined Jesus, asking for his defense against the charges, but Jesus made no reply. Now Pilate was faced with a dilemma. He did not want to appease the Jewish councilors by granting their request (it is known that he had an intense dislike for the Jews); but then it might be politically risky to release a man who had supposedly declared himself to be a king. Perhaps he could get the people themselves to let Jesus go. Since it was the custom for the governor to release

Continued on page 21

Former fishermen, Peter, Andrew, John, and James left their calling, first to follow Jesus as he preached the gospel, then to spread the word of his Resurrection and promise of salvation. The typical fisherman below, cast in bronze in the late fourth or early fifth century, has a net slung over his right shoulder and what is probably a tiller in his left hand; standing 7 inches high, he decorates a bollard—a post for mooring lines.

"I will pour out my Spirit."

The mysteries of the Last Supper, Crucifixion, Resurrection, and Ascension of Jesus Christ were "mighty works and wonders and signs" evincing the power of the Holy Spirit. The gift of tongues at Pentecost enabled the disciples to proclaim God's message to the world.

"And suddenly a sound came from heaven like the rush of a mighty wind, and it filled all the house where they were sitting. And there appeared to them tongues as of fire, distributed and resting on each one of them." Acts 2:2–3. Above, a 16th-century stained-glass depiction of Pentecost.

"Now as they were eating, Jesus took bread, and blessed, and broke it, and gave it to the disciples and said, 'Take, eat; this is my body.' And he took a cup, and when he had given thanks he gave it to them, saying, 'Drink of it, all of you; for this is my blood of the covenant, which is poured out for many.' " Matthew 26:26–28. 15th-century painting from Cyprus.

"O cross, planted upon the earth and having thy fruit in the heavens! . . . Well done, thou that didst clothe thyself with the Lord, and didst bear the thief as a fruit, and didst call the apostle to repentance, and didst not refuse to accept us! But how long delay I, speaking thus, and embrace not the cross, that by the cross I may be made alive."
Acts of Andrew, *apocryphal New Testament.*
Painting (left) by Paolo Veronese (1528–1588).

"For we know that Christ being raised from the dead will never die again; death no longer has dominion over him. The death he died he died to sin, once for all, but the life he lives he lives to God. So you also must consider yourselves dead to sin and alive to God in Christ Jesus. . . . For the wages of sin is death, but the free gift of God is eternal life in Christ Jesus our Lord." Romans 6:9–11, 23. Illustration of the Resurrection (right) found in a 13th-century Latin Psalter from France.

"When it was evening, there came a rich man from Arimathea, named Joseph, who also was a disciple of Jesus. He went to Pilate and asked for the body of Jesus. Then Pilate ordered it to be given to him. And Joseph took the body, and wrapped it in a clean linen shroud, and laid it in his own new tomb, which he had hewn in the rock. . . . Mary Magdelene and the other Mary were there, sitting opposite the sepulchre." Matthew 27:57–61. Detail from an Italian painting, 16th century.

"And while they were gazing into heaven as he went, behold, two men stood by them in white robes, and said, 'Men of Galilee, why do you stand looking into heaven? This Jesus, who was taken up from you into heaven, will come in the same way as you saw him go.' " Acts 1:10–11. The Ascension (right) from the Rabbula Gospels, Mesopotamia, late 6th century.

one prisoner during the Passover festival, Pilate asked if he shouldn't free Jesus, but the crowd refused, insisting on freedom instead for Barabbas, an insurrectionist and murderer. Pilate should have realized it would please the Jews in Jerusalem to liberate someone who had openly fought the state.

In the end, the riotous anti-Jesus crowd so unnerved the prefect that he gave orders for the prisoner to be crucified. But Pilate underscored his misgivings by publicly washing his hands in water and telling the crowd, "I am innocent of this man's blood."

The Crucifixion

Some of the men and women waiting expectantly at Pentecost had been eyewitnesses at the Crucifixion. Though they could not realize it at the time, this traumatic event, agonizing for victim and spectators alike, was to become a point around which many of Christianity's deepest beliefs would crystallize. All they knew then was that their teacher had been made to suffer the most ignominious of deaths.

The steps involved in a crucifixion were brutal. First, to weaken him, the Roman soldiers flogged Jesus with a heavy, flesh-shredding leather whip studded with lead pellets. Next the jeering soldiers placed a scarlet robe around his shoulders and circled his head with a crown of thorns in mockery of his alleged claim to kingship.

Then Jesus was forced to carry a heavy crossbeam (it may have weighed as much as 125 pounds) toward Golgotha, a hill outside Jerusalem, the place of his coming execution. When he proved too weak to carry the beam all the way, the soldiers forced a passerby, a visiting countryman, to carry it for him. At Golgotha the crossbeam was fitted onto an upright post to form a cross. Jesus was nailed to it hand and foot, after which the soldiers affixed to the cross a sign that read "Jesus of Nazareth, the King of the Jews."

Jesus suffered on the cross for about six hours, as passersby stared at the spectacle, some taunting him.

Aloe (right) and myrrh were the two spices used at Jesus' burial when he was bound with linen and laid to rest in a rock-cut tomb like the one below. Common in the first century, such tombs were fitted with a large round stone that could be rolled across the entrance to keep out scavenging animals. Short tunnels dug inside the chamber accommodated the bodies.

After he breathed his last breath at about three in the afternoon, the Roman centurion at Golgotha cried out, "Truly this was the Son of God!"

It was later recorded that at his death portentous things occurred. The earth shook, rocks split, and tombs opened. Darkness came upon the land. At the Temple in Jerusalem, the great curtain separating the outer areas from the innermost Holy of Holies was torn from top to bottom.

A wealthy sympathizer, a man named Joseph of Arimathea, claimed the body and had it wrapped in a perfumed shroud. Then, attended by some of the women disciples, he laid Jesus in a nearby tomb (probably his own) and rolled a great rock across the entrance to seal it. Matthew adds that a guard was posted to ensure that the body would not be stolen by one of Jesus' disciples. To the relief of both Jewish and Roman authorities, the career of the rabble-rouser from Nazareth was officially at an end.

The Resurrection

Now came Jesus' victory over death, which changed his disciples' outlook from mourning and despair to joy and expectation. Though the Gospels tell of the bodily Resurrection of Jesus from somewhat differing perspectives, all accounts point to a cluster of miraculous happenings that have formed the core of Christian belief from the beginning to the present day.

During his lifetime Jesus had many women followers. Prominent among them was Mary Magdalene, from whom Jesus had cast out demons. She was also one of the disciples who were anguished observers of the Crucifixion, and in all four Gospels, she is the first to whom the resurrected Jesus appears.

At blush of dawn on the Sunday following Jesus' death, Mary Magdalene, together with some other women, went to the tomb thinking to anoint his body further with various spices. There are different versions of what happened next. The women found to their consternation that the great stone sealing the tomb had been rolled back. In Luke's account, they encountered two men dressed in "dazzling apparel" at the now empty tomb. The men reassured them, saying, "Why do you seek the living among the dead? Remember how he told you . . . that the Son of man must be . . . crucified, and on the third day rise." Mary Magdalene and her companions fled the tomb and told the other disciples what they had seen.

In John's version, Mary gave the news of Jesus' Resurrection to Peter and another Apostle; they visited the tomb and confirmed her story. Then, as Mary was weeping by herself outside the tomb, the risen Jesus suddenly appeared to her alone. So little prepared was she for this manifestation, Mary actually thought at first that Jesus was the gardener. But when Jesus spoke her name, she cried out, "Rabboni!" (the Hebrew word for "teacher").

Meanwhile, Matthew's Gospel relates, the tomb's guards hastened to Jerusalem to inform the priests of what had happened. The priests in turn met with the elders and bribed the soldiers to swear that "his disciples came by night and stole him away while we were asleep." "This story," Matthew says, "has been spread among the Jews to this day."

Jesus' appearances to many of his followers

In the days following Jesus' Crucifixion, all of the disciples present that Pentecost morning had come to the startling but unshakable belief that they had seen Jesus alive again—not just in dreams or ecstasies but actually among them. None of the appearances, so fresh in their minds, had been a public demonstration meant to convince outsiders. Only their circle had shared these experiences, and thus all subsequent belief that Jesus was alive had to depend on their testimony.

The recollections of their experiences later retold in the Gospels and by Paul in 1 Corinthians varied, but all agreed that Jesus had been raised from the dead on the third day after his Crucifixion, the same day that in the Hebrew reckoning was the first of the week.

Joseph of Arimathea

Within hours after Jesus' death, Joseph of Arimathea, a rich member of the Sanhedrin who did not agree with his colleagues that Jesus should be executed, went before Pontius Pilate and asked to take the body from the cross for burial. It was an act of mercy and courage that gave Joseph lasting fame. Having received permission, he buried Jesus in his own tomb, according to Matthew. The other Gospel writers simply report that it was one hewn in rock.

So much for history. According to later legend, when the disciples went forth as missionaries, Philip led a company of believers to Gaul (modern-day France) and from there commissioned Joseph to lead a party to Britain. It is said that Joseph landed near Glastonbury and climbed its famous tor, a high grassy hill. As he stopped to rest, he thrust his staff into the ground. It took root and flowered as the Glastonbury thorn, a hawthorn that blooms twice a year, during the spring and at Christmastime.

Tradition further credits Joseph with building a structure of poles and branches that became the first church in Britain. The motive behind this legend is obvious. Every nation in Christendom wanted to trace its roots back to the Apostles. First choice would have been an actual visit by one of the Twelve. Failing that, storytellers had to settle for a second-hand connection. To compensate for this status, a later story arose that Jesus had visited England as a boy, escorted by a merchant uncle who was none other than Joseph of Arimathea.

Celtic mythology made much of a magic cup that the hero in epic tales had to seek and find. In later folklore the cup became the chalice used at the Last Supper, brought to Britain by Joseph, and then mysteriously lost. The quest for the chalice (or Holy Grail) is central to stories told of the legendary King Arthur.

In one case the testimony was handed down as a simple list: Christ had appeared to Peter, to James, to the Apostles, and to more than 500 brethren at one time.

Often the testimony involved a poignant experience. Perhaps none was more moving than that of Cleopas and a fellow disciple, described by Luke. The Sunday of the Resurrection, they had been walking from Jerusalem to the nearby village of Emmaus, when Jesus himself had joined them on the road. Thinking that he was just a passing stranger, they had told him about Jesus' Crucifixion and how some of the women disciples had claimed to have seen angels who said Jesus was alive. No one, however, had believed the women. Surprisingly, this stranger faulted them for their lack of faith and understanding. But it was only later, as they were all eating together and the stranger broke bread in the same way Jesus had often done, that suddenly "they recognized him; and he vanished out of their sight." They had immediately returned to Jerusalem remembering how his words had made their "hearts burn" within them and how "he was known to them in the breaking of the bread."

In the same vein, when Jesus appeared at a gathering of Apostles in Jerusalem, they thought he was only a vision. Luke relates what Jesus said: "Why do questionings rise in your hearts? . . . a spirit has not flesh and bones as you see that I have." He then ate a piece of broiled fish to show that he was an earthly being, not a phantom.

Jesus' further appearance to the Apostle known nowadays as Doubting Thomas was especially instructive. According to the Gospel of John, when Thomas finally acknowledged that Jesus was indeed the Lord he had known before the Crucifixion, Christ said reprovingly: "Have you believed because you have seen me? Blessed are those who have not seen and yet believe." For believers who came later, the blessing on those who believe without seeing made it

Luke tells how the risen Christ appeared as a stranger to two disciples on a road outside Jerusalem and spent the evening with them in a nearby village. Along the way he "opened" the scriptures to them, so that they felt a burning in their hearts, yet they did not recognize him until he broke bread and blessed it. Some have speculated that this event was a Eucharist, because the phrase "breaking bread" was probably used by the earliest Christians for the communion.

possible to feel that the person who was not an eyewitness had the better of it, for the purest faith was that which required no proof whatever.

No less powerful was Matthew's testimony to Jesus' appearance to his Apostles on a mountain in Galilee. Though some of the Apostles had still been filled with doubts, as Matthew recounted, Jesus assured them of his authority given by God and sent them into the world to baptize and to instruct others in his teaching. They would not be alone, he pledged: "Lo, I am with you always, to the close of the age."

One rather puzzling aspect of these reports of post-Resurrection appearances is that Mary the mother of Jesus, though present at the Crucifixion, does not figure in the appearances. And Mary Magdalene, called by some early churchmen Apostle to the Apostles, plays the most prominent role of all, before retiring to obscurity in her home village in Galilee. The sudden eclipse of the two Marys has provoked speculation by thoughtful Bible readers over the centuries.

The first proclamation of the gospel

Now, on Pentecost, as the Spirit broke like a wave around them, the disciples began to understand Jesus' promise and to fulfill his commission. The whole company could not help but speak "as the Spirit gave them utterance." In the Pentecost event recorded in Acts, the disciples' words are not recounted but only how miraculously their speech was adapted for the occasion. Among the residents and pilgrims in Jerusalem were Jews and proselytes to Judaism from the whole known world—the nations comprising the Roman Empire and from beyond the empire in Parthia and Arabia. As the crowd listened, they recognized that they were not hearing the Aramaic or the Greek common in Jerusalem but the tongues peculiar to Cappadocia or Pamphylia or whatever country they had come from.

This miracle was perhaps later understood to be more a symbol than a necessity for communication, since nearly everyone in Jerusalem could have comprehended Aramaic or Greek. But here in the first proclamation inspired by the Spirit, the divisions of humanity were symbolically overcome. Ever since the Tower of Babel described in Genesis 11:6–9, mankind had been divided and scattered by diverse languages. Now people were united, each understanding equally the utterance of God's word through the disciples. The event also focused attention on the fact that from the start, the news of Jesus was addressed to the vast Diaspora. As events unfolded, these

Appearing to the disciples on a mountain in Galilee, the risen Christ commanded: "Go therefore and make disciples of all nations, baptizing them in the name of the Father and of the Son and of the Holy Spirit." Matthew 28:19.

Mary Magdalene, one of the first people to see the risen Christ, was traditionally identified with the sinner who wet Jesus' feet with her tears and wiped them with her hair. The Latin scroll reads: "Do not despair if you are a habitual sinner; follow my example and right yourself with God." The identification of Mary Magdalene with the repentant sinner has been abandoned by many students of the Bible. So too has her designation as the woman who anointed Jesus with precious perfume in Bethany, at the house of Simon the leper. The real Mary is thought to have been from Magdala, a fishing village on the western shore of the Sea of Galilee. A story long current among Christians of the East says that when she retired she accompanied the Apostle John to Ephesus and died there.

Jews from across the world became the principal conduit for the proclamation in its early years.

But not everyone was so impressed with what was happening. The disciples had apparently moved from their house to some spot that could contain a large crowd—likely the Temple court. However, the hubbub was still such that some witnesses scoffed, "They are filled with new wine." Peter took that jibe as his opportunity. The Twelve stepped forth from the larger company and Peter shouted for all to listen.

He spoke with a voice of calm reason and explanation, for he wanted the crowd to understand what lay behind the remarkable events they had seen. Thus he began with the ancient scriptures that his hearers knew well. These people were hardly drunk, he told them; after all it was only "the third hour of the day" (9:00 A.M.). Rather the crowd was witnessing something far more profound, nothing less than the fulfillment of God's great promise that they knew from the prophet Joel—his promise that in "the last days" God would pour out his Spirit not just on a few prophets but "upon all flesh." On sons and daughters, on young men and old, even on servants, "I will pour out my Spirit; and they shall prophesy," God had said. This was a cosmic event, as significant as the sun being turned to darkness or the moon rising blood-red.

Peter moved directly, Acts recounts, from the dramatic words of scripture to the heart of his message: Jesus of Nazareth and his significance. Again he started with what they knew. They had seen the wonders and signs that had made Jesus so well known. Many had also been in the crowds, who had, less than two months earlier, turned against Jesus and shouted for his death; they knew how the lawless Pilate had crucified Jesus even though he had pronounced him innocent. What they did not know was that through it all, God was attesting Jesus' ministry, and that even Jesus' execution was "according to the definite plan and foreknowledge of God." Indeed God had gone even further, Peter told them, and raised Jesus from death.

Beliefs in the World's End and the World to Come

For centuries before Christ, Jews anticipated the world's end and the possibility of a new and better one to replace it. The term defining such matters, *eschatology,* comes from the Greek word *eschatos*, which means "last." Doctrines concerning the end of the world, the Last Judgment, death, and the resurrection of the dead are eschatological.

Because the Jews had suffered under many conquerors since the Babylonian Captivity in the sixth century B.C., they had begun to envision a return to their former glory in the time of King David (about 1000 B.C.). Gradually their hope for deliverance from oppression and restoration of Israel's dominion grew into the concept of an avenging messiah. Perhaps it would be a new King David, a saintly priest, a great prophet, or simply the intervention of God and his angels. In any case, prophets predicted that the judgment of the world's evil would be profound, with the wicked disposed of and a better world created. Influences from other cultures, particularly Persian and Hellenic, enriched Jewish eschatology. Such images as a fiery end to the world and a hierarchy of angels and demons can plausibly be traced to Zoroastrianism, the Indo-Iranian religion based on the conflict between light and darkness.

It seems natural that the early Christians, so steeped in the traditions of the biblical prophets, would be deeply concerned with these subjects, especially since Jesus' own ministry and messianic mission drew upon expectations of the "last days." His miracles were meant as signs that those days were at hand. His parables revealed the character of the coming kingdom. Even Jesus' humiliating death came to be viewed, especially in the light of the Resurrection, as a vindication of his messianic role.

As Peter experienced the marvels of Pentecost and quoted the prophet Joel in regard to the last days, he and the other disciples were profoundly convinced that the last days had indeed arrived and a new age was dawning. But they now found themselves caught in two worlds and didn't know how long this interval might last.

Would Jesus return to finish his work? Had he promised to do so? The New Testament reveals an intense expectation of Christ's Second Coming. Many disciples were preparing for the final judgment and helping others to do the same.

But expectations changed over time, partly because of what was interpreted as a delay of the Second Coming and partly because of severe persecutions. When waiting became prolonged, quite a few people were brought to the verge of doubt. Finally, when it became clear that the kingdom was not imminent, early Christians began to put more emphasis on the world mission to spread the gospel.

Peter recognized, it's implied, that such a portrayal did not fit well with the expectations of a Messiah in Israel; no one was awaiting a savior who would be crucified as a criminal. But Peter tried to bridge that gap by turning again to the Scriptures and citing a psalm, which he interpreted as a prophecy by David, concerning the death and Resurrection of the Messiah, or Christ. What David had prophesied, Peter proclaimed, the disciples had seen: "This Jesus God raised up, and of that we all are witnesses." This Jesus was now at God's right hand and had sent forth the Holy Spirit that God had promised. For Peter, the conclusion was inescapable and sure, "God has made him both Lord and Christ, this Jesus whom you crucified."

What would the multitudes at Pentecost make of all this? Surely many continued to scoff and perhaps even worried about the birth of such a dangerous superstition centered on a man who had been crucified by the Romans. But for many, Peter's words made sense. This was God's Spirit that filled these Galileans. "What shall we do?" they called out to Peter. He told them to change their lives and be baptized in the name of Jesus for the forgiveness of their sins. Then they could share the gift of the Holy Spirit, which was intended for them and for everyone. In Acts it is recorded that 3,000 were added to the band of disciples on that one day. The movement, to say the least, had experienced a potent beginning.

Jerusalem

At the time of Jesus' death, Jerusalem was a major city. Its status as the center of religious life for the Jews dated back a thousand years to the reign of King David, who had captured the Jebusite citadel of Zion and rebuilt it as the "City of David." It is surprising to consider, however, that this legendary city was, by today's standards, a vest-pocket metropolis, occupying only about 300 acres spread out along a rocky ridge in central Palestine.

After David, starting in the time of his son King Solomon, the city witnessed the rise and fall of several empires, suffering repeated captures at the hands of Egyptians, Assyrians, Babylonians, Greeks, and finally Romans. Throughout the Babylonian Captivity (586–538 B.C.), when thousands of Jews were sent into exile, Jerusalem was largely depopulated, but it was resettled when Cyrus the Great of Persia let the Jews living in Babylon return to their homeland.

During the reign of Alexander the Great (332–323 B.C.), Jerusalem came under Greek rule and remained so until a revolt in 167 B.C. led to the establishment of an independent Jewish kingdom with Jerusalem as its capital. The ruling class of this state was thoroughly imbued with Greek culture, which remained a strong influence even after the Roman conquest of 63 B.C.

Jerusalem in the time of the early Christian movement was a lively city: its narrow, steeply pitched streets were crowded with bazaars and thronged, during festival seasons, with foreign pilgrims and grumpy caravan animals. At the heart of everything was the Temple. A magnificent structure, it was the third to be erected on this site. The first was built by Solomon and had stood for nearly 400 years, until the Babylonians destroyed it. A replacement, started during the reign of the Persian king Cyrus the Great, remained intact for almost 500 years. When King Herod the Great, Rome's client king of Judea, took power, he tore down the second temple and started a new one about 20 B.C. This became the centerpiece of his ambitious building program, which included the fortified city walls with a system of three monumental towers, his own gigantic palace, and a huge fortress, the Antonia, which housed the Roman garrison. In addition, he expanded the water-supply system whereby good drinking water flowed from rain catchment pools feeding a Roman aqueduct.

The improved water supply soon supported vastly increased numbers of permanent as well as transient residents, most of them Jewish. Almost all of Jerusalem's Jewish population was engaged in one way or another in the work of the Temple—as craftsmen providing and repairing necessary ritual objects; incense makers; dealers in sacrificial animals; provisioners for the pilgrims, such as innkeepers and proprietors of restaurants and wine shops; and of course scholars and priests. There were money changers and bankers too, for the Temple was the local bank, and virtually all Jerusalemites, rich or poor, deposited their money there. Public officials kept a vigilant eye on the city's markets to safeguard the interests of both producers and consumers, and prices were controlled.

The wealthiest Jews in Jerusalem were the priestly aristocracy, great landed proprietors, and officials in the Roman tax system. Not surprisingly, members of these groups tended to identify more completely than their less well-to-do neighbors with the values and lifestyle of the Greek and Roman upper classes. For these cosmopolitans there were a Greek-style theater, a sports stadium, and many fine homes on the western hill of the Upper City.

To the Romans, Jerusalem was important largely as a good source of revenue. During this period, they did not much care how residents conducted their religious affairs, so long as they paid their taxes on time. An appointed governor, who resided in Caesarea, was in charge of the province that included Jerusalem. The Sanhedrin retained local autonomy to decide religious and legal matters in Jerusalem, but the governor reserved the right to appoint the chief priest, or head

Many of Jerusalem's markets, like this one at the western Temple wall, catered mainly to the pilgrim trade. Pilgrims sometimes far outnumbered the local population, so trade could be brisk and haggling intense.

Shops opened just after dawn, and most business was conducted during the day. Jumbled close together, they offered items of every description—fabrics, garments, pottery, glassware, brass and copperware, cosmetics, perfumes, spices, household articles, fruits, and vegetables.

Bazaars like this can be seen even today in many Middle Eastern towns. They tend to be crowded, noisy, and exciting. Since ancient times, such markets have been important gathering spots—in the New Testament are references to people sitting or standing idle in the marketplaces, exchanging salutations there. They have also been a traditional place of intellectual stimulation: "Wisdom cries aloud in the street; in the markets she raises her voice." Proverbs 1:20.

of the council, and he made his presence felt during periodic visits to the city, usually at festival times.

To the Jews, Jerusalem was the religious homeland and heartland of perhaps as many as 4 million brethren, living scattered in cities as far away as Rome and Babylon. These Jews of the Diaspora were law-abiding subjects in their adoptive lands and worshiped at their local synagogues. But they also owed allegiance to the Temple in Jerusalem. From all over the Diaspora, the Temple dues required of all Jews poured into Jerusalem; and by the many thousands, Diaspora pilgrims flowed into the city each year to attend the major religious festivals. The influx of visitors sometimes caused Jerusalem's population to increase as much as fourfold in festival seasons.

Competing faiths and cultures

The mix of cultural influences in the city made it a seedbed of new religious outlooks. One of these was Christianity. Jesus' followers were definitely set apart from other Jews by their claim of messiahship for the martyred Jesus and especially by their belief in having received the Holy Spirit. Yet the new group was just one of several sects within Judaism at the time. In addition to taking part in services in remembrance of Jesus, Jewish Christians worshiped at the Temple and observed the traditional rituals.

Prominent among the Jewish sects that existed side by side in Jerusalem were the Sadducees and the Pharisees. The Sadducees were largely aristocratic and committed to a conservative, letter-of-the-law interpretation of Moses' teachings. The Pharisees, by contrast, had a broader, evolutionary approach to Judaism. Instead of relying for guidance exclusively on the Torah, the ancient written law of the Jews, the Pharisees also took into account the more recent oral traditions of Jewish wisdom.

Another major difference between the two sects concerned their conception of God. The Pharisees saw God as infinitely wise and merciful, deeply concerned with the fate of human beings and in control of each person's life, except for the power to choose between good and evil. The Sadducees conceived of God as remote and quite uninvolved in human activities and believed that man has total charge of his life. The Sadducees also denied the possibility of resurrection, immortality, and the existence of angels.

The Pharisees' outlook was more popular and, by the first century, represented the beliefs of most of the Jewish people. But the Sadducees were a powerful force in the Sanhedrin and to protect their status, often made accommodations to the Roman occupiers.

Strongly opposed to the occupation were the Zealots, who were dedicated to overthrowing Roman rule. Still another Jewish sect, the Essenes, removed themselves from worldly concerns and were devoted to a semimonastic, communal life; the largest group lived at Qumran near the Dead Sea (see pages 34–35).

Mingled with the varying religious beliefs in Jerusalem were the cultural and political influences of the Greeks and Romans. The Greek language, manner of dressing, and architectural styles, which had prevailed there for some 300 years, remained strongly influential even after the Roman takeover. Although the Greeks had not persuaded the Jews to waver from their belief in monotheism, many elements of Greek philosophy and culture and some social customs were sufficiently attractive that many Jews tried to unite their own traditions with those of the Greeks and even went so far as to defend their Jewish heritage by means of the ideas and values of Greek culture.

Another cultural link with the Greeks was the Septuagint. This Greek edition of the Hebrew scriptures, translated in the third and second centuries B.C., had become the most widely read edition of the Old Testament by the beginning of the Christian Era. Since a great many educated men would have had an opportunity to read it, the Septuagint might even have had some influence on Gentiles, thus increasing the cross-fertilization of ideas.

Remembering Jesus

Jesus published no books nor took time from his brief ministry to compile his teachings or memoirs. After his death, all that he had done and said might have been forgotten had not his followers immediately begun to tell his story. But for decades they too wrote nothing down. For the first generation of Christians Jesus' story was transmitted by word of mouth, from heart to heart, first by disciples who had known him, and then, like spreading ripples, by hundreds of converts who retold it second, third, and fourth hand.

Christians reported Jesus' words and actions in order to win converts and instruct new believers, to guide the practices and values of the church, to interpret elements of worship such as the Lord's Supper, to convince opponents in controversy, and to understand the great events of salvation they believed God had brought about.

Often Jesus' deeds were focused into patterns that could be easily recognized and remembered. Miracle stories, for example, commonly described the disease or peril that Jesus encountered, then the miracle itself, and lastly the consequence of the miracle as people were amazed or disturbed. In another anecdotal pattern, sometimes called a pronouncement story, just enough of some situation, controversy, or teaching was described to lead to a striking saying, or pronouncement, which usually concluded the story like a punch line.

The stories most frequently recounted were important for the ongoing life of the Christian communities. Through these the image of Jesus, his voice as prophet and teacher, shone through, as his parables of farmers and pearls and the Prodigal Son were retold countless times.

When the evangelists finally began to write the Gospels toward the end of the first century, the process of retelling became even more selective. Acts relates, for example, how Paul cited orally a proverb of Jesus, "It is more blessed to give than to receive," a saying that did not find its way into any of the four Gospels. On the other hand, selected stories that were translated from Aramaic into Greek and honed and polished into crisp, incisive anecdotes and aphorisms, do survive in the written text. Thus, the rich oral tradition was passed on and has left a permanent stamp on the way Jesus is known today.

Jesus healing a blind man is just one type of miracle story that circulated orally in the decades following his death. Varying versions appear in all four Gospels.

Roman contributions to this society were law and order and political stability, the same benefits they brought to all their conquered lands. Despite the fact that Jews had considerable autonomy over their affairs through the Sanhedrin, there was always an omnipresent Roman army—on call to keep the peace and suppress overt opposition to the empire's authority, which it did swiftly and often ruthlessly. Although in most of its provinces Rome enlisted auxiliary soldiers who were native to the region, Jerusalem was an exception; Jews were usually exempted from army duty (possibly because of their observance of the Sabbath). In Jerusalem, the troops would have been foreign for the most part (that is, Roman from other regions); one historian has made a good case for their being Samaritan. But whether local or foreign, their visibility was a constant irritating reminder to the people that they were being ruled by a foreign power.

Thus the setting in which Christianity emerged was urban; it was peopled with Jews from many nations who adhered to various forms of Judaism; different cultural ideas blended here; and the atmosphere was charged with undercurrents of resentment to Roman rule. Also for many, who hoped to be liberated one day from control by foreign powers, Jerusalem represented the heart of their expectations, emotionally and theologically, for the new kingdom of Israel.

From Christianity's earliest days a regular part of the worship service was the ritual sharing of bread and wine in remembrance of Jesus. This Roman bas-relief shows the typical method of crushing grapes in the wine-making process.

Early Christian lifestyle

Within five years after Jesus' death not only had a growing and dedicated church been established in Jerusalem, but also missions had been started in Samaria and towns along the coast of Palestine. It is reasonable to suppose that the good news had been carried also to Galilee, where Jesus had spent most of his own ministry, but we know little about the early church there.

How did Christians live during these years? The question is not easily answered, because most accounts of the period were written not by eyewitnesses but by people who lived several decades later. Granted this element of uncertainty, it does seem clear that the first Christians were a deeply devout group dedicated to preparing themselves for the kingdom of God but faced with controversies and difficult decisions.

They organized their religious life around three central functions: prayer (some consider it likely that the Lord's Prayer was recited), sermons and religious instruction, and a daily common meal. The shared meals, partaken in remembrance of the Last Supper, were called the Lord's Supper. They helped strengthen communion among the followers, who believed that Jesus himself was present at the table. But this table fellowship also served another purpose; it provided sustenance for hungry Christians. Those who were attracted to the new faith came from various classes of Jerusalem society and probably included pilgrims from abroad with limited resources, as well as many who were impoverished.

Everything in common

To provide sustenance for poorer converts and for preachers, to prepare for the kingdom of Heaven that they felt was imminent, perhaps even to fulfill a Hellensitic ideal, early Christians shared their possessions. As needs arose, the faithful sold their property and gave the money realized to the Apostles for distribution. A few stories in Acts tell us something about the attitudes and problems that arose from this system.

In one account, a man named Joseph, whose character inspired the Apostles to nickname him Barnabas, meaning "Son of encouragement," sold a piece of land and handed over the proceeds. Barnabas was a Jew from the Diaspora, a native of Cyprus, but his family came from the tribe of Levi and maintained some property in Jerusalem. He had a cousin or an aunt named Mary, whose house served as a meeting place for the Jerusalem community. Barnabas was destined to become a leading Christian missionary.

Another story was far more somber. It told of a couple named Ananias and Sapphira, who likewise sold land but decided to give only part of the proceeds to the community. They evidently wanted the reputation for generosity that men like Barnabas had gained, and they agreed to say that their partial gift was the entire price of the land. The story emphasizes that such deception was wholly futile, because the Holy Spirit was so powerfully present in the Apostles. Peter immediately recognized the lie and confronted Ananias with it. Peter emphasized that a partial gift was completely acceptable, but "to lie to the Holy Spirit" was not. His accusation struck Ananias like a blow, and he fell down dead. Later that day the scene was reenacted with Sapphira, and she too died. Through the remembrance of such an event the early church reminded itself that the power of the Holy Spirit it had experienced was not to be trifled with.

It was the practice in the primitive church to help the poor, especially widows. This aid, modeled after a Jewish tradition, included a daily distribution of baskets filled with food and sometimes clothing. Flat loaves of bread (right) were staples in the baskets. Other typical food items were dried peas, lentils, or beans; olive oil; dried figs; and in season, fresh vegetables and fruits.

As the church in Jerusalem grew, all the strands of Jewish society were represented in it, including large numbers of Jews from the Greek-speaking Diaspora. Among them were many elderly people, who desired to be buried near Zion and had returned to settle there. These immigrants had their own synagogue communities that worshiped in Greek and maintained ties to the Diaspora. Many had been influenced by the powerful Greek culture in their homelands but were also deeply committed to their faith. Tensions between these Jews of Greek culture and language, called Hellenists, and the Aramaic-speaking Jews native to Palestine, known as Hebrews, were natural and inevitable.

Continued on page 36

Ancient Essene scribes wrote out their books on specially treated sheepskins and goatskins. These books were the most precious things the community owned. Members swore to safeguard the valuable scrolls and to keep their teachings secret from outsiders. A Jewish writer who sojourned in their midst says that they used their books to foretell the future and were seldom wrong.

Essenes: Sons of Light

"To the elect of righteousness you have made me a banner, and a discerning interpreter of wonderful mysteries."

—DEAD SEA SCROLLS

The Roman savant Pliny the Elder (A.D. 23–79) described the Essenes as "a solitary race," which was "strange above all others in the entire world." They were remarkable indeed, because they were monks living in a monastery—a phenomenon hitherto unknown in Judaism (and rarely seen anywhere at the time outside India). Similar to the Pharisees but much more radical, the Essenes were the most pious, rigorous, and secretive of all the Jewish sects of antiquity. Although the group is never mentioned in the New Testament, scholars have identified Essene practices and beliefs that parallel those of early Christianity.

The name *Essenes* means "the pious ones" (or possibly "the healers"). After the Jewish independence war of 167–165 B.C., the Essenes formed their own sect because they could not agree with the Pharisees on certain religious and political issues. Led by a "Teacher of Righteousness" —whom historians have never been able to identify—they set up a number of monastic communities, such as the one tentatively identified as a monastery at Qumran, in the wilderness on the west side of the Dead Sea. By the time of Christ, there were an estimated 4,000 Essenes, scattered throughout Palestine in communal enclaves of zeal and ascetic piety.

Though some Essenes did marry in order to have children, the sect was mainly a brotherhood of male celibates. The brethren concentrated on purifying themselves for what they believed was the imminent coming of the kingdom of God. They did so unsparingly in their monasteries. Their day began at sunrise, and they spoke not a word until after morning prayers. Then they spent the day toiling at their appointed tasks in the grain fields, at the pottery kilns and looms, or in the scriptorium copying sacred texts. Zealous study of books, especially the Scriptures, was an all-important activity, for their entire life centered on the effort to understand the Law of Moses. Like many early Christians, they were inclined to prophetic interpretations of Scripture, particularly ones having a bearing on the present and the immediate future. The Essene view of history as preordained by God comes through in one Dead Sea Scroll: "Assuredly, all the times appointed by God will come in due course, even as He has appointed in His inscrutable wisdom."

The Essenes were experts in medicinal herbs and the healing powers of gemstones, a science they purported to have gleaned from ancient writings. Their white linen garments were in keeping with their belief that they were the true priesthood of Israel, the righteous "faithful remnant" mentioned in earlier prophecy, who would live to witness the dawning of a new era. In this cosmic context they saw themselves as Sons of Light at war with the Sons of Darkness led by Satan.

Life in the monastery was life at the minimum, with communal property, ritual cold baths, and meager meals at midday and evening. A council of 3 priests, who stood for the 3 priestly families, and 12 laymen, who represented the 12 tribes of Israel, governed the community under strict rules, particularly for the Sabbath. When the Essenes rested on the Sabbath after six days of toil, they ate cold meals prepared beforehand and even refrained from relieving themselves, lest the waste profane God's holy day.

Their breaking of common bread was treated as a holy act, much as the shared meals of the earliest Christians were a kind of Eucharist. There were other institutional similarities. The Essene office of "overseer" paralleled the later Christian office of bishop. Like the followers of Jesus, the Essenes rejected animal sacrifice, and like them, too, they spoke of their new doctrine and mode of life as "the Way."

On entering the community, new members were on probation through three stages and then were initiated with an oath pledging piety toward God, honesty with fellow Essenes, and secrecy regarding the group's teachings—for example, the esoteric doctrine concerning the naming of angels. Initiates were bathed in flowing water, a ritual in some ways paralleling John the Baptist's rite of baptism.

Some scholars have speculated that John may have lived in an Essene community for a period of time. They note that he, too, lived an ascetic life, apparently never married, and preached repentence in preparation for the kingdom of God that was soon to come.

The brotherhood disappeared about A.D. 70, as Roman armies crushed the Jewish uprising (in which the Essenes had taken part). Several hundred documents of the zealous sectarians remained hidden in a cluster of desert locations near Qumran, where they lay buried for almost 2,000 years. Then one day in 1947 an Arab shepherd searching for a lost goat threw a stone into a cave mouth. The sound of breaking pottery led him to clay jars containing the first of the discoveries known as the Dead Sea Scrolls. Although a complete edition of the texts has not yet appeared, the so-far-published documents provide an inside view of what many Jews were thinking about in the period of Jesus' lifetime and the generation following his death.

Below is a commentary on the Old Testament book of Habakkuk, verse by verse, with an explanation of the prophecy's inner meaning and how it applies to current events.

From the beginning of Christianity, baptism was an important ritual—the means by which new converts were accepted. Little is known of the precise proceedings in the primitive church, but by the third century somewhat elaborate rules had been established. As church building developed, special receptacles for the baptismal water and a separate room or building for the ceremony were often included in the plans. This embellished baptismal font is part of a basilica in Tunisia, North Africa.

Included among Hellenist Christians were perhaps a disproportionate number of elderly widows. According to Acts, the Hellenists believed their widows were being neglected in the daily distribution of food and funds, and they complained against the Hebrews. No blame is assigned for the conflict, but the story shows how the Apostles resolved the problem. They asked the assembly of disciples to choose seven good men, "full of the Spirit and of wisdom," who could take charge of this ministry. The group selected seven leaders with Greek names—possibly they were all Hellenists—and the Apostles ordained them by laying their hands on them. But the Seven, as they are still called, were far from just a social service committee. Some became vocal and active missionaries of the early church. These were men who "did great wonders and signs among the people" and who led the first expansion of the church outside Jerusalem.

Baptism

One of the most dramatic rituals observed by the earliest Christians was baptism. Its aim was to wash away all uncleanliness resulting from sin, thus preparing the initiate for his or her new life. In its most basic form, the ceremony called for a confession of faith by the candidate, followed by complete immersion in water in the name of Jesus Christ.

Variations on simple immersion were created by the end of the first century. For example, water might instead be poured three times over the candidate's head. Eventually, special receptacles were made in which the candidate would stand. Anointing with oil either before or after baptising with water was added to some rites. And in North Africa, milk and honey representing entrance to the promised land were presented to the newly baptized.

The New Testament does not say whether Jesus ever baptized anyone (one passage in the Gospel of John says he did, then retracts the statement, claiming it was Jesus' disciples who did so), but Jesus himself was baptized by John the Baptist. Long before John even, Jews of the Old Testament had purification-by-water rituals called lustrations. Similarly, the Essenes required several ritual washings by their faithful each day. In contrast, Christian baptism was meant to be a single, stirring event in which a candidate was given access to the Holy Spirit in the name of Jesus.

Names for Christians

During the early days of the church, Jesus' followers called themselves and were called by others a variety of names. The lack of a single, central organization and title only reflected the unstructured nature of the group. One common designation was *followers of the Way*. The simpler and often used term *the Way* was possibly a shortened form of "the way of the Lord" or "the way of God." Early Christians saw the gospel of Jesus as the will of God revealed through him. The word *Christian* itself was not used until around A.D. 40.

Another name, *Nazarenes,* referred to people who, like Jesus, came from Nazareth or were—by extension—followers of Jesus. When this expression was used by tradition-minded Jews to designate early Christians, it had contemptuous overtones. In those times Nazareth was looked down upon by cultivated Jews as an insignificant backwater.

A number of designations for Christians appear in the New Testament. Among them are *God's temple, little flock, salt of the earth*, and *one body in Christ*. The term *church* (Greek *ekklesia*) also appears in the New Testament. For example, it is used by Jesus in his prediction to Peter: "You are Peter, and on this rock I will build my church." There are also numerous references to the word in the letters of the Apostle Paul. In his epistle to the Ephesians, for instance, Paul states that "Christ is the head of the church."

In the Greek translation of the Old Testament, *ekklesia* is used to represent the Hebrew word that means "assembly" or "congregation." Early Christians took over this term from the Old Testament to designate their assemblies as the people of God. In the secular sense, the Greek word means "a gathering of persons for any sort of event." But to early Christians, the church was specifically an assemblage of the faithful, united in their love for Christ.

The opposition

The strongest opponents to Christianity were the Sadducees, who did not believe in resurrection from the dead and longed to crush the infant movement. They were joined in this cause by many Pharisees, who though they believed in resurrection, were not convinced that Jesus was the predicted Messiah. Elders of both groups who sat on the Sanhedrin were alarmed by the growing influence of the Apostles. Not surprisingly, they reacted strongly to the miraculous healing of a lame man by Peter and John.

This event took place outside the Temple, where the man, crippled since birth, could daily be seen begging for alms. Instead of heeding the afflicted one's request for money, Peter commanded him to walk. "He took him by the right hand and raised him up; and immediately his feet and ankles were made strong." To all who had witnessed or heard about the

"For the instruction of the commandments of the Law." This Greek inscription marked a synagogue of Jerusalem. Greek was the common tongue for many Jews throughout the empire.

The great Rabbi Gamaliel, teacher of the Apostle Paul, was renowned for his purity and saintliness, as well as for his broad-minded views. One of his favorite phrases was "for the benefit of humanity."

miracle, Peter proclaimed that healing had been accomplished "by faith in his [Jesus'] name." The early Christians believed that the very name of Jesus could bring about a work of wonder.

Annoyed that Peter and John were preaching at the Temple, the priests and Sadducees had them arrested. But the man who had been restored to health was irrefutable proof of the Apostles' powers. The next day the council was forced to let them go with a simple stricture that they no longer teach in Jesus' name.

On another occasion Peter was again arrested, this time with the other Apostles, and put in prison. That night, according to Acts, an angel released them and told them to go preach in the Temple. Of course the Sanhedrin was astonished the next day to discover the Apostles' whereabouts. Brought before the council and admonished for teaching, Peter and the Apostles answered, "We must obey God rather than men."

Feelings were running high and the Sadducees "wanted to kill them." But at the last moment a Sanhedrin elder, the illustrious Rabbi Gamaliel, rose to speak. "Keep away from these men," he said, "and let them alone; for if this plan or this undertaking is of men, it will fail; but if it is of God, you will not be able to overthrow them. You might even be found opposing God!" The Sanhedrin was swayed, and the Christians were freed.

Martyrdom of Stephen

Ultimately, it was not with the Sadducees or the Sanhedrin that the most fateful debates for the disciples took place. Fires of conflict were kindled between Greek-speaking Jews, such as Stephen, Philip, and Barnabas, who believed in Jesus and Greek-speaking Jews who did not. These conflicts were fueled evidently by some longstanding debates that had been transferred from the Diaspora to Jerusalem. The confrontations focused on the centrality of the Temple and its sacrifices, rigorous observance of the Jewish law, and the degree to which Greek culture should be rejected or accepted—all issues for which Jews had fought and died in the two centuries before Christ.

The first and most virulent incident began when Stephen, one of the Seven, was challenged in debate by some of his Hellenist compatriots. Jews from northern Africa and Asia Minor and Jews who were former slaves, probably from Rome, were outraged at arguments that he had been making since becoming a follower of Jesus. Though tradition does not record the debate, it does describe the accusation against Stephen that grew out of it. He had evidently opened a wound on the issue of the Temple, arguing that the coming of Jesus of Nazareth rendered the Temple and its sacrifices—the glory of Jerusalem—unnecessary. Fighting words indeed! Had not their forefathers gone to war in the time of the Maccabees to reclaim God's Temple and restore its sanctity?

The Hellenists rushed Stephen before the Sanhedrin, charging that he claimed "this Jesus of Nazareth will destroy this place, and will change the customs which Moses delivered to us." Stephen's rebuttal, though not a transcript since no court records exist, encapsulates the arguments of early Christians like him. The speech is not a defense but an attack on his accusers. It begins with the common ground that they all shared as Jews—the history of God's mercy and promises to his people. But Stephen emphasizes that the people repeatedly rejected God's commands. He argues that even the building of the Temple, a house "made with hands," undermined the God-given pattern of a movable "tent of witness" that Moses had received; the God who claimed that "Heaven is my throne, and earth my footstool" does not dwell in a house. Now this pattern of denial had culminated in the rejection of Jesus, "the Righteous One," whom these leaders have "betrayed and murdered"!

Stephen could hardly have expected a kind reception. The enraged mob "ground their teeth against him," while Stephen, with perfect calm given by the Holy Spirit, had a vision and cried, "I see the heavens opened, and the Son of man standing at the right hand of God." When the crowd heard such a claim made for one who they believed had rejected God's Temple and law, they "stopped their ears," dragged Stephen from the city, and stoned him, while he prayed, "Lord, do not hold this sin against them."

Stephen is remembered as the first Christian martyr—one who bears witness to his faith by giving his life. His prayer as he died, "Lord Jesus, receive my spirit," is considered the earliest recorded prayer to Christ. Though Stephen was eliminated, the dangers to Judaism that he represented did not go away. Persecution broke out against the disciples, led by the Hellenist Saul of Tarsus (now known to us as the Apostle Paul), who was present at Stephen's stoning. Though many in the church left Jerusalem, remarkably the Apostles were able to stay. The persecution at this time was largely against Hellenist Christians, not the Hebrew Christians, represented by the Apostles.

The intensity of antagonism against the new movement by Hellenist Jews, who lost many of their number to the church, continued for decades. Later, after Saul the persecutor himself was converted, he debated with the same Hellenists who had confronted Stephen, and himself had to leave Jerusalem to avoid being killed. Even when Saul/Paul came to the end of his own ministry, it was Hellenist Jews in Jerusalem who precipitated his arrest in the Temple. The man who presided at Stephen's stoning was destined to give his life to bring Stephen's ministry to fulfillment.

Paul's conversion

Young Saul, a Pharisee, is a supreme example of Christianity's power to illuminate and transform—key words in the story of the first Christians. Jesus' message transformed the lives, values, and hopes of all who came to believe, thereby changing their personal histories and through them the history of the world.

A native of the Greek city of Tarsus in Cilicia, near the southern coast of present-day Turkey, Saul was an

The martyrdom of Stephen has often been compared to Christ's. Both were charged falsely at their trials with blasphemy against the Law of Moses and the Temple; both, too, prayed for their tormentors to be forgiven. Scholars still debate whether Stephen's execution was a legal act of the Sanhedrin (it is believed they had the authority to put a person to death for violating the sanctuary of the Temple) or if the stoning was a mob response to his speech.

Paul recalled his vision on the Damascus road as "a light from heaven, brighter than the sun shining round me and those who had journeyed with me. And when we had all fallen to the ground, I heard a voice." Acts 26:13–14.

intense young man. His family boasted descent from the ancient tribe of Benjamin, and his parents had named him for Saul, the first king of Israel, a hero of their tribe. Like many Jews of the day, Saul also had a Greco-Roman name. That name was Paul.

He was a man of two worlds. His writings show that he was educated both in the current philosophy of the Greek and Roman world and in the traditions of the Hebrew Scriptures and their interpretation among the Jews. He was also trained as a tentmaker, a sturdy craft that could earn him a living anywhere he chose to be. From his father he had inherited Roman citizenship, which gave him legal rights and protection throughout the vast realm governed by Rome.

If, however, it came to a conflict between Greco-Roman culture and their deep faith as Jews, Paul and his family sought no compromise. They were Jews first. His family was committed to the way of life of the Pharisees, and Paul was reared to be totally devoted to the law of the God of Israel, not that of Rome.

To this end, he went to study with Gamaliel, the liberal Sanhedrin elder, who was the most prominent rabbinic teacher of his time. Subsequent to his studies, Paul seems to have become a kind of Pharisaic missionary, bringing the light of God's law to Gentile converts to Judaism.

When we first meet this young man he is locked in struggle with a new sect that had arisen among his people, a group that Paul saw as a mortal threat to Israel. It was probably not simply because they claimed that Jesus was the Messiah; such an assertion might be thought foolish but was not in itself blasphemous. But when some followers of Jesus argued that the law and the Temple were no longer central, they struck at the heart of all that Paul believed.

Paul was as far from the followers of Jesus as it was possible to be; but he was also close enough to want to throttle the new movement with his own hands. When Jesus and the faith he aroused in others first became a focus of Paul's life, the young man was filled with violent revulsion.

Then one day something happened that turned Paul's values upside down. In his letters he described the experience in various ways: as an appearance of Jesus to him, as God revealing his Son to him, as seeing the Lord, as being apprehended by Jesus. The event was considered so remarkable and important by the author of Acts that in his selective narrative of the early Christian movement he made room to record the episode at length three times.

As Acts describes the vision, it overtook Paul as he was approaching the ancient city of Damascus, armed with credentials to search out and arrest followers of the Way, when he was struck down and blinded by a light that appeared brighter than the sun. An unknown but insistent voice called his name in Hebrew: "Saul, Saul, why do you persecute me?" The demanding question did not fit at all with what Paul thought he was doing as a defender of God's law, and he had to ask, "Who are you, Lord?" When the voice responded, "I am Jesus, whom you are persecuting," Paul's world was immediately overturned.

When it actually happened, Paul's vision not only illuminated him within but blinded his external sight. He was led helpless by his companions into Damascus, where he waited for guidance through three days of fasting. Then a disciple named Ananias was told in a vision to seek out Paul and restore his sight. Ananias laid his hands on Paul, and "something like scales fell from his eyes and he regained his sight."

During his fast, Paul had visions of future missions to carry the name of Jesus to the world, but he did not embark on his calling overnight. Time was needed—time perhaps for Paul's Christian victims to recover from their indignation at his cruelties, time for his Jewish ex-colleagues to get over their anger at his apostasy, time for Paul himself to ponder the step that he had taken. In a letter written years later to the Galatians, he states that he "went away into Arabia." "Arabia" probably means either the Syrian Desert or the Negev wilderness of southern Palestine. There he would have been able to support himself as a tentmaker. Later he returned to Damascus, where he preached boldly in the name of Jesus and had to flee.

All accounts of Paul's conversion and its aftermath stress two conclusions. First, Paul came to the conviction that the Jesus he had fought so strenuously was indeed God's own Messiah; Paul's ardor for God's service never wavered, but the vision redirected it completely. Second, Paul believed that the good news proclaimed by Jesus was intended not only for Israel but for the whole world, and that he was specifically commissioned as emissary to the Gentiles.

With those new realities burning forever in his heart, Paul's future agenda was set. No words seemed adequate to express his amazement at God's grace in transforming him. Every gain or advantage he had once had now seemed a total loss. It was as though he had died, and in fact been crucified with Jesus, and had been given a new life.

When Paul returned to Damascus three years after his conversion, he so inflamed some of the Jews there with his preaching about Christ that he was forced to flee for his life. This 15th-century oil painting shows how his companions helped him escape by lowering him over the city wall in a basket.

Chapter Two

A TALE OF THREE CITIES

As "the Way" moved from Jerusalem to Antioch and on to Rome, Gentiles joined the ranks, ministered to especially by Paul, the converted Pharisee. Meanwhile, Rome was ravaged by a devastating fire, and tensions in Jerusalem were building toward a disastrous conflict with the Roman Empire.

The story of how Christianity grew from a messianic sect in Palestine to a world religion is in part the story of how the Lord's Supper, celebrated by a group of Jews, came to be shared with Gentiles (non-Jews, or pagans). To those early days belongs the evolution of the faith's fundamental mystery, the Eucharist, commemorating Jesus' Last Supper and continuing communion with his disciples. The table of fellowship enjoyed daily by the first believers gradually gave way to a weekly meal, usually held on Saturday night and often referred to in later texts as an *agape*, or love feast. Most of what we know about these celebrations comes from Paul. His letters abound with instructions on how the meals were to be conducted, words of advice against eating and drinking too much, and guidelines as to the general tone of the proceedings. He clearly intended to set Christian fellowship apart from cult associations, so-called mystery religions that stressed secrecy and salvation, which were popular at the time.

Early congregations in cities across the Roman Empire shared a weekly meal, usually held on Saturday nights. During these events the faithful joined in celebrating the Eucharist, reading Scripture, singing hymns, and praying.

Caesarea, the seat of Roman government in Judea during the first century, featured an amphitheater among its typical Roman amenities. It was in this port city that the Apostle Peter converted the centurion Cornelius, thus paving the way for Gentiles to enter the church.

The celebrations seem to have been a feature especially of congregations in the Diaspora, to which Greek-speaking Christians fled after the stoning of Stephen. Typically they were held in the home of a wealthier member, who had the space to accommodate several families, and might have included people from different social strata—a gathering atypical of Greco-Roman society in general.

Breaking bread with Gentiles

To bring Gentiles into the Christian community, whereby they could partake in the Lord's Supper, was not an easy step. For Jews, who comprised all converts in the primitive church, were forbidden to eat with such people or consume food not prepared according to Jewish dietary laws. Only a pagan who had converted to Judaism, agreeing to live by its laws, would be eligible to take the next step and be baptized in Jesus' name. A dramatic event, recorded in Acts, tells us how this requirement changed.

Peter was preaching the gospel throughout Palestine, when he stopped in Joppa (present-day Jaffa), situated on a mountain overlooking the Mediterranean. Here he stayed with a tanner named Simon. It is significant that Peter chose to lodge with a tanner, for leather workers were considered by orthodox Jews to be ritually unclean because their work put them in frequent contact with the skins of dead animals. Perhaps he was following the example of Jesus, who, during his ministry, had associated with societal outcasts.

While praying on the roof of the tanner's home before the noon meal, Peter had an extraordinary vision. Acts explains: "He fell into a trance and saw the heaven opened, and something descending, like a great sheet, let down by four corners upon the earth. In it were all kinds of animals and reptiles and birds of the air. And there came a voice to him, 'Rise, Peter; kill and eat.' But Peter said, 'No, Lord; for I have never eaten anything that is common or unclean.' And the voice came to him again a second time, 'What God has cleansed, you must not call common.' This happened three times, and the thing was taken up at once to heaven." As Peter pondered this disturbing vision, he heard the voice again telling him that three men were looking for him and he should "accompany them without hesitation." At that moment three messengers arrived and asked Peter if he would go to the Caesarean home of their master, the Roman centurion Cornelius.

In Acts Cornelius is described as "an upright and God-fearing man, who is well spoken of by the whole Jewish nation." Perhaps this pious Roman had, like others at that time, become disenchanted with the polytheism of his pagan ancestors and turned to the monotheism of the Jews. But Cornelius had not yet

Life in the Diaspora

Ritual hand washing before eating was a custom among Jews, reminding them that as water cleansed their bodies so God would cleanse Israel. This was but one of many ways in which Jews of the Diaspora maintained their religious identity.

By the first century A.D., about two thirds of the world's Jews, possibly as many as 4 million people, lived outside of Palestine. Egypt had a Jewish population of perhaps a million centered in Alexandria, the most important city in the Roman world after Rome, and in Rome itself, there had been a large Jewish colony for some 200 years.

Elsewhere Jews were settled in Spain, Gaul, Northwest Africa, and Greece, as well as in the Greek-speaking Middle East and in Macedonia and the Crimea. Beyond the empire's eastern frontiers, in Parthia (modern Iran) there was a large Jewish population with roots dating back to the exile in Mesopotomia (from about 587 to 537 B.C.) known as the Babylonian Captivity.

Over the years the Jews were subject to relocations, sometimes forced and sometimes voluntary, which scattered them not only geographically but socially. When at times they found themselves on the losing side in a war, they would be displaced and enslaved. Eventually, the Jewish slaves would buy their freedom and swell the ranks of the working poor in whatever country they happened to be. But throughout the Diaspora there were also Jews who belonged to the local ruling class.

Between these two extremes were civil servants, merchants, bankers, tradesmen, artisans, farmers, shepherds, physicians, lawyers, painters, poets, actors, and singers, even a few fortune-tellers, astrologers, and itinerant quacks. Many Jews, who lived in Syrian and Parthian way stations on the silk road from China, worked in the silk business. Indeed, some of the earliest Christian missionaries to the East were originally Jewish silk merchants.

Rich or poor, every Jewish male contributed annually a half shekel to support the Temple in Jerusalem, but most religious life was focused on the local synagogues. Many did their best to follow the exacting regulations of Mosaic Law in traditional form. Others focused on the similarities between Greek philosophy and Hebrew doctrines, attempting, often sucessfully, to incorporate into their lives the best from both cultures. These adaptations set them apart from their brethren in Jerusalem.

Despite such efforts, anti-Semitism was widespread. Jews were exempted from certain civic duties and observances that would have violated their religion; many also acquired citizenship. The granting of these special privileges, combined with their refusal to mingle socially with non-Jews and to worship the state gods, often led to tensions between Jews and their neighbors.

Yet Diaspora Jews at the time of Christ were energetic and successful proselytizers. Judaism has not sought converts so actively before or since. Many Gentiles were attracted to the Jews' belief in one God, their emphasis on family, and their commitment to taking care of their own. Semiconverts to Judaism, known as God-fearers, were among the earliest converts to Christianity.

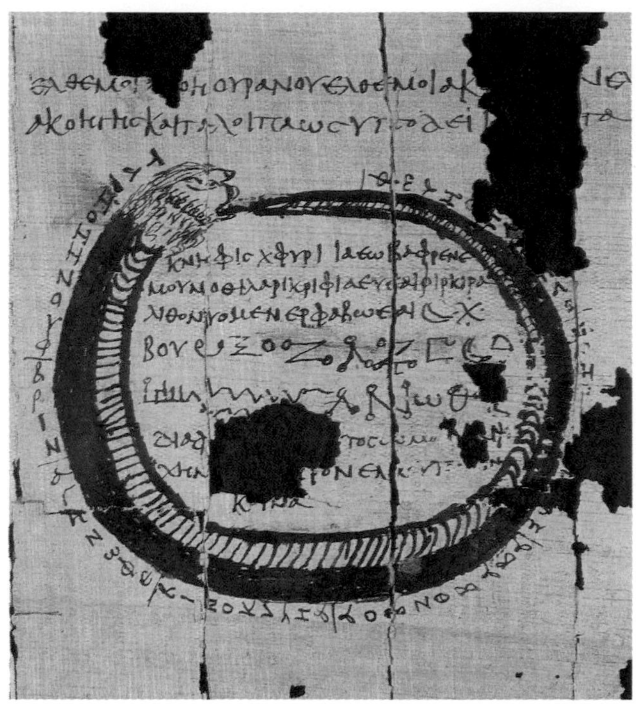

An amulet against demons, illness, and injury features magic words in Greek and a tail-eating "world serpent." For many people in Roman times the serpent held magical powers and symbolized eternity and the cyclical nature of time, with the end returning to the beginning. Belief in magic was common, but Christians taught that simple prayer could have more power than any spell, however potent.

become a full convert to Judaism. He was probably a "God-fearer," or Gentile sympathizer with Judaism.

The prospect of visiting a centurion (commander of a 100-man unit of the Roman army) in the garrison town of Caesarea should have given Peter pause. Jerusalem's Jewish Christians would surely have objected on both religious and political grounds. But he accepted. The next day when Peter, accompanied by six Jewish Christians from Joppa, reached Caesarea (35 miles north of Joppa), Cornelius prostrated himself before the Apostle. Peter helped him to his feet, saying, "Stand up, I too am a man."

Addressing a group that had gathered in the centurion's home, Peter told them: "You yourselves know how unlawful it is for a Jew to associate with or to visit any one of another nation; but God has shown me that I should not call any man common or unclean. So when I was sent for, I came without objection. I ask then why you sent for me." Cornelius explained that he had been told by an angel in a vision to send for the Apostle. Peter replied, "Truly I perceive that God shows no partiality, but in every nation any one who fears him and does what is right is acceptable to him."

Peter preached about Jesus, and "the Holy Spirit fell on all who heard the word." They began speaking in tongues (making ecstatic, probably unintelligible sounds known as glossolalia). As they spoke, the Jews who had accompanied Peter were "amazed, because the gift of the Holy Spirit had been poured out even on the Gentiles." Peter commanded that the group be baptized and stayed with them for a few days.

When he returned to Jerusalem he was criticized by his conservative Jewish brethren for associating and dining with Gentiles. But when Peter told of his vision at Joppa and the scene at Cornelius' house, "they were silenced" and said, "Then to the Gentiles also God has granted repentance unto life."

But could such a difficult issue have been so easily resolved? There is considerable evidence that it was not and that Peter himself remained ambivalent; Paul later criticized him for refusing to eat with Gentile Christians who did not observe Jewish dietary laws.

There is no denying, however, the significance of Peter's actions in Caesarea. From that time on Jewish Christians would have to consider acceptance of Gentiles who requested baptism and welcome them to full church membership. The author of Acts thought the Cornelius story so meaningful that he included two versions of it in this book, much as he had included three versions of Paul's conversion. And the remainder of Acts flowed from this one episode as the gospel spread throughout the Gentile world.

Conversion of a eunuch

While Peter's outreach to the Gentiles was a remarkable event of its kind, an act by the evangelist Philip (not to be confused with the Apostle of that name)

Within a generation after the death of Jesus, Christianity had spread throughout Palestine and many major cities in Greece and Asia Minor. Among the early missionaries were Hellenistic Jews who fled Jerusalem following the martyrdom of Stephen.

was equally significant. A close associate of the martyred Stephen and one of the seven officials appointed to oversee the funds of Jerusalem's Hellenist Christians, Philip had fled Jerusalem after Stephen's stoning. He preached in a number of towns and made quite a few converts among the Samaritans. These were Jews who did not acknowledge the Jerusalem Temple because they considered their own sanctuary on Mount Gerizim to be more sacred.

During his travels in Samaria, he met an Ethiopian (the only one mentioned in the whole of the New Testament) who was returning to Africa after a pilgrimage to Jerusalem. This official—described in Acts as a eunuch in charge of the queen of Ethiopia's treasury—was reading aloud from Isaiah about the suffering servant: "In his humiliation justice was denied him. Who can describe his generation? For his life is taken up from the earth." Philip asked him if he understood what he was reading. The eunuch answered, "How can I, unless some one guides me?" Philip explained that Isaiah was one who had prophesied the coming of Christ. After Philip had told him the good news about Jesus, the eunuch was eager to be baptized then and there.

Tyche, or Lady Luck, who was popular in the East and in Asia Minor, was adopted as the patron deity of Antioch. Here the Apostle Paul and other missionaries founded a major Christian community.

There are similarities between the conversions of the centurion and the Ethiopian. Both men were baptized on the spot. The eunuch, like the tanner, would have been considered unclean by Jews (Deuteronomy 23:1 forbids eunuchs admission to the community of Israel, because castration was viewed as a blemish). The stories of their acceptance into the church carry the message that converts to Christianity would no longer be limited by cultural, religious, or geographic qualifications.

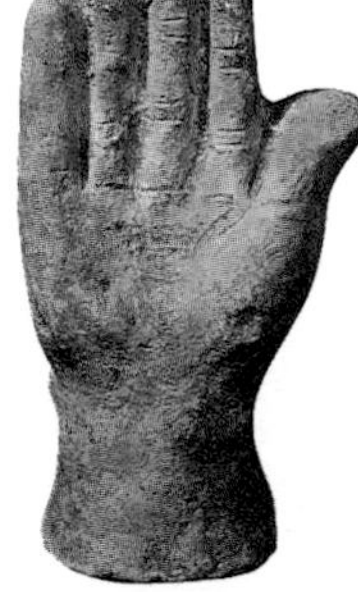

During Roman times, remedies for diseases might be sought at an asclepion, or healing center, dedicated to the Greek god of medicine, Asclepius. The treatment was free, and recovered patients donated replicas of the affected body parts to the healing center.

What it meant to become a Christian

It was a big step for Gentile converts to turn their backs on their pagan background. For one thing, each activity in life was governed, so they had believed, by a god or by fortune. Now, they had to take it on faith that this world is controlled not by chance but by the will of one all-seeing God.

Another big adjustment for many was to let go of magic—charms, spells, and curses invoked to control natural and supernatural forces. Belief in magic was almost universal in the Greco-Roman world, even though Roman law forbade its use to harm individuals or property, and its practitioners were generally held in ill repute. Many were drawn to magic because a major component of its practice dealt with illness, both physical and mental. Then as now, people afflicted with disease were apt to go to any lengths to obtain relief. Magicians, exorcists, and pagan priest-therapists offered help and often succeeded in effecting cures. (As viewed by many pagans, Christians who performed exorcisms and miracles were themselves considered to be magicians.)

Wondrous healings and miracles performed by the Apostles, which were reported in Acts, offered potential converts a viable alternative—the power of belief in Jesus and his miracles. Such belief might empower them to perform works like those of Jesus in healing the sick. The Gospel of John went so far as to report that Jesus had promised: "Truly, truly, I say to you, he who believes in me will also do the works that I do; and greater works than these will he do."

Christians of later generations were to look back on the earliest period as one in which great miracles were performed by believers. This tradition is reflected in the epilogue to Mark (16:9–20), which was added to the Gospel sometime in the second century. The passage reports a final post-Resurrection appearance in which Jesus is said to have given his disciples power to cast out demons, to pick up snakes and drink poison with impunity, to speak nonexistent languages, and to cure the sick by the laying on of hands. Acts relates: "And God did extraordinary miracles by the hands of Paul, so that handkerchiefs or aprons were carried away from his body to the sick, and diseases left them and the evil spirits came out of them."

There is some scriptural evidence that the disciples cured physical ills by three methods—prayer, the laying on of hands, and the application of oil to the sick person's body. (The oil itself, olive oil, was used for similar purposes in ancient Israel and throughout the Mediterranean world.)

As Christianity was seen to compete successfully with both Jewish and pagan miracle working, it was inevitable that other practitioners would try to steal Christian fire. Acts tells us that in Ephesus, a group of itinerant Jewish exorcists tried casting out demons in the name of Jesus. An evil spirit who possessed one man answered them, "Jesus I know, and Paul I know; but who are you?" And the man leaped on the intruding exorcists and beat them up, so that they fled naked and wounded. Word of this incident threw the townspeople into consternation. Large numbers of believers came forward to confess that they, too, had practiced magic. Some even collected their magical books and burned them publicly as an act of Christian faith.

At the same time that they rejected belief in pagan gods and magic, new converts were expected to adopt the Christian ethic, which besides avoidance of such sins as idolatry and adultery, stressed charity and brotherhood. Whatever their former lives had held, they were now part of a caring community that would look after them in times of illness or other affliction, meet their basic needs for food and shelter if necessary, and share with them love and a newfound belief in life after death.

Christian meetings

The common meeting place for Christians during the early years was a home, usually one that belonged to a wealthier member. The owner of such a house had a certain responsibility for the group, often acting as its patron. Acts, for instance, reports that Jason, a Jewish Christian of Thessalonica (modern Salonika), posted bond to guarantee his guests' good behavior.

Households formed the basic cells of the expanding church. A wealthy one included not only immediate family but often slaves, freedmen, hired workers, and even business partners, all of whom joined in the worship or baptism. Thus Paul writes, "I did baptize also the household of Stephanas." In Acts we read that "Lydia . . . was baptized, with her household."

In his first letter to the Corinthians, Paul outlined the early Christian service: "When you come together, each one has a hymn, a lesson, a revelation, a tongue, or an interpretation. Let all things be done for edification." From Paul's description it is clear that these early gatherings were dynamic and exciting and encouraged every worshiper to participate.

One of the great healing centers was the asclepion at Pergamum, which featured therapeutic springs. The picture shows part of the vast rotunda used for medicinal bathing. Patients would have incubated, or slept, in the nearby temple, for a dream received there was of central importance in obtaining a cure.

The homes of the wealthy in second-century Rome were usually quite elaborate. The fancifully named nymphaeum, or shrine of the sea nymphs, was a common feature of many villas. In the open-air dining room above, the far wall features a nymphaeum richly adorned with a hunting mosaic. Adjacent to the grotto is another mosaic representing sea gods. At right, by way of contrast, is a humble, two-family house that lodged working-class people in the same period.

There is little record of what original hymns the earliest Christians sang. Many believe that one is quoted by Paul in Philippians 2:6–11 and another in Colossians 1:15–20. But we assume that traditional hymns and psalms were also borrowed from Jewish services. Early Christian worship was closely related to synagogue worship also in its emphasis on prayer and interpretation of Scriptures.

Speaking in tongues (or glossolalia) was prevalent, and the phenomenon was somewhat disparaged by Paul. He explained that prophecy is preferable, because it benefits the entire community: "For one who speaks in a tongue speaks not to men but to God; for no one understands him. . . . On the other hand, he who prophesies speaks to men for their upbuilding and encouragement and consolation." Chanting, singing, and preaching were rituals meant to unite the congregation. Speaking in tongues, Paul believed, could be valuable only if someone in the congregation were able to interpret the meaning.

Antioch, a first outpost

As the church continued to grow, its members were adopting or creating an evolving mix of rituals and gradually reshaping the worship. Nowhere was this process more evident than in Antioch, capital of the Roman province of Syria and third-largest city in the empire after Rome and Alexandria. Many converts there probably came from among the "God-fearers," Gentiles, such as Cornelius, who adopted the Jewish beliefs but did not submit to circumcision and become full proselytes. But in Antioch a number of Gentiles were also baptized and the young church's mission to non-Jews began in earnest.

Members of the church in Jerusalem were curious when they heard that Hellenists were accepting Gentiles into the Christian community at Antioch. They had good reason to question the missionary activities, for it was clear that the Hellenists were baptizing new converts without requiring circumcision. Eventually this practice would lead to dissension between conservative and more forward-looking Jewish Christians. In the meantime, the Jerusalem church dispatched Barnabas to investigate. Barnabas was so pleased to find the community thriving, thanks to its openness, that he brought Paul to Antioch, and the two lived and preached there for a year. Owing to the combined missionary efforts of this pair and others, the new congregation at Antioch swelled with converts.

Indeed, they became so prominent that they were called, for the first time, Christians, to differentiate them from the Jews. Some scholars claim that Antioch's disciples were scornfully called Christians because they talked so much of Christ. Others speculate that since the term *Christian* in its original Greek form contains a Latinate ending, it could have been used by Roman officials to pinpoint members of a potentially subversive new movement. Still others believe that the disciples themselves proudly coined the word.

Although there is no record of the exact size of the Christian community at Antioch, it apparently attracted all classes from patrician to slave. We do know that it counted a number of wealthier citizens among its converts, for about A.D. 46, the community sent a famine-relief contribution to Jerusalem.

After their successes in Antioch, the disciples moved farther afield to spread the good news. Barnabas and Paul sailed to Cyprus, the third-largest island in the Mediterranean and site of the Roman Empire's prosperous copper mines. They preached first in synagogues, then perhaps in the homes of converts. The pair continued into Asia Minor (modern Turkey) and in less than three years had established several Christian communities there as well as in Cyprus. Other missionaries went forth into North Africa and Rome. "I renounce thee, Satan, and all thy servants and all thy works" or similar words echoed throughout these regions as more and more Christian converts turned their backs on the pagan world and pledged to follow the teachings of Jesus.

A cloth merchant plies his trade in this Roman bas-relief. Prominent among Paul's early converts was a businesswoman named Lydia, a seller of purple goods. Her house at Philippi served as the meeting place for the congregation addressed in Paul's letter to the Philippians.

The church in Jerusalem

Although the congregation in Antioch had become the most dynamic of the Christian communities by A.D. 40 or so, Jerusalem was still the headquarters of the movement. The group that remained after many had fled the persecutions led the Jerusalem church down a more conservative road.

James, whom Paul describes as Jesus' brother in Galatians, governed the Jerusalem church as chairman of its council of elders, a sort of Christian Sanhedrin. Although it is not recorded how James came to rule the Jerusalem church, his family connections probably would have played a key role. (James was succeeded later by Simeon, a second cousin of Jesus.) James acted as mediator between those powerful Jewish Christians who were opposed to welcoming Gentiles into the movement and the church members who were willing to receive them.

The fourth-century church historian Eusebius quotes a fascinating description of James by Hegesippus, a second-century Christian convert: "But James,

The emperor Caligula (above) went insane as the result of an illness, according to Philo, a Jewish philosopher from Alexandria. Lead poisoning may have been the cause —it is suspected to have been widespread at the time. The picture below shows typical lead pipes in Roman plumbing.

the brother of the Lord, who, as there were many of this name, was surnamed the Just by all, from the days of our Lord until now, received the government of the church with the apostles. This apostle was consecrated from his mother's womb. He drank neither wine nor fermented liquors, and abstained from animal food. A razor never came upon his head, he never anointed [himself] with oil, and never used a bath. He alone was allowed to enter the sanctuary."

While James was entrusted with the Jerusalem church, Paul, journeying far and wide to spread the gospel, was named as Apostle to the Gentiles. Peter similarly spread the gospel to the Jews. This division was not strict, however, for Peter sometimes ministered to Gentiles and Paul often began his work in a city by first meeting with the Jews there.

An insane emperor

The brief and stormy reign (37–41) of the emperor Gaius Julius Caesar Germanicus, better known as Caligula ("Baby Boots"), had a particularly damaging impact on the Jerusalem church. Relations between Rome and the Jews became more hostile, thanks at least in part to Caligula's insanity.

"Height: tall. Complexion: pallid. Body: hairy and badly built. Scalp: almost hairless, especially on the poll." That is how the Roman historian Suetonius described Caligula. "Because of his baldness and hairiness," Suetonius continued, "he announced it was a capital offence for anyone either to look down on him as he passed or to mention goats in any context."

Caligula became obsessed with the idea that he was a living god, and he demanded that his subjects acknowledge his divinity. Most people had no problem with complying. The divine status of an emperor was a matter of civic observance; to venerate the office of emperor was to do no more than one's duty as a good citizen, at least for any pagan. And so, during the winter of 39–40, a group of Gentiles in Jamnia took the emperor at his word and erected an altar to him. Local Jews, who far outnumbered their pagan neighbors, were enraged and immediately toppled the altar. When the incident was reported to Caligula, he commanded that a colossal golden statue of himself be erected at the Temple in Jerusalem.

Anticipating the Jews' hostile reaction, Caligula ordered Petronius, the Roman governor of Syria, to lead an army into Judea. If any refused to admit the soldiers, Caligula ordered, they were to be killed and the whole nation enslaved. When Petronius asked to have the order reversed, because of the Jews' outrage, Caligula commanded him to commit suicide.

A delegation of Jews from Alexandria, headed by Philo, a Hellenist Jewish philosopher, was no more successful. Caligula reportedly said to them, "You are the wretches who do not believe that I am a god, although I am recognized as such among all the rest of mankind." The mad emperor was assassinated before his statue could be erected in Jerusalem, but the damage had been done. The relationship between the Jews and the government continued to deteriorate.

Tensions lessened somewhat during the reign of Caligula's successor, Claudius, who ruled from 41 to 54. He appointed Herod Agrippa I, himself a Jew, as king of Judea and Samaria. Herod Agrippa pursued a pro-Jewish policy and to gain the respect of the Pharisees was willing to attack any sects that they viewed as radical. Thus he began persecuting members of the church and even ordered the beheading of the Apostle James the son of Zebedee. He also jailed Peter, who was rescued but forced to go into hiding. These two events shook the Christian movement.

When Herod Agrippa I died in 44, Claudius returned Palestine to Roman rule. Herod Agrippa's rule, which had included a strict adherence to religious principles, was now replaced by foreign misrule. The first procurator, Fadus, outraged Jews when he confiscated the high priest's ceremonial robes. Successive governors ranged from unaware to inept to corrupt—often a combination of all three. The Jews started to raise their voices in dissent, as extremists exhorted them to wage a holy war against Rome. Tension and resentment filled the air and led to numerous uprisings. Eventually relations between Jerusalem and Rome were stretched to the breaking point.

During this troubled time, the young church was also the victim of divisions. After Paul's first missionary journey, a team of Jewish Christians from Judea traveled to Antioch and insisted that Gentile converts there be circumcised. In Galatians Paul writes that these "false brethren" slipped into the church "to spy out our freedom which we have in Christ Jesus, that they might bring us into bondage." They proclaimed that unless you are circumcised, you cannot be saved. To Paul's opponents in this matter, circumcision was an outward sign of membership in God's covenant that represented the physical continuity of the Jews' salvation history. Jesus had followed the rules of the Torah, went their argument, and so must his followers. Their teaching was, of course, in direct contradiction to Paul's view, and this controversy threatened to divide the young church.

After "no small dissension and debate," it was decided that the issue should be resolved by a conference of "the apostles and the elders" in Jerusalem. This Council of Jerusalem, as it has come to be called, proved to be a watershed in the development of Christianity. Paul, Barnabas, and Titus, an uncircumcised Gentile convert, had a mixed reception in Jerusalem. The "church and the apostles and the elders" welcomed them, but some Christians who were Pharisees like Paul insisted: "It is necessary to circumcise them, and to charge them to keep the law of Moses." Paul, however, "did not yield submission even for a moment, that the truth of the gospel might be preserved."

Paul told the group of his work and how he "had been entrusted with the gospel to the uncircumcised, just as Peter had been entrusted with the gospel to the circumcised." Peter supported Paul, and James acted as spokesman for the council. In a compromise that

Sharing with Peter the leadership of the Jerusalem church in the early years was James, known as the brother of the Lord. To him is traditionally attributed the teaching that "faith apart from works is dead." James was martyred by stoning in A.D. *62.*

An inscription from Corinth, (above) reads "Place of the Hebrews." There was a sizable Jewish community in Corinth when Paul arrived, and he preached in a synagogue there for more than a year. At right is the Appian Way, typical of the Roman roads Paul traveled during his missionary journeys. Near the end of his life, when he made his way to Rome from the seaport of Puteoli on the Bay of Naples, he came up the Appian Way. Members of Rome's Christian community walked some 30 to 40 miles from the capital to meet him.

was reported in Acts, the opposing parties agreed that Gentile converts would not have to be circumcised but should remain chaste and abstain from "unclean" meat. Paul mentions that their sole obligation was to contribute money for Jerusalem's poor.

Paul had won the day, and, more important, he had preserved the unity of the church. His fervent mission to spread the faith among the Gentiles had received Jerusalem's approval, and a possible schism between Jewish and Gentile Christians had been averted. Jewish Christianity continued to flourish. For the next several hundred years, large numbers of Jewish Christians, especially in Palestine, and later in Babylon and other areas outside the empire's eastern frontiers, maintained their separateness as a community.

Paul's efforts had helped establish, at least in principle, that in the new faith "there is neither Jew nor Greek . . . you are all one in Jesus Christ." The Council of Jerusalem prevented the followers of Christ from dissolving into just another historical religious cult. As Paul would later write to the Galatians: "For neither circumcision counts for anything, nor uncircumcision, but a new creation."

This first of apostolic councils set another important, far-reaching precedent. When the Jerusalem church sent a letter to Antioch summarizing its findings, it wrote, "For it has seemed good to the Holy Spirit and to us to lay upon you no greater burden than these necessary things."

Later theologians understood this wording to imply that a properly constituted council—one inspired by the Holy Spirit—carries with it the right to speak with the Spirit just as the Spirit spoke in Scriptures. Such a council could promulgate doctrine and practices and interpret dogma. Thus, subsequent councils, held after the Apostles had died, would base their legitimacy and authority on this first one in Jerusalem.

Paul's missions

"A man small of stature, with a bald head and crooked legs, in a good state of body, with eyebrows meeting and nose somewhat hooked, full of friendliness; for now he appeared like a man, and now he had the face of an angel." The subject of this portrait, found in the apocryphal *Acts of Paul and Thecla,* is the converted Pharisee Paul. This vivid description is one of the few that we have of any of the Apostles.

His looks were certainly deceiving. On missionary journeys throughout the Mediterranean—scholars estimate that he covered some 10,000 miles over his lifetime—Paul displayed almost superhuman energy and endurance. He suffered shipwrecks, a stoning, beatings, jailings, humiliations, the rigors of primitive traveling conditions, and a great deal more in his mission to spread the word of Christ. His capacity for survival was coupled with an ability to touch people's souls as he preached the gospel.

Perhaps the best clue to his success—as missionary, evangelist, writer, administrator, and defender of the faith—is found in one of his own letters to the church at Corinth: "I have made myself a slave to all, that I might win the more. . . . I have become all things to all men, that I might by all means save some. I do it all for the sake of the gospel, that I may share in its blessings." By the time of his martyrdom (believed to be about A.D. 62), Paul, more than any other follower of Christ, had helped to create and nurture a network of Christian communities that would blossom into a universal church. Indeed, during the century following his death, some Christians referred to Paul as "the Apostle" as if there had been no others.

How did this man, born a Roman citizen, raised as a Jew, and educated with Greek influences, succeed in developing such a widespread and varied collection of Christian communities? He was, to put it simply, a man with a mission. First, he ardently believed that Jesus was the Messiah of both Jews and Gentiles and that the good news of Jesus' coming had to be proclaimed throughout the world: "For I will not venture to speak of anything except what Christ has wrought through me to win obedience from the Gentiles . . . so that from Jerusalem and as far round as Illyricum I have fully preached the gospel of Christ." Second, he was driven to spread that gospel as quickly as possible, since, as he writes to the Corinthians, "The appointed time has grown very short. . . . the form of this world is passing away."

Paul traveled widely to accomplish his goal. From the time of his conversion to his imprisonment, he preached and, with his assistants, founded churches in at least 20 cities. Acts breaks down his travels into three journeys. However, on closer examination, it is apparent that the Apostle interspersed his travels with extended stays in various cities. For example, after establishing churches on Cyprus and in Asia Minor on his first journey, he paused for 18 months in Corinth on his second journey. His so-called third journey was more an extended stay in Ephesus than an ongoing tour. It was in Corinth that Paul encountered some of his greatest challenges—and victories.

On the east coast of Greece at the head of a gulf, Corinth was a crossroads between the eastern and western halves of the Roman Empire. A constant stream of travelers and cargo flowed through this hub and made it one of the great commercial centers of the

Paul preached to and engaged in debates with Jewish teachers in synagogues wherever he went. Not all received him warmly. In Jerusalem a group of Asian Jews denounced him and accused him of bringing Gentiles into the inner sanctuary of the Temple; this was a crime that was punishable by death.

Paul: The First Great Christian Thinker

When he first put pen to papyrus in a letter, Paul had been a Christian for 15 years; his reflections were mature and profound, and his manner of expressing them was idiomatic, for he often dictated his letters to an amanuensis, or secretary. At the core of Paul's thinking was the fiery illumination that was his personal vision of Jesus Christ. The medium in which he communicated it was the Greek language. That medium colored Paul's message, for his style was that of a cosmopolite who could and did quote from Greek literature.

No question was more central for early Christianity than understanding who Jesus was. Paul's faith centered on the Crucifixion. The hanging of God's Messiah as an accursed criminal was so inconceivable to Paul as a Pharisee that it had been a very big stumbling block to his acceptance of Christ. But in his conversion he had come to believe the unthinkable *was* true; the God whom he had always obeyed had revealed himself in the death of Jesus—a sacrifice made for all the weak and ungodly, both Jews and Gentiles. Furthermore, God had shown that Jesus was his own son by raising him from the dead.

Paul says little about Jesus' teachings or life; no Gospels had yet been written, and he may not have had much information. But his faith in God as seen through the death and Resurrection of God's son was enough for Paul and had vast implications for Christianity in centuries to come.

That faith changed the way he viewed the law given to Moses. Since God had sacrificed his own son to free people from sin, Paul believed, it was clear that neither the Mosaic Law nor any law among the Gentiles had been adequate to reconcile people to God. The law was holy and good, he argued, but it could not break the enslaving power of sin, even for Jews, like himself, who were its faithful adherents.

Paul saw problems of Christian relationships through a prism of Christ crucified. Life for a Christian was to embody the love expressed in Christ's death; all self-promotion should be rejected in favor of service that builds up the community.

Although Paul's letters were written to diverse and particular audiences, a distinct vision of the gospel penetrated them all. It was that of the first Christian theologian, a man whom Albert Schweitzer called "the patron saint of thought in Christianity."

time. But like other bustling port cities, Corinth was notorious for the profligacy of its lifestyle. Paul would later write of Corinthians who "have not repented of the impurity, immorality, and licentiousness which they have practiced." Also, the city attracted a host of itinerant magicians, mystagogues, and philosophers representing pagan beliefs from Stoicism to mystery cults. Corinth presented an intriguing challenge to Paul. If he could establish a Christian congregation in such a wild town, then surely it would shine brightly throughout the empire as an example of the reforming power of Jesus' message.

Paul lost no time laying the foundations for his community of believers at Corinth. The audience for his preaching included sailors; merchants; pilgrims heading for the nearby shrine of Asclepius, the Greek god of healing; and visitors attending the Isthmian Games, held every two years. Paul's later letters confirm that the church in Corinth was composed largely of converts from the poor and even the slave classes. "Not many of you were wise according to worldly standards," writes Paul, "not many were powerful, not many were of noble birth."

A few Christians were already there when Paul arrived; by the time he departed he had built up a sizable community of new converts. While Acts offers only a few glimpses into Paul's year and a half in Corinth, his subsequent letters to the church there—written while he was based in Ephesus—provide many insights. First Corinthians warns the congregation about the dangers of immorality. Paul writes to a church divided, in which even his own authority as an Apostle was being challenged: "I appeal to you, brethren, by the name of our Lord Jesus Christ, that . . . there be no dissensions among you, but that you be united in the same mind and the same judgment." There is only one solution to the growing problem of dissension, "for no other foundation can any one lay than that which is laid, which is Jesus Christ."

Throughout his letter, Paul returns to this theme of surrender to the message of the cross. He addresses also some specific problems within the community, concerning permissiveness, freedom, civil law, marriage, eating the meat of sacrificed animals, and methods of worship. His epistolary advice is indicative of questions that early Christians were undoubtedly asking about practices in their young church. While Paul's letters offer insights into the troubles that faced the churches in those days, they also stand as testaments to the Apostle's remarkable literary skills. His highly individual style, characterized by striking imagery, artfully chosen phrases, and subtle parenthetical asides, is immediately recognizable. Indeed, some scholars believe that certain letters which bear his name, Ephesians, 1 and 2 Timothy, 2 Thessalonians, and Titus, for example, were not actually written by him, because they don't have these characteristics.

A number of the most inspired and poetical passages in the Bible flow from Paul's pen: "If I speak in the tongues of men and of angels, but have not love, I am a noisy gong or a clanging cymbal. . . . Love is patient and kind; love is not jealous or boastful; it is not arrogant or rude. Love does not insist on its own way. . . . When I was a child, I spoke like a child, I thought like a child, I reasoned like a child; when I became a man, I gave up childish ways."

On the road again

From Corinth, Paul traveled to Ephesus, then to Caesarea. In the early 50's he set out again for Ephesus, where he stayed for nearly three years, establishing a vibrant Christian community. He seems to have stopped next at Philippi, Thessalonica, and Beroea, to strengthen Christian groups. Then he returned to Jerusalem.

Healing was part of the apostolic ministry. While on Malta, Paul was called to the bed of a man "sick with fever and dysentery; and Paul visited him and prayed, and putting his hands on him healed him."

This sixth-century mosaic, which depicts the Port of Classis in Ravenna, Italy, reveals the look of ancient sailing ships. In Paul's day, traveling by sea was risky business; Paul himself was shipwrecked four times.

Paul was a survivor. His life, punctuated by life-threatening encounters and arduous journeys, has the makings of a biblical thriller. "Five times I have received at the hands of the Jews the forty lashes less one. Three times I have been beaten [by Romans] with rods; once I was stoned. Three times I have been shipwrecked; a night and a day I have been adrift at sea; on frequent journeys, in danger from rivers, danger from robbers, danger from my own people, danger from Gentiles, danger in the city, danger in the wilderness, danger at sea, danger from false brethren; in toil and hardship, through many a sleepless night, in hunger and thirst, often without food, in cold and exposure. And, apart from other things, there is the daily pressure upon me of my anxiety for all the churches."

How did Christianity's most successful missionary survive such hardships? His devotion to spreading the gospel apparently strengthened his nerve. Paul describes himself thus as a messenger of God, "We have this treasure in earthen vessels, to show that the transcendent power belongs to God and not to us." It is clear also that Paul took pains to plan his travels carefully. He journeyed along major Roman highways and favored regular sea routes.

There is no denying, however, that travel in Paul's day was anything but easy, especially for an itinerant preacher with little money, only his feet for locomotion, and a large stake in getting from one place to the next in the shortest possible time. Take, for example, Paul's trip from Tarsus to Iconium (Konya in modern Turkey), made during his second journey. The Apostle's route very possibly took him through the rugged Taurus Mountains in Anatolia, which rise to 7,000 feet. The rocky terrain, often covered with snow, surely made for slow going, so he would have been able to manage far less than a typical daily average of 25 miles. Spring floods, hailstorms, extremes in temperature, and rock slides were common occurrences. Other hazards included highwaymen and such wild animals as bears, wolves, and wild boars. It is not surprising that travel was considered so dangerous in Paul's day that people made certain they had settled their legal affairs before beginning a journey.

Yet Paul had certain attributes to help him withstand the rigors of his missionary travels. His Roman citizenship protected him in civil crises; his knowledge of Greek enabled him to preach to the Hellenistic converts; and his training as a tentmaker supplied him with a lifelong source of income. Tentmakers were much in demand not only for making tents but also for their skills in repairing all kinds of leather goods. In fact, during his 18-month sojourn in Corinth, he earned his living as a tentmaker, for he would never accept money from a congregation during the period he was ministering to them.

The Marketplace of Beliefs

When Christian preachers, such as Paul or Peter, proclaimed their message, competing voices could always be heard. In the synagogues, challenges were limited to debates about Scripture and Jewish tradition, but when these men stepped out into the *agora*, or marketplace, of a Greco-Roman city, they confronted a dissonant chorus of philosophers and religious guides, as well as astrologers, exorcists, fortune-tellers, and healers all competing to show their intellectual and religious wares.

In the New Testament itself we read, for example, about a slave fortune-teller possessed by a familiar spirit, a team of Jewish exorcists who presented themselves as sons of the high priest, a magician who was counselor to a Roman governor, and people who thought Paul and Barnabas were Greek gods in human form. We also read of a hall, evidently used for lectures by a man named Tyrannus, which Paul rented for part of each day. Familiarity with these religious, philosophical, and occult claims was bound to affect the way people heard the preacher's message about Jesus.

Christian missionaries in the Greek cities found perhaps their most serious competition in the legions of traveling philosophers, especially Cynics and Stoics. Almost any major public square could boast one or more. Some were charlatans who would make converts, get money from them, and then clear out. Others were serious and effective teachers, who believed they were called to guide people toward purpose and contentment in life and to help them escape a sense of helplessness in a world they perceived as empty of meaning and dominated by blind chance. Some of the more reflective listeners turned to these philosophical guides or perhaps to the ancient monotheism and high ethics found in Judaism. But for many, a belief in astrology, an understanding of demonic forces in the cosmos, or the experience of ecstatic worship of Cybele, the great mother goddess of Asia Minor (see page 122), provided a sense of meaning in the world. As Christianity made its way into this marketplace of beliefs, it had to join the already hot debate over what were true manifestations of God, what could bring salvation, and what was mere deception and foolishness.

Wherever he went, Paul preached. "I do not account my life of any value," he said, "if only I may accomplish my course and the ministry which I received from the Lord Jesus, to testify to the gospel of the grace of God." Although his usual audiences were Jews in synagogues and Christians in house-churches, he was known also to argue in the marketplaces with Stoics and Epicureans.

All roads lead to Rome

"I mention you always in my prayers, asking that somehow by God's will I may now at last succeed in coming to you. . . . that we may be mutually encouraged by each other's faith." So wrote Paul to the church at Rome. For some time he had hoped to realize his dream of visiting Rome so that he might help shape the Christian faith in the empire's most strategic city. Paul implores the Romans to pray for him, "that I may be delivered from the unbelievers in Judea."

Shortly after writing these words, Paul traveled to Jerusalem in time for the feast of Pentecost. At several stops along the way he was warned not to proceed there. In Caesarea Paul brushed aside one warning, saying, "I am ready not only to be imprisoned but even to die at Jerusalem for the name of the Lord Jesus." His words were prophetic.

In Jerusalem Paul was warmly welcomed by James and others in the Jerusalem church. He delivered the money he had collected from the Gentile churches and related what "God had done among the Gentiles through his ministry." When Paul went to the Temple for the purification rites, a group of Asian Jews, probably from Ephesus, spotted him and shouted: "Men of Israel, help! This is the man who is teaching men everywhere against the people and the law and this place; morever he also brought Greeks into the temple, and he has defiled this holy place." Although Paul had not brought any pagans into the Temple—a crime that was punishable by death—the angry crowd attacked him.

The Apostle would surely have been beaten to death by the crowd if Roman troops had not intervened. Paul was arrested and hurried up the steps of the Antonia fortress. He was about to be interrogated under flogging, when he claimed immunity from such punishment—his right as a Roman citizen. After threats against his life, Paul was transferred to a prison in the coastal town of Caesarea. Here he was tried before the procurator, Felix, on charges of defiling the Temple and provoking civil disorder. A delegation of Jews headed by the high priest, Ananias, came to Caesarea to present the Jews' case against Paul. Felix postponed his decision and Paul spent the next two years imprisoned in Caesarea.

Felix was eventually replaced by Porcius Festus, who, after Ananias and others demanded Paul be returned to Jerusalem for trial, asked Paul if he wished to comply. Paul knew that he stood little chance of a fair trial in Jerusalem. As a Roman citizen, he had the right to appeal to Rome. "If then I am a wrongdoer, and have committed anything for which I deserve to die," said Paul, "I do not seek to escape death; but if there is nothing in their charges against me, no one can give me up to them. I appeal to Caesar."

Finally, Paul would realize his dream of journeying to Rome. The conditions of his travel, however, were far from what he must have hoped. He left Caesarea a prisoner on board a merchant ship, which stopped at the coastal towns of Sidon and Myra. After transferring to a large grain ship, Paul and his guards sailed for Crete. The ship was buffeted by strong winds, and a northeaster blew it off course. It drifted for two weeks before being wrecked off Malta. That the crew and passengers survived was largely due to Paul's mastery of the situation. This was, after all, his fourth shipwreck! Finally, Paul arrived in Rome.

There he was placed under house arrest. Our last picture of Paul—as described in Acts—is of the evangelist, about 60 years old, carrying out his mission with the same energy he had displayed over the last 30 years. "And he lived there two whole years . . . and welcomed all who came to him, preaching the kingdom of God and teaching about the Lord Jesus Christ quite openly and unhindered."

Paul's last days are a matter of conjecture. Some, such as Clement of Rome, who is traditionally held to have known the Apostle, tell us that Paul fulfilled his ambition to reach the "extreme limit of the west" (possibly Spain). Eusebius, the fourth-century church

Shortly before Paul was sent to Rome on his appeal to Caesar in the case of accusations made against him by the Jews, he was granted an audience by Herod Agrippa II, ruler in Palestine. Herod dismissed him saying, "In a short time you think to make me a Christian!"

historian, writes that "after pleading his cause, he is said to have been sent again upon the ministry of preaching, and after a second visit to the city, that he finished his life with martyrdom." Rome's present-day Basilica of St. Paul Outside the Walls stands on the site where Paul is believed to be buried.

The former Pharisee had traveled a long and arduous road from his days in Tarsus. His churches, which he labored so diligently to found and nurture, would grow and prosper as testaments to his inspired preaching. His eloquent letters to the faithful would survive for centuries to enlighten Christians in their search for the meaning of Christ's gospel.

Part of Clement's epistle serves as an appropriate epitaph: "He gained the illustrious reputation due to his faith, having taught righteousness to the whole world . . . and suffered martyrdom under the prefects. Thus was he removed from the world, and went into the holy place, having proved himself a striking example of patience."

Continued on page 64

Peter was sleeping in prison between two guards, when "an angel of the Lord appeared . . . and woke him. . . . And the chains fell off his hands." Acts 12:7. The angel then led him out of the prison.

Christ promised the disciples immunity from snake poison. The promise held good for Paul when he was shipwrecked on Malta and was struck by a viper. Unharmed, Paul shook the snake off into the fire, and the local people said that he was a god.

" 'Tabitha, rise.' And she opened her eyes, and when she saw Peter she sat up. And he gave her his hand and lifted her up. Then calling the saints and widows he presented her alive. And it became known throughout all Joppa, and many believed in the Lord." Acts 9:40–42. A paragon of good works, Tabitha was also known by her Greek name, Dorcas—both names mean "gazelle," symbol of beauty, gentleness, and speed.

An Age of Miracles

The days when the Apostles spread the gospel were remembered later as an age of miracles; wonders attributed to the Apostles were seen as signs that Jesus was still among them. Paul held miracle working to be only one of many spiritual gifts.

Opposed by a magician on Cyprus while preaching to the Roman proconsul, Paul became filled with the Spirit and struck the man blind for "making crooked the straight paths of the Lord." Acts 13:10.

"They even carried out the sick into the streets . . . that as Peter came by at least his shadow might fall on some of them." Acts 5:15. The healing was by the Spirit, Peter said, not by his own power.

This gold coin depicts Claudius surrounded by a protective wall of Praetorian Guards. The historian Suetonius claimed that "Claudius was so timid and suspicious" that "he never attended a banquet unless with an escort of javelin-bearing Guards, and waited upon by soldiers." On hearing of a plot to overthrow him, Claudius "fled ignominiously to the Guard's Camp, asking again and again as he went: 'Am I still Emperor?' "

The Christian community in Rome

"And so we came to Rome." With these six words, Acts records Paul's arrival in the imperial city. While it is likely that Paul reached Rome about A.D. 60, we are less sure of when Christianity first arrived. In his letter to the Romans, written sometime between 54 and 58, Paul notes, "I have longed for many years to come to you, [and] I hope to see you . . . as I go to Spain." So we can surmise at least that a Christian community predated the writing of this letter. One popular theory speculates that Christianity was introduced to Rome by Jews after their return from a pilgrimage to Jerusalem, perhaps in the early 40's, possibly as early as the 30's.

Claudius, Caligula's successor, ruled as emperor from 41 to 54. His reign was marked by numerous successes, among them the addition of Britain to the Roman Empire in 44, the expansion of road building, improved communications, development of an imperial administration not unlike the American civil service system, and reorganization of the treasury. He was an able administrator who brooked no agitations. When the Jews and Greeks clashed in Alexandria and Antioch, Claudius backed the Jews but also sent a letter admonishing the Alexandrians to live peacefully or face his wrath. He then warned the Jews against bringing more of their brethren into these cities.

Suetonius, in his biography of Claudius, wrote, "Because the Jews at Rome caused continuous disturbances at the instigation of Chrestus [possibly a misunderstanding of Christus, or Christ], he expelled them from the city." This expulsion apparently took place in 49, indicating that Roman authorities did not at that time differentiate between Jews and Christians. How many were expelled? Acts records that Claudius "commanded all the Jews to leave Rome," but it is unlikely that total expulsion could have been enforced. Probably Claudius sent away those Jews who were especially involved in the conflicts over Christ. For among those forced to leave Rome were Aquila and Priscilla, the tentmakers who became Paul's companions in Corinth. Certainly, they were vigorous supporters of the Christian movement.

The statue, right, that commemorates Claudius as a god, features the eagle linking him to Jupiter, the supreme deity of the Roman pantheon. The downfall of Claudius started about A.D. 48, when he married Agrippina, mother of Nero. Two years later, she persuaded Claudius to adopt Nero as his heir. He died in 54 after eating, it is believed, poisonous mushrooms given to him by Agrippina. Upon the accession of Nero, Claudius was officially deified.

Pagan life

Jupiter, Juno, Mars, Hercules, Pomona. To a first-century Roman, these were but a few of the gods that populated the heavens and ruled his life. Throughout the Roman world, pagans, who far outnumbered the monotheistic Jews and Christians, worshiped a pantheon of gods with vastly different characteristics and origins. In addition to major deities, such as Jupiter and Juno, they heeded a host of household gods, spirits of the countryside, spirits of ancestors, protectors of towns, even deified emperors.

A typical Roman believed that gods controlled nearly every activity in the world and that paying homage to them would guarantee success or at least stave off disaster. For example, a Roman farmer solicited Pomona, goddess of fruit, and Ceres, goddess of creation and growth, for a successful harvest; while a homeowner might make offerings to Janus Patulcius, charged with opening doors, or Janus Clusivius, responsible for closing them.

Though the Romans appeased their gods through prayer and sacrifice, their religion had little relation to moral actions, which were determined more by social or familial codes of behavior. Success, not sin, was the prime concern. Cicero writes, "Jupiter is called Best and Greatest because he does not make us just sober or wise but healthy and rich and prosperous."

Some gods were known by several names, and communicating with them could be a tricky business. For example, a prayer to the goddess Diana might be addressed to "Diana, Latonia, Juno Lucina, Trivia, Luna," with perhaps a phrase such as "or whatever name you wish to be called" added at the end.

While prayers were an integral part of pagan worship, most people believed that sacrifice was the truly effective way to influence the gods. In Roman temples, oxen, cows, goats, lambs, horses, bulls, rams, and even dogs were sacrificed regularly. For one special event—Caligula's coronation—160,000 cows were offered up in a three-month period!

Complex rules and elaborate rituals governed the ceremony; a mistake in form or the presentation of an imperfect offering would void the effort. Presiding at the event could be either an official of the government or a private citizen, anyone who was requesting a special favor or giving thanks for a prayer fulfilled. A procession that included the worshipers, the sacrificial

Concern with the gods permeated pagan Roman life. The painting on this bedroom wall from first-century Pompeii depicts a round-walled tholus, *or altar enclosure, of an open-air sanctuary, with suspended branches and fruit on the altar as offerings.*

Children march in a pagan religious procession depicted on a wall in Ostia. Located at the mouth of the Tiber, Ostia was Rome's harbor. Christianity arrived there probably in the second century, competing with other popular religions imported from the Middle East as well as the old Roman cults.

animal—often decorated with ribbons—and perhaps a band of musicians would approach the temple of the god to whom the sacrifice was being made. The animal was led to an altar outside the temple, where the priest, after washing his hands, would sprinkle its head with sacred flour and salt, as attendants steadied it. A prayer would be offered, the animal would be dealt a swift blow to the head to stun it, then it was slaughtered and cut in pieces. Attendants made certain that the organs were faultless, because any imperfection would invalidate the ceremony. Finally, the offering was burnt on an altar.

For household oblations, the object offered did not have to be an animal—the family gods might be presented with grain or wine—as long as it connoted life and contributed to the god's vitality. An undernourished deity would be too weak perhaps to guarantee good results. Thus those animal parts believed to be the most vital—kidneys, liver, heart—were usually proffered to the gods, while the rest was eaten by worshipers, or the meat was sold.

And what of daily life among Roman pagans? First-century Rome, the capital of an enormous empire that stretched from Britain in the west to Cappadocia (in modern Turkey) in the east, was a cosmopolis of more than 1 million people. To call its residents Romans may be a mistake, for, as Seneca tells us, more than half the population came from abroad. A typical street scene might include "Moorish slaves leading elephants about; fair-haired Germans of the Imperial Guard; Egyptians with shorn heads; a Greek professor, his scrolls in charge of the Nubian slave at his heels; Oriental princes . . . wild men from Britain."

The majority of Rome's citizens in the first century were poor and depended on the government for free grain and such amenities as public baths and entertainment. Most lived in overcrowded tenements, and many were disease ridden. At the same time, there existed a new elite of high government officials (often wealthy former imperial slaves), military leaders, nobles from the provinces, and rich businessmen, who enjoyed many of the same benefits that had heretofore been reserved for the urban aristocracy.

Life revolved around the family household, which consisted of the father, mother, children, and often various other relatives, as well as several slaves and perhaps a dozen or so freedmen. The father, or *paterfamilias*, dominated. He could decide whether or not to accept and raise a newborn infant, and all his sons remained under his authority until his death.

Peter in Rome

Although tradition from the late second century onward holds that Peter was head of the Roman church, the New Testament does not mention him in that city. Scholars have long differed over *when* Peter arrived in Rome and some question *whether* he ever did.

Mysteriously, Peter disappears early from Acts, which merely reports that "he departed and went to another place." Given his prominence in the four Gospels, this is puzzling. Four times, a list of Apostles appears in the New Testament; each time Peter heads the list. His influence during the lifetime of Jesus was unmatched, and of the Twelve, Peter was the most important during the church's early days in Jerusalem, acting as spokesman, leader, miracle worker, chief evangelist, and mediator.

Some have argued that Peter left for Rome after his last appearance in Acts. Yet Paul makes no mention of Peter when he writes his letter to the Romans. Surely he would have at least sent greetings. Peter's own first letter, if it was, in fact, written by him, may provide a clue to his whereabouts. Addressed to the "exiles of the Dispersion in Pontus, Galatia, Cappadocia, Asia, and Bithynia," the letter implies that he at least visited Rome, for it sends greetings from "Babylon," used in Revelation as a code name for the city.

Not until the second century do written clues appear, presented as derivations of earlier oral tradition, concerning Peter's whereabouts. Irenaeus speaks of "Peter and Paul . . . preaching at Rome, and laying the foundations of the Church." The early Christian theologian Tertullian refers to the martyrdom of Peter, Paul, and John in Rome. Origen, quoted by Eusebius, claims Peter was crucified—head downward—in Rome. Eusebius himself writes that Peter and Paul were killed in Rome, and their names "still remain in the cemeteries of that city."

In the 1940's excavations beneath St. Peter's Basilica, built on the site of a shrine to Peter erected by the fourth-century emperor Constantine, unearthed a long row of mausoleums. Archaeologists uncovered a grave containing, so they thought, the bones of Peter. However, closer examination proved them to be the bones of a woman. Later, a Vatican official rescued other bones from an opening in a wall exposed during the earlier excavations. After careful checking, the bones were found to match Peter's description—a powerfully built man in his late sixties. Have Peter's remains been found at last? Archaeologists, scholars, and theologians are still debating the find.

As Rome burned

A full summer moon hovered in the predawn sky over Rome on July 19, 64. Suddenly, flames enveloped a row of shops in the vicinity of the Circus Maximus, the great arena near the Palatine Hill. Fanned by winds, the fire quickly spread to adjoining shops and swept the length of the Circus. Before long it had become a conflagration raging out of control. The historian Tacitus recorded the scene: "First, the fire swept violently over the level spaces. Then it climbed the hills—but returned to ravage the lower ground again. It outstripped every counter-measure. . . . Terrified, shrieking women, helpless old and young, people

The above carving of a pagan altar may have belonged to the family of Quintus Aurelius Symmachus, a Roman senator who despite friendship with Christian converts remained a stubborn defender of paganism and an opponent of Christianity all his life. The painting, left, from a house at Pompeii, adorns a shrine where offerings of food would have been left for the household gods. The shrine is part of the atrium, which served as both central hallway and a room for receiving guests.

intent on their own safety, people unselfishly supporting invalids or waiting for them, fugitives and lingerers alike—all heightened the confusion."

The fire spread furiously. When some citizens tried to fight back the flames, others stopped them. Still others threw lit torches to feed the conflagration. Tacitus notes that these arsonists claimed "they acted under orders. Perhaps they had . . . or they may just have wanted to plunder unhampered."

Nero rushed to Rome from his palace at Antium, reaching the city just in time to see the Palatine palace engulfed in flames. The Domus Transitoria, a mansion he had only just built, was a pile of smoldering ash. The emperor wasted no time before directing the fire fighting and supervising the provision of shelter and food for the homeless. The fire burned for nine days and left most of the city—10 of its 14 regions—in ruins. Thousands lost their lives and the streets were filled with distraught, displaced persons.

Scapegoats found

Although Nero had come quickly to his subjects' aid, a rumor accusing him of ordering the fire circulated through the burnt-out streets. Indeed, an embellishment of it alleged that Nero had burst into song in his palace tower as he watched the fire envelop the city. The emperor immediately began detailed planning for Rome's reconstruction, but the rumors continued. According to Tacitus, "to suppress this rumor, Nero fabricated scapegoats—and punished with every refinement the notoriously depraved Christians (as they were popularly called)."

Christians were arrested, and as Tacitus explains, "their deaths were made farcical." Nero reveled in their persecutions and offered his gardens in which to stage the grisly spectacle. In the barbaric tortures, some victims were sewn into animal skins and torn apart by dogs as crowds jeered. Others were crucified. Still others were set afire and used as torches while the horrors stretched into the night. Through it all, Nero mingled cheerfully with the crowd and even mounted his chariot, dressed as a charioteer.

Nero's persecution of the Christians was a gruesome testament to growing resentment against the early church. It was also proof that in the 20 years since the reign of Claudius, Rome's Christians had been recognized as a group distinct from the Jews. But why were they the object of such wrath?

For one thing, they were a minority; for another, they refused to participate in pagan religious rites. Tacitus provides other clues. He describes them as "depraved" and labels their religion "deadly superstition," "mischief," and "shameful practices." He states that they were convicted "not so much for incendiarism as for their anti-social tendencies," an explanation that mirrors the Greeks' *misanthropia* ("hatred of mankind") label, which was attached originally to the Jews. Tacitus' opinion is telling, for he was more than a historian; he was a member of the aristocracy and a friend of several emperors. Hence his feelings toward Christians may reflect the aristocratic viewpoint. Suetonius, a writer and government official, also justified Nero's crucifixion of the Christians by explaining they were proponents of "a new and mischievous religious belief." The accusations were false; but in the long run, the suspicions that had been aroused by them could be justified, as Christians began to subvert the values and beliefs of pagans.

Official Rome, before Nero's persecution, had generally singled out Christians only when their actions threatened the empire's peace or security, and in this the Jews sometimes aided them. In Acts, for example, a group of Jews takes Jason and some of the brethren to the local magistrate and proclaims, "These men who have turned the world upside down have come here also . . . and they are all acting against the decrees of Caesar, saying that there is another king, Jesus." Thus, as Christianity began to blossom, it evoked a growing measure of hostility among both Roman officials and former Jewish colleagues.

Simon Magus

Peter is in Rome to refute the apparent miracles of a false messiah, Simon Magus. As a massive crowd awaits the outcome, Simon, who has won the initial skirmishes already, is now pushed to the brink and boasts he will prove his divinity by flying "up unto God." Leaping from a wooden tower, the Magus [magician], aided either by magic spells or by demons, sails across the sky, seemingly victorious. The crowd looks to Peter for his reaction. The Apostle implores the Lord Jesus to have Simon "fall from the height and be disabled; and let him not die but . . . break his leg in three places." The imposter plummets to the ground. He is carried off, his leg broken in three places, at last humiliated. This tale, from the apocryphal *Acts of Peter,* is one of many Simon Magus stories.

Simon Magus falls from the sky as Peter calls on Jesus to strike him down. An early Christian account of this amazing event asks if it was a sin to believe Simon, since he apparently did perform miracles. If so, then was it not sinful to have believed Jesus on the strength of his signs and works of power?

There may have been more than one Simon. In Acts, a Simon without the epithet of Magus appears as a Samaritan magician converted to Christianity by Philip the Deacon. Later, Simon offers to buy from Peter the apostolic power of bestowing the Holy Spirit through the laying on of hands. Peter rebukes him fiercely, and Simon repents. From this episode we derive the term *simony*, the buying and selling of ecclesiastical powers or offices.

While there is no reason to assume that Simon's conversion and repentance were not genuine, some early Christian writers seized upon the character of Simon and transformed him into the founder of a rival, heretical sect. Whether or not he was the same as the one in Acts is uncertain. It may have been another or even mythical Simon who made a number of pronouncements concerning himself and his consort, Helena. She was a former prostitute whom he proclaimed as the Holy Spirit.

This Simon claimed that the God who created this world was not the highest God, "but that the highest God is another who alone is good and who has remained unknown up to this time." He proclaimed himself the unknown God, saying he had descended from heaven through a succession of cosmic spheres to this earth in order to be reunited with Helena, who in earlier lives had been Helen of Troy and, before that, the mother of the angels and other divine powers. This man's followers were the Simonians, a Gnostic sect that remained active throughout late antiquity. (See pages 128–131 for more on Gnosticism.)

The pleasure-loving Nero

Who was this man, who could glory in crucifixions and reputedly fiddle while Rome burned? Only 16 in A.D. 54, when he inherited the emperor's mantle from his adoptive father, Claudius, Nero looked like a worthy successor. He was described as handsome and headstrong and interested in improving Rome's arts and education. Owing to his youth, control of the empire was at first in the hands of his mother, Agrippina, his prefect of the Praetorian Guard, Burrus, and his tutor, Seneca. Under their direction, Rome prospered. But the good times were not to last.

The young emperor apparently both loved and hated his mother, who clearly dominated him. By 59 he had tired of her oppressiveness. Anxious to assert his own independent authority, he ordered her death. Three years later Burrus died and Seneca retired. Nero's rule rapidly degenerated.

The emperor Nero was already unpopular for his many misdeeds by the time that the great fire of A.D. *64 destroyed half of Rome. Nero blamed the Christians for the fire, and Peter and Paul are thought to have perished in the ensuing persecution.*

Nero gloried in the enormous wealth of his position; he used gold thread for his fishing nets, never wore the same robe twice, and had his mules shod with silver. An unabashed hedonist, the emperor reveled in orgies and debauchery. He had his 19-year-old wife murdered so that he could marry his current mistress, then later killed the mistress.

For all his wantonness, Nero had a lifelong interest in the arts. He was an ardent admirer of all things Greek—much to the dismay of his Roman subjects. He introduced Greek games and arts contests to the Romans, wrote poetry, played the lyre, and also fancied himself a talented singer. Both architecture and town planning seemed to fascinate him.

Unfortunately, Nero's hedonism and interest in the arts were not matched by attention to the details of empire. Unlike his predecessors, for example, he never visited the legionary camps. The Roman Senate hated him for his abuses and his cavalier attitude toward the once august body. A senatorial conspiracy against him was discovered in 65, and its organizers, including Seneca, were killed or banished.

Nero became even more tyrannical, claiming he was the equal of Apollo and the other gods. He fanned the flames of discord by encouraging the cult of emperor worship and erected a huge statue of himself in Rome. Revolts broke out throughout the empire, but Nero seemed not to care.

The end was fast approaching. When his trusted body guards deserted him, Nero's death was assured. He fled Rome, and the Senate declared him a public enemy, ordering his arrest. Hiding from his pursuers, Nero soon realized he had little hope of escape. In despair, he foresaw his death and cried out repeatedly, "Alas, what an artist is dying in me." Suicide appeared to him preferable to death by public flogging (standard punishment in Rome for enemies of state), yet Nero—dagger in hand—hesitated.

"How ugly and vulgar my life has become! This certainly is no credit to Nero." As the horses of the Praetorian Guard approached, Nero raised the knife to his throat and, according to Suetonius, whispered a line of poetry: "Hark to the sound I hear! It is hooves of galloping horses." Trembling, he seized the dagger and plunged it into his throat.

At the time of Nero's death in 68, the Roman Empire was poised on a dangerous precipice. The threat of civil war was hanging heavy in the air, and the Jews in Judea had already begun a revolt that would forever alter the face of Christianity.

The Jewish War

Nero's reign was marked by an amazing indifference to the troubles that were brewing throughout his vast empire. But nowhere were the threats more serious to the stability of the *Pax Romana* than in the province of Judea. Since the time of Tiberius, the Jews in Palestine had suffered the corruption and excesses of a series of inept, and worse, Roman governors; they were losing patience with their rulers and beginning to rebel.

By 66, during the term of Gessius Florus, the Jews decided they had had enough. In response to a pagan sacrifice that was set deliberately in front of a synagogue in Caesarea, a delegation of Jews protested to Florus. He had them arrested, and further fanned the flames of rebellion by taking money from the Temple treasury. Then he ordered Roman troops to raid the markets in Jerusalem, with the result that some 3,600 Jewish men, women, and children were slaughtered. Judea's Jews, led in part by the intensely rebellious sect called Zealots, took up arms against the Romans in a widespread revolt.

But they were not wholly united in their determination to topple Roman rule. Many of Jerusalem's leaders and the high priests, who had long collaborated with the Romans, counseled peace. They were opposed by the Zealots and the Sicarii (from Latin *sica*, a dagger). This latter group, with daggers concealed in their garments, assassinated Roman collaborators.

Rebel successes

The Roman client king Herod Agrippa II sent 2,000 horsemen to assist the leaders and priests, who were occupying the upper city, while the lower city and the Temple were already controlled by rebels. The insurgents scored a series of surprising victories. They drove the cavalry out of the upper city and set fire to the archives, where all debts were recorded, hoping to encourage the poorer citizens, out of gratitude, to join them in their rebellion. They also captured and set fire to the Antonia fortress. By late summer the revolutionists had taken over the whole of Jerusalem. Cestius Gallus, the Syrian military governor, led the crack 12th Legion down the coast from Antioch to suppress the rebellion in Jerusalem. Miraculously, the outnumbered, undertrained Jews held off Gallus' legionnaires and auxiliaries and forced them to retreat. The rebels then pursued Gallus and killed his entire 400-man rear guard. Reassured by their victories, the Jews went so far as to mint their own coins.

Two of the few surviving parts of Nero's Golden House are the lavishly decorated underground room, above, and the octagonal hall, below. His enormous palace featured a circular dining room with a revolving roof, sulfur and seawater baths, a park with an artificial lake and a zoo, and a 120-foot-tall statue of Nero himself. Nero reportedly said on moving in, "Good, now I can at last begin to live like a human being!"

When Nero heard of the defeat, he dispatched his top commander, General Titus Flavius Vespasian, to quell the rebellion. The skilled military strategist, accompanied by three legions of infantry, plus cavalry and engineers, advanced on Galilee. Despite the string of fortresses that Josephus, commander of the Jewish forces in Galilee, had built there, the region fell to the Romans. (Josephus was captured and saw the remainder of the war, which he later documented, as a prisoner; he then defected to the Romans.) Vespasian's troops seized the coast road next and moved inland, retaking territory after territory until, by A.D. 68, the Romans were ready to isolate Jerusalem.

Nero's suicide on June 9, 68, led to a temporary lull while Vespasian awaited orders. Three emperors came and went before Vespasian himself was named head of the realm. He sailed for Alexandria and Rome in 70, leaving his command—and the final siege of Jerusalem—in the able hands of his son Titus. When Titus reached the outskirts of the city, he had 80,000 troops with him. He would need them.

Jerusalem, while not impregnable, was heavily fortified. On three sides, steep valleys provided natural fortifications. Troops could attack only from the north, where staunch walls and towers created three lines of defense. Titus mounted a classic military siege and after two weeks, Josephus records, his troops

Struck by Jerusalem authorities during the second year of the Jewish War, this silver coin bears a bunch of fruit, perhaps pomegranates. The fruits are surrounded by the words "Jerusalem the Holy" in old Hebrew script.

During the last desperate siege of Jerusalem, the Temple itself was finally assaulted and burned, against orders from Titus. In a reenactment of part of the battle, left, Roman soldiers rain arrows and javelins down upon the rebels from atop the Temple altar, while their comrades below attack the defenders in hand-to-hand combat. According to Josephus, "No pity was shown for age, no reverence for rank; children and greybeards, laity and priests alike were massacred."

These potsherds, each inscribed with a single name, may be some of the lots that, according to the Jewish historian Josephus, were drawn by the last survivors at Masada to choose the person who would kill the others and then himself before the Romans broke through their defenses.

"became masters of the first wall." Five days later the second wall fell and the legionnaires rushed in, but "the Jews, constantly growing in numbers and greatly at an advantage through their knowledge of the streets, wounded multitudes of the enemy."

The defenders' victory was short-lived. Titus sealed off the town with a five-mile earthen wall and killed anyone caught attempting to breach it with supplies. The tactic yielded quick results. The inhabitants were soon wracked by starvation and disease. Thousands of corpses festered throughout the city and were tossed over the walls to the valleys below.

Within a month Roman troops had reached the Temple. Titus offered to spare this holy sanctuary if only the rebels barricaded within would come outside to fight, but his offer was refused. Instead, the Jews themselves set fire to portions of the edifice rather than let the enemy take possession. When Roman troops, against Titus' orders, continued the burning, he tried in vain to stop them. The Temple was pillaged and torched, never to be rebuilt. "As the flames shot up, a cry, as poignant as the tragedy, arose from the Jews, who flocked to the rescue," wrote Josephus, "lost to all thought of self-preservation, all husbanding of strength, now that the object of all their past vigilance was vanishing."

The entire city was razed except for three staunch pillars in the northwest corner. Those Jews not slaughtered were carried off as slaves. Later, Titus marched triumphantly through Rome, bearing the golden menorah (candelabrum) from the Temple and parading before him hundreds of Jewish captives.

The fortresses of Herodium and Machaerus were captured in Jerusalem's wake. Only the now legendary Masada, set atop a steep rock outcropping, remained to be vanquished. Although the Romans had occupied the mountaintop fortress for 60 years, the Zealots had captured it in A.D. 66 and managed to hold it throughout the war. More of their group fled to Masada during Jerusalem's fall and it was here they made their final stand. Flavius Silva, Judea's new procurator, came up with an ingenious plan for breaching this heretofore impregnable fortress and snuffing out the Jewish rebellion. First, taking his cue from the siege of Jerusalem, he built a wall around the base of the mountain. Then he ordered his troops to begin work on a massive earthen ramp. Little by little, the ramp grew until it climbed 300 feet, with a platform and tower on top, and reached the fortress.

A huge iron battering ram was wheeled up the ramp and used to crash through the main wall. Inside, a second wall of timber and earth, behind which the defenders were barricaded, was set ablaze. Masada's occupants were doomed. Of some 960 men, women, and children all but 2 women and 5 children took their own lives, rather than submit to their Roman captors. The seven-year war had come to an end.

What happened to the Christians

While we know that the fall of Jerusalem and the Temple's destruction dealt a severe blow to the Jews, it is less certain what happened to the Christians as a result of the conflict. Because so many were associated with the Temple, some scholars believe that they probably perished along with their Jewish brethren. However, according to the historian Eusebius, the Christians, "commanded by a divine revelation," left Jerusalem prior to the siege and settled beyond the Jordan in a town called Pella. Later tradition has it that some returned to Jerusalem after the war, but it was no longer the nucleus of the church.

Jesus himself predicted that the Temple and even Jerusalem would be destroyed one day. Matthew recorded his words: "So when you see the desolating sacrilege spoken of by the prophet Daniel, standing in the holy place . . . then let those who are in Judea flee to the mountains. . . . Pray that your flight may not be in winter or on a sabbath. For then there will be great tribulation, such as has not been from the beginning of the world . . . and never will be."

If Christians saw destruction of Jerusalem and the Temple as God's punishment of Jews who rejected Jesus, Jews supporting the revolt would have seen as betrayers those Christians who remained neutral during the war. Later the rabbis added to the synagogue liturgy a prayer that condemned Jewish Christians. Henceforth, they could hardly join in worship at the synagogues. From now on, Christianity would develop separately from Judaism. Likewise, Judaism would undergo a momentous transformation.

Mark's Gospel

It was during the turbulent times of the Jewish War that the first of the New Testament Gospels, the Gospel according to Mark, was probably written. Most biblical scholars believe it was composed around 70, though others think it could have been written as early as 45 to 60. The claim for 70 is based on Mark's description of the destruction of the Temple, as prophesied by Jesus, in Chapter 13: "And as he came out of the temple, one of his disciples said to him, 'Look, Teacher, what wonderful stones and what wonderful buildings!' And Jesus said to him, 'Do you see these great buildings? There will not be left here one stone upon another, that will not be thrown down.' " And a parenthetical note that Mark adds in verse 14 indicates he knows his readers will understand the meaning. Additional references in Mark to persecutions of the Christians and the flight of the Jews also point to an authorship around 70.

Though the author was a contemporary of the Apostles, his identity is a matter of scholarly debate. An influential second-century tradition points to Mark, Peter's companion in Rome, who supposedly wrote down what Peter preached. Other early church historians followed this tradition and claimed the Gospel was written in Rome specifically for the church there. The congregation presumably would have been a mixture of Jews and Gentiles, for Mark assumes that his readers are familiar with the Jewish Scriptures and frequently alludes to them without direct quotation. At the same time, he carefully explains Jewish customs and translates Aramaic phrases into Greek.

The evangelist Mark is pictured with his Gospel. According to the early church leader Papias (about 60–130), said to have known some of the people who actually saw Jesus, Mark was Peter's interpreter in Rome and took down Peter's recollections of Jesus as the basis for his Gospel. This view is accepted by many scholars.

Considered the earliest of the Gospels, Mark's work apparently was used as a source for the longer accounts of Matthew and Luke. It thus represents the first surviving attempt to commit to writing the oral traditions about Jesus' life and the beginning of what came to be known as the New Testament.

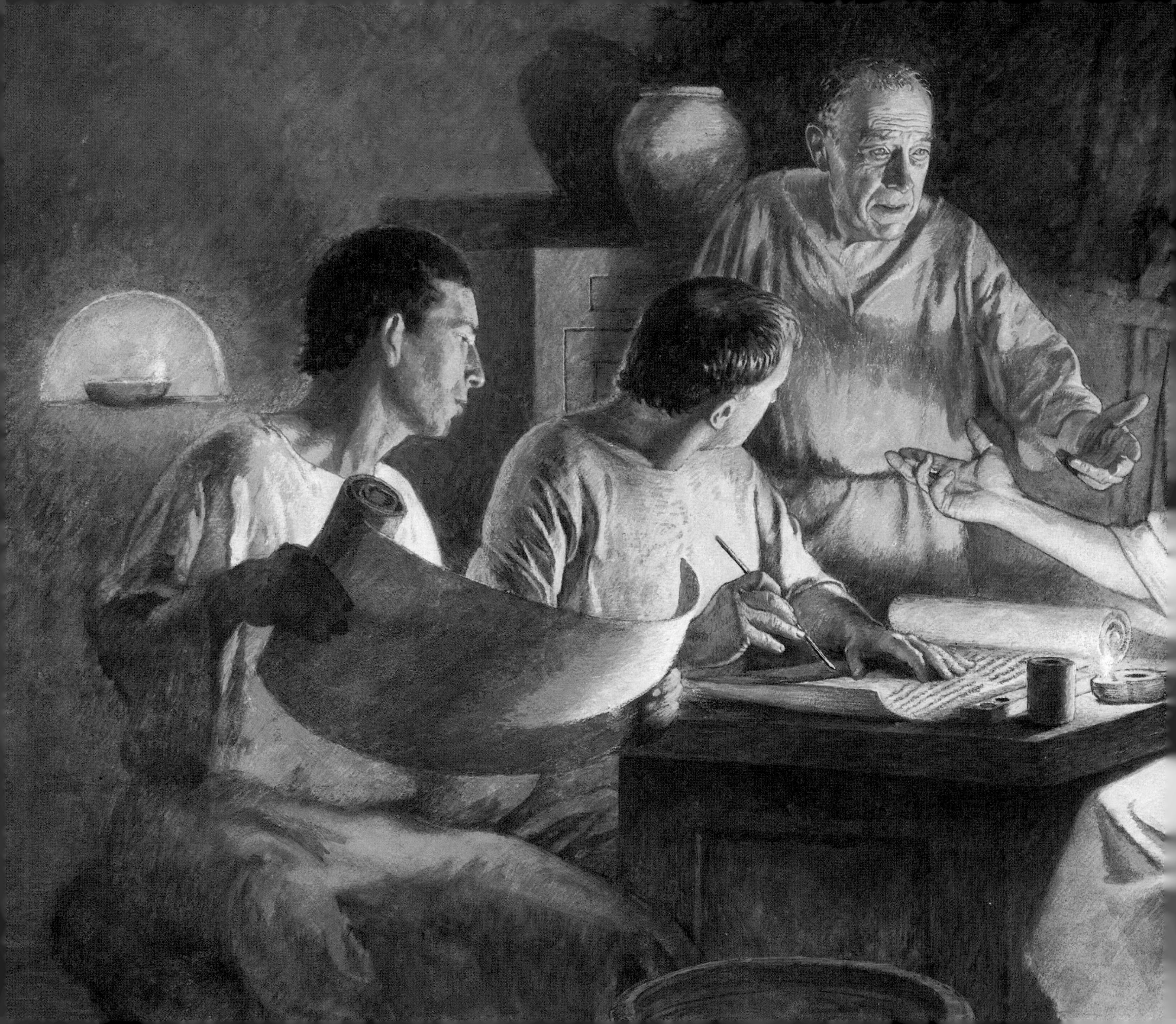

Chapter Three

HEIRS OF JESUS CHRIST

As Christianity passed the half-century mark, the churches organized to meet new challenges. At the same time, the inspired work of writing down the "memoirs of the Apostles" got under way.

About 50 years after the Crucifixion, a certain Christian in Rome, or perhaps it was Ephesus or Antioch, started writing an account of the beginnings of the faith that was the center of his life. Like others before him, he set out to recount the story of Jesus in order to show the divine character of Jesus' mission. But he went further than others and also described the later deeds of the Apostles to demonstrate the power that he saw at work in the infant church. The result was a narrative in two volumes, which constitute the third of the New Testament Gospels and The Acts of the Apostles. Together they form the largest portion of the New Testament written by a single author. Each volume was about the length that would fill one large papyrus scroll.

The author addressed his work—as was the custom in literary circles of the time—to a friend or patron, in his case a fellow Christian probably of considerable social standing, whom he calls "most excellent Theophilus." The name *Theophilus* was popular among Greek-speaking Jews as well as non-Jews, and its meaning, "lover of God," made it strikingly appropriate for the patron of such a

The author of the Gospel of Luke and the Acts of the Apostles is traditionally believed to have been a Gentile physician from Antioch who was an associate of the Apostle Paul. Here he is shown dictating his version of the story, assisted by fellow workers in Christ, including a scribe.

A doctor treats a child at the sanctuary of Amphiaraus, an ancient Greek healing center, in this detail from a bas-relief. Possibly, the work was dedicated as an offering by the child's grateful parents. Paul's "beloved physician" Luke might have been the first Christian medical missionary. According to the church historian Eusebius, Luke was close not only to Paul but to other Apostles as well and learned his "spiritual healing art" from them.

work. All we know for certain about Theophilus is that he had received instruction in the Christian faith.

Though the author named the person to whom his work was addressed, he kept himself anonymous. At no point in his extensive work did he provide his name or specify his background or the city where he lived. It is apparent, however, that he was well educated and a talented writer. Evidently he wished to draw attention not to his own identity but to the great story of Christ and his followers. Later generations could not honor his anonymity, however, and by the end of the second century the tradition was permanently established that the author was Luke, identified in the New Testament as "the beloved physician" and one of Paul's "fellow workers." Accordingly, the theologian Irenaeus, bishop of Lugdunum (present-day Lyons) late in the second century, wrote that "Luke, also, the companion of Paul, recorded in a book the Gospel preached by him [Paul]." Medical terminology sprinkled throughout the third Gospel once confirmed for many that the Luke referred to as the beloved physician was the book's author. Such medical terms, however, would have been known to any educated person in the Roman world, so they are far from conclusive evidence. With the passage of centuries the tradition was further embroidered, and in later ages Luke became the patron saint of physicians, surgeons, and painters.

According to one ancient source, which reflects how the legends about this man grew, Luke never married and lived to the age of 84. In 356 or 357 the emperor Constantius II had what were thought to be Luke's relics moved from Thebes (in Greece) to Constantinople. In art, Luke is traditionally associated with the figure of an ox, one of the four creatures (man, lion, ox, and eagle) singing at the throne of God in Revelation 4:6–9, which is interpreted as an allegory of the four evangelists. The ascription of these anonymous writings to Luke is a reasonable conjecture, however, and even scholars who question the accuracy of the tradition still call the anonymous author Luke for the sake of convenience.

The purpose of Luke's writings

Though Luke does not tell us his name, he does reveal many things about his purposes. In the first words of his Gospel he refers to the fact that "many have undertaken to compile a narrative of the things which have been accomplished among us." Before and after Luke's time other Gospels were written, all of them anonymously. Luke knew of these works and used at least some of them. Probably he had before him as he wrote a copy of what we know as the Gospel of Mark. His writing shows that he had studied it and felt free to take over much of its structure and language as a kind of skeleton for his longer Gospel. He was also familiar with a great many of Jesus' deeds and teachings not included in Mark. Both the narratives in Mark and these extra stories had been handed down to Christians of Luke's generation, he says, "by those who from the beginning were eyewitnesses and ministers of the word." The Gospel writer recognized that he was in the church's second or third generation, looking back across events, striving to understand them in the light of God's purposes.

Luke wrote as a committed Christian to other Christians. He indicates that he had learned well the tapestry of tradition and wanted to write an orderly account that showed the truth of what had been taught. The word Luke uses here, which is commonly translated as "truth," actually means "certainty." What he had in mind was not to pass along facts that anyone might grasp but rather to relate those events that demonstrate the certainty of God's participation in the story from beginning to end. At practically every turning point in the narrative, Luke saw a divine intervention, a fulfillment of what he called "the definite plan and foreknowledge of God."

Luke was writing in a time when the earliest Christian community in Jerusalem had, as far as we know, ceased to exist, because the city was destroyed in 70. What had begun as the fulfillment of Jewish hopes for a Messiah was becoming primarily a Gentile movement. How could such a change take place?

Through his two volumes Luke showed how God had brought Christians from the heart of Judaism to the heart of the Roman Empire. His story begins in the Jerusalem Temple with the priest Zechariah, who faithfully keeps God's law. It describes Jesus' birth as a descendant of David and his acclamation in the Temple both as an infant and as a boy. It tells how God's Spirit filled him at his baptism, but when he began to preach in the power of that Spirit he was rejected by the people of Nazareth among whom he had grown up. Though Jesus taught and healed and gathered disciples, conflict continued to arise until he recognized that the time for his end had drawn near, and he began a circuitous journey back to the center of Judaism, "for," according to Luke, "it cannot be that a prophet should perish away from Jerusalem."

Many Christians from ancient times to the present have assumed that the Gospels were written by Apostles. Some Church Fathers themselves bolstered that assumption. For instance, the second-century Christian apologist Justin Martyr referred to the Gospels as "memoirs composed by the Apostles." Actually, the Gospels of John and Matthew are the ones traditionally attributed to Apostles. Mark and Luke derive their apostolic authority by their association with Peter and Paul respectively.

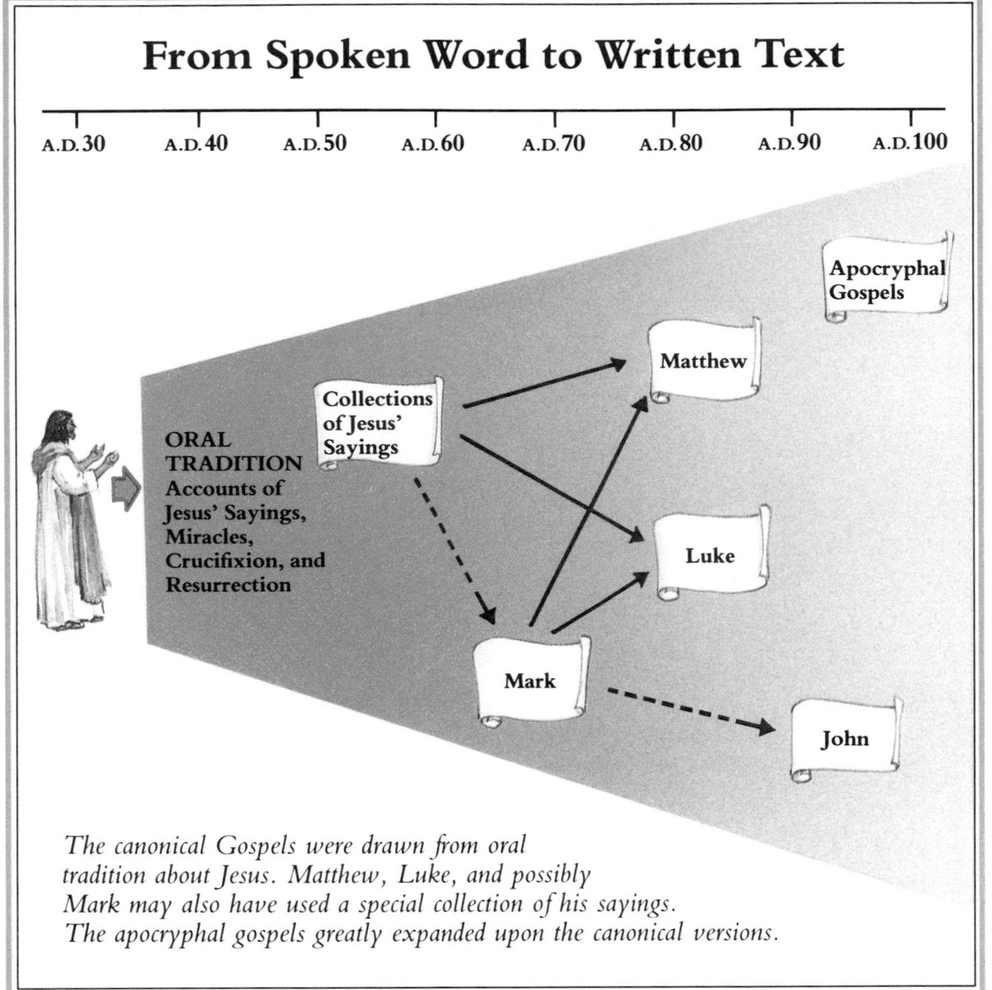

The canonical Gospels were drawn from oral tradition about Jesus. Matthew, Luke, and possibly Mark may also have used a special collection of his sayings. The apocryphal gospels greatly expanded upon the canonical versions.

Luke had no desire to write something new. But, like the other Gospel writers, he shaped the tradition in retelling it so that his readers could see patterns, purpose, and meaning in it. His story is unified by numerous threads that run through the tapestry from beginning to end. He stresses the universality of the new faith, the power of the Holy Spirit, the importance of prayer, the dangers of wealth. He shows that both Jesus and later his followers were friends to the poor, to the outcasts of society, to sinners, lepers, tax-collectors, Samaritans, and Gentiles. He emphasizes the importance of women among the disciples who traveled with Jesus, a role unprecedented in the ancient Mediterranean world. By recounting the teachings of Jesus and the sermons of the Apostles, Luke makes his work as much a body of instruction and exhortation as of narrative and description.

Meeting a need

All the New Testament authors wrote not primarily for posterity but for contemporary Christians, endeavoring to instruct, inspire, solve a problem, or chastise. The writings on the life of Jesus are called Gospels because they relate the "good news" of Christ's teachings, life, death, and Resurrection. The word *gospel* comes from Old English *godspell*, "good news," translated from Late Latin *evangelium* or Greek *euangelion*, both of which mean "good news."

Written versions of the traditions concerning Christ's life and teachings almost certainly existed before the Gospels and epistles were written, but none survived. They may have been compilations of Jesus' sayings and parables or collections of key passages from the Scriptures with notes giving interpretations of them. For example, such a collection might have contained passages from the psalms and prophets showing how they were related to each other and to Christ. These collections came to be known as *testimonia*, or "testimonies." However, all of the material committed to writing—sayings and parables of Jesus, stories about his life, interpretations of Old Testament passages relating them to Christ—had originally been handed down by word of mouth (see page 31).

In the early days of the church, oral tradition often enjoyed a higher prestige than any writing. Even when the epistles and Gospels began to circulate, the spoken word continued to be powerful. In those times, when every book had to be laboriously copied by hand, manuscripts were expensive and hard to obtain and people were used to learning stories and teachings by heart.

There is little evidence that early Christians memorized lengthy passages of Jesus' words or deeds, like the Greek minstrels who committed Homer to memory or the rabbinic disciples who could recite the traditions of the sages. Rather Christians continued to relate their traditions about Jesus mostly in short pieces, retelling individual stories or groups of sayings for a particular purpose. For reference they relied on the way these authoritative words were told to them, rather than looking them up in a book. Almost a century after Mark wrote the first Gospel, Papias, bishop of Hierapolis in Asia Minor, still instinctively believed that the ear and the heart were much better carriers of tradition than papyrus: "Things out of books," he averred, "did not profit me so much as the utterances of a voice that lives and abides."

As time went on, however, people felt a need to preserve the oral tradition concerning Jesus' life and teachings in written form. The Gospels and important sections of Paul's letters were the result.

Different points of view

It is hardly surprising that the Gospels, written by different authors, at various times, and for a variety of purposes, exhibit some discrepancies. While they all focus on the life and teachings of Jesus, each presents a different point of view. Matthew and Luke most likely had read the Gospel of Mark, but neither felt obliged simply to repeat the traditions verbatim. Both writers changed the order of some events. Luke moved the rejection at Nazareth from the middle to the beginning of Jesus' ministry. Matthew grouped miracles from various sections of Mark in one section after the Sermon on the Mount. Both revised, sometimes extensively, the accounts they had received. All of them probably realized that these were narratives they had heard numerous times in many forms. It is important to remember that while the evangelists did base their stories on accepted tradition, they were not biographers. Rather, they carefully crafted their Gospels to serve the different needs of their audiences. The overriding purpose was to win converts and strengthen the faith of believers. Therefore, each evangelist emphasized different aspects of Christ's life.

Matthew addressed his Gospel to Jewish Christians involved in the conflicts between Christians and Jews in the troubled period after the destruction of the Jerusalem Temple. He presents Jesus as the long-awaited Messiah promised in the Old Testament. Fittingly, his work begins by tracing "the genealogy of Jesus Christ, the son of David, the son of Abraham" and includes numerous references linking the new church to the old Israel. He shapes his narration to emphasize Jesus as the authoritative teacher. Five times Jesus gives extended speeches to teach his disciples their responsibilities as his followers.

Like Matthew, John wrote to a church in conflict with Jewish synagogues as both were struggling for their existence after the Jewish War. In John's Gospel, Jesus' divine nature is revealed: "And the Word became flesh and dwelt among us, full of grace and truth; we have beheld his glory, glory as of the only Son from the Father." John's narrative is dramatically different from those of Matthew, Mark, and Luke (he probably did not know them). He includes none of the parables or exorcisms that are common in the first three Gospels. Instead, his Gospel is built around seven miraculous "signs" that Jesus performs and numerous extended discourses in which Christ reveals his divine nature and mission. John's aim, as he notes near the end of his work, is "that you may believe that Jesus is the Christ, the Son of God, and that believing you may have life in his name."

The Synoptic Gospels

Since the 18th century, scholars have termed Matthew, Mark, and Luke the Synoptic Gospels. This means that they share a single basic outline and many agreements of language and detail. If episodes from the three Gospels are scanned simultaneously with

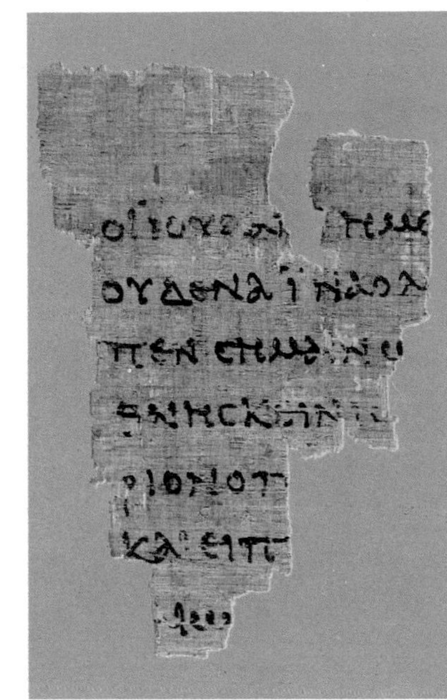

This scrap of a page from an Egyptian papyrus book, dating from the first half of the second century, is the oldest surviving piece of any New Testament book. The words are from John 18:31–33. Early Christian writings were usually circulated in what was then the innovative format of a book with pages, rather than the traditional scroll used by both Jews and pagans of the Roman world.

their texts side by side, it is quickly apparent that they contain very similar material. In many places, whole sentences and even paragraphs are practically identical in the Greek original. (First used in this sense by the German Bible scholar J.J. Griesbach in 1776, *synoptic* is based on the Greek word *synopsis*, "view at the same time, simultaneous viewing.") In fact, 606 of Mark's 661 verses appear in some form in Matthew. Likewise, 380 of Mark's 661 verses can be found in Luke's Gospel. The most widely accepted explanation for these relationships is that Mark's was the first Gospel to be written and that both Matthew and Luke revised and expanded Mark's version. In addition to the material they have taken from Mark, both Matthew and Luke have also incorporated about 250 verses of other material that is very similar in both books. This material comprises much of Jesus' teaching, most of the Sermon on the Mount, including the Lord's Prayer and the Beatitudes, and such miracles as the healing of the centurion's servant.

The great majority of scholars agree that, in addition to Mark's Gospel, there had to be a second source used by Luke and Matthew but one that was not complete and thus has not survived the centuries. Scholars have dubbed this long-vanished source Q from the German *Quelle*, "source," and believe it to have been a compendium of Jesus' sayings.

One solution to the problem of four Gospels was hit upon by an Assyrian-born, Greek-educated man named Tatian, who lived in Rome between 150 and 165. Tatian took the texts of the four Gospels and melded them into one continuous text, the *Diatessaron*, literally "through four." This harmony, or synthesis, became the standard Gospel text for several hundred years in many Christian communities of the East. (It may have been used, for example, by the congregation based in the Dura-Europos house-church described on pages 145–146.)

The canon of four Gospels

Almost since their creation, the works that comprise the New Testament have been controversial. Debates on the evangelists' sources began in earnest about 200 years ago (they were anticipated by Augustine's *The Harmony of the Gospels*, however, written in 400). But

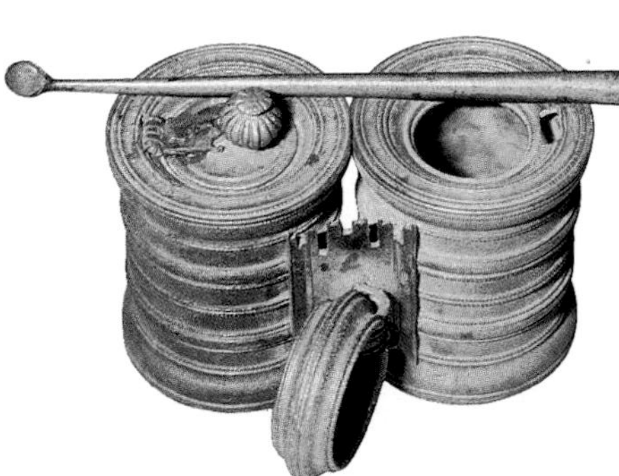

A Roman amanuensis (secretary) took notes on a wax tablet that served the same purpose as a modern scratch pad. Only when the writing reached the stage of a finished draft was pen put to papyrus. The ink wells and pen at left are no doubt similar to those used by Mark and Luke in their capacity as assistants to Peter and Paul.

arguments over which texts were legitimate, or canonical, go back nearly 2,000 years. The term *canon* comes from Greek *kanon*, "carpenter's rule," but by late antiquity the word was used in both Greek and Latin in the sense of "model, standard, norm."

About 140 Marcion (see pages 131–132), the son of a bishop in northern Asia Minor and himself a wealthy shipowner, tried to reform the church by rejecting the Old Testament and drawing up a list of authoritative Scripture to replace it. He named only one of the Gospels—a version of Luke, edited to remove what he thought were false additions. And he included 10 of Paul's letters. Marcion's proposals set off a fierce controversy and helped to clarify the views of many Christians even as they rejected Marcion's ideas.

Near the end of the second century, the Gospels of Matthew, Mark, Luke, and John were proclaimed to be canonical by Bishop Irenaeus. He explained, "Since there are four zones of the world . . . and four principal winds, while the Church is scattered throughout all the world . . . it is fitting that she should have four pillars. . . . [God] has given us the Gospel under four aspects but bound together by one Spirit." The New Testament, built around the core of the "fourfold gospels," was beginning to take shape.

By the year 300, all four of the Gospels, The Acts of the Apostles, and most of Paul's letters were generally accepted as authoritative. There were, however, other works—the *Gospel of Peter,* the *Epistle of Barnabas,* The Letter to the Hebrews, and Revelation—that were appproved by some and questioned by others.

Thanks to a fragment of a late-second-century document known as the Muratorian Canon (from the name of the Italian librarian, Lodovico Muratori, who discovered it in the Ambrosian Library in Milan in 1740), we know which works were accepted by the early Roman church. The list, written in very poor Latin, probably a translation from Greek, includes the four Gospels; Acts; 13 letters of Paul (Hebrews is not mentioned); Jude; 1, 2, and perhaps 3 John; and The Revelation to John. It says that John the Apostle was the author of the fourth Gospel *and* Revelation and recounts a colorful legend about how John decided to write a Gospel. Perhaps surprisingly, it also includes in the New Testament the *Apocalypse of Peter* and *The Wisdom of Solomon.* (The latter is now in the Apocrypha. See pages 134–137 for other early Christian writings.) The Muratorian Canon calls the latter work "Wisdom, written by the friends of Solomon in his honor." Later lists varied somewhat.

It was only in 367 that a list of 27 books identical to the present-day New Testament appeared, as part of an Easter festival letter written by Athanasius, bishop of Alexandria. In 397 the Council of Carthage published an identical one. While the Church Fathers and local councils pronounced on the legitimacy of Christian writings, it was really the communities themselves that provided the true tests of what would be included in the canon. The New Testament was based finally on writings that had proved popular and useful for reading in the scattered congregations. This can be seen in the long-standing reluctance to approve the shorter epistles—2 Peter, 2 and 3 John, James, and Jude—which were circulated less widely in the early church. Thus, the canon of Christian writings came from the bottom up, instead of being handed down by the church authorities.

What the letters teach us

"I, Paul, write this greeting with my own hand," notes the Apostle at the conclusion of his first letter to the church in Corinth. Letters make up about a third of the New Testament; 13 are ascribed to Paul, 1 each to Jude and James, and 2 to Peter; 3 are anonymous but have traditionally been attributed to John, and Hebrews is anonymous but was traditionally credited to Paul. These 21 works reflect the life of the church in its early years, when so many issues and problems were being threshed out in the daily lives of Christians. They are anything but dry theological treatises.

Paul's letters read, for the most part, like the candid, unceremonious communications he intended them to be. Although many of them are addressed to Christian communities troubled by one conflict or another, most contain the warm tone of a friend writing to a friend. Difficulties in understanding the letters often arise because today we are reading only one side of a two-way conversation. The original addressees would have recognized allusions and references that remain obscure to us.

In Paul's day a typical letter in Greek contained an introductory section, a main body, and a conclusion. Paul modified that style slightly, beginning with an opening, followed by a thanksgiving or blessing, the body, an advice section, and a closing. His format became a standard that was copied by others to communicate within the early church. Paul's letters reflected such a highly personal style that many of his readers must have felt his very presence, as one of his emissaries read his words out loud to a congregation. He wrote to these converts like a father addressing his children, here filled with pride and love, there angered over some of their failings.

In the years after Paul's death, a large number of coworkers continued his ministry, and some of the letters attributed to Paul have been thought to come from this period. Although 1 and 2 Timothy and Titus, for example, are labeled as Paul's work, they are so different in style, vocabulary, and content from Paul's other letters that many scholars doubt that he was the author. Since the 18th century these have been called pastoral letters because they were written to advise church leaders on pastoral and ecclesiastical matters. Among their distinctive characteristics, the

Sayings of Jesus Not Included in the Gospels

A rich body of sayings and parables attributed to Jesus but omitted from the four Gospels of the New Testament lived on in oral tradition. Known as *agrapha,* "unwritten things," some came to be included in writings of other Christian authors:

No man that is not tempted shall obtain the kingdom of heaven. This saying is quoted by Tertullian, the first major Christian author to write in Latin.

Ask ye for the greater things, and the small shall be added unto you: and ask for the heavenly things, and the earthly shall be added unto you. The third-century theologian Origen of Alexandria preserved this saying, which he quotes in his treatise *On Prayer.*

A letter attributed to Clement of Rome says that "when the Lord himself was asked by someone when his kingdom would come, he said: *'When the two shall be one, and the outside as the inside, and the male with the female neither male nor female.'* "

He that is near me is near the fire. He that is far from me is far from the kingdom. This saying, along with more sayings and parables attributed to Jesus, appears in the noncanonical book the *Gospel of Thomas.* Some of the material could possibly be authentic, but there is no way of knowing for certain. Here, from the *Gospel of Thomas,* is another example, a parable that might have been told by Jesus. It follows directly after the parable of the leaven, which is also found in Matthew 13:33 and Luke 13:20–21. All of these parables deal with the hidden ways that God's rule may work in people's lives.

The Jar of Flour

The kingdom of the Father is like a woman who was carrying a jar full of flour. While she was walking on a road far from home, the handle of the jar broke and the flour spilled behind her on the road. She did not know it: she had not noticed the problem. When she reached her house, she put the jar down and discovered that it was empty.

In other words, the kingdom of heaven may be lost if we are negligent.

three letters, which are addressed to Paul's companions Timothy and Titus, contain some 175 words that appear nowhere else in Paul's writings. Furthermore, they do not fit in with what we otherwise know of Paul's life. To have written them he would have to have been released from prison in Rome and have traveled extensively in the Aegean area that he had planned never to visit again.

The origin of the Letter to the Hebrews is another mystery. In the second and third centuries, the churches in the Eastern empire attributed it to Paul, while churches in the West denied that Paul was the author. It is unlike Paul's letters in both style and ideas. Indeed, it is more a treatise—arguing the significance of Christianity's new covenant over the old covenant of Israel—than a letter and does not open with an address to a specific church.

The remaining letters, James, 1 and 2 Peter, 1, 2, and 3 John, and Jude—often called the general letters or catholic epistles because they were thought to be for general circulation among the Christian communities of their day—raise similar questions. First Peter was probably written from Rome to encourage believers in Asia Minor who were being persecuted and was widely read in the early church. In 96, Clement of Rome (later known as Pope Clement I) referred to it, as did the subsequent Church Fathers Polycarp and Irenaeus. The latter claimed it was written by the Apostle Peter. Scholars have had difficulty accepting his assumption, however, because the letter's polished Greek seems unlikely as the product of an uneducated fisherman. Some believe that his secretary, Silvanus, who is mentioned in the last verses of the letter, wrote it based on Peter's teachings. In any event, its companion letter, 2 Peter, which was written to warn Christians against false teachers, is strikingly different in both style and purpose. The short, 25-verse letter, Jude, is similar in content to 2 Peter and is traditionally thought to have been written by Jude, who was a kinsman of Jesus.

A tradition claiming that James, head of the Jerusalem church, is the author of the letter bearing his name, has little support. More a collection of wise sayings and exhortations than a letter, it sets guidelines for Christian living. Within its 108 verses are about 60 commands urging the practice of a life of faith. Among these are: "Let the lowly brother boast in his exaltation, and the rich in his humiliation, because like the flower of the grass he will pass away. . . . Let every man be quick to hear, slow to speak, slow to anger, for the anger of man does not work the righteousness of God." The letter is also memorable for its teaching on the relationship between faith and works: "Faith by itself, if it has no

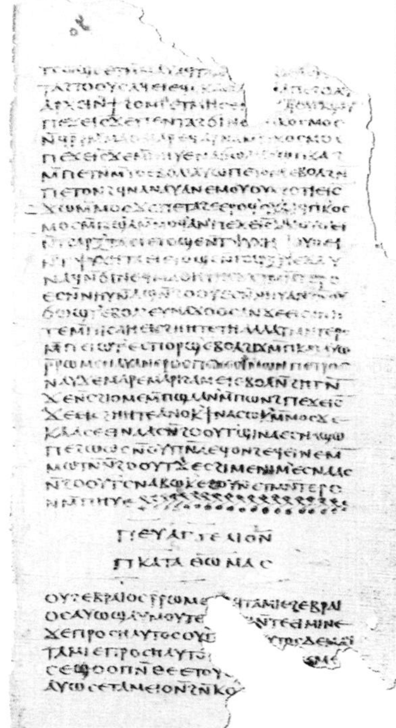

At right is the title page of the noncanonical Gospel of Thomas *(a collection of Jesus' sayings). A similar compilation was the* Secret Book of James, *which contains the mysterious parable of the date palm suggested by a fifth-century mosaic (far right): "Do not let the kingdom of heaven waste away. For it is like a palm shoot that dropped its dates all around. It produced buds, and after they had grown, the stalk dried up. . . . After it was harvested, more dates were produced by many new shoots. It certainly would be good if this new growth could be produced now, so that you might find the kingdom." (4:10–12).*

works, is dead. . . . For as the body apart from the spirit is dead, so faith apart from works is dead." Some have argued that the letter is more Jewish in character than Christian. Martin Luther considered it a lightweight missive alongside the rest of the New Testament, calling it "a right strawy epistle . . . for it has no evangelical manner about it." A number of other scholars have not shared Luther's opinion, however, since this epistle is close in content and style to Jesus' Sermon on the Mount.

Three short letters are attributed to the same person who wrote the Gospel of John. Both the fourth Gospel and 1 John make striking and repeated reference to the idea of spiritual illumination from God, of light shining in darkness; and they use the word *light* in this sense more often than any other New Testament writings. Reflecting these similarities in vocabulary, both the Gospel and the letters express comparable theological ideas. The first letter may even have been intended as a commentary on the Gospel.

A noncanonical gospel

"These are the secret sayings that the living Jesus spoke and Judas Thomas the Twin recorded." So begins the *Gospel of Thomas,* a late-first-century or early-second-century collection of sayings attributed to Jesus, which has only recently come to light. Although this intriguing work was mentioned by church writers of the third and fourth centuries, and fragments of the original Greek text were recovered around the turn of the 19th century, a complete version became available only after a chance discovery in 1945. That year a Gnostic library of parchment books in Coptic translation were found preserved in a sealed jar near Nag Hammadi, Egypt.

The sayings attributed to Jesus in the *Gospel of Thomas* have many parallels in the Synoptic Gospels but probably derive from a separate oral tradition, one that is in fact more primitive. Most remarkably, it contains not a word about the Resurrection of Jesus Christ. Like the sayings, or Q, source most likely used by Matthew and Luke, it has no narrative linking the 114-odd sayings, nor is there any logical or expository thread tying them together.

Many of the sayings in *Thomas* pertain to the kingdom of God. Instead of treating it as something that will come to the faithful, the sayings urge that one must know oneself to achieve salvation: "The kingdom is inside you and outside you. When you know yourselves, then you will be known." Elsewhere: "His disciples said to him, 'When will the final rest for the dead take place, and when will the new world come?' He said to them, 'What you look for has already come, but you do not know it.' "

Some leading Bible scholars think that part of the material in *Thomas* was written within 10 to 20 years of Jesus' death. In this view, the earliest Christians believed that Jesus' own words were their source of life and salvation, and that a true grasp of his teaching that the kingdom of God was already in their midst would empower them to transcend mundane existence. Though some facets of this teaching remain unclear, many early Christians seem to have understood and valued the *Gospel of Thomas*.

Revelation

The Revelation to John is a stirring conclusion to the New Testament. Among scholars there is wide agreement that the book was composed in the 90's, near the end of the reign of Domitian. The author is identified only as "John," and all we know for sure is that he was a first-century Jewish Christian prophet of Asia Minor. He is often called John of Patmos, after the island of Patmos, where he received the vision (see page 90). From the mid-second century onward, Christian writers began to equate him with John the Apostle and supposed author of the fourth Gospel, despite the extraordinary differences in style between the latter book and Revelation. Even such sensitive and critical writers as Irenaeus and Origen seem to have accepted the identification without question. It was not until the third century that a bishop of Alexandria, Dionysius the Great, set forth powerful arguments against the common authorship of the two books. His reason for doing so was polemical. A sect proclaiming the imminent Second Coming and the millennium was pointing at the Revelation to John as its authority. Dionysius responded with an attack on Revelation itself, which was destined to jeopardize the book's canonical status for a long time. (In the 16th century such figures as Martin Luther and John Knox expressed similar doubts about Revelation.)

The Apocalypse of Peter

Another visionary book, the *Apocalypse of Peter,* competed in popularity with The Revelation to John for acceptance as a book of the New Testament; it was listed in the Muratorian Canon, with the comment that "some of us are not willing to have [it] read in church." In this book, which dates from the early to mid-second century, Jesus describes to his disciples on the Mount of Olives the signs of his Second Coming and of the Last Judgment. The disciples also receive a vision of the eternal punishments and rewards of saints and sinners. The vision is more specific than any passage in the Bible about heaven and hell as real places. The book also sets a precedent for gruesome descriptions of infernal punishments, a theme that would be continued in Christian apocalypses of later antiquity and derivative visionary literature of the Middle Ages, including Dante's *Divine Comedy*. A late-second-century Church Father, Clement of Alexandria, believed that it was actually written by Peter and should be accepted as Scripture. Within another hundred years its canonicity was considered doubtful by most, but as late as the fifth century it was still being read on Good Friday in some churches in Palestine. Most notably, the concluding chapter of the *Apocalypse of Peter* promises that all sinners will eventually be saved because of the prayers of the righteous.

Continued on page 92

Early Christianity developed a complex picture of hell and its torments, which became further elaborated in later centuries. This miniature from a medieval book of hours draws on a variety of sources for its imagery. The figure of Satan in Revelation 20 is merged with the image of the Leviathan from the Book of Job: "Out of his mouth go flaming torches; sparks of fire leap forth." The Leviathan is a mighty sea monster that in the Old Testament is equated with Satan. Christian apocalyptic literature inherited this and other similar traditions.

Apocalyptic Visions

In Revelation, spectacular visions highlight a stirring message to believers—the Lamb with the 144,000 faithful, the beast from the sea, the woman and the dragon, the new Jerusalem, and others.

"And I saw, and behold, a black horse, and its rider had a balance in his hand; and I heard what seemed to be a voice . . . saying, . . . 'do not harm oil and wine!' " Revelation 6:5–6. The black horse symbolizes famine caused by war; the balance stands for the rationing of food and drink rather than for justice, as might be supposed. The voice could be an allusion to Titus, who during the siege of Jerusalem ordered that vineyards and olive groves be spared.

"The second angel blew his trumpet, and something like a great mountain, burning with fire, was thrown into the sea; and a third of the sea became blood, a third of the living creatures in the sea died, and a third of the ships were destroyed." Revelation 8:8–9. The image of a burning mountain may refer to the A.D. *79 eruption of Vesuvius. Or it may be that the author is speaking not of something past but rather of something that is still to come.*

The vision of the woman, the child, and the dragon (Revelation 12:1–6) reflects the struggle between Christ and Satan. The woman is identified both with Israel as parent of Christ and with the Christian Church. Some Christian interpreters have also seen her as a personification of the church in Mary the mother of Jesus.

"Then I looked, and lo, on Mount Zion stood the Lamb, and with him a hundred and forty-four thousand." Revelation 14:1. The number 144,000 symbolizes perfection and stands for the whole number of the faithful led by Christ the Lamb.

In the vision of two beasts (Revelation 13), the beast from the sea represents the Roman Empire. The beast from the earth represents Satan and his mouthpieces, such false prophets and wonder-workers as Simon Magus, Apollonius of Tyana, and other astrologers, priests, and magicians of the day. Its number, 666, possibly stands for "Nero Caesar."

"Then I saw a new heaven and a new earth." Revelation 21:1. The vision of new Jerusalem embodies the promise of renewal and transcendence at the heart of Christ's message to humanity: the city of God is descending from heaven to become the city of man.

Who wrote Revelation and the Gospel According to John?

A Christian, known only as John, was exiled to Patmos, a rocky penal colony in the Aegean Sea, probably during the persecutions of the late first century. Since banishment was the customary punishment for many offenses, including prophesying, a number of historians believe that he was charged with prophesying the return of Jesus as King.

While on Patmos, John had several glorious prophetic visions, which he wrote down in vivid detail. His stupendous book of Revelation, called an apocalypse from a Greek word meaning "reveal," describes in symbolic images God's cosmic plans for mankind. Among other things, it offers hope, through an event in which Satan is sealed in a bottomless pit for 1,000 years, that God will overcome both Satan and his dark forces. According to the apocalypse, a spirit also showed John "the holy city Jerusalem coming down out of heaven from God, having the glory of God, its radiance like a most rare jewel."

Unlike the apocalpyses of the Old Testament, these revelations were not to be hidden away but were to be read immediately in order to bolster the faith of early Christians. If it is true, as many believe, that John wrote during the reign of Domitian (81–96), he would have known that refusing to worship Domitian as a living god could put a Christian's life in danger. Nero and Caligula, two of Domitian's predecessors, had made the same demand. Some biblical scholars think that John is referring to these despotic emperors when he describes a series of evil beasts in Revelation. One beast is given the number 666. Using the numerical equivalents assigned to Hebrew letters, the number can be converted to the name *Nero Caesar*—one of the worst persecutors of them all.

Much about the author of Revelation continues to elude biblical scholars. Because the writer gives his name as John, many early Christians assumed that he was John the Apostle. However, the style and grammar in Revelation are very different from those in the Gospel attributed to John. Consequently, as early as the second century, some scholars surmised that the author of Revelation was not the Apostle but another Christian of some influence. Whoever he was, he has come to be known as John of Patmos.

In Revelation 10, *a voice told John to take the little scroll (or book) from the angel. It would be sweet because it contained God's words, and bitter because it involved his judgments.*

The Fourth Gospel

"In the beginning was the Word, and the Word was with God, and the Word was God." So begins the magnificent fourth Gospel. But who was its author? Was it John the Apostle or the visionary of Patmos? Or could it have been some unknown Christian disciple? Historians to this day are not certain, for the simple reason that the author apparently wished to remain anonymous. However, within 50 years after the book first appeared in about 95, a tradition was already established that the work was written by the Apostle John, near the end of his long life.

Several early Christian writers confirmed another tradition that John settled in the Christian community at Ephesus, where he is said to have written his Gospel and three epistles. Jerome, the fourth-century theologian, told of an elderly John being carried to Ephesian church gatherings, where he would say to the congregation, "My little children, love one another." Irenaeus, the bishop of Lyons in the late second-century, wrote that John refuted heretics and lived on till the days of Trajan, who reigned from 98 to 117. This would make John the last surviving Apostle and perhaps the only one to die of natural causes.

Some contend, however, that John died a young man, which they believe Jesus foretold in Mark 10:39: "The cup that I drink you will drink." Indeed, a few historians maintain that John the Apostle was persecuted under Herod (41–44) and died a martyr, along with his brother James. They therefore question whether Irenaeus was speaking of John the Apostle or another John, known as the Elder. Could this disciple have written the fourth Gospel *and* the epistles? It is impossible to know for sure because it was difficult in ancient times to determine precise authorship of a work. Most scholars then and now, however, remain convinced that John the Apostle is the "beloved disciple" and author of the powerful testimony to Jesus known to us as the Gospel According to John.

A powerful parable of repentance, from the writings of Clement of Alexandria, is depicted here in this 13th-century illustration. It relates how John the Apostle entrusted a bishop to teach a young man the way of God. The bishop then relaxed his care. Unused to such liberty, the youth fell in with a band of robbers. When John learned of this, he pursued the fallen youth, who felt so ashamed he began to tremble and weep.

Christianity in Rome

The period after the fall of Jerusalem in 70 was a time of growth for the Christian movement, especially in Rome. Although the origins of the church there are obscure, it grew quickly in both numbers and importance. By the end of the first century, the congregation had adopted a leadership role in the affairs of the church throughout the empire. The church's claim that Peter and Paul were buried in Rome gave it added prestige, as did its location in the capital city of the world. Eventually, the Roman church prospered enough to become known for its generosity. In the late second century, Dionysius, the bishop of Corinth, commended it for sending "contributions to many churches in every city."

In the epistle 1 Peter, probably written from Rome, Christians were counseled: "Be prepared to make a defense to any one who calls you to account for the hope that is in you . . . and keep your conscience clear, so that, when you are abused, those who revile your good behavior in Christ may be put to shame." This was timely advice, because Christians everywhere, but especially in Rome, were being derided for their devotion to a "superstition," for that was the pagan view. According to Acts, Paul, while a prisoner in Rome, was questioned about the local Christian community: "With regard to this sect we know that everywhere it is spoken against." For some, their profession of faith would become a death warrant.

Rome's first-century Christian community came from all sectors of society. The majority were low-paid, Greek-speaking immigrants. Many lived in the poorest neighborhoods, such as Transtiberim (present-day Trastevere). This was a harbor and working-class quarter across the Tiber from the heart of Rome, where seamen, potters, tanners, leather workers, peddlers, and dock workers crowded the streets. Others, especially women, were of upper-class origin.

As elsewhere, congregations worshiped in small groups, usually meeting in privately owned house-churches scattered around the capital. Paul refers to one of these in Romans: "Greet Prisca [or Priscilla] and Aquila [her husband], my fellow workers in Christ Jesus . . . greet also the church in their house."

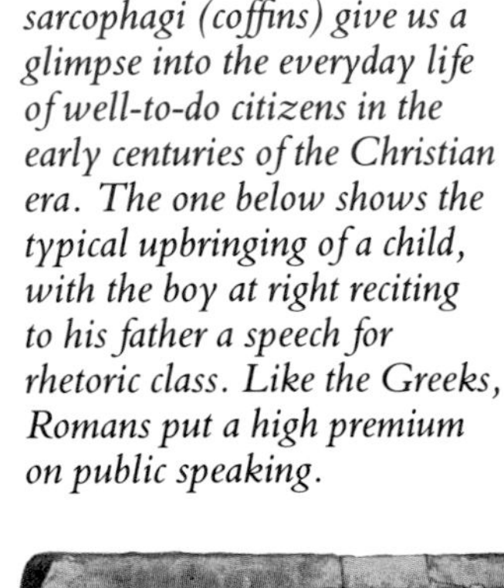

Scenes carved on Roman sarcophagi (coffins) give us a glimpse into the everyday life of well-to-do citizens in the early centuries of the Christian era. The one below shows the typical upbringing of a child, with the boy at right reciting to his father a speech for rhetoric class. Like the Greeks, Romans put a high premium on public speaking.

Unfortunately, despite the best efforts of historians and archaeologists, there are many unanswered questions about the day-to-day lives of first-century Romans. Much of the physical evidence that could detail their lifestyles disappeared, deteriorated, or was destroyed as new buildings were constructed on the foundations of older ones. In one Roman city, however, a natural disaster has provided an intimate, but eerie, glimpse into the lives of its residents. The city is Pompeii, which, along with the neighboring Herculaneum, was completely devastated by the eruption of Mount Vesuvius on August 24, 79.

Pompeii and Herculaneum

Pompeii, a fishing and manufacturing city on the coast 14 miles southeast of Naples, was still recovering from an earthquake that had rocked the area in 62 or 63, when the earth again began to vibrate on that fateful August morning. In the early afternoon the top of the mountain blew off and filled the sky with ash, pumice, and smoke. Pliny the Younger, who was an eyewitness, noted that the cloud looked like a giant pine tree: "For it shot up a great height in the form of a trunk, which extended itself at the top into several branches. . . . It was at one moment white, at another dark and spotted, as if it had carried up earth or cinders." Scientists estimate that thc powerful blast blew pumice and debris 12 miles up into the stratosphere. For the next 17 hours it rained back down on the surrounding countryside, burying the city.

Even at a distance of 20 miles from Vesuvius, in Misenium, the scenes were terrifying. Pliny wrote: "Ashes now fall upon us, though as yet in no great quantity. I looked behind me; gross darkness pressed upon our rear, and came rolling over the land after us like a torrent. . . . You could hear the shrieks of

At far right a wealthy Roman matron of nearly 2,000 years ago reclines on a couch with her infant son. Perhaps his favorite toy was one like the terra-cotta horseman, below, mounted on wheels so that it could be pushed around. The doll, right, also of terra-cotta and with movable limbs, might have possessed a whole wardrobe of graceful robes.

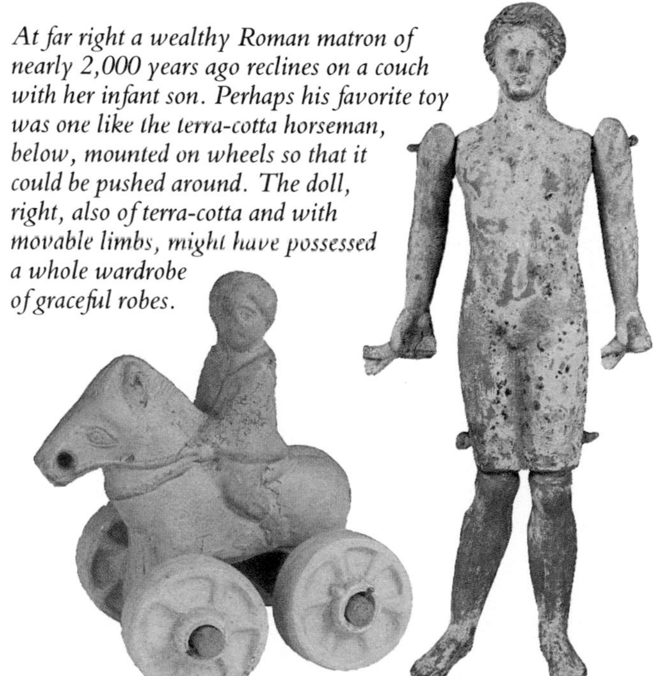

women, the crying of children, and the shouts of men; some were seeking their children, others their parents, others their wives or husbands . . . some praying to die, from the very fear of dying; many lifting their hands to the gods; but the greater part imagining that there were no gods left anywhere, and that the last and eternal night was come upon the world."

Glowing avalanches slithered toward the two cities. An oozing brown mixture sealed Herculaneum's doors and streets and entombed many of its citizens. In Pompeii, rough seas and earthquakes ravaged the dock area, cutting off the townspeople's most obvious escape route. Most fled the city, but hundreds were trapped by flames and choking sulfurous vapor. Pliny's uncle, the famous naturalist Pliny the Elder, died on a nearby beach, having sailed there in a naval galley in order to observe the cataclysm from the closest possible vantage point. He died either overcome by the poisonous fumes or from a heart attack.

As many as 2,000, or one-tenth of the local population, may have perished at Pompeii. At Herculaneum, scarcely five miles below the peak of Vesuvius, the loss of life is unknown. But the hot noxious debris of ash, stones, and steam—up to 65 feet deep in some places—killed everyone who remained in the city.

Excavations at Herculaneum and Pompeii have produced veritable time capsules of first-century life. The skeleton of a baby lies in a fragile but well-preserved cradle. A cluster of skeletons, probably those of a family fleeing the choking ash, seem frozen at the moment of death. A wooden cabinet, a marble wash basin, a bed with a graceful latticework pattern, a bronze bathtub, striking wall paintings depicting hunting scenes, gardens, and theatrical themes—all form a tableau of life at that time.

In an excavated home in Herculaneum, the imprint of a shape like a cross appears on one wall. Were Christians there in the first century? Historians have

Vesuvius dominates the skyline behind Pompeii in these pictures, one a present-day photograph, the other a fresco of a seaside villa done shortly before the volcano erupted. Remains of such villas can still be seen within the Bay of Naples.

been skeptical, because it is not on the *eastern* wall (many early Christians faced east when they prayed). Also, though the cross has been employed almost universally since ancient times as a magical and religious symbol, there is no evidence that Christians used it at this early date. It came into use in the church only after the victory of Constantine, who became the first Christian emperor early in the fourth century. Perhaps further excavations at Herculaneum and Pompeii will provide hard evidence of some other kind that there were indeed Christians living there.

A new emperor's healing touch

Vespasian, the military commander appointed in 67 by Nero to suppress the rebellion in Judea, entered Rome as emperor in 70. The city cried out for his administrative skills. Nero's excesses and the civil wars that followed his death had left the state treasury in shambles, parts of Rome in ruin (the Capitol and the Archives had been demolished), and morale among the citizenry and armed forces low.

As the biographer Suetonius noted, the new emperor wasted no time: "Throughout his reign [Vespasian] made it his principal business to shore up the moral foundations of the state, which were in a state of collapse." To rebuild Rome, he announced hefty tax increases, in some instances doubling rates. He also set an example by personally helping to clear away rubble during the building of the new Capitol. Romans must have been amazed at the sight of him with a basketful of debris on his shoulders. As the historian Tacitus wrote, "No one promoted simplicity more than Vespasian." His building program flourished as work began on constructing the Colosseum and the Temple of Peace and restoring the Forum. He also instituted prizes for poets and artists, paid an annual salary to Latin and Greek teachers, and proved to be "a devoted patron of the arts and sciences."

The outspoken emperor did not suffer fools gladly. When a young soldier who reeked of perfume visited him to thank him for his promotion, Vespasian canceled it on the spot, explaining, "I should not have minded so much if it had been garlic." When a brigade asked for a special shoe allowance, claiming that their duties called for them to be constantly on the move, he turned them down and ordered them to march barefoot. Nor was he overawed by powerful figures. Some years earlier, while accompanying Nero on a trip to Greece, he fell soundly asleep during one of the eccentric emperor's artistic performances. Suetonius noted that he was "square-shouldered, with strong, well-formed limbs, but always wore a strained expression on his face."

Vespasian was credited with the performing of two miracles in Alexandria, prior to his arrival in Rome as emperor. Such reports helped establish his authority and majesty. Both Tacitus and Suetonius write that aided by the god Serapis, he healed a blind man by spitting in his eyes and a cripple by touching the man's leg. But at the end of his life, Vespasian scorned any notions of his own divinity (emperors were usually deified after their death). Fatally ill, he managed a wry joke moments before dying: "Dear me! I must be turning into a god." Explaining that "an emperor ought to die on his feet," he struggled to a standing position and died in the arms of his aides.

Putting forth new roots

By A.D. 70 Christianity had established roots in many of the empire's most important cities. "The Word" spread quickly as both Jews and Gentiles eagerly embraced the faith. Egyptians were no exception. If we are to believe the legend recorded by Eusebius, the fourth-century church historian, the evangelist Mark himself brought Christianity to Egypt: "The same Mark . . . first established churches at the city of Alexandria." Whatever the truth of the tradition about Mark, we know Christians were present in first-century Egypt. In Acts, Luke notes that residents of Egypt (Jews or proselytes to Judaism) were present during

In a second-story room in Herculaneum, at the time a volcanic eruption destroyed the city in A.D. 79, there was a cross-shaped object on the wall, whose outline remains today. Although there may have been Christians in Herculaneum, the cross symbol comes three centuries too early. Most scholars believe that Christians did not use the symbol at all in the first century.

Pentecost. It is possible that some of these Jewish Egyptians were baptized and began preaching upon their return home. Acts also mentions "a Jew named Apollos, a native of Alexandria," who "had been instructed in the way of the Lord" apparently in his native land. A letter attributed to the emperor Hadrian in the second century also refers to "Christians, and those who call themselves bishops of Christ" in Egypt.

Throughout the New Testament, especially in Acts and in the epistles, there are numerous references to Christianity's rapid spread into Syria, Asia Minor, and Greece. In 1 Corinthians, Paul writes of "the churches of Asia" and the "wide door for effective work," which has opened for him there.

Solid documentation of Christianity's spread across Asia Minor in the first century is provided by the New Testament's concluding book, Revelation. Its author, John (see pages 90–91), says that he was instructed: "Write what you see in a book and send it to the seven churches." These seven churches were in Ephesus, Smyrna, Pergamum, Thyatira, Sardis, Philadelphia, and Laodicea. The problems of each are briefly described, in a letter dictated in John's vision by an angel sent by Christ, and advice is offered along with encouragement and rebuke. For example, Christ warns the community at Thyatira to shun a false prophetess who had a following there.

Whoever John entrusted with delivering copies of his visionary message to the seven churches would have left the small island of Patmos in the Aegean off the coast of present-day Turkey and made his way to the nearby mainland metropolis of Ephesus. With a population of possibly 250,000 in the first century A.D., Ephesus was the fourth largest city in the empire and the capital of the province of Asia. Living there were a number of Jews, Jewish Christians, Gentile Christians, Christians who followed John the Baptist, and, at the end of the century, Nicolaitans (apparently a Gnostic sect).

From Ephesus, John's envoy probably traveled north a few miles by road to the busy seaport of Smyrna. Here a fairly new community of Christians was in danger from the town's large Jewish community. "Behold, the devil is about to throw some of you into prison, that you may be tested," wrote John, "and for ten days you will have tribulation. Be faithful unto death, and I will give you the crown of life." Half a century later Smyrna's Jews did join with the pagan populace in attacking Christians; and about 156 the city's bishop, Polycarp, was martyred for confessing his faith (see page 114). To the Christians of Pergamum, north of Smyrna and 15 miles inland, John's messenger brought the warning, "Repent." A center of emperor worship in Asia Minor—"where Satan's throne is," wrote John—Pergamum had residents who were tempting Christians to "eat foods sacrificed to idols and practice immorality."

After delivering John's revelation to the church at Thyatira, where a prophetess (whom John calls Jezebel after an idolatrous queen of ancient Israel) tempted the faithful to compromise their piety by worshiping

An ancient tradition says that Mark traveled to Egypt, where he became the first bishop of Alexandria and wrote another, "secret" gospel. In this medieval mosaic his ship sails past the Pharos lighthouse at the entrance to the Alexandria harbor. The lighthouse was destroyed by an earthquake in the 14th century.

This mosaic depicting daily life on a big country estate in Roman North Africa dates from the second century A.D. *It represents the good life that many people, including Christians, who were already established in this prosperous region, doubtless enjoyed.*

idols, the envoy would have continued southeast to Sardis, about 50 miles from Smyrna. A thriving town built at the base of Mount Tmolus, Sardis was home to a group of Christians that John felt needed revitalizing. "I know your works," he wrote; "you have the name of being alive, and you are dead. Awake, and strengthen what remains and is on the point of death, for I have not found your works perfect in the sight of my God." The church in nearby Philadelphia was next to hear John's revelation. This small congregation had remained steadfast in their faith despite persecution. Lastly, the revelation would have been carried still farther south to the church in Laodicea. John tried to breathe some life into this community by exhorting, "I know your works: you are neither cold nor hot. Would that you were cold or hot!"

Conversion of the kingdom of Osroene

Antioch's key role in the spread of Christianity is well known. According to legend, however, another city can claim to be the first center of Christianity outside Jerusalem. That city is Edessa, a thriving crossroads of commerce and the capital of the kingdom of Osroene, just outside the empire's eastern frontier.

Eusebius records the fascinating legend about Osroene's conversion to Christianity. Agbar, its king, "had been wasted away with a disease, both dreadful and incurable by human means." Having heard of the miracles that Jesus had performed, the king wrote a letter to Jesus and summoned him. Jesus made this reply, "Blessed are you, since you have believed in me without seeing me. . . . In regard to what you have written, that I should come to you, it is necessary that

I should fulfil all things here, for which I have been sent." Jesus promised, however, that after ascending to heaven he would send a disciple to heal Agbar. After the Ascension, the legend continues, the Apostle Thomas sent Thaddeus, one of the 70 disciples, to Edessa. Thaddeus "began in the power of God to heal every kind of disease and infirmity." He healed Agbar, and "many of the same city were also healed by the same apostle . . . who proclaimed the word of God." The legend about Agbar probably was not created until the third century, and the early Christians in Osroene seem to have followed ascetic and Gnostic teachings. It is likely that the *Gospel of Thomas* (see pages 85–86) originated in the region.

In this official bas-relief dating from Domitian's reign, Vespasian places his hand on the shoulder of his younger son, Domitian, to signify that Domitian is his choice to succeed him as emperor after his older, childless son, Titus. Domitian did indeed come to power after Titus; some believe he may even have hastened Titus' death. Though he is remembered now for cruelties during his reign, many contend that he began his rule with a firm but equitable hand.

All these references to established Christian communities point to an ever expanding frontier and help gauge Christianity's development after the Pauline period. The list of churches in Revelation, for example, confirms that by the end of the first century Christian communities were established in the most important cities of Asia Minor. Indeed the church had expanded through most of the Roman Empire.

Titus and Domitian

Vespasian's older son, Titus, is best remembered for waging a brilliantly effective campaign to subdue the rebellious Jews of Judea in 70 (see pages 73–74), a success that is memorialized on the Arch of Titus, still standing in Rome. After his return in triumph to Rome, he shared many of the emperor's duties with his father, then became sole ruler on his father's death in 79. His love of music and poetry, coupled with a reputation for ruthlessness, caused some apprehension among his subjects that he might become a second Nero, but the worries were unfounded. He was a well-respected ruler who continued many of Vespasian's enlightened social and cultural policies. During his reign, Titus devoted much time and energy to helping the victims of the Mount Vesuvius eruption, of a fire that ravaged Rome, and of a plague. Himself a victim of a fever, he died in September 81, just short of 27 months after his rise to power.

Titus' brother, Domitian, shared few of Titus' finer attributes. Indeed, there were rumors that Domitian had a hand in Titus' death. Suetonius states, "He never once stopped plotting, secretly or openly, against his brother. When Titus fell suddenly and dangerously ill, Domitian told the attendants to presume his death by leaving the sick-bed before he had actually breathed his last." On the very day of Titus' death, Domitian ordered the Senate to install him as emperor.

Domitian's reign was a combination of successes and failures. He continued the rebuilding of Rome, consolidated Roman rule in Germany and Britain, and strengthened the empire's administration. He also cracked down on Rome's loose morals, curtailing prostitution and executing any Vestal Virgins who were found guilty of unchastity.

Domitian's policy on public morality was unpopular; at the same time, in his own private life he was notoriously depraved, a point that was emphasized by his increasingly numerous opponents. "For a while he governed in an uneven fashion," wrote Suetonius; "that is to say, his vices were at first balanced by his virtues. Later, he transformed his virtues into vices." One of those "vices" was his insistence that he be addressed as "*dominus et deus*" ("Lord and God"). He began a letter supposedly written by his procurators, "Our Lord God instructs you to do this!"

Rome's temples were filled with statues of Domitian, and anyone who refused to offer sacrifice in front of them was charged with treason. The emperor decreed that all statues of him in the Capitol had to be made of gold or silver, of not less than a specified weight. He presided over festivals and other public events wearing a purple robe, buskins, and a gold crown engraved with the images of various gods. He insisted on renaming September and October, the months of his accession and of his birth, Germanicus (a surname he had adopted) and Domitianus.

After a failed revolt against him in 88 or 89, Domitian ordered large numbers of nobles and even some members of his own family banished or executed. From 93 until his death in 96, Domitian's reign became literally a reign of terror. "All this made him everywhere hated and feared," wrote Suetonius.

Christians also were the targets of Domitian's fury. Though he never instituted an organized or empire-wide campaign, several sources refer to persecutions of Christians during his reign. The emperor banished his cousin's wife because she was believed to be a Christian and ordered other Christians killed. Some 200 years later Eusebius wrote: "He was the second that raised a persecution against us."

Epictetus

Epictetus was a leading Greek philosopher in Rome during the time when much of the New Testament was being compiled. A freedman, he studied and later taught Stoicism, often using the diatribe, a form of ironic criticism, to capture the attention of his students. The Apostle Paul used this technique frequently when writing his letters to the early churches.

Stoicism held that only by using reason could one see through false appearances. Epictetus taught his students to use their reasoning power to change for the better those things under their control (such as attitudes and opinions) and to be unmoved by those things that were outside their control (for example, illness and death). Thereby one could find happiness and calm. True fulfillment, he believed, could only be found by living in accord with nature, which was identical with the will of God.

A philosopher of Epictetus' time was readily recognized by his distinctive garb.

Epictetus was lame, some believe as the result of mistreatment when he was a slave. According to Epictetus: "When you have shut the doors and made a darkness within . . . you are not alone, but God is within." Wrongdoers, he believed, should not be punished as criminals but pitied, because they are more unhappy than their victims. When the emperor Domitian expelled all philosophers from Rome about 90, Epictetus left for Nicopolis, Greece, where he opened a school, which drew many devotees. Although the emperor Hadrian lifted the ban on philosophers in 117, Epictetus remained in Nicopolis until he died, sometime in his eighties, around 130.

While at the time, the Stoicism of men like Epictetus may have been a moral alternative to Christianity, some historians contend that it was helpful in developing a climate in which Christian teaching could take hold more firmly.

On September 18, 96, Domitian was assassinated. The conspirators, who included his wife, had already picked a successor. The general public was indifferent. Domitian's death marked the end of the Flavian dynasty—so-called because *Flavius* was the name of the clan to which Vespasian and his sons belonged. The news brought cheers in the Senate. "[Senators] thronged to denounce Domitian in the House with bitter and insulting cries," wrote Suetonius. "Then, sending for ladders, they had his images and the votive shields engraved with his likeness, brought smashing down; and ended by decreeing that all inscriptions referring to him must be effaced, and all records of his reign obliterated."

The 66-year-old Nerva, a respected senator, became emperor in 96. He re-called those whom Domitian had exiled and instituted an expensive land reform program. As if to symbolize the emperor's reforms, the imperial mint issued coins bearing the legend, "*Roma Renascens*" ("Rome reborn"). Under Nerva, Christians were free from the terror they had known under Domitian. Though incidents of persecution did occur here and there, they were more localized and sporadic. By avoiding offense to their neighbors, Christians could live in peace, build up their organization, and broaden their membership. Their leaders urged them, in the words of 1 Peter, to "maintain good conduct among the Gentiles, so that in case they speak against you as wrongdoers, they may see your good deeds and glorify God."

The dynamic life of the church

It is Wednesday in Rome's Transtiberim district. A dozen men—dressed in dark wool tunics and leather sandals—and seven women gather in the home of a fellow Christian, a prosperous local merchant. The day is one of fasting and the group has assembled to offer a prayer to God. Their voices join in reciting familiar words that carry into the courtyard: "Father, hallowed be thy name. Thy kingdom come."

In the Macedonian town of Philippi, an elder stands in front of a room full of Christians and reads from Paul's letter to the Philippians: "Rejoice in the Lord always; again I will say, Rejoice."

On a Sunday in Corinth a group of slaves and freedmen, paupers and aristocrats fill a home. A tall, middle-aged man, his weathered face framed by a fringe of black beard, stands and begins speaking in tongues.

Others recite prayers, lead hymns, or give instruction. Later the entire community joins in a meal that begins with bread blessed as the body of Christ and ends with wine identified with his blood.

Scenes like the above occurred throughout the Roman Empire during the latter part of the first century, as Christians began to disassociate themselves from synagogues, and as Jews themselves also sought to cut off their former brethren. (About A.D. 85 a formal anathema was added to the synagogue liturgy: "May the Nazarenes [Jewish Christians] and the heretics be suddenly destroyed and removed from the Book of Life.") These "brothers and sisters" or "the holy and beloved" gathered in the homes of more prosperous members, such as those of Gaius in Corinth, Nympha in Laodicea, or Philemon at Colossae.

As Christianity spread throughout the empire, it was inevitable that some families would be divided between those who embraced the new faith and those who held with the old gods. In many cases the menfolk remained pagans while the women listened to Christian proselytizers, converted with or without their husbands' consent, and then brought up the children as Christians. In the Roman household shown here, the father makes offering at a family shrine, as women of the house listen to a teacher of the gospel; a statue of Mercury as a youth adorns the portico.

Apollonius of Tyana

Many pagan holy men lived in the first century A.D. A most remarkable one was a widely traveled sage named Apollonius. The son of wealthy parents in Tyana, a small town in what is now central Turkey, he gravitated as a youth to the teachings and ascetic lifestyle associated with the sixth-century B.C. Greek philosopher Pythagoras. He let his hair grow long, was a strict vegetarian, wore no article of clothing made from an animal substance, went barefoot, and remained celibate. He spent a few years at a healing center (see pages 48–49), where he studied medicine, and afterward went to India, where he spent some months in an ashram as a guest of the resident ascetics. Returning home, he then went on to Greece, Italy, and Spain, and from there to Egypt. Apollonius practiced what he preached and was outspoken in his message, believing himself divinely inspired to set erring humanity straight. He is reported to have successfully defied both Nero and Domitian.

Legend credits him with miraculous cures, such as healing lame and blind people, and other displays of divine power. In the first half of the third century, some 100 years after Apollonius' death, the emperor Alexander Severus reportedly worshiped at a private shrine in which were images of the mythic Greek poet-seer Orpheus, putative founder of a religion named after him; Abraham, patriarch of Israel; Jesus Christ; and Apollonius of Tyana. Alexander's great aunt, the empress Julia Domna (wife of Septimius Severus), had shared his admiration for Apollonius. A quarter-century earlier she had commissioned a popular writer and lecturer of the day, Philostratus, to do a *Life of Apollonius*. The book, a highly readable blend of fact and fancy that has come down to us nearly intact, was such a eulogy of Apollonius that it moved pagans to compare him to Jesus Christ. Around 300, Hierocles, governor of Bithynia and one instigator of the Diocletianic persecutions, wrote a treatise, *Lover of Truth*, which claimed that Apollonius was superior to Jesus. It is thanks to the refutation by the church historian Eusebius that so much material about Apollonius was preserved.

By the end of the first century, Christians had established certain rituals for worship that led to the more structured liturgy of later periods. There are hints in the New Testament at the form of this early worship. Paul's letter to the Colossians notes: "Let the word of Christ dwell in you richly, teach and admonish one another in all wisdom, and sing psalms and hymns and spiritual songs." Passages from several hymns he mentions are quoted in New Testament letters, for example, 1 Timothy 3:16. While historians know that these early services included readings from the Scriptures, prayer, and celebration of the Eucharist, the full details are unknown.

An early manual of Christian worship

Only after the discovery of the *Didache* ("Teaching of the Twelve Apostles") did scholars begin piecing together the puzzle of first-century Christian worship services. This slim manual of worship and church order, probably compiled around 100, was found in the library of a Middle Eastern monastery in 1875. From the *Didache* it is clear that in the latter part of the first century Christians were still following many Jewish forms of worship, even though they were attempting to distance themselves from the Jews. "Mondays and Thursdays are their days for fasting, so yours should be Wednesdays and Fridays," the manual states. "Your prayers, too, should be different from theirs," it adds, and recommends recitation of the Lord's Prayer three times a day. This advice was possibly a reflection of the synagogue tradition of thrice-daily services. The *Didache* also offers guidelines for baptism and indicates that different forms of the ritual were possible. (See pages 36 and 145–147 for more details on baptism.)

The Eucharist, a reference to the past as well as the future, was the central part of Christian worship. Christians following the outline that was detailed in the *Didache* offered this prayer during the celebration of the Eucharist: "We give thanks to thee, our Father, for the holy Vine of thy servant David, which thou hast made known to us through thy servant Jesus." The Eucharist, as described in the *Didache*, does not mention the Last Supper or the death or body and blood of Jesus but is focused mainly on the coming kingdom. Another prayer was offered for the consecration of the bread, and the service ended with a blessing for the survival of the church: "O Lord; deliver it from all evil, perfect it in thy love, sanctify it, and gather it from the four winds into the kingdom which thou hast prepared for it."

By the end of the first century, Christian worship had evolved into distinctive liturgies. Prayers, hymns, baptism, the Eucharist, teaching, the reading of Scripture, and the making of offerings were being tailored to specific beliefs and needs of the growing communities. Although congregations no doubt varied in their observances, many would have met the test of Clement of Rome, who in a letter to the Corinthian church about 96 reminded the community that the Lord "has enjoined offerings [to be presented] and service to be performed . . . and that not thoughtlessly or irregularly, but at the appointed times and hours."

Evolving leadership

Just as the liturgy evolved, so did the church's leadership and organization. When Paul wrote to the church in Rome in the 50's, he mentioned no ecclesiastical hierarchy. Rather, he referred to "kinsmen" and "fellow workers in Christ Jesus." Apparently at that time, these "fellow workers" who were "led by the Spirit of God" provided the leadership of the church. By contrast, according to Clement's letter to Corinth near the end of the first century, just as Christ had commissioned the Apostles, so the Apostles had in turn "appointed the first fruits [of their labors] . . . to be bishops ["overseers"] and deacons ["ministers"] for those who should afterwards believe." Clement also refers to the bishops as presbyters or elders. (By the middle of the third century these titles had become completely distinct from one another, and the Roman church boasted 1 bishop, 46 presbyters, 7 deacons, 7 subdeacons, 42 acolytes, plus exorcists, readers, and doorkeepers—52 in all.) The pastoral epistles likewise mention bishops who are also called presbyters or deacons or ministers, and they detail the necessary qualities for each.

This ancient Roman wall painting represents a typical harbor somewhere in southern Italy. Puteoli, where Paul landed en route to Rome, probably looked quite similar. Christian missionaries saw many harbors like this one.

In some regions after the beginning of the second century, church leaders were working to develop a hierarchy of authority. In order to avoid division and maintain the strength to withstand attacks by its enemies, including those in the imperial government, and also to avoid becoming a private cult that could be subject to the whims of capricious charismatic leaders, they argued that Christianity needed a clear center of authority in each city.

The duties of bishops and deacons

Bishops or presbyters were in this period leaders of local churches. The Greek term *episkopos*, from which our word *bishop* is derived, means "overseer, guardian, inspector." In the everyday Greek of the time it was used for a variety of public offices. First Timothy lists a few requirements for, and responsibilities of, the position. A bishop "must be above reproach, the husband of one wife, temperate, sensible, dignified, hospitable, an apt teacher, no drunkard, not violent but gentle, not quarrelsome, and no lover of money. He must manage his own household well . . . for if a man does not know how to manage his own household, how can he care for God's church?" The church had had different needs in the early decades when the seven leaders of Greek-speaking congregations were chosen to distribute church funds to those in need. The qualifications as reported in Acts 6 were that they should be "men of good repute, full of the Spirit and of wisdom." Now the church required leaders who embodied even more: stability, continuity, and acceptance in the community at large.

According to the letter to Titus, one of a bishop's duties was to "hold firm to the sure word as taught, so that he may be able to give instruction in sound doctrine and also to confute those who contradict it." At the end of the first century, there appears to have been a growing movement to recognize one presiding bishop as supreme authority in a city and to designate other leaders as elders or presbyters. As noted in the letters of Ignatius, written early in the second century, the churches in Antioch, Philadelphia, Smyrna, Ephesus, Magnesia, and Philippi were led by single bishops at this time. In his letter to Rome, however, Ignatius, who strongly favored rule by one bishop, did not single out one person who was in charge of the church there. Nevertheless, it should be remembered that church organization varied widely from place to place, that it was everywhere relatively unstructured, and that the writings of the period are frequently unclear about what authority was attached to particular titles.

Deacons (from the Greek word *diakonos*, "servant, minister") ranked after presbyters or bishops. As detailed in 1 Timothy, they had to be "serious, not double-tongued, not addicted to much wine, not greedy for gain; they must hold the mystery of the faith with a clear conscience." We know little about the duties of these early deacons, but they appear to have ranged from assisting the bishops to caring for the poor to overseeing the community's meals. By the third century, deacons were described as unordained administrative assistants to bishops.

Women's changing role

The early church also offered women opportunities to emerge from their age-old condition of subjugation. This was perhaps owing to Christ's encouraging attitude toward women, which was in marked contrast to prevailing definitions of a woman's role in the community. The first century witnessed changes at different levels of society throughout the empire, and points of view regarding women were diverse in both Judaism and Christianity. Jewish women were subject theoretically to their husband's wishes and enjoyed only lowly status within the synagogue. Indeed, a noted rabbi said of women in a statement that has been tentatively dated about A.D 90: "Better burn the Torah than teach it to a woman." However, inscriptions from the same period show that women were leaders of synagogues in some places.

Among Christians, the status of women partially reflected their place in Roman society. A free-born Roman woman had many of the same rights and privileges of citizenship accorded to men. In fact, the women formed an important part of Rome's labor force, filling jobs as artisans, shopkeepers, textile workers, and employees in other businesses. Some well-to-do Roman women who turned to Christianity married converts of a lower class.

Nevertheless, there was tension and contention over the role of women within Christian communities from a very early period. This is evident from Paul's references to the status of men versus women in his letters. Despite his general statement that all are one in Christ, "There is neither male nor female; for you are all one in Christ Jesus," Paul ruled in favor of men over women. To the Corinthians, he wrote, "For man was not made from woman, but woman from man. Neither was man created for woman, but woman for man." He immediately qualified the statement, to guard against misunderstanding: "Nevertheless, in the Lord woman is not independent of man nor man of woman; for as woman was made from

Itinerant prophets played a leading role in early Christianity, but some congregations had a rule that they could stay only overnight or for two days if really necessary. On leaving, they were to be given just enough provisions to last to the next night's lodging. Those who asked for money were likely to be challenged as impostors.

man, so man is now born of woman. And all things are from God." Another passage says: "The women should keep silence in the churches. For they are not permitted to speak, but should be subordinate, as even the law says. If there is anything they desire to know, let them ask their husbands at home. For it is shameful for a woman to speak in church." Since this passage directly contradicts what Paul says in 1 Corinthians 11:5 about women praying and even prophesying in the presence of men, many scholars believe that it was inserted in the letter, possibly by the author who wrote the pastoral epistles. If the statement enjoining the subjugation of women in 1 Corinthians is indeed by Paul, it probably reflects the Greco-Roman tradition that women were not allowed to participate in a public assembly.

Paul's admonition may also have been in response to a specific problem in Corinth; too many worshipers were speaking in tongues or otherwise disrupting the services. Apparently a group of women were among the offenders. Whether or not its original target was local and short-term, Paul's rebuke had a powerful long-term effect. A passage in 1 Timothy, which is attributed to Paul but possibly was inserted by a later writer, underlines the message: "Let a woman learn in silence with all submissiveness. I permit no woman to teach or to have authority over men; she is to keep silent." In time, women lost much of their status within the church, and by the end of the first century, most churches had silenced women as effectively as synagogues ever had.

This early Christian painting of a woman who is praying comes from the catacombs of Rome. The purple stripes on her tunic indicate that her family is of equestrian rank. (Equestrians were just below the patrician, or senatorial, class in Roman society.) The word GRATA, written above her head, means "pleasant."

"Render to Caesar"

The first-century Christian owed allegiance to two masters. As a citizen or resident of the Roman Empire, he was bound to follow the dictates of the state and the emperor. As the author of 1 Peter wrote, "Be subject for the Lord's sake to every human institution, whether it be to the emperor as supreme, or to governors as sent by him to punish those who do wrong and to praise those who do right. For it is God's will that by doing right you should put to silence the ignorance of foolish men. Live as free men, yet without using your freedom as a pretext for evil; but live as servants of God. Honor all men. Love the brotherhood. Fear God. Honor the emperor."

While Christians may not have engaged in emperor worship, they were not rabble-rousers, and their religion, while odd and at times offensive from the pagan

Judaism After the Jewish War

Judaism was never the same after the fall of Jerusalem. By destroying most of the city and, more important, by burning the Temple, the Romans brought to an end some of the age-old Jewish rituals. No longer would millions of Jews from the Diaspora make their yearly trek to the hallowed place of worship. Nor would they observe the Temple's animal sacrifices, a ritual for more than 1,000 years. Destruction of the Temple also ended the time-honored right of priests to judge the civil and religious affairs of the Jewish people. Nearly all members of the Sanhedrin were killed during the war. One who survived the slaughter was Rabbi Johanan ben Zakkai, whose escape is a revered legend. A moderate voice during the Jerusalem siege, he tried in vain to convince the rebels to make peace with the Romans in order to avoid the downfall of the city. They refused and questioned his loyalty. Realizing the danger of his position, he said to two disciples, "Make a coffin for me that I may lie in it." With Johanan hidden inside the closed coffin, the disciples got as far as the gates of Jerusalem when gatekeepers questioned them. "It is a dead man," they explained. "Do you not know that the dead may not be held overnight in Jerusalem?" The gatekeepers let them pass to safety. With Jerusalem in ruins, Rabbi Johanan then set about creating a new school for rabbis in Jamnia, 30 miles away. The study of the Torah was strongly emphasized. During this period Jewish militancy gave way to openness and a renewed effort toward proselytizing. The transformation of Judaism was exemplified by the rabbi's response to a student's lament upon seeing the Temple in ruins. Charity, said the rabbi, was as important as acts of worship, and he quoted Hosea 6:6, in which the Lord says, "For I desire steadfast love and not sacrifice."

A floor mosaic from an ancient synagogue shows the curtained sanctuary for the Torah, flanked by lions, birds, and menorahs.

point of view, posed no real threat to the empire. They did, of course, serve also another master, whose kingdom was not of this world. They fully expected Christ to return to earth and replace the Roman Empire with one of his own design. Some (but by no means all) seem to have expected even an earthly kingdom of Christ. Nevertheless, they steadfastly kept their pledge to "render to Caesar the things that are Caesar's." In order to survive and to strengthen their young church, Christians had to be both exemplary citizens and moral individuals. As the author of 1 Peter puts it, "Let none of you suffer as a murderer, or a thief, or a wrongdoer or a mischief-maker; yet if one suffers as a Christian, let him not be ashamed, but under that name let him glorify God."

The definitive split between Jews and Christians

The fall and destruction of Jerusalem in 70 led to a split between Christians and Jews in many cities of the Middle East and coincided with a progressive distancing between them in other places. The Jewish War had been marked by massacres in which Gentiles killed large numbers of Jews, and the radical parties among the Jews had answered in kind. It was inevitable that Jewish Christians especially would become embroiled in the conflict. The Gospel of Matthew, written perhaps in Antioch, reflects the split. It refers to "their synagogues" and "my church." Evidently in times past the community of Jewish and Gentile Christians in Antioch had maintained some ties to the synagogue. Now it was a separate congregation.

The Gospel of John, possibly written in Ephesus a short time later, reflects even sharper conflicts with local synagogues. This explains the tone of outright hostility against the Jews that appears at several points in John. Looked at with modern-day hindsight, this tone could easily be mistaken for anti-Semitism. It is not that, however. The condemnations were the reflections of Jewish Christians who had gone through years of bitter controversy within the synagogues and had finally been excluded from them by Jewish communities who found their claims for the divinity of Christ incompatible with Jewish monotheism. The whole story of how Christians and Jews drifted apart in those early years has not yet been reconstructed. It may never be fully known. Recent archaeological findings suggest that in some places, at least, Jews and Christians lived in close harmony with one another for long periods. Many details of their day-to-day culture seem to have overlapped to the point of being indistinguishable from one another. The surviving evidence gives us sharply focused glimpses of specific situations, but it does not provide a reliable basis for generalizing on the grand sweep of events.

In this detail from a medieval French tapestry, John of Patmos faces the seven Asian churches in Revelation. Three details are wrong: the buildings, their crosses, and the halos. None of these things were used by Christians in John's time.

When they were no longer viewed as a Jewish sect, Christians lost the protection that excused Jews from worshiping the emperor, freed them from military service, and permitted them to celebrate the Sabbath. At the same time, they did not enjoy the ancestral status of the Jews, whose faith was respected for its venerable antiquity. As its status changed, the church came to be considered an illegal sect. Christians had to become more cautious than they had been.

Throughout the epistles there are exhortations to Christians to lead exemplary lives. First Peter offered also a household code for husbands, wives, and servants. For example, to wives it says: "Let not yours be the outward adorning with braiding of hair, decoration of gold, and wearing of fine clothing, but let it be the hidden person of the heart with the imperishable jewel of a gentle and quiet spirit." The message from these writers was straightforward. Christians should follow Christ's example in accepting suffering but also live moral, upright lives and not offer the state an excuse to single them out for punishment. Keep a low profile, they were told. "Be sober, be watchful. Your adversary the devil prowls around like a roaring lion, seeking some one to devour."

Vision of coming triumph

Not every Christian, however, was content to "be sober, be watchful." During Domitian's persecution of Christians, there was one who wielded his pen as a soldier might his sword and wrote a dramatic attack

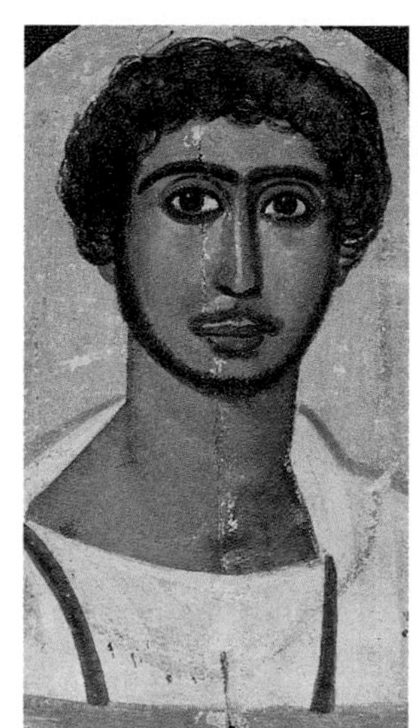

An idea of what some typical early Christians looked like can be gained from these lifelike funerary portraits of Greeks who resided in Egypt. (The portraits have survived because of the dry Egyptian climate.) Though it is impossible to say which, if any, of these men and women were actually Christians, Greek-speaking city dwellers who made up most Christian congregations of the first two centuries A.D. *would have dressed and worn their hair like the people depicted here.*

on the injustices of the Roman Empire. The writer is John (see page 90), and his work, Revelation, assured Christians that their suffering was only temporary. "I will keep you from the hour of trial which is coming on the whole world, to try those who dwell upon the earth." This is what the angel who conveyed Jesus' message said in John's vision. "I am coming soon; hold fast what you have, so that no one may seize your crown." In this startling work, John paints a dramatic picture of Christ triumphing over evil. Rome is described as "fallen . . . Babylon . . . a dwelling place of demons," and the church is "a great multitude which no man could number." Revelation, rich with visions and symbols, was intended to instruct and inspire. Most important, it was written to embolden a threatened community.

John wrote Revelation as Christians, especially in Asia Minor, were refusing orders to worship the emperor. He used elaborate symbols and images, drawn extensively from the Old Testament prophets, to convey his message. A "beast rising out of the sea, with ten horns and seven heads" represented the Roman Empire. Another beast, which rises "out of the earth" and "cause[s] those who would not worship the image of the beast to be slain," symbolized the false prophets who helped enforce emperor worship.

The beasts are eventually overthrown. Then appears "the holy city, new Jerusalem, coming down out of heaven from God." John's message was clear: Christ would return soon and reign in a new world. As 1 Peter had exhorted, "The end of all things is at hand; therefore keep sane and sober for your prayers." John writes at the end of Revelation, "He who testifies to these things says, 'Surely I am coming soon.' Amen. Come, Lord Jesus!"

Christians who faced the harshness of Roman oppression would surely have taken comfort and courage from John's awesome vision. They would need such courage to defy the empire. Christians were beginning to pay dearly for their beliefs. During the second century, the pages of church history would be stained with the blood of many martyrs. Some doubtless recalled the promise recorded in Revelation: "Be faithful unto death, and I will give you the crown of life."

Chapter Four

DEFENDING THE FAITH

Throughout the second century, the church struggled to come into its own amidst a flourishing revival of paganism. New Christian writings served to inspire and defend the faithful, but it was the courage of the martyrs that gave them the strength to continue.

"Come fire, come cross; grapplings with wild beasts, cuttings and manglings, wrenching of bones, hacking of limbs, crushing of the whole body; let cruel torments of the devil come upon me; if only I may attain unto Jesus Christ." With this fervent appeal, Ignatius of Antioch embraced his martyrdom. His death, at the beginning of the second century, demonstrated such piety and courage that future Christian martyrs sought to imitate his bravery. Ignatius had been the bishop of the church in Antioch for 40 years when he was denounced as a Christian during a short but intense period of persecution in the reign of Emperor Trajan. According to legend, Ignatius was cross examined by the emperor himself and still refused to follow Trajan's orders to worship the Roman deities. No doubt Trajan thought to make an example of this zealous Christian bishop, who was probably a converted pagan. Ignatius, who was more than 70 years old, was given a brutal sentence: he was to be bound in chains and taken to Rome, where he would be devoured by beasts for the entertainment of the public. Unafraid, Ignatius regarded his punishment with joy,

For his refusal to worship pagan deities, Ignatius, bishop of Antioch, was sentenced to die in Rome. During the long journey there, he was treated badly by his squad of Roman guards, but their cruelty only made him feel "still more a disciple."

thanking the Lord for providing this opportunity, the better to prove his love for his Savior. The sentence extended Ignatius' life by many months, for the trip was a long one by land and sea. During this arduous journey, Ignatius authored seven spirited letters, which historians date to about the year 107. He addressed them to several churches in Asia Minor and to Polycarp, bishop of Smyrna, who helped to preserve them. The letters are considered among the most significant Christian documents of the period.

In each one Ignatius stressed the importance of preserving unity among the faithful. To that end, he exhorted Christians to obey their bishops, just as God is obeyed in heaven. Being something of a prophet, Ignatius referred to himself as Theophorus, meaning "God-bearer," and shared a divine revelation from the Spirit that followers of Jesus were to "pay heed to the bishop, the presbytery, and the deacons."

Ignatius was equally concerned that Christians not be led into error by ideas he judged heretical. One group, for example, wanted to meld Jewish practices, such as Sabbath observances, with Christian ones. Ignatius warned new believers not to be led astray, "For if we go on observing Judaism, we admit we never received grace." He opposed also another heresy, later called Docetism, which denied that Jesus had a true physical body. Adherents of this view argued that since the material world is inherently evil, Jesus must have been a pure spirit who only seemed to die on the cross. Ignatius was outraged. An essential tenet of the bishop's faith was that Jesus did have a human body, suffered the tortures of the Crucifixion, and then was resurrected after death.

The letters are also the final testament of a believer facing martyrdom. He urged his followers to do nothing to rescue him. Bound in chains he called "spiritual pearls," vexed by 10 soldiers that he referred to as "leopards," he traversed much of Asia Minor by foot, before setting sail for Rome.

Scores of grieving believers sought out Ignatius during his difficult trek. To all who came to see him, he explained that his martyrdom would lead to a union

Accused Christians were tried in courtrooms much like the one pictured in this fresco from Pompeii. The power of the Roman court is evident in its very design. The magistrate sits on a dais between two assessors, who will help him decide the case, while the accused kneels far below. Christians who refused to deny their faith were usually sentenced to death.

with God at the instant of death, what he called "attaining to God." According to legend, when he reached Rome, Ignatius was devoured by two ferocious lions in the Flavian amphitheater (Colosseum).

Pliny the Younger

As the Roman Empire expanded, it accommodated a variety of religions and cults. Their adherents had only to recognize the supremacy of the state and agree to honor the traditional Roman deities, whose goodwill was considered necessary for the prosperity of the empire. Two troublesome exceptions were Jews and Christians. Both groups were considered atheists because they refused to acknowledge the divinity of the Roman gods. And both were believed politically threatening to the state. The Jewish faith at least had the advantage of being an ancient national religion; while the relatively new Christianity to many seemed a dangerous and subversive superstition.

The ignorance of nonbelievers fostered gossip and ugly rumors. For example, word spread that Christian rites included cannibalism. This misunderstanding was likely due to confusion over the Christian teaching that the body and blood of Christ are represented in the Eucharist. Christians were also accused of incest because they called one another brother and sister and exchanged the "kiss of peace," or holy kiss, before celebrating the Eucharist (see page 141). As Christians grew in number, so did the accusations against them, forcing at least one Roman governor to investigate the legal implications of Christianity.

That governor was Pliny the Younger, an accomplished lawyer from the aristocracy and a nephew of the writer Pliny the Elder. Trajan put him in charge of the combined provinces of Bithynia-Pontus on the Black Sea (present-day northern Turkey). Early in Pliny's tenure, in 112, a number of Bithynians were accused of being Christians. Upon hearing them assert their devotion to their faith, Pliny had those who were not Roman citizens executed, not for any crimes they had committed but for obstinately refusing to deny their faith. By this time, being a Christian was considered a crime against the Roman Empire. (Some historians have speculated that the people who instigated the accusations were merchants who were upset over falling meat prices, since the Christians would not purchase meat left over from pagan sacrifices.)

C. PLINIUS CALUISIO SUO SALUTEM

The letters of Pliny the Younger tell us much about the life of a Roman nobleman in the second century. In the letter above, Pliny writes to a friend for advice about buying the land next to his estate. Money is not a problem. "My mother-in-law will accommodate me, whose cash-box is as much at my service as my own."

Soon, anonymous accusations spread, and a number of Christians were hauled into court. Those who recanted, cursed Christ, and made an offering to the pagan gods and a statue of the emperor, Pliny set free. But he wondered whether the deniers were still guilty for having engaged in Christian activities in the past.

When Pliny investigated exactly what these Christian doings entailed, he discovered that the accused

Like his friend Ignatius before him, Polycarp, the elderly bishop of Smyrna, sought to imitate Christ, even in his death. "If we suffer for the sake of his name, let us glorify him," wrote Polycarp in a letter to the Philippians. On a February afternoon in 155 or 156, Polycarp entered a crowded stadium and refused yet again to blaspheme Jesus. As Polycarp had foreseen in a dream, the rabble demanded that he be burned alive. Confident that Jesus would give him the power to endure the flames without moving, he asked not to be nailed to his wooden pyre.

met innocently before dawn to "chant verses" in praise of "Christ as a God." The food they shared together was "ordinary and harmless." Such activities could not technically be considered crimes.

Pliny knew that in the past, adherents of other religions had been punished for their activities, not their beliefs. He was in a legal quandary. The question he posed to Trajan was whether he should continue to prosecute Christians for the name only (that is, for simply *being* Christians) or for their so-called crimes.

Trajan replied that those convicted of *being* Christians must be punished. However, those who made a sacrifice to the Roman gods, proving they were no longer Christian, were to be pardoned. Trajan made it clear that simply bearing the name "Christian" was a capital offense. He also wrote that Christians were not to be sought out and hunted down, and anonymous accusations were no longer permitted, "for they are unworthy of our time." In one short paragraph, which Pliny preserved for posterity, Trajan laid down a precedent that forestalled widespread governmental persecution but, nonetheless, left Christians under a continual threat of execution should any one bring charges against them.

The martyrdom of Polycarp

In 155 or 156, some 40 years after the martyrdom of Ignatius, a wave of persecution suddenly swept Smyrna (present-day Izmir in Turkey). A number of Christians were martyred, among them the gentle but tough-minded bishop of Smyrna, Polycarp. He was so revered that he never had to take off his own shoes, as he was always surrounded by the faithful, who were eager to serve him. According to the second-century theologian Irenaeus, Polycarp, as a young man, had known several Apostles. From his *Epistle to the Philippians,* Polycarp's only extant writing, it is clear that his faith was a blend of compassion and exhortation and his style very similar to that of the pastoral letters in the New Testament.

Polycarp's ordeal was recorded in great detail in a letter from the church of Smyrna to that in another town of Asia Minor. This moving document, *The Martyrdom of Polycarp,* is the oldest known account of a Christian martyrdom. It graphically describes the persecutions of a dozen Christians and then focuses exclusively on Polycarp. Though not intimidated, the elderly bishop heeded his followers' urging to go into hiding. As Polycarp prayed night and day for the deliverance of others, he had a vision that his pillow burst into flames, and he knew he would be burned alive—a form of execution at the time.

The letter recounts that when Polycarp was arrested and brought before the crowd filled with loathing for the atheist, he refused the Roman proconsul's pleas to curse Christ, declaring, "Eighty-six years I have served him, and he never did me any wrong. How can I blaspheme my King who saved me?" The provincial city's one lion was sated from previous spectacles, and Polycarp was, as he had foreseen, burned at the stake. He requested not to be nailed in place, promising that "he who grants me to endure the fire will enable me also to remain on the pyre unmoved." When the piles of wood were lit, the flames formed a wall around him; only after the executioner reached into the pyre to stab him, did he die.

The devotion of Polycarp's followers was so great, the governor was warned not to allow Christians to take his remains, "else they will abandon the Crucified, and begin worshiping this one." His disciples managed to gather from the pyre a few of his bones, which were considered "more valuable than gold." This is perhaps the first reference to the reverence early Christians had for the relics of martyrs.

The martyrs of Lyons

Sporadic persecutions followed, but none was as brutal as the one at Lyons, in Gaul (present-day France), a thriving Roman province. In the summer of 177, hatred toward Christians there mysteriously erupted. As with Polycarp, the trials and tribulations of the Lyons martyrs were carefully preserved. The accused were mostly immigrants who had become prosperous tradespeople. Some of their pagan slaves were tortured by the authorities until they confessed that their masters practiced cannibalism and incest. As a result, Christians were subjected to terrible punishments.

The 90-year-old bishop Pothinus was beaten so severely that he died two days later. Many of the victims were confined to dank and airless underground dungeons, where they succumbed to inhuman conditions or were strangled by their jailers. Other "athletes of faith," as they referred to themselves, were whipped repeatedly and roasted on a red-hot iron chair before being torn apart by wild beasts.

The most poignant martyr of all was the delicate young Blandina, who endured incredibly painful and protracted tortures without complaint. Her prayers inspired strength in her companions. Even the pagans were moved by her unusual courage.

The more the faithful confessed to being Christian, the more they were brutally tortured. Even a number of those who recanted were punished, in defiance of Trajan's policy to spare those who denied the faith.

Why were the people of these cities in ancient Gaul so full of hatred toward Christians? Some historians have speculated that in this case those who were persecuted may have fulfilled an economic function of sorts. Whereas rich landowners were expected to furnish professional gladiators for public entertainment, condemned criminals, such as Christians, could be used instead, and for a tenth of the cost.

Throughout the orgy of hate in Lyons, the martyrs never vilified their barbarous torturers; instead, they prayed for them. To the Christians, the war was against Satan, not the Roman people or their government. Indeed many Christians longed for the chance to be martyrs in order to imitate the death of Jesus on the cross. Their faith proved so steadfast that Roman guards refused to return to the Christians any of the martyrs' remains for fear that they would rise again. Instead, the guards threw the bones into a river.

The third-century theologian Tertullian noted, "The blood of the martyrs is the seed of the church." Their deaths not only inspired countless other believers, and possibly helped attract new converts, but also served to underscore the growing spiritual desperation and insecurity lurking beneath the surface of the ever prosperous Roman Empire.

High tide of the empire

The Roman Empire enjoyed unparalleled peace and prosperity during the second century. Diverse nationalities mingled easily under the umbrella of imperial protection, and talented provincials rose to power in Rome itself. One such outsider was Marcus Ulpius Trajanus, better known as Trajan. A nobleman born in the Spanish territories, he was the first emperor to come from the provinces. Assuming power in 99, Trajan proved a conscientious administrator and able politician. He restored confidence to the state and repaired the damage done during Domitian's reign.

At heart, Trajan was a soldier, and as emperor, he spent more than half of his 20-year rule leading military expeditions to extend the empire's boundaries. Just and kind, Trajan earned the loyalty of his soldiers by living alongside them in hardship, even ripping up his own clothing to help bandage their wounds.

After two wars with the aggressive Dacians, whose territory included present-day Rumania, he won a region rich in gold and silver mines, which he used to replenish Rome's depleted treasury. In celebrating the victory, he delighted the Roman populace with four months of public games. About 10,000 gladiators fought, and 11,000 animals were slaughtered. A more lasting gift to the citizenry was his far-sighted building program with its unprecedented achievements in engineering, town planning, and architecture. A noteworthy example is the Forum of Trajan, or marketplace, parts of which still stand in Rome today.

Unfortunately, what had succeeded in the West floundered in the East. Trajan tried to take control of Armenia and Parthia (modern-day Iran), but his resources were overextended, and revolts sprang up. His conquests in the East also depleted the number of peacekeeping soldiers, who guarded the ever expanding empire. When a violent uprising of Jews erupted in Cyrenaica (modern-day Libya) in 115, the few troops available were powerless to stop it. The revolt spread quickly to regions in the Mediterranean and assumed the character of a formal war. Cyprus was devastated when the Jews attacked Greek inhabitants there and wrecked roads and buildings. Trajan's generals, in turn, executed thousands of Jews.

By 117 the Jewish rebellion was all but over when Trajan had a stroke. Too ill to continue, he turned the army over to his younger cousin and ward, Hadrian, and set off for Rome. A few days later Trajan died. The very next day, it was announced that Hadrian had been adopted as his imperial successor.

Trajan's Column, right, stands over 100 feet high. Erected in Rome sometime between 106 and 113, it tells the story, in spiraling scenes, of his army's heroic victory over the warring Dacians. Once capping the column was a bronze statue of Trajan himself, but in 1588 it was replaced with one of Saint Peter. In a detail from the pillar, above, Trajan (fourth from right) offers a sacrifice to pagan gods. An image of the monument, which symbolizes Trajan's military might, appeared on a coin that also bore his likeness.

During his later years, the emperor Hadrian eschewed traveling for the pleasure of his villa in Tivoli, outside Rome. It was a spectacular complex of buildings and gardens, more than a mile long. A lover of Greek art, he had copies of famous Greek statues set along the edge of the villa's reflecting pools.

Hadrian, the great conciliator

Following such an esteemed leader would be difficult for anyone, but it was especially so for Hadrian. Dark rumors spread in the Senate that Hadrian was romantically involved with Trajan's wife. Many felt she had engineered his imperial adoption by forgery.

Army commanders were distressed when the first thing Hadrian did was give up territories that Trajan had fought to acquire. He abandoned Trajan's policy of expanding the empire through conquest. Making peace and consolidation his goals, he decided to keep only those territories that could be securely defended. Thus, Armenia went back to the Parthians.

Hadrian transformed the aims of the army from conquest to border control, yet he managed to introduce a code of discipline that maintained the peacetime military at peak efficiency. He also invested in impressive defensive works, such as the stone wall that runs through northern Britain. Money that had once paid for battles was now poured into construction of new buildings. Hadrian rebuilt, among other things, the renowned Pantheon in Rome, a temple dedicated to all the pagan gods and goddesses.

A cultured man, Hadrian performed music, painted with sensitivity, and tried his hand at writing. On his deathbed he wrote these lines:

Sweet little soul, flitting, fair,
My body's guest and friend,
I wonder where you'll end.
A little ghost, stiffened, bare?
You'll miss your jesting there.

The cosmopolitan Greek lifestyle appealed greatly to Hadrian, who spent much time visiting Athens. Where Trajan had traveled for conquest, Hadrian traversed the empire to absorb its beauty and culture. Though open-minded, Hadrian found it difficult to tolerate the religious separatism of the Jews, which continued even after nearly two centuries of Roman rule. He had fought them during the Jewish rebellion in 115 and perhaps felt little concern for such combative people. Many historians argue, however, that news of Hadrian's plans to rebuild Jerusalem as a pagan city dedicated to the god Jupiter precipitated the Bar Kokhba revolt of 132 (see box on page 128). After the war, he did indeed build a pagan city, with a temple to Jupiter on the sacred site of the Jewish Temple and a sanctuary to Venus on the spot where tradition holds that Jesus was crucified.

However, Hadrian's legal actions toward Christians were moderate. Like Trajan, he received a letter from a local governor asking for guidance on how to treat Christians. Hadrian replied: "By Hercules, you must be very careful to see that if anybody accuses one of them falsely, you assign *him* severe penalties in proportion to his malice."

Hadrian began the long process of making Roman law more uniform. In the past, whenever a local magistrate had taken office, he had issued edicts regarding his interpretation of specific civil laws. Because these edicts were customarily renewed by incoming magistrates, their interpretations became part of the Roman civil law. However, some magistrates did not renew the old rulings but instead issued new ones that reversed or contradicted those of their predecessors. The result was legal instability. To eliminate this confusion, Hadrian commissioned a group of Rome's best jurists to unify existing decrees into a definitive code, which only the emperor could alter.

His personal life, however, was far from consistent. Midway through his reign in 124, Hadrian, whose marriage was correct but cold, fell in love with a handsome young page named Antinoüs. Some six years later, as the emperor's entourage was traveling up the Nile to visit famous sites, the youth drowned. Grief-stricken, Hadrian declared him a god. Many cities built temples in the youth's honor, and Hadrian commissioned portrait statues, 500 of which still exist today. Apparently, many people responded to this new cult and avidly worshiped the new deity.

The revival of paganism

From its earliest beginnings, the worship of numerous divinities had been part of the social and political fabric of Rome. As far back as the fifth century B.C., Romans had sacrificed to Apollo, an Olympian god, to rid the land of pestilence. Augustus Caesar, emperor at the time of Jesus' birth, is credited with returning pomp and splendor to the state religion. He even went so far as to add his murdered great-uncle, Julius Caesar, to the pantheon of gods to be worshiped.

Starting with Julius Caesar, a number of Roman rulers were deified, usually *after* their deaths. In the first century, the emperor Domitian had scandalized his contemporaries by demanding deification while still alive. In Athens, Hadrian was proclaimed "the Olympian" and honored alongside the god Jupiter. These are but a few examples of the emperor cult, which provides evidence that for Romans there was virtually no distinction between the state and religion or between political and spiritual allegiances.

The peace and prosperity achieved by Trajan and Hadrian spurred new spiritual and intellectual developments. Traveling merchants and soldiers brought different religions from the East, while philosophy students from all provinces flocked to Athens to be educated in the teachings of Plato or the Stoics.

Hadrian's Wall spans 73 miles in northern Britain, near the Scottish border. Hadrian had the 20-foot-high defense work built to hinder continuous attacks from warring barbarian tribes, namely the Scots and the Picts. Protected by numerous forts, the wall marked the northern boundry of the Roman Empire.

Indeed, members of all classes sought answers to the search for meaning in an age that offered material well-being but little spiritual fulfillment.

In such a time of religious questioning, spiritual charlatans abounded. One notorious scoundrel, Alexander of Abonoteichos, convinced the gullible that a captive snake wearing a model of Asclepius' head could reveal the future. Alexander displayed the snake and through a hidden tube, spoke, as if he were an oracle. Alexander was richly rewarded for such magical powers. Despite the rumors that his practices were corrupt, he was highly successful.

Pagans believed in fate and looked to the gods for aid. They gave heed to prophecy, which helped to warn and advise, often seeking predictions at the shrines of oracles. And they believed in astrology, which was considered a science. Astrology, they thought, could reveal the course of an individual's life determined by the movements of celestial bodies. But none of these things could answer the deeper spiritual questions or provide freedom from the control of fate or the stars. Perhaps in an attempt to find answers, an increasing number of pagans turned to the mystery religions of Demeter, Isis, and Cybele.

The wrath of the goddess Demeter

The Greeks had long believed in an afterlife, with the deceased descending into the underworld to exist as shadowy beings. It was an ancient myth, concerning the ruler of the underworld, Hades, that gave rise to the cult of Demeter and the promise of a happy afterlife. In this story Hades abducted Persephone, the daughter of the Greek grain goddess, Demeter, and kept her in his gloomy domain. Demeter was so outraged that she refused to return to Mount Olympus and resume her role as goddess of the harvest. As she roamed the world looking for her daughter, the earth suffered such terrible famine that Zeus (also known as Jupiter) ordered Hades to return Persephone to her mother. Unfortunately, Persephone had been tricked into eating pomegranate seeds during her imprisonment, not knowing that partaking of food in the underworld would make her escape impossible. Zeus imposed a compromise. Persephone could leave, but each year, during the four winter months, she would have to return to Hades. This cycle accords with the growing of grain in ancient Greece. Seeds were planted in autumn, the plants flourished under the warm winter sun, then were harvested in spring and kept underground in storage during the hot summer months.

Demeter had supposedly instructed the noblemen of Eleusis, a town near Athens, in her sacred rites. To perpetuate her teachings, the citizens of Athens built a huge sanctuary in Eleusis to honor the goddess and reenact the secret rituals she had introduced. Initiation into the Greater Mysteries began in September and included a festive 14-mile procession from Athens to Eleusis that ended in all-night dancing and singing. The initiates went through rituals involving fasting, sacrificing a pig, and drinking a mixture of barley, water, and mint. Some scholars believe that this potion contained a hallucinogen, possibly ergot, which provoked rapturous visions. To attain the highest level of secret knowledge, initiates returned a year later to participate in more rituals and to view, for the first time, sacred objects of the mysteries.

The Eleusinian mysteries were considered so sacred that initiates were forbidden to speak about them. The initiation could be expensive, but it was considered worth the price. On one of his many journeys through Greece, Hadrian himself became an initiate, and even the Stoic Marcus Aurelius was admitted into the inner sanctum at Eleusis.

Isis, an Egyptian goddess

One of the most successful religions of the second century was devoted to Isis, an Egyptian goddess, who, it was believed, could grant her followers success and freedom from fate in this world and protect them when they arrived in the underworld. According to ancient myth, Isis had been married to her brother Osiris, a wise and beneficent ruler who was murdered by his jealous brother, Set. While searching for the body of Osiris, Isis discovered that Set had cut it into 14 parts, which he had scattered all over the country. She was able to retrieve all but the genitals. These she replaced with a gold image, replicas of which were carried in ritual processions of the Isis cult. Osiris became ruler of the underworld and took care of Isis' followers when they reached the world below. In the Greco-Roman world, Osiris was renamed Serapis and was worshiped throughout the empire.

The goddess Isis was praised with daily worship services held in her temples. She required chastity of her priests and repentance from her followers, who might do penance by crying their sins aloud in the

To reach the fearful oracle of Trophonius (in central Greece), a person had to climb down into a stone pit, where he was then drawn through a small opening into a dark passage. Clutching honey-cakes to feed any mythical serpents along the way, the terrified supplicant later emerged, feet first, through the same opening, having triumphantly obtained visions of the future.

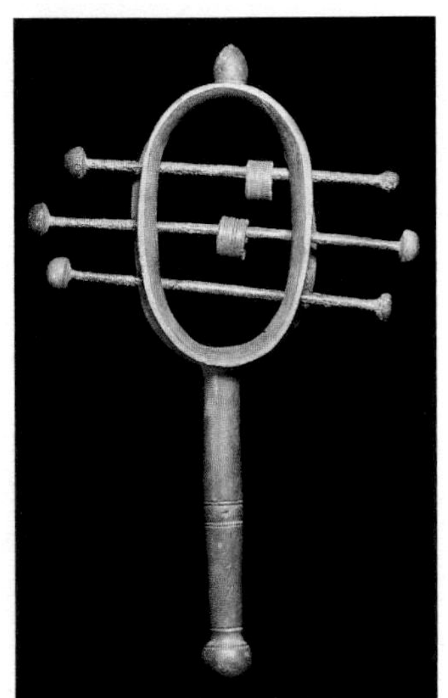

White-robed followers of Isis, Egyptian goddess of life, walk behind a priestess, who wears a snake, sacred to Isis, wrapped around her arm. Devotees often carried in processions musical instruments, such as the sistrum, directly above. The cult of Isis was extremely popular during the second century.

streets. One initiate described a powerful dream in which Isis revealed that she had the power to save him from fate as well as the vagaries of magic but only if he remained her loyal servant.

Cybele, the ancient fertility goddess

The mystery religion of Cybele, or the Great Mother, was brought to Rome in 204 B.C. during the Punic Wars. At the time, Hannibal seemed poised to conquer the city. When the Senate consulted the *Sybilline Books*, ancient texts containing prophecies, it was advised to enlist the aid of Cybele, the mother goddess from Phrygia (a region now part of central Turkey). A black meteorite, identified as the image of the goddess, was brought to Rome. After years of warfare, Hannibal was finally turned back, and a temple to the Great Mother was built in Rome. Eventually, a festival to commemorate the coming of the goddess was held each year from April 4 through 10.

Spring festivals also centered around her consort, Attis, whose sacred symbol was a pine tree and whose priests were eunuchs, known as *Galli*. From March 15 through 27, Attis was honored in a series of rituals, including the decoration of a pine tree with ornaments and self-flagellation by the mendicant priests. They let their hair grow long and donned female garb, perhaps to identify with the Great Mother, acknowledged as the creator of all gods and all mankind.

Romans were both repelled and fascinated by this Eastern religion. In a ceremony called the *taurobolium*, an initiate waited in a deep pit beneath a wooden lattice, upon which a garlanded live bull was laid. When the animal was slain with a spear, the participant lifted up his face to the shower of blood, drinking it as it anointed him. This ritual was possibly a kind of purification in preparation for the afterlife and was apparently good for a 20-year period, after which an initiate would have to repeat it. The religion became so entrenched in Roman life that in the mid-second century the image of the Great Mother appeared on coins.

"In the mysteries," wrote one pagan, "we learn not only to live happily but to die with fairer hope." The mysteries provided a way to satisfy deep spiritual longings, as well as circumvent the finality of one's fate. Moreover, they sanctioned new roles for Roman women, some of whom served as priestesses.

It was common for wealthy Romans to be initiated into several mystery religions. Only Christians and Jews refused to share in the revival of ancient religions that was sweeping the empire in the second century. Their uncompromising monotheism led them to view the many gods of the empire as demonic.

The religious policies of Antoninus Pius

Because of its exclusivity, Christianity remained a banned superstition and continued to be perceived as inimical to the state. However, during the reign of Hadrian's successor, Antoninus Pius (138–161), there were few outbreaks of persecution against Christians. In fact, Antoninus Pius discouraged them. He also modified Hadrian's ruling that in effect forbade circumcision, allowing Jews to circumcise their sons but not Gentile converts. With this policy, further expansion of Judaism was prevented. However, he upheld Hadrian's edict that barred Jews from their holy city of Jerusalem and enforced it by building a ring of military posts around the city.

Antoninus was not Hadrian's first choice for successor. The man whom Hadrian had been grooming for the job, Lucius Verus, died suddenly. Hadrian, suffering from a fatal illness, chose Antoninus, a lawyer from a senatorial family, who was a fine judge and capable adminstrator. Apparently, Antoninus deliberated for some time before accepting Hadrian's offer. He was granted supreme administrative authority on February 25, 138, and took the title *Imperatoris* as part of his own name—the first ever to do so. When Hadrian died four months later, he became emperor.

Although Hadrian had repeatedly challenged the Senate's authority, Antoninus managed to convince Rome's ruling body to deify his late adoptive father. For this action and for his devotion to state religion, the name *Pius* (or "pious") was added to Antoninus' name. With deft political and administrative abilities, Antoninus quickly gained the Senate's respect, and using great diplomacy, he was able to contain or limit many military conflicts.

Antoninus continued Hadrian's effort to codify the Roman law, working to remove any inconsistencies. More important, he anticipated two basic principles of civilized justice when he decreed that a man is to be considered innocent until proven guilty; and in cases where there is any doubt, the verdict should be resolved in favor of the accused.

Throughout his 23-year reign, Antoninus Pius did not once leave Italy, preferring to live unpretentiously in his villa just outside Rome. He despised political

Continued on page 127

A priest of Cybele, the Asian fertility goddess, is shown in full vestments. He holds a pomegranate (symbol of life) and a dish of pine cones and fruit (symbolizing fertility). Beside him are objects used in the cult rites, a tambourine, flutes, cymbals, and a whip for self-flagellation.

To many pagans, nature was the supreme good—"the mighty parent of the gods." Indeed, nature was a favorite subject in Roman decorative arts. This lifelike mosaic of ducks swimming may show the influence of Egypt and its great river, the Nile.

The walls of the Stabiae, a fashionable resort near Pompeii, were decorated with exquisite frescoes—here a woman gathers wildflowers. The dedicated naturalist Pliny the Elder went to the Stabiae to observe the eruption of Mount Vesuvius and died there while investigating the volcano's terrible fury.

This painting of a glass bowl with fruit is from the house of Julia Felix in Pompeii. It demonstrates that the Romans were not only fine painters but masters at glasswork. Roman glass was renowned for its beauty.

The eruption of Mount Vesuvius preserved for posterity much of Pompeii, including some 3,500 frescoes on the walls of villas. This fresco shows beautifully rendered little birds.

Roman Decorative Arts

The marvelous paintings, mosaics, and decorative objects that have survived from Roman times attest to the pagan love of beauty as well as the extraordinary skill of the empire's artists and artisans.

Decorative flooring was as much a part of Roman architecture as columns and arches. The tiling in an octagon-shape is a centerpiece in an elaborate floor design. Below is a fragment of pavement from the palace of Tiberius in Rome.

This painting of a vase from the house of Uccelli in Pompeii reveals the great debt Roman art owed to Greece. The classic shape of the urn shown above resembles Greek vases of previous centuries. Urns such as these were used to hold either wine or water.

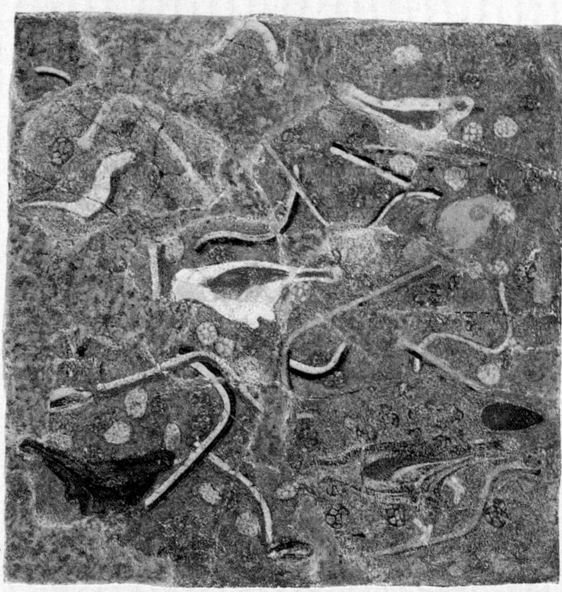

This charming glass mosaic of birds among branches once graced the wall of a villa or perhaps even a palace.

A Philosopher-Emperor

By birth a member of the circle that surrounded Hadrian, Marcus Aurelius was educated for high office from earliest childhood. Following his accession, he came closer to the old ideal of philosopher-king than any of the other Roman emperors. His watchword was "to worship and bless the gods, and to do good to men."

In private life, he endured much disappointment. His beloved adoptive brother, Lucius Verus, with whom he shared the imperial post for a time, was unfit for power but luckily was carried off by a stroke before it became necessary to remove him. An unworthy wife and an infamous son (Commodus, who became one of the worst emperors) were lifelong burdens that he bore without complaint.

Although famous for benevolence, piety, and clemency, Marcus Aurelius could not have felt he had anything in common with the Christians. It seems never to have dawned on him that many of them were, like himself, brave, dedicated, highminded, and pure of heart. Like many other Romans of his day, he considered Christianity to be a superstition and its adherents unintelligent fanatics.

He believed in a divine purpose. "We all work together toward one final end, some with knowledge thereof and conscious intelligence, and some in ignorance." This was his prayer: "Give what Thou wilt, take back what Thou wilt."

His Stoic philosophy, expressed in his diary, published as the *Meditations*, called for high ethical self-government by an individual. Many of its precepts coincide with Christian teachings, but the two ways of life were worlds apart. As a Stoic, Marcus Aurelius believed that "it is enough to abide with the Divinity that is within," in other words, that salvation is an individual affair, between a man and the divine light within himself. His social credo was simple: "Love the human race!" Christians, on the other hand, believed that God's saving grace, not only inside the individual but present in the group and the outside world as well, had come in the person of Jesus Christ. Salvation came from communion with him and loving one another.

A generous ruler, Marcus Aurelius increased the number of people who were eligible for free corn from the state. He forgave unpaid taxes during his reign and provided many games and spectacles.

corruption and once said, "Nothing is meaner, indeed more heartless, than to nibble at the property of the State without adding to it by one's own efforts." He encouraged the rich to be as generous as he in making donations to better the empire. When his beloved wife, Faustina, died in 141, Antoninus Pius endowed an institution for poor Roman girls in her honor. He did much to improve the empire, finishing the baths at Ostia, which Hadrian had begun, and constructing countless roads and bridges.

While always generous, Antoninus was loath to show signs of extravagance. During the 900th anniversary of Rome's legendary founding, he celebrated modestly by issuing a series of commemorative medallions that paid honor to the history of Rome.

Antoninus Pius died, childless, in 161. His final watchword, "peace of mind," was an inspiration to his adoptive son and son-in-law, Marcus Aurelius. The wise Antoninus had made a deep impression upon Marcus Aurelius, who later wrote: "Remember his qualities, so that when your last hours come your conscience may be as clear as his."

When Marcus assumed the imperial robes, he surprised everyone by appointing Lucius Verus the Younger, his adoptive brother, as his full colleague, thus introducing dual emperorship. However, the peace Rome had enjoyed under Antoninus Pius was soon overturned. Marcus and Lucius had to protect the Eastern provinces from the Parthians. Lucius successfully routed the invaders but died in 169. Marcus, now sole emperor, not only had to fend off a serious threat to the empire from invading Germanic tribes but also was forced to deal with the aftermath of a plague that had decimated the ranks of the army. No doubt his Stoic philosophy helped him prevail through these difficulties (see box, opposite page).

Though sickly, Marcus Aurelius never shied from physical hardship. Most of his 20 years as emperor were spent campaigning against Germanic tribes. In spare moments during the years 169 to 175, he wrote his *Meditations*, a collection of thoughts and observations by one who seemed more suited to philosophy than war. Though just and compassionate, Marcus had little patience for Christians, whose teachings he viewed as a threat to society and an affront to the gods. It was during his reign that the Christians of Lyons suffered persecution and martyrdom.

The challenge of heresy

As the church spread to all parts of the empire, the customs and cultures of regional groups exerted a powerful impact on its development. Factions began to form, claiming different interpretations concerning Jesus and his Apostles. But instead of weakening the church, dissenting opinions and beliefs seemed to spur the development of a creed and canon that unified and strengthened the more dominant segments of Christianity. In the ensuing battles, however, the groups that lost ground had much of their literature either destroyed or lost. History, as one sage quipped, is written by the winners, not the losers. To the victor goes an assured place in the annals of history.

Certain sects of Jewish Christians posed a special challenge to the emerging church. They considered themselves descendants of the earliest Christians in Jerusalem, yet they tried to combine Jesus' teaching with the religion of the Old Testament and its laws. Unfortunately, much of the writings of these Jewish-Christian sects has been lost. From a few surviving fragments, historians have managed to piece together a broad outline of their thought. One group, known as the Ebionites, apparently had their own book, the *Gospel of the Ebionites*, written probably about the middle of the second century. Fortunately, a few quotations from this fascinating work have been preserved in the writings of an early church historian.

The Ebionites saw Jesus as the latest in a long line of prophets. Apparently, they did not believe he was born the divine Son of God, but rather that when at his baptism the Holy Spirit descended on Jesus in the form

Although Antoninus Pius was not the first choice of Hadrian for emperor, he proved to be worthy of the task. Thanks to Antoninus' diligence and keen sense for politics, the empire enjoyed more than 20 years of peace. During his reign, Rome celebrated the 900th anniversary of its founding.

"Son of a Star": The Tragic Coming of a Would-be Messiah

Jewish zealots had suffered crushing defeat in their first great rebellion against Rome between 66 and 73, yet many Jews had still not resigned themselves to living under Roman rule. Jewish insurrection broke out anew in 115, and it took the Romans two years to put down the revolt.

Another uprising, which was to prove the last, flared in Palestine probably about 132. It seems to have coincided with the emperor Hadrian's intention to build a pagan city on the ruins of Jerusalem and with his edict that effectively banned the rite of circumcision. But the date for this unhappy stroke of policy is not precise—it may have come *after* not *before* the rebellion.

The Jews of Judea and Galilee rose under the leadership of Simeon Ben Kosiba, known to posterity by his messianic title Bar Kokhba, which translates as "son of a star." The name is based on the prophecy: "A star shall come forth out of Jacob, and a scepter shall rise out of Israel" (Numbers 24:17). It is difficult to form a clear idea of Bar Kokhba from the mass of folklore and sparse historical references concerning him. Many of his followers apparently thought he was the Messiah, while some Christians saw the man as a murderous impostor. Recently discovered letters by him confirm the image of a Napoleonic leader who kept a tight grip on both the economy and the armed forces, busied himself with details, and denounced lazy commanders: "You are living well, eating and drinking off the property of the house of Israel, and care nothing about your brethren."

The Romans failed to take the rebellion seriously at first, and the insurgents took Jerusalem and much of the surrounding territory in Judea. Bar Kokhba proclaimed an independent state, issued new coinage, and imposed controls on the economy.

His success was short-lived. Rome brought in reinforcements from as far away as Britain. Avoiding pitched battle, the legions laid siege to Jewish strongholds. One by one they fell. About 135 the Romans stormed the fortress Bether. Bar Kokhba died in the battle, and the revolt ended.

According to the Greek historian Dio Cassius, 50 fortresses and nearly 1,000 villages had been destroyed by the time it all ended, and half a million Jews had died. So many of those who survived were carried off as slaves that the price of a Jew in the slave market was less than that of a horse. (This last legend was recorded by Jerome, the Bible translator, who lived in Bethlehem during the late fourth century.)

The psychological consequences for the Jews went far beyond the destruction and loss of life. Bar Kokhba's revolt marked the last serious attempt until modern times to found an independent Jewish state.

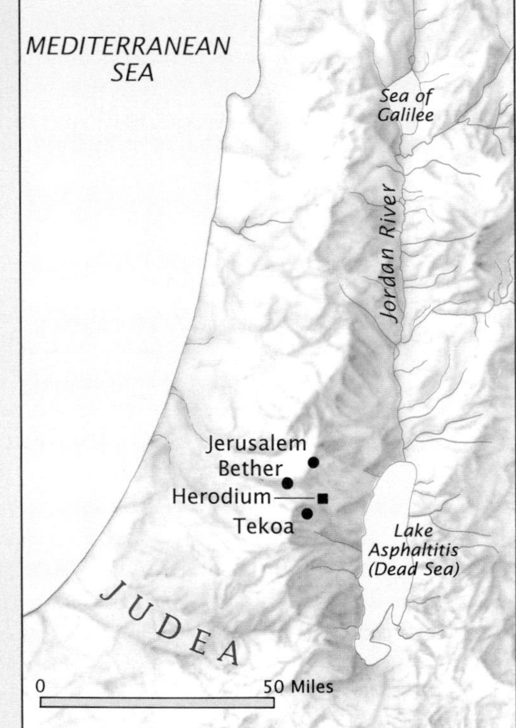

In the last days of the Bar Kokhba revolt, rebel-held territory shrank to the Judean mountains and included rebel strongholds at Herodium, Bether, and maybe a third one near Tekoa. Eventually, the Romans destroyed them one by one.

Bar Kokhba struck over old coinage with new inscriptions. The silver denarius shown here (left) bears Simeon's name, while the other side (right) reads: "For the freedom of Jerusalem." Other coins were inscribed "Simeon prince of Israel," and still others were dated, for example, "Year one of the redemption of Israel."

of a dove, it signified his adoption by God. Ebionites continued to adhere to many rituals prescribed in the Old Testament, such as observing the Sabbath. They disliked the Apostle Paul, for he opposed the observance of certain Jewish practices, such as circumcision. But while they revered the Torah, the Ebionites believed that Jesus had done away with all Temple sacrifices and had called them to an ascetic life. As the church became more and more Gentile in composition, such Jewish-Christian sects lost their influence.

Justin and Trypho

Though the great majority of Jews were unconvinced by the message of Christianity, there is evidence that early Christians were still intent on spreading the gospel among them. Justin, later known as Justin Martyr because of his martyr's death (see page 140), was a second-century philosopher who converted to Christianity as a young man. He wrote a number of works, including a fascinating rendition of a debate with a Greek-speaking Jew named Trypho.

Justin's *Dialogue with Trypho* may have been written around 155, during the reign of Antoninus Pius, though the actual debate supposedly took place some 20 years earlier. Throughout this work, he repeatedly argues that the coming of Christ was the fulfillment of Old Testament prophecies. In one passage, for instance, Justin has Trypho question how Jesus could be the *Christos* (the Greek word for "Messiah") when, according to Jewish law, death by crucifixion is demeaning and, therefore, unworthy of the Messiah. Justin explains that the mystery of the cross can be traced to the Old Testament, when it is understood symbolically. To make his point, he interprets a passage in which he says Moses stretched out both arms for hours, a sign that assured the Israelites' victory over a warring enemy. To Justin, that symbol of extended arms signified Israel's salvation—a sign that Christ on the cross ultimately fulfilled. The church is the new Israel, Justin goes on to explain. He urges Trypho and other Jews to accept the fact that Christ came for all people: "The Lawgiver is come but you discern him not; the poor have the Gospel preached to them, the blind see, but you understand not."

The *Dialogue* is a gentlemanly encounter between a Jew and a Christian that is free of the virulent attacks against Judaism that characterized the work of many later writers. Justin is sympathetic to Trypho's confusion over the various and sundry beliefs that were inundating the church. He assures Trypho that Jesus himself had prophesied, "Many false prophets will arise and lead many astray."

Gnosticism

One religious movement that profoundly challenged orthodox Christianity was Gnosticism (from the Greek word *gnosis*, which means "knowledge"). The Gnostics of the second century saw themselves as an elite group that held the key to the secret of salvation. Only their own mystical knowledge of an otherwise unknowable God would bring inner peace and salvation. Many Gnostics considered themselves to be Christians but strongly believed that their unique spiritual *gnosis* differentiated them from the masses.

Inspired by a longing for spiritual knowledge and mystical experience, Gnostics were concerned with the mystery of good and evil. The movement was considered so radical that it was eventually driven underground, and most of its writings were destroyed. For centuries, much of what was known about Gnosticism had to be gleaned from the writings of critics and opponents. Then in 1945 an astonishing discovery was made at Nag Hammadi in Egypt. Found inside an ancient earthen jar were 13 books, or codices, that included Gnostic writings. These books were compilations of some 50 texts, which described, among other things, Gnostic rituals, apocalyptic visions, and creation stories. Several texts claimed to be gospels preserving sayings of Jesus. This find tells us much about the radical nature of Gnostic theology.

Essentially, Gnostics believed that there are two separate realms. One is the world of spiritual light, ruled by a single, transcendent, and utterly indescribable Being. The other is the material world of darkness and ignorance, in which mankind dwells. Knowledge is the bridge that permits one to escape from the realm of blind materiality into the realm of spirit.

Some Gnostic leaders were originally members of mainstream Christian communities. One was Valentinus, a theologian in Rome from around 140 to 150. He was a brilliant intellectual, who was perhaps even considered for the post of bishop of Rome; his influence on Gnosticism was so profound that those who followed his teaching were called Valentinians. Like other Gnostic leaders, Valentinus formulated stories that expressed a vision of the creation of the world.

Gnosticism was a major religious movement in the second century. Bird masks, such as the one depicted in this mosaic, were part of a ritual disguise thought to be used in Gnostic ceremonies. Two griffins, fantastical animals with wings, appear to be guarding a temple.

His myth holds that through countless ages, 30 spiritual beings issued from the supreme Father in pairs of male and female; these couples were the personification of divine qualities, such as goodness and truth. The last female to appear was Sophia (*sophia* is Greek for "wisdom"). In her desperate passion to know the unknowable Father, she rejected her partner and conceived by herself a malformed child whom she called Ialdabaoth (most probably translated as "Child of Chaos"). While her passions produced elements of the material world, her recalcitrant child shaped them into the dark world of mankind. Ignorant of the powers above him, Ialdabaoth thought that he was the only god and urged people to worship him. From Sophia, however, a spark of the true divine realm was trapped deep within the heart of man.

Salvation comes when Jesus is sent by the God of Light to lead Sophia into enlightenment and separate her from her passions. To the Gnostics, Jesus was not the Son of God in human form. He was instead the great revealer of *gnosis*—the flame of illumination from the divine realm that continues to burn in truly spiritual people. Not everyone was capable of receiving *gnosis*, they believed, but only a select few who managed to recognize within themselves the spark that was their true identity. The revelation by Jesus of the true God helped such seekers to awaken from the stupor caused by Ialdabaoth and turn toward a mystical vision of their original Father and true self.

Gnosticism was a fascinating blend of Christianity, religious speculation, mysticism, Greek philosophy, and Judaism. According to Irenaeus, Valentinian Gnostics claimed "to know the deep things of God" and to have "perfect knowledge of God."

How did one become a member of a Gnostic sect? Methods varied. Some groups drew up instructions for elaborate initiation rituals, many of which included a second baptism. Others eschewed formal rites and emphasized self-knowledge. One Gnostic writer explained, "It is not the . . . [baptism] which liberates, but it is gnosis [knowledge] of who we were, what we have become; whence we were; into what we have been cast; whither we hasten; whence we are redeemed; what birth is; and what rebirth."

Church leaders were disturbed by the rapid growth and widespread popularity of Gnosticism, and early Church Fathers were quick to pen treatises attacking the Gnostics as heretics. Gnostics denied the potential goodness of humanity, since it sprang from the material realm. Because they believed that their actions in life bore no connection to their spiritual destiny, a few felt free to live immoral lives. Most Gnostics, for the same reason, however, practiced asceticism. They also denied the reality of the Incarnation and the promise of the Resurrection, as both entailed mingling the spiritual with the despised material world.

Despite Christian opposition, this unusual religion was to have a lasting impact on Christianity. Apparently, some early Christian hymns were deeply influenced by Gnosticism. There are even a few traces of Gnostic terminology in the New Testament. Timothy, for example, was instructed to "avoid the godless chatter and contradictions of what is falsely called knowledge [*gnosis*], for by professing it some have missed the mark as regards the faith."

The Gnostics may also have affected the church's attitude toward women. Because women played such a prominent role in Gnostic sects, the second-century church may have begun to exclude women from performing in church services, in an effort to distance itself from this dissenting movement.

Marcion

Another faction proved to be even more challenging to the early church than the Gnostics. These were the Marcionites, a radical group named after their founder, Marcion. Born around 85 in Sinope, in Asia Minor, Marcion moved to Rome sometime in his fifties. There he taught and encountered the Syrian Gnostic teacher Cerdo. Marcion had already begun to develop his own theology, which proved to be so threatening to traditional Christian views that he was excommunicated by the church in 144.

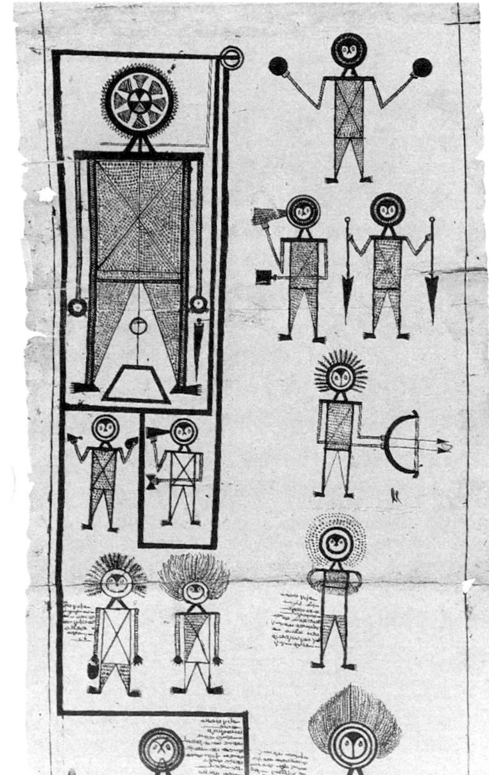

Only one Gnostic group, the Mandeans, have survived to the present day. Living in southern Iraq, the Mandeans, whose name means "the knowing ones," are only 15,000 in number. They believe in a unique cosmology. Before a soul can ascend to heaven, it must pass through various planetary levels, which are guarded by demons, such as the ones pictured to the left. Below is a Gnostic amulet thought to have magical powers.

Like Valentinus, Marcion constructed his own version of creation. He believed that there were two gods—the God of the Old Testament and the God of Jesus. The first one is a Creator-God, whose nature is a mixture of righteous justice and harsh vindictiveness. The second one, the God of Jesus, is pure grace, love, and goodness. According to Marcion, these vastly different deities personify the contrast between the law and grace found in Paul's letters. Marcion asserted that while the Creator-God was often depicted in the Old Testament as petty and wrathful, Jesus had revealed a God who was previously unknown and who would graciously free humanity from the stern demands of the Creator-God's laws.

According to Marcion, because Christ came from the spiritual God, he could not really have been of the flesh. Otherwise he would have been part of the old God's creation. Neither was he the fulfillment of the Old Testament's messianic promises.

Marcion was deeply influenced by the writings of the Apostle Paul, who, in his letters, contrasted the gospel of grace in Christ with the laws of Moses. But where Paul saw Christ as the fulfillment of promises given to Abraham and to Israel, Marcion saw an absolute contradiction between the gospel of Christ and the Old Testament. Thus, the Old Testament could never be Christian Scripture for Marcion, and even many Christian writings, such as certain Gospels, he felt were contaminated with falsehoods when they declared that events in the life of Jesus fulfilled certain Old Testament prophecies. In fact, Marcion rejected all of the Gospels except for Luke's, which he attempted to purify of Old Testament connections. Marcion was also suspicious of many letters that were supposedly written by the Apostles. His canon contained only 10 letters of Paul and Luke's Gospel and nothing at all from the Old Testament.

In his own way then, Marcion made the first attempt to compile a Christian canon, for at that time, the church had no formal list of accepted New Testament Scriptures. All of the early churches simply made use of whatever Christian writings they found appropriate. (During this period a standard canon was beginning to develop, however, and most scholars agree today that it was Marcion who provided some of the impetus for it.)

After the church expelled Marcion, he created an ecclesiastical structure for his own sect, complete with bishops, presbyters, deacons, and deaconesses. Moreover, he commanded that his followers adhere to a strict code of discipline. Where Paul had merely recommended sexual abstinence, Marcion demanded it. He forbade marriage and allowed married persons to be baptized only if they agreed to abstain forever from sexual relations. He also forbade the consumption of meat and wine, using water instead of wine in his version of the Eucharist.

Following Paul's example of traveling widely to gain converts, Marcion established churches in Italy, North Africa, Egypt, Syria, and Cyprus. Around 154 Justin noted that Marcion had attracted followers from every race, and Tertullian later wrote that he had established churches "as wasps make nests." The seriousness of his threat to the church was expressed by Polycarp, the bishop of Smyrna. When Marcion met him he asked, "Do you know me?" Replied Polycarp, "I know the first-born of Satan."

The widespread popularity of Marcionism was evident by the number—and ferocity—of its opponents. After Marcion wrote *The Antitheses*, listing what he saw as contradictions between the Old Testament and the Gospels, he was vehemently attacked. Irenaeus, Justin Martyr, Origen, Eusebius, and Hippolytus all wrote diatribes against him.

Marcion died about 160, but his sect continued to flourish for more than 200 years. The longevity of the community was a remarkable accomplishment considering that it did not permit marriage and had to replenish itself by attracting new converts. In the fourth century, the emperor Constantine outlawed Marcionism along with other heretical groups and ordered that all Marcionite meeting houses should be handed over to the orthodox church.

Once a part of several competing streams in Christian literature, many Gnostic writings were either lost or destroyed. Then in 1945 a huge cache, in the form of leather-bound documents, was rediscovered at the foot of some cliffs near Nag Hammadi, Egypt. They had been sealed in a jar since the fourth century. Coptic translations of earlier works written in Greek, these books are the most important single source of Gnostic scripture available today.

There is a legend that Jesus sent a holy man to heal the dying king of Edessa, in Syria. When the king recovered, the whole city converted to Christianity and became the first to adopt it as an official state religion. Historians believe that it was actually the heretic Marcion who brought Christianity to Edessa sometime in 150. This third-century mosaic depicts an Edessean funerary couch.

The church's response

In the second century, church leaders realized the dangers posed by groups with divergent theology, all claiming to be true Christianity. In debate with these challengers, church leaders were forced to define their doctrines and firmly establish an ecclesiastical organization. The development of the Apostles' Creed is an example of the church's response to these threats. Though one tradition holds that the Apostles themselves composed this profession of faith, with each one contributing a clause, the creed probably grew out of a series of baptismal questions, which were developed to affirm traditional beliefs. Formulated sometime around 150, these questions also weeded out those who were loyal to Gnosticism and Marcionism. For example, the one being baptized avowed that Christ was born of the Holy Spirit and the Virgin Mary, thus affirming that Jesus was born on earth and did not, as the Marcionites believed, simply appear. Moreover, the baptismal candidate had to state that he or she believed in "the holy church."

As the heresies of the second century probably spurred the development of a Christian creed and a canon, the very organization—and authority—of the

The Protevangelium of James, *a popular early Christian story, told how the Virgin Mary came to be the mother of Jesus. In this medieval tapestry, Mary's own birth is depicted. Because Mary was God's chosen one, she was conceived free from original sin, hence the term "immaculate conception."*

church also gained strength from its contest with controversy. In order to support the church's claim that it and not Marcion or the Gnostics represented the unbroken line of Jesus' authority, leaders of the church attempted to demonstrate that its own bishops were successors of Christ's Apostles. The churches in Rome, Ephesus, and Antioch, for example, produced records that confirmed they were founded by Apostles. In contrast, the Gnostic churches claimed to have possession of secret writings from the Apostles, which supported their teachings.

Popular Christian writings

Like a raw recruit after his first battle, the church emerged from the second-century disputes a stronger and more disciplined organization. It began to depend less on oral tradition and more on an increasing number of written works. Christians in this period were familiar with nearly all of the 27 books that make up today's New Testament, but historical records show they also read other works for both instruction and inspiration. Quite a few of these books were deemed authoritative because they were supposedly written by Apostles, and many were very popular.

The Protevangelium of James (also known as *The Protogospel of James*) was especially favored because it contained events that presumably occurred before those related in other gospels (*protos* is Greek for "first" or "before"). This intriguing account focuses on the Virgin Mary, beginning with the story of her parents, Joachim and Anna, and their anguish over being childless. According to the protogospel, when Joachim was told that it was not fitting for him to offer gifts at the Temple because of his childlessness, he fled to the wilderness, where he fasted for 40 days.

During her husband's absence, Anna was visited by an angel, who told her, "Anna, the Lord has heard your prayer. You shall conceive and bear, and your offspring shall be spoken of in the whole world." Anna replied, "If I bear a child, whether male or female, I will bring it as a gift to the Lord my God, and it shall serve Him all the days of its life."

Joachim and Anna were overjoyed at the birth of their child, Mary. As promised, they gave Mary to the Temple when she was 3, and she lived there until she was 12 years old, when the priests decided that it was time for her to be married. Joseph, an elderly widower, was chosen by God to become Mary's husband. He protested to the priests that he was old and already had sons of his own. "She is a girl, I fear lest I should become a laughing stock to the children of Israel." In trepidation of the Lord's wrath, however,

Joseph did agree to marry the child of the Temple and act as her guardian and preserve her virginity.

When Mary was 16, an angel appeared to her. Here the protogospel borrows from the Gospel of Luke as it relates the angel's message: "A power of the Lord shall overshadow you; wherefore also that holy thing which is born of you shall be called the Son of the Highest . . . you shall call his name Jesus." As her guardian, Joseph was angered that someone had taken advantage of Mary and believed that the priests would fault him for not providing better protection. Indeed, the priests did order Joseph and Mary to undergo the ordeal of bitter water, which, according to Jewish tradition, would reveal sins in the guilty. They drank the water and were proven innocent.

To comply with the Roman census, Joseph and Mary traveled to Bethlehem, where they sought shelter in a cave and she gave birth to the infant Jesus. The protogospel relates that at the moment of Christ's birth the entire world momentarily stopped. Joseph, who was out looking for a midwife, "looked up at the vault of heaven, and saw it standing still and the birds of the heaven motionless . . . sheep were being driven and [yet] they did not come forward; . . . and the shepherd raised his hand to strike them with his staff, but his hand remained up. . . . And then all at once everything went on its course [again]."

The protogospel draws from both oral and written traditions. Details about Mary's parents and her childhood, for example, were based on oral legends, while the story of Christ's infancy was borrowed largely from the Gospels of Matthew and Luke. Most likely *The Protevangelium of James* was written in the middle of the second century. Apparently at that time it was used widely in Christian liturgies. The numerous Greek editions and ancient translations indicate that it was something of a best-seller in its day.

Another lost work, possibly from this period, is a collection of hymns called *The Odes of Solomon.* They were mentioned in several fourth-century works, but until the 20th century the hymns themselves had not been found. In 1909, thanks to some dogged scholarly detective work, 40 of the hymns from *The Odes of Solomon* were discovered in a Syriac manuscript.

Although their authorship is unknown, it is clear that many were modeled on Old Testament psalms. The image-rich songs give thanks for protection from persecutors, honor God for conquering death and hell, and praise Christ for offering his Word. Others celebrate Christ's Passion and Crucifixion. One hymn reflects a passage from Matthew's Gospel (16:18): "And the foundation of everything is thy rock./ And upon it thou has built thy kingdom,/ And it became the dwelling-place of the holy ones."

Scholars have noted elements of Gnosticism in many of the hymns and believe that their presence reflects the influence of the Gnostics at the time these

The Bible tells us little about Jesus' childhood. In the second century, legends were written describing Jesus' years with Joseph the carpenter.

The Infancy Gospel of Thomas *describes miracles, such as bringing clay sparrows to life, that Jesus performed as a young boy.*

This is a fragment of the oldest extant Christian hymn with musical notes. The hymn was jotted down in Greek on the back of an Egyptian bill of sale sometime in the late third century. Because there are holes in the papyrus, the modern translation given above is only an approximation. The melody was written for tenor voices.

hymns were composed. One notes, "It is enough to have gnosis and to find rest." Whatever their origin, the hymns provide a rare insight into early Christian worship. In the words of J. Rendel Harris, the scholar who discovered them, they are "redolent of antiquity and radiant with spiritual light."

An early Christian novel

The Shepherd of Hermas was extremely popular during the early centuries of the church. Unlike other Christian works, it reads more like a novel than a gospel or an epistle. Many modern scholars liken it to John Bunyan's *Pilgrim's Progress*, the popular 17th-century story of the spiritual trials of a devout Christian.

Most likely written in the first half of the second century, the *Shepherd* was considered a primer in Christian ethics. From historical evidence, scholars have concluded that it was read aloud at church services. The story describes the mysterious visions of Hermas, a Christian man with a wife and family. It begins with Hermas accidentally seeing a beautiful woman bathing. Because he does not act on his lust, he believes he is free from sin. But then he begins to have a series of visions. In one, the woman he saw bathing appears and cautions him that until he cleanses himself of inner sin and seeks righteousness, he will not be able to sit with those who have pleased God, namely the martyrs. Hermas realizes that in this revelation the woman symbolizes the church.

Subsequent visions reveal that Hermas also must correct the ways of his sons, who have denied the faith, possibly during a period of persecution. Moreover, in his visions, Hermas learns that while God forgives all sins that occurred before baptism, there is no forgiveness for those committed afterwards. In his last vision, Hermas sees "the shepherd" for whom the work is named. This shepherd instructs Hermas in Christian morals and ethics and gives him special commandments as well as parables, which portray human life as a journey through an alien world.

An oral history of the Lord

During the reign of Hadrian, a work called *Expositions of the Oracles of the Lord* in five books was written. The author of this work was Papias, the bishop of Hierapolis in Asia Minor—not far from Smyrna—where his friend and colleague, Polycarp, was bishop. Sadly, this potentially fascinating work has never been found. Bishop Ireneaus and the church historian Eusebius preserved the only fragments of the *Oracles* that are known to scholars today.

Papias was born about A.D. 70 and is said to have been "a hearer of John," though the John in question was probably not the Apostle. Living in the last days of the apostolic age, Papias was deeply impressed with the oral tradition concerning Jesus' life. As he wrote in the preface to his lost work: "I will not hesitate also to set down for your benefit, along with my 'Expositions,' everything that I carefully remembered from the elders, guaranteeing its truth."

Papias was the source for several, mostly faulty, traditions concerning the authorship of the Gospels. For instance, he recorded that Mark, the secretary of the Apostle Peter, wrote down accurately all that Peter had to say about the sayings and doings of Jesus but not necessarily in their proper order. He also wrote that Matthew "composed his history in the Hebrew dialect, and everyone translated it as he was able." Most biblical scholars concur, however, that the Gospel of Matthew, to which Papias apparently referred, was written originally in Greek.

The writings of the second century reveal the tremendous amount of change and experimentation that was taking place during this period. Debate and conflict seemed the norm. It would be decades before a solid body of sacred literature was judged authoritative. Until then, Christian writings remained a mixed bag of doctrine, theory, and inaccuracies. Throughout the second century the church faced the almost daily task of making up its collective mind about which writings best expressed Christ's message.

Attack and defense

Rumors that Christians were involved in outrageous activities, such as cannibalism, debauchery, and incest, were not uncommon in Rome. Marcus Aurelius' beloved tutor, M. Cornelius Fronto, reported sometime in the 150's that Christians gathered at lavish banquets and after feasting, "the light is upset and extinguished, and in the shameless dark lustful embraces are indiscriminately exchanged; and all alike, if not in act, yet by complicity, are involved in incest."

Most well-educated Romans tried to dismiss Christians as ignorant riff-raff because so many converts were poor, female, and uneducated. (Usually, only men from rich families received a good education.) Perhaps some Romans mistook this religious sect for one of the popular burial societies of the era, whose members met at dinners where they listened to speeches by their colleagues. Burials were expensive in Rome; these societies collected money to furnish decent ones for their members. To outsiders, the Christian practices of sharing the Lord's Supper and listening to the gospel might have resembled activities of a burial club. Since Christians felt that to deprive a person of an honorable burial was an affront to God, they too provided burials for poorer brethren.

Some scholars estimate that the number of Christians in most cities in the second century was small compared with the overall population. But in Rome, the number was growing, causing concern among Rome's pagan intellectuals. One possible reason for alarm was that many Romans perceived Christianity to be a Jewish splinter group. Memories of bloody Jewish rebellions in 115 and 132 were, no doubt, still fresh in people's minds (see box, page 128). Both rebellions were crushed without mercy, but Christians may have incurred a taint of guilt by association, even though they did not participate in either revolt.

What truly set Christians apart from other groups, however, was their zeal to imitate Christ even to the point of martyrdom. They were willing to die rather than deny their faith. Many educated Romans, including the emperor Marcus Aurelius, believed that one should despise the vanity of the world and not fear death. But the eagerness of Christians to die for their faith appeared vulgar and theatrical.

Christianity was a radical belief to many people. Aside from their willing acceptance of martyrdom, a number of Christians took the unsettling attitude that natural disasters, such as earthquakes and floods, were welcome as signs that Judgment Day was at hand. They considered famine an omen that the rulers of secular society were about to be overthrown. These interpretations were very specious to the pagans, many of whom thought that such misfortunes were an indication that their own gods were offended by the atheism of the Christians.

Pagan critics

By the 160's the opposition to Christianity had become more articulate. Lucian of Samosata was one outspoken critic. He dismissed Christians as gullible fanatics of a mystery sect, claiming that "they have transgressed . . . by denying the Greek gods, worshipping the crucified sophist." Lucian wrote about the Christians in his satirical portrayal of a confidence man named Peregrinus Proteus, a sometime Christian, who lived in the first half of the second century.

The story goes that Peregrinus, a wealthy young man from Asia Minor, fled to Palestine, possibly after murdering his father. There he converted to Christianity and became a revered teacher and author of religious texts. When Peregrinus was arrested for his faith, widows and children waited outside his prison cell to help him. Lucian reports that after bribing the guards, Christian officials brought Peregrinus meals and read the Scriptures to him. Meanwhile, Peregrinus amassed a small fortune from his supporters. Lucian sarcastically comments, "[Christians] despise all things indiscriminately and consider them common property. . . . So if any charlatan . . . comes among them, he quickly acquires sudden wealth by imposing upon simple folk." After his release from prison, Peregrinus fell out of favor with his fellow Christians, possibly for eating meat that had been offered to the idols. He then tried asceticism in Egypt before taking up the philosophy of Cynicism.

The Cynics mocked all societal conventions and political authority. They strove to live a natural, self-sufficient life, believing it was far more virtuous. Some Cynics took the teaching of Diogenes, the most famous Cynic of all, to an extreme and renounced all worldly goods. Several critics at the time noted that there was little difference between Christians and Cynics. Indeed, both groups eschewed worldly goods. A thin, humble old man, leaning on a stick and trudging from town to town to preach, might as likely be taken for a Cynic as a follower of Jesus.

Peregrinus next appeared in Athens to preach the virtues of Cynicism. In an effort to demonstrate inner strength in the face of death, he announced at the Olympic Games of 161 that he would burn himself to death at the next games. Four years later as crowds gathered round a huge pit, some jeering and others begging him to change his mind, this strange character, now 65 years old, flung off his meager garb and leapt into a sea of flames.

Another critic, named Celsus, attacked Christians with vigor, convinced that this new sect was advocating disrespect for the empire and its ancestral gods. In his *True Doctrine*, written around 178, Celsus argued that Jews and Christians were wrong in assuming there could be such a thing as a "chosen race." He wrote that each race should honor its own god, for all divinities were subject to the same God above. All of humankind, indeed all of creation, received justice in equal measures from divine Providence. "Why, if God wanted to deliver the human race from evils did He send this spirit into one corner?" he asked, referring to Jesus. To preserve the laws and piety of Rome, Celsus wanted Christians to integrate their beliefs into the

In Roman times, the customs governing Christian and pagan marriages were quite similar. One was the joining of the couple's right hands during the ceremony, as depicted on the funeral stone, shown here. In Christian marriages, wedding bands were worn by brides in the West and by both partners in the East probably from imperial times onward. They were placed on the middle finger, from which a nerve was believed to lead directly to the heart.

state's cooperative polytheism. But Christians still remained apart, continuing to support one another not only in religious convictions but in social services as well. To finance their programs they adopted the Jewish practice of tithing, or giving a tenth of their income to the community. A few believers even went so far as to sell themselves into slavery to raise money for the needs of others.

Christian apologists

If Christianity was in opposition to the accepted religion of the Roman Empire, it was even more radical when compared with pagan philosophy. For educated Greeks and Romans, philosophy itself was a religion. Students of Plato, Aristotle, Diogenes the Cynic, or Epictetus the Stoic were as passionate and adamant about their systems of belief as Christians. But by the second century, many of Christianity's strongest supporters were converted philosophers.

To defend Christianity, a few Christian philosophers wrote intellectually sophisticated arguments aimed at demonstrating the validity of their beliefs. This school of writing, called *apologia* from the Greek verb meaning "to defend," relied heavily on logic and reasoning. Though the apologists were seeking to sway the opinion of the best-educated and most powerful leaders of society, their philosophical arguments also served to bolster the Christian community.

Philosophy was a crowning achievement of Roman and Greek education. Regardless of whether a young man studied Platonism, Cynicism, or Stoicism, he was assured a thorough grounding in logic and rhetoric, as well as ethics.

The most famous of the early apologists was Justin Martyr, who taught Christian philosophy in his rooms above a bathhouse in Rome. A pagan, born about 100 in Flavia Neapolis (in present-day Jordan), he was trained in Greek philosophy, especially in the teachings of Plato, and converted to Christianity while a young man, when its truth was revealed to him in a chance discussion with an anonymous old man.

In an attempt to impress Antoninus Pius with the virtues of Christianity, Justin addressed his *First Apology* to the emperor in 155. It is a somewhat lengthy essay defending Christians from charges of atheism. Using his philosophical training, Justin lambasted the idea of pagan piety and stated that Christians are indeed guilty of atheism—if piety is based only on the worship of corrupt pagan gods.

Justin acclaimed the superiority of a Christian way of life, especially when compared with certain immoral practices of magicians and devotees of mystery religions. Developing a tactic that he also used in his *Dialogue* with the Jew Trypho (see page 129), Justin tried to prove the truth of Christian belief by relating how Christ fulfilled the prophecies of the ancient Jewish prophets. Perhaps to refute incessant rumors that Christians were guilty of cannibalism, he explained the Eucharist, writing that it consists only of bread and of wine mixed with water. Justin also tried to reconcile Christianity with Greek philosophy by arguing that Jesus embodied the philosophical concept of divine reason referred to as the Logos. Jesus, he said, is the incarnation of the Logos in human form.

Around 161, Justin wrote a second apology, this time addressing Marcus Aurelius. In this shorter work he decried the persecution of Christians by showing the injustice of condemning those whose only crime was confessing the truth of their belief.

Soon after writing his second apology, Justin was denounced by a personal enemy, the Cynic philosopher Crescens. An anti-Christian whom Justin had defeated in a debate years before, Crescens had tried once already to have Justin arrested but to no avail. In 165, when Romans were suffering from a plague, Crescens accused Justin again. His action cost Justin his life. Justin was tried before Q. Junius Rusticus, a stern but fair-minded magistrate who had great influence with Marcus Aurelius. When threatened with scourging, or flogging, Justin responded: "We ask nothing better than to suffer for the sake of our Lord Jesus Christ and so be saved." He refused to deny the faith he had so brilliantly and ardently defended and so was martyred by beheading.

Another apologist, Athenagoras, started where Justin had left off. Well-schooled in philosophy, he was considered the most eloquent of Christian apologists. In *A Plea for the Christians*, he appealed to Marcus Aurelius and his son, Commodus, for civil toleration. The year was 177. Athenagoras pointed out that since many different religious doctrines were tolerated within the empire, it was only just that Christianity be tolerated too. He then tackled the common accusations of atheism, incest, and cannibalism by showing that Christian standards of conduct were morally high. Using his vast knowledge of Greek philosophy, he explained how the Christian belief in the one God was similar to the classical concept of the unity of God. He was possibly the first to make a philosophical defense of the Trinity by attempting to demonstrate that the Father, Son, and Holy Spirit are one Being.

The aim of the apologists was to demonstrate that Christianity embodied the Greek ideals of virtue and reason. But a few Christians disagreed. They thought that philosophy was far too mired in pagan culture and objected to having their new, revealed belief in Jesus buttressed by philosophical arguments.

Trouble on the horizon

Sometime in the early 170's, a miracle that was later claimed by both pagans and Christians occurred just when the emperor Marcus Aurelius was in trouble on the northern frontier. His reign had been hampered by a number of misfortunes. Prolonged warfare

The Holy Kiss

"Having ended the prayers, we salute one another with a kiss," wrote Justin Martyr in his defense of Christianity. The kiss, a traditional greeting among family members, became a powerful symbol of unity and reconciliation when exchanged among Christians. It was commonly given before the sharing of the Eucharist to celebrate the fact that the men and women of the congregation were brothers and sisters, in spirit, through the love of Christ.

The kiss was a reminder of Jesus' love for his church. In fact, the Greek word used in the New Testament for "kiss" is *philema*, derived from the verb *phileim*, "to love." The Apostle Paul repeatedly instructed the faithful to "greet one another with a holy kiss." No doubt, the practice helped fuel rumors of Christian incest. But kissing on the mouth posed other, more serious problems for early Christian men and women, namely, how to keep holy kisses from becoming carnal. The fact that some "brothers and sisters" liked holy kisses so much they came back for more, led the second-century apologist Athenagoras to urge that a liturgical kiss be "carefully guarded." He warned that a defiled kiss "excludes us from eternal life."

In time, rules were drawn up that permitted men to kiss only men, and women to kiss only the covered hands of men. Licinius, co-emperor with Constantine from 311 to 324, forbade worship by Christians in mixed congregations, due to rumors of wild kissing and general promiscuity.

Despite false rumors of licentiousness spread by nonbelievers and the physical temptations among the faithful, the early church firmly upheld the practice. But, gradually, the exchange of the mouth-to-mouth kiss was modified.

In the latter part of the Middle Ages, the church began to encourage embracing instead of kissing. Worshipers were instructed to place their hands on the shoulders of the recipient, who in turn placed his or her hands on the elbows of the giver, each one bowing the head toward the other. In more recent times, churches have urged their worshipers, before sharing the Eucharist, to celebrate the spirit of Christian unity by shaking hands. This gesture is known as the "sign of peace."

against insurgents in the East and a raging plague had depleted the army of both money and men. Worse still, several Germanic tribes had banded together to invade the provinces south of the Danube. To raise money and to set an example of thrift and self-denial, the emperor auctioned off treasures of the imperial palace, including his wife's jewelry and silk robes.

To fight the invaders, Marcus had to patch together an army that included slaves and gladiators as well as foreign mercenaries. They succeeded in pushing the Germanic tribes back across the Danube. Then, following the classic Roman strategy of dividing the enemies by penetrating deep into their territories, Marcus advanced along the Morava River in northern Moravia (part of present-day Czechoslovakia). But one of the warring German tribes, known as the Quadi, turned and attacked the Roman camp. Soon, the imperial troops were trapped by the encircling Quadi, who cut off all their sources of water. As the Roman army slowly succumbed to thirst and battle weariness, surrender seemed inevitable.

The Thundering Legion

As legend has it, a group of Christian soldiers in the 12th Legion prayed to God for help. The legionnaires knelt down together, a sight that surely must have mystified the fierce Quadi. Suddenly, the heavens burst open and life-giving rain poured down upon the

The life of a Roman legionnaire was one of training, privilege, and discipline. Young recruits were subjected to rigorous mock battles and had to swear an oath of allegiance, which was re-sworn every New Year's Day. During the reign of Marcus Aurelius, the imperial army was called upon to defend the northern borders of the Roman Empire from fierce Germanic tribes. The fighting called for arduous hand-to-hand combat, as portrayed on this Roman sarcophagus. Most likely, the soldiers used swords and daggers, similar to the ones pictured above.

parched soldiers. Delirious, the Romans "turned their faces upwards and received the water in their mouths, then some held out their shields and some their helmets to catch it," wrote the Roman historian Dio Cassius. Lightning and hail stormed down on the Quadi, who surrendered on the spot. The prayers of the so-called Thundering Legion had been answered.

The incident was carved in relief on the column erected before the Roman Pantheon to celebrate the emperor's military successes. Though Dio Cassius credited the miraculous rain storm to the powers of an Egyptian magician in Marcus' entourage who was present at the event, Christians everywhere who heard the story felt the victory was surely theirs. Nonetheless, the god who is portrayed showering water upon the thirst-ridden soldiers is Jupiter, the chief divinity of the Roman state.

The story of the Thundering Legion says much in regard to how Christians felt about the Roman Army. For the first time known to us, they were broadcasting an anecdote that revealed two very important facts: Christians were serving in the armed forces, and they were doggedly loyal to the emperor.

Still, many Christians were morally opposed to serving in the army. They saw themselves as peacemakers, who honored the commandment against killing, even in self-defense. But try as they might, Christians could not ignore the power of the military. In fact, they borrowed heavily from the military vernacular. Consider these expressions: *Militia Christi* meant "soldiering for Christ," heretics were rebels, those who denied the faith were called deserters, and a believer in the old gods was a *paganus,* or "civilian."

Conflicts of conscience

The life of a Roman soldier had appeal. It offered automatic Roman citizenship and retirement after 20 years with a sizable sum of money and a plot of land. But as more and more soldiers within the ranks converted to Christianity, a few wondered if they should resign. The consequence would be dishonorable discharge with loss of all benefits earned. Of course, a common soldier was probably not concerned with the intellectual issues that occupied theologians. Perhaps many a Christian military man felt he could worship Jesus in hope of eternal life, while continuing to venerate the old pagan gods who had always been in charge of assuring victory in the field.

The theologian Tertullian was the first to address the issue of Christians and their relationship to the military. In 211 he wrote, "The oath of allegiance to God and that to man are incompatible. . . . All uniforms are prohibited to us, since they are the signs of a forbidden calling." Tertullian feared that because military life was rife with pagan ritual, a Christian soldier would have to participate in two sinful activities: making sacrifice to the Roman gods and administering torture and capital punishment. Even the military oath of allegiance, or *sacramentum,* represented idolatrous power, he felt. Tertullian was evidently aware that Christians were serving in uniform, and he rebuked soldiers who honored the military code by wearing the crown of laurels after a victory. This practice was most certainly wrong, he argued, because it was too much like idolatry.

However, not all Christians agreed with Tertullian that the teachings of Jesus suggested military service was intrinsically sinful. And since the Second Coming no longer appeared as imminent as the early disciples had believed, it seems likely that Christians had to consider participating more fully in the affairs of the world. As their numbers grew, it would be less possible to abstain completely from involvement in the government and the military. New social and political challenges in the next century would give birth to new interpretations of the Christian view of both warfare and service to the state.

To protect themselves from arrows and javelins, Roman legionnaires wore armored tunics. The chest and upper back plates were riveted onto leather straps, which had buckles at their ends so a soldier could fasten the armor plate onto his body for a close fit.

thompson

Chapter Five

BEARING THE CROSS

The church grew steadily, becoming a state within a state, as more and more pagans entered the Christian fold through baptism. Meanwhile, the empire developed into a military dictatorship and persecutions worsened.

As Christianity advanced, its rituals underwent transformations. Baptism, for example, steadily evolved into a more complex rite than it had been in the age of the Apostles. The practice of spontaneous baptisms, such as that of the Ethiopian eunuch mentioned in Acts, did not last long. By the second century, the church required that converts be instructed in the faith and fast for a specific period before being baptized. By the third century, baptismal rites were even more elaborate. In 232 the earliest known baptistery was built inside a house-church at the doomed Roman outpost of Dura-Europos on the Euphrates. Dura fell to a Persian army in 256 or 257; but the Christian house-church chanced to be preserved in good condition.

Baptisms varied from place to place, but in their main elements, rituals in the third century probably resembled those described by Tertullian in Carthage or Hippolytus in Rome. Prospective converts, or catechumens (the term means "persons under instruction"), spent a three-year instruction period known as the catechumenate to prepare for initiation into the church.

A baptism is in progress at the oldest known Christian church on earth. Converted from a house in 232, it stands amid the ruins of Dura-Europos, an ancient Roman outpost in the Syrian desert. The church was used for only about 24 years before the Persians destroyed the town.

Normally, baptisms were performed on Easter, though possibly also at Pentecost. The catechumens were instructed to bathe on Thursday; they fasted on Friday and Saturday and spent Saturday night in a prayer vigil. As the sun rose on Sunday, the baptismal waters were blessed; candidates took off their clothes and one by one entered the baptistery. (Men and women were baptized separately at this time.)

As a candidate answered each of three questions of the confession of faith, the person was immersed—or water was poured over his or her head—and then he or she was anointed with the oil of thanksgiving. At some point in the ceremony, each candidate renounced Satan, his servants, and his works and was thereupon anointed with more oil.

Hippolytus recorded a baptismal confession used in the Roman church. Although each church had its own confession of faith, the Roman version would have been fairly typical of baptisms being performed elsewhere. These confessions were early prototypes of the later Apostles' Creed.

"Do you believe in God the Father Almighty?" the candidate was asked.

"I believe."

"Do you believe in Jesus Christ the Son of God, who was born of the Holy Spirit and Virgin Mary, who was crucified under Pontius Pilate and died, and rose the third day living from the dead, and ascended into heaven, and sat down at the right hand of the Father, and will come to judge the living and the dead?"

"I believe."

"Do you believe in the Holy Spirit, and the holy church, and the resurrection of the flesh?"

"I believe."

Finally, after the newly baptized were dressed in white garments, symbolizing purity and rebirth, the

Near the house-church at Dura was a magnificently decorated synagogue. This mural from the synagogue illustrates an oral tradition that expands on The Book of Esther, according to which the Jewish hero Mordecai was served by his vanquished Persian opponent as a menial. The image of the conquering monarch on horseback comes from Persian art. It was eventually recast by non-Persian artists to represent Old Testament heroes, Christian saints, and even Byzantine emperors.

bishop laid his hands on each by way of confirmation, and all participated for the first time in the Eucharist.

At Dura-Europos baptismal candidates had only to look at the decoration of the baptistery to be reminded of the significance of the sacrament they were receiving. The baptismal font there resembled a sarcophagus, symbolizing the idea that one is "buried with Christ" in baptism. Frescoes depicted scenes of Christ walking on water and the Samaritan woman at the well, water-related reminders of God's power. A portrayal of the Good Shepherd suggested to candidates that their baptism was their entry into the flock of Christ. The theme of baptismal resurrection was symbolized by a scene of women at Christ's tomb.

Not all of those baptized in the early church had undergone instruction in the faith. At least in some places, infant baptism was begun during the second century. Scriptural warrant for it included Jesus' blessing of the children in Mark 10:13–16 and an episode in Acts wherein an entire household was baptized at once. The testimony of three leading third-century Christians provides some understanding of how the custom developed. Writing in Carthage, Tertullian deplored infant baptism as a senseless novelty and recommended delaying it until the child was old enough to understand and believe. His contemporary, Origen of Alexandria, stated that infant baptism went back to apostolic times; he nonetheless wondered why babies should be baptized, since they were sinless. Half a century later, Cyprian of Carthage answered that question. Infants must be baptized, he wrote, to cleanse them not of their own but of Adam's sin, "the contagion of the ancient death." He regarded the newborn as innately sinful and in the clutches of Satan until baptized. The doctrine of original sin had not yet been propounded, but this view came close.

Given the widespread expansion of the church by the early third century, with cities as varied as Rome, Carthage, Alexandria, Antioch, and Jerusalem boasting flourishing communities of Christians, there was a remarkable amount of agreement about ritual. Nonetheless, different languages, traditions, and customs in far-flung provinces invariably resulted in a number of inconsistencies. Firmilian, a third-century bishop of Caesarea, noted, "All things are not observed [at Rome] alike, which are observed in Jerusalem, just as in very many other provinces also many things are varied because of the difference of the places and of the names." Sometimes, as happened with the controversy over the celebration of Easter, these disparities threatened church unity.

Dispute over Easter

Known as the Quartodeciman controversy, the dispute over the celebration of Easter pitted the church in Asia Minor against the church in Rome. The Eastern church commemorated Easter with a vigil on the same night that the Jewish Passover was celebrated,

Another of the Dura synagogue murals shows the Ark of the Covenant being taken away on a cattle-drawn cart from the land of the Philistines. The lords of the Philistines watch, as the Ark leaves behind the wreckage of the heathen god Dagon's cult. The Jews of Dura doubtless felt themselves to be part of a beleaguered outpost in a world-wide fight against idolatry.

regardless of what day of the week it happened to fall on. The Roman custom, also observed in some parts of Asia Minor, held that Easter fell on the Sunday following Passover. When Polycarp, bishop of Smyrna, visited Anicetus, Rome's bishop, around 155, the two discussed the conflict but reached no solution.

Throughout the latter half of the second century, the dispute even divided the Roman church. The controversy was most noticeable every seven years, when thanks to East-West calendar differences, the large Christian community from Asia would be commemorating the death of Christ, and therefore still fasting, while Rome's other Christians were commemorating the Resurrection. Something had to be done. Victor I, a native of North Africa and the first Latin-speaking bishop of Rome, in 190 called on all churches to follow Rome's lead by observing Easter on the Sunday after Passover. He called synods, regional councils of bishops, in Rome, Palestine, and elsewhere to establish the new rule. When congregations in Asia Minor refused to follow his edict, he excommunicated them. They remained unmoved; however, Polycrates, the bishop of Ephesus, wrote to Victor, saying, "I am not scared of threats."

The dispute simmered off and on until it was finally resolved—in favor of Rome—by the Council of Nicaea in 325 (see pages 218–220). Although Victor's edict was widely disregarded in Asia Minor, it is significant because it shows that the church in Rome and its bishop were beginning to claim authority in the disparate lands of third-century Christianity.

By 200 the church had been planted throughout Egypt, Italy, Asia Minor, and North Africa and was growing in both Spain and Gaul. Its members belonged to a vibrant organization that boasted its own leaders, properties, and rituals. But as the church grew stronger, the empire was beginning to weaken.

Septimius Severus appears as emperor, right, and in the imperial family portrait, above, along with his wife, Julia Domna, and their sons, Caracalla and Geta (obliterated face). Geta was murdered by Caracalla after the death of Septimius.

Beginning of "decline and fall"

Most historians agree that the close of the second century marks the start of the empire's decline. Consider the reign of Commodus, the dissolute tyrant who in 180 succeeded his illustrious father, Marcus Aurelius. Commodus' rule was marked by economic decline, palace conspiracies, threats from barbarians, and widespread executions. With casual disdain, he ordered the murder of senators. To amuse himself, he dressed in gladiatorial armor and slew unarmed opponents in the Flavian Amphitheater, now known as the Colosseum. For a dozen years the empire suffered under Commodus. Then, on New Year's Eve 192, his wrestling partner was induced to strangle him.

Paradoxically, though Christians had suffered under the benevolent rule of Marcus Aurelius, they were hardly ever persecuted by his malignant son. Commodus' chief concubine, Marcia, apparently favored Christians and used her influence to protect them.

Near chaos followed the death of Commodus. Pertinax, the prefect of Rome and an experienced army

Remains of a gate arch span the Roman road in Dougga, Tunisia, not far from where Septimius Severus was born. He was the one who had the arch erected in 205.

commander, was installed as emperor with the help of the Praetorian Guard and the concurrence of the Senate. But less than three months later he was killed by the Guard, presumably because he tried to enforce some disciplinary measures. The Praetorians next demonstrated their low esteem for the emperorship by auctioning it off to the highest bidder. The bidding was won by Didius Julianus, who lasted for just 66 days after purchasing the purple robe. Next, Lucius Septimius Severus, an African-born military commander, was proclaimed emperor by his troops. He marched on Rome declaring that he would avenge the death of Pertinax and claim imperial power.

Severus, commander of 12 legions in southeast Europe, reached Rome in 193. There his forces overpowered the scandal-ridden Praetorian Guard. He wasted no time in dismissing the Guard and replacing it with men handpicked from his own legions. Severus came from a prominent North African family that included several senators. He himself had entered the Senate in about 173 and had risen quickly through government and military ranks, becoming consul in 190. Although well educated, with a solid grounding in Latin and Greek literature, Severus brought to his role as emperor a mind-set that had served him well in the military. His philosophy of governing was simple, expressed in his deathbed advice to his sons. He enjoined them to live in peace, enrich the soldiers, and despise the rest of the world.

Early in his reign, Severus set up a military dictatorship and catered to his troops, the real source of his power. The soldiers' pay was raised by almost a third, and they were given a number of special privileges. Herodian, the historian, commented: "[Severus] was the first to increase their grain ration, and [he] permitted them to wear gold rings and to live with their wives . . . all of which used to be considered incompatible with military discipline and with preparedness and readiness for war. He was the first to undermine their famous vigor . . . teaching them to covet money and turning them aside to luxurious living."

To secure the empire's borders, especially against the Parthians in the East, Severus added three legions to the army. All of these expenditures depleted the treasury. To raise revenues Severus hiked taxes and devalued the Roman currency. Nevertheless, the economy worsened and inflation soared. Military campaigns continued to drain the treasury. Severus, ever the soldier-emperor, led his troops against rival claimants to the imperial power and restive barbarians. He died in 211 in Britain, where he had become embroiled with an unsuccessful invasion of Scotland while endeavoring to quell a native uprising.

For the next 24 years the Severan dynasty presided over a slowly deteriorating empire. Caracalla inherited his father's mantle and took

Julia Domna's horoscope indicated that she would be the wife of a sovereign prince. On the strength of this prophecy, the widowed Septimius Severus married her while still aspiring to imperial office. Once she became empress, Julia Domna surrounded herself with a circle of savants and was called Julia the Philosopher. Her efforts to reconcile her sons were in vain. Stricken with cancer, she reportedly starved herself to death in 217 after her second son, Caracalla, was assassinated.

to heart his advice to "enrich the soldiers." Army pay was increased by an additional 50 percent, and the new emperor announced that he looked to the soldiers as his power base, not to the aristocracy and the urban upper middle class. A saying of his was, "No one but myself ought to have money, and that in order to give it to the soldiers." Taxes on the wealthy were again raised and the currency devalued.

In 212 Caracalla granted Roman citizenship to virtually all free men throughout the empire. According to Dio Cassius this measure added large numbers of people to the tax rolls, but it did nothing to raise their real political or legal position. From a privileged status, Roman citizenship had now become a mere label.

In spite of a faltering economy, Caracalla decided to launch some costly and ostentatious building projects, a few of which, notably the famous Baths of Caracalla, survive in Rome. He thought of himself as a second Alexander the Great. The ailing empire desperately needed such a man, but Caracalla could not measure up to his dream. He hoped to emulate Alexander by uniting Rome with the East and bringing under one rule the two great civilized peoples, the Greco-Roman and the Parthian. But his dreams came to nought. He was finally assassinated at the instigation of one of his Praetorian prefects in 217.

This third-century tomb relief depicts a banker and two laborers. The Roman world was in serious economic trouble throughout most of the century. Imperial currency no longer enjoyed public confidence, and many people took to paying in kind. Some emperors tried to ease the plight of the poor, but few of their policies succeeded.

Continuation of the Severan dynasty

The unfortunate story of the Severan dynasty continues with the rise to power of a 14-year-old cousin of Caracalla. The child-emperor had been brought up in Emesa (modern Homs), an important city in Syria. While still a young boy he was installed by his mother as the high priest of the Syrian sun god, Elagabal, whose principal temple was in Emesa. Assuming his deity's name, the boy became Elagabalus (or Heliogabalus, as he has been popularly named in ancient as well as modern times).

Once he was confirmed as emperor, Elagabalus fancied himself the founder of a new world religion based on Elagabal, with himself as the god's representative on earth. He built a temple to Elagabal on the Palatine Hill and plundered temples of Roman gods to embellish it. The black cone that symbolized the Syrian god began to appear on his coinage. According to some historians, he had a penchant for extravagances and for dressing in women's clothes that further scandalized conservative Romans. After three and a half years his grandmother and aunt maneuvered his younger cousin into position to serve as a replacement, under the name of Alexander Severus. When the 18-year-old Elagabalus resisted the move, he was murdered together with his mother, and their bodies were thrown into the Tiber River.

Alexander Severus, who reigned from 222 to 235, was the last of the Severan emperors. Although intelligent and high-minded, Alexander was only 14 when he replaced his eccentric cousin, and he remained for the rest of his life the pawn of his elders and advisers. His adopted name—Alexander—is a clear reflection of the old Severan dream to unite the East and the West. At the age of 27 he was killed by his own troops when he tried to placate barbarians on the German frontier with a settlement of money.

Christianity attacked by a pagan philosopher

"Whenever they get hold of children in private and some stupid women with them, they let out some astounding statements as, for example, that they must not pay any attention to their fathers and school-teachers, but must obey [the women]. . . . the more reckless urge the children to rebel." In this attack against Christians, written probably in Alexandria around 180, the philosopher Celsus echoed a sentiment that had been widely held for the past 100 years and was gaining more ground during the late second century.

As the church spread throughout the empire, more people began to speak against Christians for refusing to serve the state or pay homage to the Roman gods and—as Celsus claimed—disrupting the bonds of society. Now, said Celsus, the time had come to eradicate Christianity in order to save the empire. He was writing for an audience already predisposed in his favor. Christians had often been blamed for everything from famines to fires. Sometimes, especially during troubled periods, they were vilely persecuted. While persecutions in general were not widespread in the early third century, they did occur.

The Passion of Perpetua

A famous Christian martyr was Perpetua, a married 22-year-old Carthagenian woman who was a catechumen when arrested along with four companions in 202 or 203. Perpetua and her maid, Felicitas, received baptism in jail and, together with several companions, were put to death in an arena that may be the one still standing near present-day Tunis.

This crude drawing, left, of a man gesturing at a crucified figure with a donkey's head and beneath it the words "Alexamenos worships God," was discovered when servants' quarters of the ancient imperial palace on the Palatine Hill in Rome were excavated in 1856. It is an anti-Christian, or possibly anti-Jewish, cartoon. (A tracing of it appears above.) Many pagans believed that the Jews and Christians worshiped a god in the form of a donkey.

The story of their sufferings, published soon afterward as *The Passion of Perpetua and Felicitas*, opens with Perpetua's pagan father attempting to persuade his determined daughter to renounce Christianity: "Lay aside your pride, do not ruin us all, for none of us will ever speak freely again if anything happens to you." Although she grieves for her father, Perpetua still refuses to change her mind: "It shall happen as God shall choose, for assuredly we lie not in our own power but in the power of God."

Highlighting the *Passion* are four vivid dreams recorded in prison by Perpetua herself during the last days before her martyrdom. These extraordinary documents offer us a sharply detailed picture of what went on inside an early Christian's mind in the supreme crisis of her life. In the first dream, Perpetua saw a ladder covered with "swords, lances, hooks, daggers—so that if anyone went up carelessly, or without looking upwards, he was mangled and his

The Mishnah

In Roman times the history of the Jews already stretched back some 2,000 years. Governing their lives through much of this period had been the laws that tradition holds were revealed by God to Moses on Mount Sinai. Some of these commandments were written in the Torah, or Pentateuch (the first five books of the Old Testament), while others were transmitted orally by rabbis, through study and repetition. The oral law expanded and interpreted the written law and together they formed the Halakah.

By the end of the second century A.D., the oral tradition had become enormously complex and cumbersome. In fact, though custom forbade the practice, some rabbis had begun to keep notes so they would not forget its intricate provisions. With the Temple lying in ruins since the Jerusalem War and the Jews further disorganized after the Bar Kokhba revolt, there was a great need at this time to record the laws and customs for future generations.

Finally, learned rabbis organized a massive compilation, the Mishnah (from an ancient Hebrew word meaning "to repeat," or "to recite," and later, "to teach"). This exacting task was done under the leadership of the most famous Jewish sage of his time, Judah ha-Nasi (about 135–220).

The Mishnah's six sections cover the full range of Jewish life from proper celebration of religious holidays to correct relationships between husband and wife. There are rules for agriculture, guidelines for celebrating the Sabbath and holy days, instructions on obtaining a divorce, and explanations of the proper way to draw up contracts. The book even includes precise instructions on the treatment of criminals and appropriate donations to make to the poor.

Detailed as it was, the Mishnah was just the beginning of the codification of oral law. Its precepts stimulated continuing debate among Jewish scholars. By the fifth century these debates themselves had been collected in the Gemara. Together the Mishnah and the Gemara were published in learned tomes that comprise the Talmud, a book of law and lore still vital to the practice of Judaism today.

This illuminated page from a commentary on the Mishnah is the opening of a section dealing with problems that may arise when a man is bidden to marry his deceased brother's widow.

flesh caught on the weapons." The ladder had a dragon at its foot and led to heaven. Perpetua had no trouble climbing it to see "a large garden, and sitting in the midst a tall man with white hair in the dress of a shepherd, milking sheep; and round about were many thousands clad in white. . . . And he called me and gave me some curds of the milk he was milking, and I received it in my joined hands and ate; and all that were round said, Amen. At the sound of the word I awoke, still eating something sweet."

Interpreting the dream as a portent of her coming martyrdom, Perpetua went on to have a nightmare in which she saw, still suffering in the darkness of the pagan afterlife, a younger brother who had died of cancer as a small boy. In the third dream, Perpetua saw the same brother restored to health, drinking water from a golden bowl and playing like a normal, healthy child. In the fourth and final dream a few hours before her death, Perpetua saw herself changed into a man, pitted against an ugly Egyptian gladiator in the arena. Just before she was to face her enemy, a friendly giant appeared, carrying a green bough with golden apples, which he promised to give her if she was victorious. As the fight progressed, she found herself floating in midair striking her foe. Having won at last, she obtained the bough and began to walk toward the gate of life. Upon awakening, Perpetua interpreted the dream to mean that she was not going to fight wild beasts but the Devil himself.

Perpetua entered the arena singing a psalm and "abashing with the high spirit in her eyes the gaze of all." A savage cow, unleashed on Perpetua, knocked her down. Undaunted, she stood up and bound her disheveled hair, "for it was not proper for a martyr to loosen her hair, lest she seem to mourn at the moment of her glory." Then she went over to her maid, Felicitas, and the pair stood still. The crowd shouted that the women should be spared, then turned ugly and called for blood. Perpetua and Felicitas exchanged the kiss of peace and then were killed by gladiators.

The story became a staple of early Christian literature. In the fourth century it was read during church services in Africa. After 200 years, *The Passion of Perpetua and Felicitas* was still so highly revered there that Augustine had to warn worshipers not to accord it the same status as the Scriptures.

Debates on how God the Father relates to the Son

In addition to pagan attacks on their faith, Christians of the early third century faced a crisis of belief within their ranks. Debates about the divinity of Christ and the question of the Trinity forced the young church to attempt to clarify its teaching. Many Christians resisted the idea of a triune Godhead consisting of the Father, Son, and Holy Spirit—to them, that seemed too close to the polytheism of their pagan neighbors. Some of these people were called Monarchians, because they stood for the "monarchy, " or one origin, one rule of the one God.

Monarchianism consisted of two schools of thought. The first was brought to Rome from Asia Minor around 190 by a leather worker from Byzantium named Theodotus. It taught that Christ was a mortal until his baptism at about age 30, at which time the Holy Spirit made him the Son of God by adoption. The words "You are my Son, today I have begotten you," quoted from Psalm 2:7 and spoken by the voice heard at the moment of Jesus' baptism in a variant account from Luke 3:22, lend themselves to this "adoptionist" theory. Like the Ebionites, who also denied the innate divinity of Christ, the Adoptionists were widely condemned by the church.

The second school of Monarchianism proved more popular. It taught that Christ was divine but regarded the Trinity as three manifestations of a single divine being, rather than as three distinct selves; in other words, the Father and Son were seen as distinct *modes* of existence of the one God. This view, known as modalistic Monarchianism, was brought to Rome from Smyrna about the year 200. Noetus, who had been excommunicated for his beliefs, was the bearer. Opponents gave this brand of Monarchianism yet another name, *Patripassianism,* which means "suffering-fatherism." Probably because it did not deny the divinity of Christ, Patripassianism soon gained many followers. Meanwhile, Hippolytus in Rome, Tertullian in Carthage, and Dionysius in Alexandria vigorously attacked it. From these early debates grew controversies—and heresies—concerning the Trinity

While visiting Alexandria about 215, Caracalla arranged for a massacre to punish the inhabitants for laughing at him. Here he is seen on his arrival at night, visiting the tomb of Alexander, where he will leave his imperial robe and jewels as an offering. Next, having assembled the citizenry, he will order the attack and observe the killing from the Temple of Serapis. (Here he consecrated the dagger with which he had killed his brother, Geta, three years earlier.) Notwithstanding his many crimes, Caracalla was deified by a decree of the Senate after his assassination in 217.

and Christ's nature that dominated Christian theology for the next two centuries. Already, as it happened, passionate and skilled defenders of the faith were springing up eager for the fray. Alexandria and Carthage boasted the ablest of these defenders.

Founded in 332 B.C. by Alexander the Great, the city of Alexandria in Egypt swiftly grew into one of the busiest and most important ports of the ancient world. Its strategic position, at the mouth of the Nile on the Mediterranean, made it a major crossroads and transshipment point. From there to the corners of the empire went vast cargoes of Egyptian grain, olives, grapes, dates, and the like; Chinese and Indian gold, gemstones, cotton, spices, and condiments; as well as linen, papyrus, and other goods created in the workshops of Alexandria itself. Such enormous quantities of Egyptian wheat were shipped from this port, it was known as the granary of the empire.

But Alexandria was more than a commercial hub. It was also a marketplace of the mind, an intellectual center that boasted a rich commerce in ideas. Its famous library, founded in the third century B.C. by Ptolemy I Soter (Alexander's lieutenant), had attracted some of the world's finest minds and had made the Mediterranean port a vibrant center of philosophical, literary, and scientific activity.

Although Rome inherited Alexandria's preeminence as the literary capital of the Roman world after the fall of the Ptolemaic dynasty in 30 B.C., Alexandria remained an important intellectual center. In particular, philosophical debate flowered there, and from the second through the fifth century, neo-Pythagoreans, Neoplatonists, Gnostics, and Christians competed for the hearts, minds, and souls of Alexandria's large population of spiritual seekers, most of whom were Greek-speakers, many of them Jews.

At right, a bird's-eye view of Alexandria is combined with a map outline of the metropolitan region, in an illustration from a Latin manuscript. Below, a vase dating from the third or fourth century features a painting of Alexandria's famous lighthouse, the Pharos.

Christianity's origins in Alexandria are obscure. Tradition holds that the Evangelist Mark made his first convert there in A.D. 45. Acts speaks of an Alexandrian Jewish Christian named Apollos, whom Paul described as his coworker in Corinth (1 Corinthians 3:5–6). When Hadrian visited Egypt in 130, he found a Christian community of mixed Greek and Jewish background. "Those who call themselves bishops of Christ are, in fact, devotees of Serapis," a letter ascribed to Hadrian reads. At exactly the same time, a Gnostic Christian philosopher, Basilides, was active in Alexandria. His followers claimed that he had received his Christianity from a certain Glaucias, who they said had been an interpreter of the Apostle Peter.

The movement founded by Basilides lasted in Egypt until the fourth century. His commentaries on Christian Scriptures are among the earliest. To live in harmony with the will of God, he taught, was to love the whole universe, to desire nothing, and to hate nothing. He also believed in reincarnation. Like some other Gnostics, he declared that both the Jewish covenant and the teachings of Jesus were superfluous for persons who were "by nature faithful and elect."

We are more certain about the latter part of the second century. By that time enough Christians were living in Alexandria to justify the existence of a privately operated theological academy, the Catechetical School, headed by the Christian teacher and missionary Pantaenus, who is said to have preached the gospel in India. Classes probably met in a private house, perhaps in the teacher's own dwelling. Students received a firm grounding in the Christian faith through the study of Scriptures and philosophy. This modest center became noteworthy for the extraordinary young Christian intellectuals it attracted.

Portrayed at left in a Greek illuminated manuscript is the theologian Clement of Alexandria, who wrote mainly for intellectuals, both pagan and Christian. At right is "Agathangelos," the pseudonymous author of a Life of Gregory the Illuminator, the third-century "Apostle of Armenia."

Clement of Alexandria

The first of these outstanding people was Clement of Alexandria. Born around A.D. 150 to pagan parents, probably in Athens, Titus Flavius Clemens seems to have been driven by a never ending quest for knowledge. After converting to Christianity and studying with a series of six teachers in Greece, southern Italy, and Palestine, he arrived in Alexandria around 180, where he found what he had long been looking for, a master teacher. Of Pantaenus, Clement later wrote, "The last that I met with was the first in excellence. Him I found concealed in Egypt; and, meeting him there, I ceased to extend my search beyond him, as one who had no superior in abilities." Clement proved an outstanding student and after 10 years succeeded his teacher as head of the Catechetical School.

For the next 20 years Clement taught, studied, and wrote. While in Alexandria, he drew upon his wide learning to write an *Exhortation to the Greeks*, a wholesale attack on popular paganism that at the same time acknowledges the divine inspiration of the higher doctrines found in Greek philosophy and poetry. As Philo had sought to harmonize pagan philosophy and Jewish Scripture, Clement attempted to demonstrate the compatibility of both with Christianity.

Other surviving works by Clement include the *Educator*, a treatise on morals and manners; the *Miscellanies*, which further developed his claim that pagan philosophy and culture have a legitimate place in Christian life; and a sermon addressed to the wealthy class of Alexandria, the *Rich Man's Salvation*. In this last dissertation, he considered a question that must have been troubling many members from the well-to-do and cultured social strata of the Greco-Roman world who were well disposed toward Christianity: Could a rich person find a place in the church of Jesus Christ? Clement's answer is emphatically affirmative. The possession of wealth and the cultivated way of life that should accompany it are no obstacle to salvation; if a rich man uses his wealth responsibly and not frivolously, he is fully entitled to a place among the followers of Christ.

The famed and controversial Origen of Alexandria was said by the Church Father Jerome to have been the greatest teacher since the Apostles. Although others labeled Origen a heretic, he had a deep influence on later Christianity.

Clement was a voracious reader. Throughout his works he displayed a sweeping mastery of ancient writers and peppered his work with quotations from them. His *Exhortation to the Greeks* and *Miscellanies* include hundreds of quotations from pagan authors that would not otherwise have survived.

Just as Alexandria served as a meeting place of Western and Eastern thought, Clement's works presented Christianity as a blend of faith and knowledge. All stages of learning, said Clement, lead inevitably to Christ. "The way of truth is one," he wrote, "but into it, as into a perennial river, streams flow from all sides." The Old Testament and the writings of Greek philosophers, especially Plato, he argued, had laid the groundwork for Christ's message.

Why did Clement stress the intellectual aspects of Christianity by invoking Plato in his writings? Clearly, he was writing in response to critics who claimed that the church was founded upon only a rudimentary faith. The pagan philosopher Celsus, for example, had written that "some Christians do not even want to receive a reason for what they believe, and use such expressions as 'Do not ask questions; just believe' and 'Your faith will save you.' "

If the church appeared simplistic, it would not attract intellectuals, who might otherwise be drawn to other, more philosophical paths, reasoned Clement. He left Alexandria in 202 or 203, apparently to escape persecutions, but it is not clear where he went. About 211 he probably carried a letter to the church in Antioch. The letter (quoted by the church historian Eusebius) describes its bearer as "Clement the blessed presbyter, a virtuous and esteemed man . . . who upheld and extended the Church of the Lord." A few years later the same writer, in another letter, speaks of Clement and Pantaenus as "those blessed men who have trodden the road before us." The likeliest conclusion that can be drawn from this reference is that Clement had died sometime between 211 and 215, when the second letter was written.

The influence of Origen

After Clement's departure from Alexandria, his post as head of the Catechetical School was given to a precocious 18-year-old Alexandrian named Origen. A passionate scholar, a daring philosopher and theologian, Origen was destined to be remembered as the greatest Christian scholar before Augustine. He was the first Christian to analyze the Bible systematically; at the same time, he created a spiritual theology that has never ceased to enrich the Christian world.

A gifted child, adored by his parents, Origen was 16 in 202, when Emperor Septimius Severus decreed a persecution. Origen urged his father, Leonidas, to die for the faith. The father embraced martyrdom, and according to legend the son would have followed suit, had his mother not hidden his clothes in order to keep him in the house. With Leonidas dead and all of his property confiscated, Origen became the head of the family, supporting his mother by finding a wealthy patroness who included him in her intellectual salon. During these same years he attended lectures by the Platonist teacher Ammonius Saccas. (Some 25 years later Ammonius taught Plotinus, whose Neoplatonism along with Origen's theology eventually provided the foundations on which Christian philosophy was later built.) The teenage Origen embraced the ascetic way wholeheartedly, eating little, going barefoot, and sleeping on the floor.

Then came an incident that, if true, shows the ardent asceticism to which Origen was committed. He is said to have castrated himself as an act of obedience to Jesus' saying that "there are eunuchs who have made themselves eunuchs for the sake of the kingdom of heaven" (Matthew 19:12). The church historian Eusebius explains that this act was "both to fulfill the Savior's saying, and also that he might prevent all suspicion of shameful slander on the part of unbelievers (for, young as he was, he used to discourse on divine things with women as well as men)." Eusebius also says that Origen's act was approved by Demetrius,

Pious Animal Stories

High on the best seller list in the Middle Ages was a collection of animal fables called *Physiologus*. The tales, derived from ancient folklore of Egypt and perhaps other countries too, were written by an unknown author. Some believe he lived in Alexandria during the second century A.D., when allegorical exegesis of the Scriptures was common among scholars there. Working with allegories about real animals and birds, such mythical creatures as the phoenix and unicorn, and occasionally plants or stones, the author imbued these pagan stories with Christian teaching and morals.

They became popular far and wide. By the fifth century, the tales had been translated from Greek into Ethiopian, Armenian, Syriac, and possibly Latin. They were available by the late Middle Ages in virtually every European language as well. These later versions, known as bestiaries, were almost as widely circulated as the Bible itself.

The subjects in some fables represent an aspect of human nature. For example, in a story about the hedgehog, believers are exhorted to stop behaving in the busy manner of these animals and pay more attention to spiritual matters. In other accounts the beasts stand for the Devil or Christ. In each story an animal or other creature is introduced and its character described. This is followed by an allegorical interpretation of that character, or behavior, sprinkled with quotations from both Old and New Testaments, and an appropriate conclusion.

Typical is this tale about the stag. "It is said in Psalm 41, 'As the stag longs for flowing streams, so longs my soul for thee, O God' [Ps. 42:1]. The stag is an enemy of the dragon . . . the dragon flees from the stag into the cracks in the earth, and the stag, going and drinking from a stream until his muzzle is full, then spits out the water into the cracks and draws the dragon out and stamps on him and kills him.

"Thus did our Lord kill the huge dragon, the devil, with heavenly waters of indescribable wisdom. The dragon cannot bear water, and the devil cannot bear heavenly words. If you also have intelligible dragons hidden in your heart, call upon Christ in the Gospels with prayers and he will kill the dragon. . . . You will never find a dragon in the house where the stag's hair appears. . . . Likewise, if the traces of God and fear of Christ are found in your heart, no impure spirit will enter you."

Here, the story continues with an account of Jesus casting demons out of a man into some swine and sending the herd into the sea, where they drowned. It concludes with: "He calls the apostles and prophets mountains, and stags he calls the faithful men who attain to knowledge of Christ. . . . It is written in the psalm, 'I have lifted my eyes up to the mountains whence my help will come' [Ps. 121:1]."

"Of the stag," reads the text in this illuminated manuscript, "Physiologus says that since he is an enemy of the dragon and hunts him down he wants to kill him." The stag symbolizes Christ, and the dragon is the Devil.

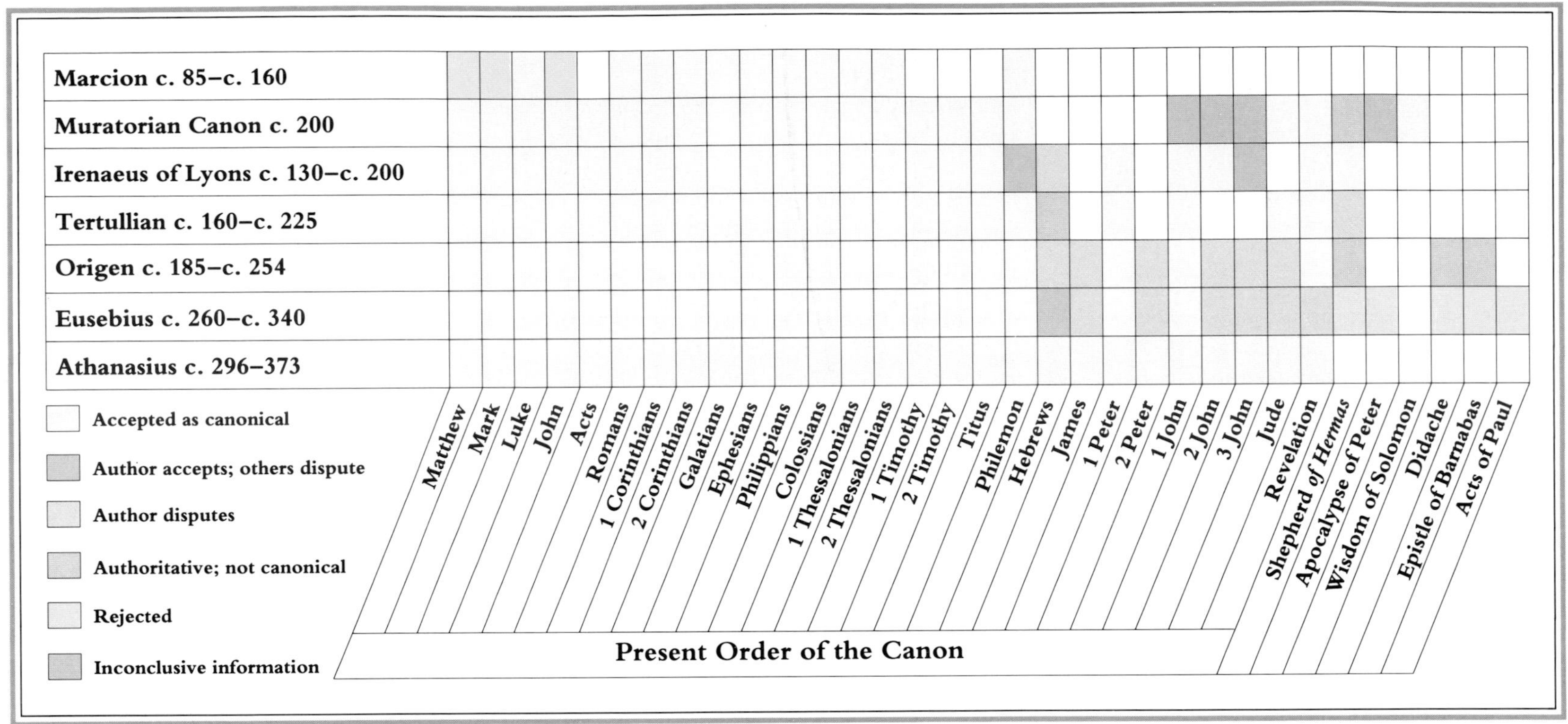

The New Testament grew up around the Gospels and Paul's letters. By the early third century, Christian theologians had begun to identify those writings deemed authoritative and approved for use in worship services, but they were still in doubt as to which were canonical and which were not. This chart presents a simplified overview of the complex process of evolution that led to the New Testament text as we know it.

bishop of Alexandria. Some historians have rejected the story as an invention of later anti-Origen polemicists. It was believable perhaps because of Origen's highly ascetic life. Even his defenders, such as Eusebius, could accept it by attributing the act to youthful rashness. Origen himself, however, when he wrote his commentary on Matthew 19:12, forcefully repudiated any literal application of the text.

Several years after his appointment as head of the Catechetical School, Origen turned the job of routine instruction over to a fellow teacher and devoted himself to scholarship. He began work on the *Hexapla*, the vast edition of the Old Testament with various versions arranged in six parallel columns; it occupied much of his energies over the next 40 years. In addition to his work on the Old Testament, Origen also developed a New Testament canon; indeed, he was perhaps one of the first to use the term *canon* (literal meaning, "measuring stick"). In these labors he was subsidized not by a church organization but by the private patronage of a wealthy couple.

Origen began to travel as a lecturer and spokesman for Christianity. In these roles he sojourned about 230 with the powerful and influential Julia Mamaea, mother of the reigning Alexander Severus, and expounded the faith to her. Eventually Origen settled in Caesarea, where he spent the remaining 20 years of his life writing, lecturing, restudying the pagan classics he had forsaken in youth, and conversing with a stream of visitors. He became one of the most prolific authors in history. More than a dozen stenographers and copyists spelled one another to keep up with him.

On First Principles is Origen's most controversial work, a testament to his unique systematic theology and the first such work in Christian history. Written when Origen was about 40 and at the height of his powers, *On First Principles* addresses such fundamental questions as What is God? What is the Holy Spirit? Why was the universe created? In the universe as Origen saw it, the sun, moon, planets, and stars were all God-created beings endowed with free will.

He wrote that there might come a time when the sun would exclaim, "I would desire to be dissolved, to return and be with Christ, which is far better." Behind this idea was his conviction that the material universe was created for the education of all souls on a long homeward journey back to God, back to the spirit world that was our original dwelling and is our final goal. This process, Origen said, involves the entire cosmos. Our bodies are merely a temporary garment for the souls that have existed since before the creation. The heavens and earth meant by the opening verse of Genesis, "In the beginning God created the heavens and the earth," is an immaterial, purely spiritual place. There we will regain the paradise we lost when our spirits lost their white-hot focus and by a "cooling" process were changed from spirits to souls. They fell from the immaterial world into the evil, material creation. The process of divine ascent will redeem all beings. Even the souls of the damned, and the Devil himself, will be saved.

A tangible, almost sacramental presence of the Son as well as the Holy Spirit fills the Scriptures, Origen believed. He taught that there are three levels of meaning in a biblical text: the literal, the moral, and the spiritual. The literal, or outer, meaning is to the other two levels what our body is to our soul and spirit, an ephemeral envelope. The moral meaning is the soul of the text, its teaching for our life in the here and now. The spiritual level is the text's core, transmitting the divine presence into our lives and putting us in conscious contact with that presence. Origen foresaw the controversies that his teachings would provoke. "I wish to be a man of the Church," he wrote, "not the founder of heresy."

Origen was labeled a heretic many times in ensuing centuries, even though some of the greatest Church Fathers—men such as Jerome, Ambrose of Milan, Basil, and Gregory of Nazianzus—acknowledged his influence and copied and transmitted his works. Also falling under Origen's spell were many of the desert monks, who were free to read his books in Egyptian monasteries before the anti-Origenist crackdown that began about 400. These ascetics strove to liberate themselves from all forms of experience, to achieve what Origen called *apatheia*, or "passionlessness." In this state they hoped to become one with God.

In the sixth century, the Byzantine emperor Justinian anathematized anyone who accepted Origen's doctrines. Justinian's 10 anathemas condemned, among others, the doctrines that in some future world Christ will be crucified again, this time to save the demons; that in the general resurrection all people's bodies will rise to judgment in the shape of spheres; and that every sinner, without exception, will eventually be saved.

When Origen came to Rome in c. 212, one of those who heard him preach was the theologian Hippolytus, who later quarreled with the bishop of Rome and was apparently elected as a rival bishop. At that time, there were strong personalities in prominent positions who often did not agree with the mainstream. Origen and Hippolytus were such men. Hippolytus was later reconciled with the Roman church leadership and died a martyr. This statue was probably made during his lifetime.

A great theologian

As the church was flourishing in Alexandria, it was also flowering throughout North Africa. In Carthage, which by the third century contended with Alexandria for "second city" status within the empire, the church had gained a faithful following sometime during the second century. By 225 there were some 70 Christian bishops in the North African provinces of Proconsularis and Numidia.

Like Alexandria, Carthage produced noted defenders of the faith. One of the earliest and most famous of these was Tertullian. Disenchanted with the pagan way of life and struck with admiration for the courage of the Christians, he embraced Christianity about 195, when he was around 30 years old.

Some 30 works by Tertullian survive. Of varying length, they fill several hundred printed pages. In his early *Apology,* written in 197 to protest persecution, Tertullian argues that Christians are not bad citizens but good and useful ones, and he appeals to the Roman sense of justice: "If it is certain that we are the most guilty of men, why do you treat us differently from . . . other criminals? . . . When others are accused on the charges which are brought against us they employ their own tongues and hired advocacy to plead their innocence. . . . Christians alone are not allowed to say anything to clear themselves, to defend truth. . . . That alone is looked for, which the public hate requires—the confession of a name, not the investigation of a charge."

Little is known of his life except that he came from a middle-class pagan background and seems to have been trained in the law. A married man, he possibly was ordained as a presbyter before he became a follower of a radical movement called the New Prophecy, or Montanism, a decade after his conversion. Eventually, he started his own Tertullianist church, which was even more rigorously purist than the Montanist church. Despite his ardent advocacy of martyrdom, he appears to have survived to a ripe old age.

Tertullian wrote primarily in Latin. He was in fact the first Christian writer of importance to write in this language and is sometimes spoken of as the father of Latin theology. His point of view was down-to-earth compared with that of his Alexandrian contemporaries. He disagreed with their presentation of Christianity as a new philosophy: "What indeed has Athens to do with Jerusalem," he demanded to know, "what the Academy with the Church?" Elsewhere he stated that Greek philosophy is the source of all heresy.

Where the Alexandrians went in for allegorical and philosophical interpretations of the Scriptures, Tertullian insisted on a literal reading of them as history. At the same time, he emphasized the primacy of faith over reason: "Away with all attempts to produce a mottled Christianity of Stoic, Platonic, and dialectic compositions! We want no curious disputation after possessing Christ Jesus, no inquisition after enjoying the gospel! With our faith, we desire no further belief." Over the ages Tertullian has been remembered for his bold paradoxes of faith: "The Son of God died; it is by all means to be believed, because it is absurd. And he was buried and rose again; the fact is certain because it is impossible."

When it came to combating heretics, such as Marcion or the Gnostic teacher Valentinus, Tertullian was at his advocatorial best. He argued that not only were heretics wrong but they did not even have the right to dispute with the church. He claimed that the church's interpreting of the Scriptures in a consistent manner from the time of the Apostles proved its sole ownership. Further, since heretics have no right to Scriptures, the church need not argue with them.

Tertullian also urged that Christians should strive to live apart from the rest of the world. He believed that the faithful should not serve in the military or anywhere within the government, which was pagan. Nor should believers attend any sort of public entertainment, because these events were celebrations in honor of the pagan gods.

Gradually, Tertullian became disenchanted with what he perceived as laxity on the part of Christian leadership. This defender of the church and scourge of heresy became attracted to Montanism and its fiercely ascetic ethic. The Montanists claimed that Christians had to live a life totally free from sin after baptism; there was no such thing as a chance for a "second repentance." When a church elder, whom Tertullian described as a "bishop of bishops," declared that the church could remit sins such as adultery or apostasy, Tertullian broke with the church.

It is a tribute to Tertullian's genius that, although he died outside the church, he continued to exert an influence on later theologians. Cyprian, the bishop of Carthage, called him "the master" and read his works daily. The argumentations that Tertullian made concerning the Trinity and the person of Christ have been echoed by other leading Christian thinkers down through the centuries.

The earliest leading Christian to write in Latin, Tertullian, above, was born a pagan in Carthage, where he spent most of his life. Well-to-do Romans of Tertullian's period adorned their villas with mosaic depictions of everyday life as they knew it. In the top scene, three men are enjoying a board game. At left, servants are bringing drinks to guests. Many more of these mosaics still exist, and the lifestyle they depict is hedonistic but mildly so. Tertullian railed against worldliness and luxury, defending the simple life as a better alternative.

Wreaths of laurel or gold were an omnipresent feature of pagan life in the Roman Empire. They were placed on statues of gods, donned by important persons at public ceremonies, awarded to victorious athletes and soldiers, and worn at festive events. Some Christians in the Roman Army refused the military wreath when it was awarded. They were applauded by Tertullian, who was uncompromising in his opposition to military service.

The mainstream threatened by the fringe

"All who destroy the form of the Gospel are vain, unlearned and also audacious," wrote Irenaeus, the bishop of Lugdunum (modern Lyons), in his lengthy treatise *Against Heresies.* The barbed phrase "destroy the form of the Gospel" refers to the editorial activities of various influential contemporaries who were taking it upon themselves to expand or abridge the then accepted body of inspired writings. According to Irenaeus, either way was a path of heresy (from Greek *hairesis,* "choice," "school of thought," "sectarian opinion"). Those heretics who expand on Scripture, Irenaeus said, do so "that they may seem to have discovered more than is of the truth." And the ones who abridge it do so, he explained, "that they may set the dispensations of God aside."

Irenaeus' defense of Christianity was not limited to the Gospels; this skilled apologist and innovative theologian lent his talents to the resolution of several theological issues of the day. He is remembered primarily for a monumental tour de force in which he attacked the Marcionites (those who abridged Scripture) and the Gnostics (those who expanded on it).

Born in Asia Minor around 130, Irenaeus (his name means "man of peace") grew up in Smyrna, where he knew Polycarp, who was martyred. Irenaeus once described his childhood: "I remember the events of those days more clearly than those which happened recently. . . . I can speak even of the place in which the blessed Polycarp sat and disputed . . . the discourses which he made to the people, how he reported his converse with John and with the others who had seen the Lord."

Little else is known of Irenaeus' early life. He moved to Gaul and was appointed bishop of Lugdunum to succeed Bishop Pothinus, who had been martyred during a persecution in 177. Perhaps Irenaeus' role as head of a martyr church inspired him to launch his attack against Christian heretics. In any event, he produced *Against Heresies* from about 180 to 185. This work, which Irenaeus originally intended as an attack on Gnosticism, grew to include his understanding of Christianity. It is one of the earliest works of Christian theology, and at the same time it is one of the richest extant sources of information on Gnosticism and the Gnostic scriptures.

Irenaeus emphasized that the church is founded on tradition, which he termed the "rule of faith." It had spread Christ's message via the unbroken line of succession from Christ to the bishops of all the churches, especially that in Rome. (For good measure, Irenaeus included a list of Roman bishops from apostolic times to his own day.) Heretics had no such authority, argued Irenaeus. Nor did they have any place in the church, for Christianity was a faith "spoken with one voice." Irenaeus appealed to church unity, basing his argument on the rule of faith, the Scriptures, and the principle of apostolic succession.

The "New Prophecy" of Montanus

Gnosticism (see pages 129–131) and Marcionism (see pages 131–132) were not the only movements that threatened to split the late-second-century church. The New Prophecy—better known as Montanism, after its founder, Montanus—sprang up in Phrygia, a region of Asia Minor in present-day Turkey that was long known for its pagan ecstasy religion centered on the Great Mother Cybele. Montanism soon posed a challenge to mainstream Christian communities in the region. Reportedly an ex-priest of Cybele, Montanus was a convert to Christianity who proclaimed he was an instrument of the outpouring of the Holy Spirit as foretold by John: "When the Spirit of truth comes, he will guide you into all the truth; for he will not speak on his own authority, but whatever he hears he will speak, and he will declare to you the things that are to come" (John 16:13).

While the church had no blanket proscription against prophets—prophecy had, after all, been a long-accepted practice within it—the prophecies of

The rites for the mother goddess Cybele, above, featured prophetic utterance and healing. Rooted in the same region of Asia Minor as Cybele was the cult of Dionysus, or Bacchus, god of nature and wine. The mosaic, left, shows Bacchic dancers. Christianity's first great revival movement, Montanism, with its ecstasy and inspiration in worship, also developed in this region.

Montanus elicited almost instant condemnation. His message was as simple as it was revolutionary: The world as we know it would soon come to an end, Christ would return, and the heavenly Jerusalem would descend to earth at Pepuza in Asia Minor. The language of Montanist prophecy was at times electrifying. Montanus and his listeners seem to have believed the words were not his but those of the Holy Spirit speaking through him. He made such startling statements as this: "I am the Lord God Almighty dwelling at this moment within a man."

There had been growing unease in the church at the commonly perceived fading of faith in Christ's imminent return and at the increasing worldliness of Christians, both the leadership and the rank-and-file. These changes combined with a noticeable cooling of the enthusiasm that had in earlier times been felt as a sign of the Holy Spirit's working in their midst. Many readily accepted Montanus' prophecy of a speedy Second Coming and abandoned their homes and work to follow him to the countryside. Montanists lived rigorously ascetic lives and, in their preparation for the

After 30 years of royal favor, Mani died in a Persian prison, put there at the instigation of Zoroastrian magi who feared his religion. As was the custom, his body was mutilated and exposed. Believers said he ascended to the realm of light.

coming last days, separated themselves from society. They welcomed martyrdom. Montanus encouraged them, "Do not desire to die in bed or in abortions or in debilitating fevers, but in martyrdom so that he who suffered for you may be glorified." They advocated celibacy and endured long fasts. Montanus was joined by two women, Maximilla and Priscilla, who also claimed the gift of prophecy. As a sign of their new faith, they left their husbands.

Montanism spread throughout Asia Minor and into Syria. It also reached the West, and in North Africa its strict moral code attracted Tertullian. About 207 this advocate of orthodoxy became Montanism's most eminent convert. He later founded his own denomination of Montanist (strictly speaking, Tertullianist) churches, which lasted until late imperial times.

Tertullian continued to write after his conversion to Montanism. From this period comes a detailed and sympathetic first-hand account about a charismatic church member: "We have among us now a sister who has been granted gifts of revelations, which she experiences in church during the Sunday services through ecstatic visions in the Spirit. . . . And after the people have been dismissed at the end of the service it is her custom to relate to us what she has seen. . . . 'Among other things,' says she, 'there was shown to me a soul in bodily form, and it appeared like a spirit; but it was no mere something, void of qualities, but rather a thing which could be grasped, soft and translucent and of ethereal color, in form at all points human.' "

In Rome there was ambivalence on Montanism. Eleutherus, the late-second-century bishop of Rome, was at first conciliatory toward the group but later condemned it. While Eleutherus' successor, Victor, acknowledged Montanus' prophetic gifts, there is evidence that he also spoke against Montanism. Theologians had a hard time refuting the Montanist message; much of their refutation was simply a mudslinging campaign, loudly alleging scandalous improprieties by the New Prophecy's leading lights. The prophetess Priscilla accepted offerings of gold and silver and expensive clothes, wrote the Christian polemicist Apollonius around 200. Another Montanist, the same writer charged, had been haled before a Roman magistrate for robbery, and after some members of the local Christian community had used their influence to get the case dismissed, he went about claiming he had faced persecution for his belief in Christ. It was further alleged that yet another prominent Montanist (possibly Montanus himself) had dyed his hair, worn eye makeup and fancy clothes, lent money at interest, and frequented gaming tables and dice games.

It is impossible to determine how many of these accusations were based on facts. Belief that the world was coming to an end was not in itself heretical, however, and the church was reluctant to be seen as a "slayer of prophets." Even the archenemy of heretics himself, Irenaeus, did not hesitate to mention that many church members also had miraculous powers of prophecy, healing, raising the dead, and speaking in tongues through the operation of the Holy Spirit.

Unlike the Marcionites, Montanists did not reject the Old Testament. On the contrary, a noted hunter of heretics, Epiphanius, acknowledged from a distance of some 200 years' hindsight that they received "the whole of the Scriptures." Also, their strict ascetic code was difficult to fault. Nevertheless, the church did condemn Montanism. Bishops attempted, unsuccessfully, to exorcise Priscilla and Maximilla. The latter complained, "I am driven away like a wolf from the sheep. I am not a wolf; I am word and spirit and power." She also declared: "After me shall be no more prophets, but the end of the world."

The church saw in Montanism not only a disruptive force but a deception of those who followed it. "They magnify these females [Priscilla and Maximilla] above the Apostles and every gift of Grace, so that some of them go so far as to say that there is in them something more than Christ."

It is not clear what became of the three—Montanus, Maximilla, and Priscilla. Documents that have survived from early in the third century speak of them as recently dead. The church historian Eusebius, writing more than 100 years later, reports a tradition that Montanus and Maximilla hanged themselves "like the traitor Judas."

Although the Montanists were vilified by the church, and neither wars and natural catastrophes nor a speedy Second Coming materialized as predicted, Montanism managed to survive. It lived on, especially in the countryside in one form or another, for several hundred years. It was only in the mid-sixth century that the New Prophecy was at last forcibly put down. And when that happened, according to Procopius, historian of Justinian's reign, the last of the Montanists burned themselves alive in their churches to avoid capture by their fellow-Christians.

Mani's "call in the world"

About half a century after the death of Montanus, yet another influential religious movement was born. It was called Manichaeism after its founder, Mani, who was born in 216 in Babylonia. His mother was said to be of Parthian royal lineage, and his father was a member of the Elkesaites, a Gnostic baptist sect within the Jewish-Christian community.

Mani had a vision at age 12 in which he saw his heavenly double, or "twin," who promised to stay at his side as a helper and protector. He later interpreted this to have been a vision of the Holy Spirit. Mani boasted, "The writings, wisdom, apocalypses, parables, and psalms of all previous religions, gathered from all parts, have come together in my religion, in

This Manichaean book illustration shows the "elect," or "perfect," copying sacred writings—the only form of work that they were allowed. They were famous for the excellent quality of their writing materials.

the wisdom that I have revealed." Mani went on to proclaim himself the last and greatest of the prophets from a line that included Zoroaster, the Buddha, and Jesus. In a hymn, Mani proclaimed:

I was born in the land of Babylon
and I am set up at the gate of truth.
I am a singer, a hearer,
who has come from the land of Babylon.
I have come from the land of Babylon
to send forth a call in the world.

Mani's teaching was a rigorously dualistic form of Gnosticism; his primary thesis was that the present world order results from a conflict between the principles of light and darkness. In the past, Mani taught, the worlds of light and darkness were completely separate. Then darkness captured part of the light world, and the resulting mixture of light and darkness led to the creation of the world as we know it, including all living things and such inanimate substances as metals. All contain properties of light. The goal of Mani's teaching was to distill light from darkness, good from evil, so that the mixed universe could split into its original parts, which would then go their separate ways. Man's key role in Mani's vision is summed up by the historian Kurt Rudolph: "The universe and earth and man are subject to a process which has as its goal the liberation by God of God, and in which man is a decisive means to that end."

Believers were divided into two main classes, those who renounced the world entirely, the "elect," and a less strict class, the "hearers." The elect owned nothing, rejected marriage, and did not work but were supported by the "hearers." They ate only light-containing food (it was a vegetarian diet; melons and radishes were believed to contain more light than

This mosaic from Roman North Africa shows Dionysus as a man with luxuriant beard and hair. Pagans of later antiquity tended more and more to the worship of gods whose presence could be felt in all parts of life. Dionysus' influence extended not only to wine but to religious fervor, prophecy, and the care of souls in this world and the next.

The triumphal progress of Dionysus from Greece to India and back again was a favorite theme in pagan art and literature of late Roman times. It served as an allegory of the spread of a new religion from one end of the known world to the other. Christianity itself was spreading in this fashion, as were offshoots, such as Montanism and Manichaeism. Some Christian teachers tried to portray their own religion as a sober equivalent of the Dionysian mysteries, in which they could spiritually dance with angels around the true God.

most foods) and drank no wine. The rank-and-file membership were free to marry, work, and enjoy some luxuries, but they too were bound by a moral code that enjoined monogamy and the renunciation of fornication, lying, hypocrisy, idolatry, and magic.

Thanks to the appeal of Mani's message—it explained the existence of evil and offered a program of salvation through knowledge—and his genius at organization, Manichacism prospered. Missionaries traveled throughout the known world spreading the word. A hierarchical church was organized, with deacons, priests, bishops, and even apostles. The movement spread through Asia Minor eastward through the Persian Empire and on as far as India and China, and westward all the way around the Mediterranean as far as Spain. Persecution of Manichaeans began in Persia in Mani's lifetime; he himself died after having been thrown in jail on the orders of a new king.

Manichaeism essentially disappeared in the West in the sixth century, only to resurface during the Middle Ages in Asia Minor, the Balkans, southern France, and Italy. It survived on the outskirts of China until the 14th century. Manichaean scriptures, including writings by Mani himself, recovered over the past 100 years, have not yet been fully edited and published. Originally composed in Syriac and Persian, they were first published in a new script devised by Mani. The titles of Mani's scriptures include *Living Gospel*, *Book of Mysteries*, *Book of the Giants, Treasure of Life*. A curious innovation was an illustrated book, *Image*, setting forth Mani's worldview in pictures. In later ages, the calligrapher-prophet came to be known by a nickname: The Painter.

The continuing pagan revival

Challenges to the church came not only from within. The revival of pagan religions, which had begun in the second century, lingered on in the third. Eastern cults were emphasized after Septimius Severus (see page 149) married Julia Domna, the daughter of a Syrian hereditary priest-prince. They imported the sun god of Syria to Rome. Their son, the emperor Caracalla, later erected a temple to Serapis, an Egyptian sun god who also encompassed fertility and medicine.

Septimius Severus was sometimes, but not always, sympathetic to Christianity. When he was dangerously sick, a Christian slave anointed him with holy oil, and he believed that he had benefited from the slave's ministrations. His son Caracalla's nurse and preceptor were both Christians. His great-nephew Alexander Severus liked to castigate the venality of the pagan priesthood with a verse from the first-century satirist Persius: "Tell me, priests, what's gold doing in a holy place?" At the same time, the Severan dynasty also intensified public devotion to the sun god and blended it with emperor worship. Coins minted during this time picture the sun god with the characteristic beard of the emperor. Christians remained aloof from this revival of paganism. Previously, their refusal to participate in the state religion had simply marked them as troublemakers. Their continued refusal would have much more serious and far-reaching consequences.

The worst persecutions to date

The year is 248 and Rome is aglow with the flickering lights of thousands of torches. Crowds pack the Campus Martius, a site of holy pageants. The Palatine and the Capitoline hills are also teeming with people; they are laughing, dancing, and imbibing, as government workers distribute free wheat, barley, and beans to the revelers. On the riverbank overlooking the Tiber, the emperor in his role as *pontifex maximus*, or high priest of the Roman religion, sacrifices lambs and goats to the Fates, the goddesses who control human destiny. Massive white bulls are paraded along the river and sacrificed to Jupiter, the patron god of Rome. An immaculate heifer is cleanly killed as an offering to Juno, sister and wife of Jupiter. Nearby, a chorus of boys and girls, chosen from the aristocracy, chants ancient hymns to Apollo and Diana.

The seven-pointed star on this man's forehead identifies him as a priest of the sun god from Roman Egypt. Sun worship, a monotheistic religion which originated in Persia, had become a chief imperial cult by the middle of the third century. It was to remain the predominent religion of the empire, until replaced by Christianity in the decades following 312.

The eagle symbolized Rome's power and readiness to strike her foes. During Rome's 1,000th year, legions were fighting invaders from the north and east. Each legion had its sacrosanct eagle standard.

The merrymaking, sacrifices, and prayers were all part of the celebration of Rome's 1,000th anniversary. Although it had to be delayed for a year because the emperor Philip was off in the Danube region leading his troops against invading barbarians, it was nonetheless spirited. The celebration also included a renewal of the Secular Games, the Roman centennial festival held on and off since republican times to honor the gods and to mark the end of one century-long age, or *saeculum*, and the beginning of another.

Not all Romans, however, took part in the festivities. Christians avoided the pagan rites and no doubt offended many by their refusal to participate. Romans typically viewed the Christians as "atheists," who showed disrespect to the gods. A dishonored god was a dangerous deity, the pagans believed. Famine, plague, and drought were commonly thought to be caused by angry gods. A common phrase, "no rain, because of the Christians," attested to this belief. These were increasingly dangerous times for Christians throughout the empire. Although there was no widespread persecution, localized attacks were not uncommon. Shortly after the celebration, the empire was once more in crisis. Philip appointed Decius, at that time a distinguished senator, to lead an army against the Goths on the Danube. So successful was he, that he won the empire from Philip in 249.

This ancient carving depicts the infants Romulus and Remus, the mythical founders of Rome, who were nursed by a she-wolf. Citizens of the empire, from poets to imperial officials, referred to Rome as the "Eternal City."

Persecution by Decius

Decius' accession proved disastrous for the Christians. Origen foresaw the troubles: "It is probable that the secure existence . . . enjoyed by believers at present will come to an end, since those who calumniate Christianity in every way are again attributing the present frequency of rebellion to the multitude of believers, and to their not being persecuted by the authorities as in the old times." He then predicted "persecutions no longer local as hitherto, but universal."

On January 3, 250, Decius performed the annual sacrifice to Jupiter and presented the imperial offerings to the gods. At about the same time he also ordered every resident of the Roman Empire to follow his example. For the first time ever, Christians everywhere were forced to prove their loyalty to the state. To do so they would have to deny their Christian beliefs and take part in pagan sacrifices. Commissions were set up in each town to administer Decius' edict. Each person who sacrificed was issued a certificate (*libellus*) to prove that he had obeyed the emperor's command.

Legal procedures that had long been followed with accused Christians remained in effect throughout the Decian persecution. The aim was not necessarily to kill Christians but to convince them to turn to the state religion. Many who would have been persecuted eluded the legal process by fleeing, by subterfuge, or by outward conformity. Most of the martyrs were persons who made the heroic decision to defy the Roman state in a public and provocative manner.

The government wasted no time in arresting those who chose the path of defiance. Fabian, the bishop of

Rome, was arrested, put on trial before Decius himself, and executed on January 20, 250. The bishops of Antioch and Jerusalem were arrested and died in custody. Dionysius of Alexandria escaped arrest, thanks to the help of country people in the district to which he fled. In Asia Minor one bishop fled to the safety of the hills and urged his congregation to do likewise. Cyprian of Carthage also went into hiding.

Some Christians bribed officials for the certificates. Others hoped to avoid detection. In June 250, however, enforcement stiffened, and the local commissions intensified the search for anyone who had not sacrificed. Neighbors informed on neighbors. Many Christians, fearing torture, and even death, completed the sacrifice. Others refused. They were tortured until they recanted their Christianity or died.

In Caesarea, Origen was arrested and tortured. He refused to renounce his faith yet somehow survived, only to die after his release from jail. The martyrdom he had once written of—a brave death in full view of multitudes of bloodthirsty pagans and enthusiastically applauding angels—eluded him.

In Alexandria, Dionysius described how Christians were forced to sacrifice: "When called by name, they approached the impure and unholy sacrifices. But pale and trembling, as if they were not to sacrifice, but themselves to be victims and the sacrifices to the idols, they were jeered by many of the surrounding multitude, and were obviously equally afraid to die and to offer the sacrifice." Other Alexandrian Christians who refused to sacrifice suffered for their faith. Two were put onto camels and paraded through the city. People mocked them and hit them with sticks as they passed. They were then burned alive. A soldier, probably a Christian, who intervened was beheaded.

In some places a majority of Christians obeyed their emperor's command. In Carthage, for example, so many Christians crowded the pagan temples that magistrates pleaded with them to return later. In other cities entire congregations, in some cases led by their bishops, renounced their faith. Euctemon, the bishop of Smyrna, openly sacrificed. After an initial flurry, the state relaxed its offensive. By the end of the year, Christians who had fled or hidden reemerged.

The end of the Decian persecution

When Decius' attention was again diverted to invading Goths, the Christian communities breathed a collective sigh of relief. The church of Rome felt confident enough to elect Cornelius bishop in the spring of the year 251, and the church of Carthage held a synod not long after that. But the persecutions during Decius' reign had cost the church more than the loss of many staunch members; they had also divided it. When the clouds had lifted, the church found itself faced with a complex disciplinary problem: How should it treat the *lapsi* ("lapsed [Christians]"), who had renounced their faith during the persecutions? Factions emerged; they represented three opposing views.

The most lenient position was that any confessor (one who had suffered for the faith) could readmit a lapsed Christian without penance. In opposition to this view was the second one, held by Cyprian, the bishop of Carthage, who thought that church unity and the

Continued on page 175

The celebrations for Rome's 1,000th year were launched by the soldier-emperor Philip (pictured on the coin), who may have been using the pageantry to consolidate his own shaky position. He had recently instigated the murder of his imperial colleague and predecessor, Gordian III, and the Roman Senate had deified Gordian. Philip himself was killed soon afterward.

Cruel Games

"The gladiatorial games are prepared," wrote a third-century church leader, "that blood may gladden the lust of cruel eyes." Though some pagans opposed the games, most favored them. Church Fathers wrote fierce tracts to discourage Christians from attending the gory rituals.

This bas-relief shows gladiators pitted against wild beasts, a favorite spectator sport for Romans. Huge numbers of animals and men died in the encounters. Sometimes even emperors fought beasts in the arena, much to the disgust of traditionalists.

This mosaic from North Africa depicts a prisoner, possibly a Christian, being driven to face a lunging lion. In his Exhortation to Martyrdom, *Origen wrote: "A great theater is filled with spectators to watch your contests and your summons to martyrdom. . . . And no less than Paul you will say when you enter the contest, 'We have become a spectacle to the world, to angels and to men.' " 1 Corinthians 4:9.*

After the second century, games and wild-beast shows could be given only by emperors, except in provincial towns, where they were sponsored by rich men or high-ranking officials or priests. On occasion they were organized by private businessmen who were granted government permission. The spectacles were always popular.

This mosaic from an imperial villa shows circus hands loading an antelope onto a cargo vessel for shipment to Rome.

A gladiator knocks down his opponent as the band plays on. Scenes like this help explain the distaste of early Christians for public shows. When the crowd wanted the loser's life spared, the sign was thumbs down. Thumbs up meant he should be dispatched.

Roman hippodromes held crowds of more than 200,000. Chariot racing, the featured sport in these huge stadiums, was a business in the hands of competing companies. Teams were identified by color—the reds, whites, blues, and greens—and fans displayed their colors and placed bets on them. Admission to arenas and other Roman theaters was by token. The horn token below bears an image of Hercules.

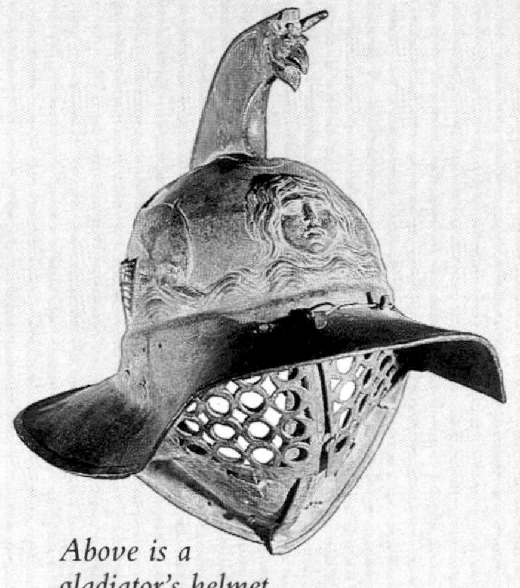

Above is a gladiator's helmet, one of several types of elegantly fashioned protective gear worn by these highly trained combatants.

A treatise attributed to Bishop Cyprian of Carthage states that idolatry is the mother of public amusements, and it may entice faithful Christians with delights of the eyes and ears. His catalog of depraved spectacles included even jugglers.

At left, a fourth-century Roman consul, Julius Bassus, rides in an arena with circus teams.

The Flavian Amphitheater in Rome was a regular scene of gladiatorial combats and wild-beast shows. Its name since medieval times has been the Colosseum, as in the prophecy attributed to the eighth-century historian Bede: "While the Colosseum stands, Rome shall stand; when the Colosseum falls, Rome shall fall; and when Rome falls, the world shall fall." The emperor Commodus (below) entered the arena dressed as Hercules.

authority of the bishops must be maintained; he therefore insisted that only a church synod should decide on the treatment of the *lapsi.* Under his leadership, the synod at Carthage set periods of penitential exclusion, varying with the degree of the individual lapse. Designated as *sacrificati* were those who had actually sacrificed on Roman altars; the *thurificati* were those who had burned incense before the emperor's image; and the *libellati* included anyone who had not complied with the imperial command but had obtained, through bribery or deception, a certificate that falsely attested to compliance. These degrees were to be considered in setting penances, and the decision on how to apply them was to be left to the discretion of the clergy.

A third view, that of hard-liners led by the Roman presbyter Novatian, insisted that none of the lapsed could ever be readmitted to the church. Rejection of the Spirit's promptings to confess Jesus as Lord when tried by persecution was viewed by Novatian's followers as an unforgivable sin. They denied that any bishop had the power to remit such a sin, when Christ himself had said, "Whoever denies me before men, I also will deny before my Father who is in heaven."

It is noteworthy that so many of the lapsed were clamoring for readmission. Their eagerness to get back into the Christian community may be a measure of how bad times had become in the Roman Empire. There had been no great debates over readmissions a century and a half earlier, when Pliny the Younger wrote to Trajan that he had

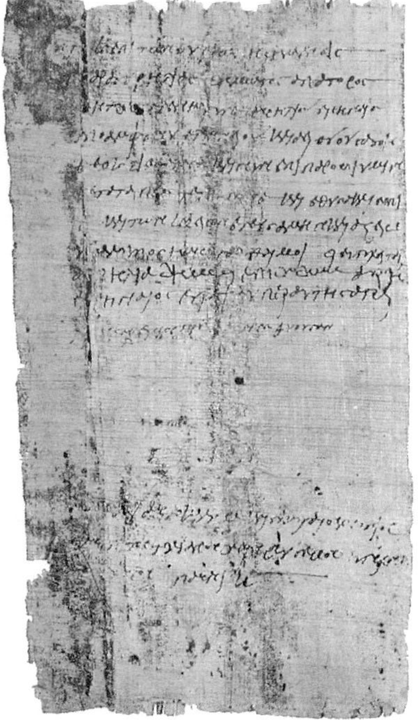

Decius, depicted on the coin, ordered everyone to sacrifice to the gods (objects used are shown on the relief above right) and obtain certificates of compliance. The certificate reads: "Here present and conforming to the order, I have sacrificed and made a libation. I, Aurelia Demos, present this declaration."

dismissed charges against those who denied they were or had been Christians. Possibly, a pleasant life outside the community was available to many a lapsed church member in the more prosperous and peaceful world of the second century. By the year 251 only the oldest people alive could remember those happy times. Most of those who lived during this period knew only misrule, social upheaval, economic collapse, civil wars within, and invasions from without.

The Christian church had become a warm nest for many in hard times. "One cannot have God for one's father unless one has the church for one's mother." Cyprian wrote these words during that same year in his tract *On Church Unity*. He accused the Novatianists of telling the lapsed (and now excluded) church members, in effect: "Go ahead, beat your breast, shed tears, groan day and night . . . you will still die outside the church; you will do everything conducive to peace, but none of the peace that you seek will you find."

The chasms among these three views widened when Cyprian, after hesitation, supported Cornelius as head of the Roman church, and Novatian claimed the same office. Novatian, who was able and erudite, was justified in expecting election as bishop of Rome. Cornelius probably was chosen because his more lenient attitude toward lapsed Christians was favored by large numbers of church members. Novatian promptly sent a delegation from Rome to Carthage to establish his authority there. Though a synod in Rome supported Cyprian's view on the lapsed and, in October 251, excommunicated Novatian, nonetheless, Novatianist churches sprang up in North Africa, Gaul, Spain, the East, and even in Rome itself.

To orthodox Christians, Novatianists were beyond the pale. Speaking for the mainstream, Cyprian wrote, "There is no salvation outside the church." Yet the only issue that differentiated Novatianists from the main body of believers was their policy on lapsed Christians. The issue, however, brought forth fundamentally different images of the church on both sides. Was it to be a community of the pure or a hospital for sick souls? Novatianist churches survived in some places until the seventh century.

Persecution under emperors Gallus and Valerian

After Decius died in battle in June 251, his successor, Gallus, renewed the persecutions, but they were sporadic and relatively mild. Most were limited to the major cities and were more the result of localized mob violence than universal edict. When Valerian assumed power in 253, he was at first friendly to the Christians. Bishop Dionysius went so far as to claim that Valerian was more favorably disposed to the church than any previous emperor had been: "All his house was likewise filled with pious persons and was, indeed, a congregation of the Lord." However, for reasons that are not clear, Valerian's attitude toward the

Christians changed remarkably in the summer of 257, when he ordered church leaders to acknowledge the traditional gods: "Those who do not profess the Roman religion must not refuse to take part in Roman religious ceremonies." Christians were also forbidden to assemble in either churches or cemeteries.

Bishops Cyprian and Dionysius boldly refused to comply. They were banished. In August 258 Valerian issued a much more severe edict, a violent attack on the church's leadership. Bishops, priests, and deacons who refused to obey the earlier decree were to be killed. Christians of senatorial and equestrian rank (the upper classes) were to lose their property; if they did not renounce Christianity, they too were to be executed. Christian matrons would lose their properties and be exiled, while lower-ranking civil servants faced slavery if they refused to renounce their faith. On August 8, Sixtus II, bishop of Rome, and four deacons were arrested for celebrating the Eucharist in a catacomb; they were executed.

Five weeks later, Cyprian was summoned from his exile to the proconsul's residence in Carthage and told, "The most sacred Emperors have commanded you to conform to the Roman rites."

"I refuse," replied Cyprian.

"You have long lived an irreligious life, and have drawn together a number of men bound by an unlawful association, and professed yourself an open enemy to the gods and the religion of Rome," accused the proconsul. "You shall be made an example to those whom you have wickedly associated with you. . . . It is the sentence of this court that Thascius Cyprianus be executed with the sword."

"Thanks be to God," answered the bishop.

On September 14, Cyprian became Africa's first bishop-martyr. The persecution spread to Spain, where Fructuosus, bishop of Tarragona, and two of his deacons were burned alive. In the East at Caesarea still more churchmen died for their faith. Persecutions ended in 260 with the death of Valerian after his capture by Persians in Edessa. Since Valerian was the first Roman emperor ever taken captive in battle, his fate was interpreted by Christians as divine retribution. While the persecution may have added some much needed money to the state's treasury (from confiscated properties), it did not stop Christians from meeting together, and it failed to destroy the clergy. In one regard, it may even have enriched the church by adding to the long roster of Christian martyrs.

Gallienus, Valerian's son and successor, apparently viewed the Christians as an asset rather than a liability. With its military position in the East weakened by the ever threatening Persians and others, Rome began to court the loyalty of Christians in the Eastern provinces. The new emperor restored their property and halted persecutions. For the next 40 years, Christians enjoyed what has been called "the long peace."

The only time in history that a Roman emperor fell into enemy hands was when Shapur I of Persia captured the emperor Valerian in battle in 260. The event is commemorated on this relief found near the ancient city of Persepolis. Shapur went on to launch three more campaigns against the Romans; he took many captives, including a bishop of Antioch and members of his flock. These captives may have been the founders of Iran's Christian communities.

Chapter Six

UP FROM THE WILDERNESS

By the end of the third century, the enduring faith of the first Christian monks had inspired countless new converts. Then, without warning, Diocletian initiated the last great persecution. Only the rise of Constantine, the first Christian emperor, stopped the bloodbaths.

Jesus had enjoined his followers to be *in* the world but not *of* it. Perhaps no one took this more to heart than Antony, the father of Christian monasticism. Born in Coma, Egypt, about 250, of well-to-do Coptic Christian parents, he was a sensitive young man who shunned school and companions of his own age, preferring to lead a simple life at home. When he was about 20, his parents died, leaving him sole guardian of his younger sister and their estate. According to legend, Antony was reflecting on the lives of the Apostles some months later, when he entered his local church during a reading of the Gospel of Matthew. What he heard changed his life and set the course of Christian monasticism: "If you would be perfect, go, sell what you possess and give [it] to the poor . . . come, follow me." Antony divided the 200 acres of his fertile family farm among the citizens of his town. Then he sold his belongings and gave the proceeds to the poor, keeping a little money for his sister. But, again, another reading in church seemed directed to his ears alone: "Do not be anxious about tomorrow." He knew then that the material world was not for him.

Toward the end of his long life, Antony often received visitors at his humble desert dwelling. His simple, monastic life became an example to other desert monks. Soon after his death in 356, monasteries sprang up throughout the deserts of Egypt.

He entrusted his sister to a group of religious women and adopted a life of strict self-denial, dwelling alone in a shed near his parents' house. Because in his day there were no monasteries, Antony sought spiritual direction from a recluse in a nearby town. Day by day, he learned how to be an ascetic, spending his time in solitary prayer, with periodic fasting and manual labor. His saintliness was so evident that the townspeople began to call him God's friend.

According to Athanasius, a fourth-century Church Father who wrote a biography based on the lore surrounding Antony's life, the young ascetic was soon set upon by the Devil, who tried to tempt him with visions of fame and a comfortable home. The Devil masqueraded as a woman, then a dragon, and finally a young boy, who spoke disparagingly to him. "Who are you who speak thus to me?" asked Antony. The boy replied, "I am called the spirit of fornication." Antony stood his ground and said, "The Lord is my helper and I will despise my enemies." Upon hearing these words, Athanasius writes, the boy fled. It was Antony's first victory over the Devil.

Antony fought valiantly against the Devil, who appeared in terrifying disguises. Though greatly tempted, the ascetic was not induced to forsake his faith. He told the Devil: "It is a sign of your helplessness that you ape the forms of brutes."

To withstand the demons better, Antony went into the Egyptian desert and had a friend lock him away in an abandoned tomb. There, for perhaps 15 years, he struggled against temptation, often keeping vigil the entire night and eating only once a day. He had only bread and water brought by an obliging sympathizer, and usually slept upon the bare ground. Once, a friend found him unconscious. When Antony revived, he said that a legion of devils had lashed him with supernatural violence. Wracked with pain, Antony continued his fight against evil, even when apparitions of savage beasts assaulted him throughout the night.

These struggles led him to deep psychological insights. "As the demons find us," Antony once said, "so they behave towards us, and according to the thoughts which are in us they direct their assaults."

One day, the demonic visions vanished, and, Athanasius tells us, a light shone into Antony's cell. "Why did you not appear at the beginning to stop my pains?" asked the exhausted recluse. "I was right here," intoned a voice, "but I waited to see you in action. And now, because you held out and did not surrender, I will ever be your helper and I will make you renowned everywhere."

The extraordinary Paul of Thebes

When he was past 90, Antony may have thought that he had endured the ascetic life longer than anyone else, but there was another who had surpassed him. According to legend, in 342 Antony was enjoined in a dream to search for a solitary "more perfect than himself." The man's name was Paul of Thebes. Back in 250 he had gone into hiding to escape persecutions sparked by Decius. Paul's brother-in-law, hoping to confiscate his estate, decided to betray him, but Paul, then 22, fled to a cave in the Egyptian desert to live as a hermit. (The word *hermit* is derived from the Greek word for desert, *eremia.*) The story goes that a spring provided fresh water, and a palm tree furnished food and clothing for the next two decades. When he was 43, a raven began to appear daily, bringing half a loaf of bread, just as ravens had fed the Old Testament prophet Elijah. By the time Antony found him, Paul was 113 years old and had lived and meditated alone for some 90 years.

When Antony finally reached Paul's abode, the two men knew each other's names by revelation. Then the raven suddenly appeared, bearing a full loaf of bread, rather than the usual half ration. The frail hermit, foreseeing his death, asked Antony to go and fetch a cloak for his shroud, but Paul died before the monk returned. As he was hastening back to the cave, Antony saw Paul's soul ascending to heaven, accompanied by angels, Apostles, and prophets. After he reached the body, two lions appeared and dug a grave. For the rest of his life, Antony treasured Paul's tunic, which was fashioned from woven palm leaves. He wore it on both Easter and Pentecost.

Antony and Athanasius

Though he preferred seclusion, Antony did make at least two trips into the outside world. Hearing that believers were being persecuted in Alexandria and hoping to be martyred, he led a delegation of monks there. He boldly ministered to Christians in the mines and prisons but was not chosen for martyrdom. When the persecution ebbed, he found a new desert spot, which he called Inner Mountain. There he planted a small garden and resigned himself to being a "daily martyr to his conscience, ever fighting the battles of the faith." He went to Alexandria another time to condemn the Arians (see pages 225–226). Before he died at the age of 105, Antony bequeathed his cloak and sheepskin to Athanasius, the bishop of Alexandria, and bade two fellow monks to bury him secretly and never reveal the site.

When he was 113 years old, the solitary Paul of Thebes, depicted here in his legendary tunic of woven palm leaves, was visited in his desert cell by the recluse Antony, then 90 years old. Knowing that he was near death, Paul said to his visitor, "Thou hast been sent by God to shelter this poor body in the ground."

In many ways Athanasius was the exact opposite of Antony. He led an active life within the church, until his intransigent politics forced him to flee for a few years to the desert. There he met Antony, some 40 years his senior. Though of different backgrounds, the ascetic and the pugnacious theologian became fast friends. In fact, our knowledge of Antony comes almost entirely from Athanasius, who wrote *The Life of St. Antony* about 357, within a year of the monk's death. This biography was extremely popular; later it became a basic document from which the monastic movement in the West took its first, most powerful inspiration. At a time when the empire was shot through with anarchy and corruption, the story of so upright a man was an inspiration to many Christians.

Desert fathers

Indeed, Antony's courage became so well known that others followed his example. Many sought him out in the desert to learn how to live like a "monk." (The word comes from the Greek word *monachos*, which means "single.") His followers believed that those who endured the rigorous life of an ascetic, who were victorious in their physical and spiritual ordeals, would be blessed with the freedom to speak directly with God. The wisdom of the desert fathers became legendary, and their advice on the ascetic life was recorded in a book called *Sayings of the Desert Fathers*. One example from the book, attributed to Arsenius, advises, "Be solitary, be silent, and be at peace."

Sayings of these *abbas*, or desert "fathers," often concerned ways to find *hesychia*—Greek for "quietness." One abba, Basil of Caesarea, was asked by a disciple for a word of guidance. "You shall love the Lord your God with all your heart," the abba said. The young monk went away for 20 years and then returned to report, "Father, I have struggled to keep your word; now speak another word to me." Basil responded, "You shall love your neighbor as yourself." The monk repaired again to his cell. Such was the arduous road to spiritual peace and perfection.

As the number of monks increased, the desert fathers had to consider how far apart to build their cells. A distance of one day's walk was deemed ideal, for it allowed monks to keep in touch with one another without distraction. An imagined view of these early desert monasteries is shown here in a medieval rendering.

A number of desert fathers told how they came to seek God in the wilderness. One was Abba Macarius, a former camel driver. When he was a young anchorite, or religious hermit, an unmarried girl who was pregnant named him as her seducer. The townspeople beat Macarius nearly to death. But when the girl went into labor, the infant remained in the womb for days. "I know what it is," she finally said; "it is because I slandered the anchorite, and accused him unjustly." Before the townspeople could reach him to make their amends, Macarius had fled to the barren serenity of the desert.

As he devoted himself to God, it became known that Macarius could perform miracles. Once a man died after taking a sum of money in trust, and his widow could not find it. She and her children were about to be sold into slavery to make good the debt when Macarius was called. He went to the grave and called out, "Where have you put the deposit?" The answer came: "It is hidden in the house, at the foot of the bed." His disciples were frightened, but Macarius explained the event's spiritual meaning: "It is not for my sake that this has happened, for I am nothing, but it is because of the widow and the orphans that God has performed this miracle. . . . God wants the soul to be without sin and grants it all it asks."

Repentance of past sins was a major element of monastic life. Some ascetics came to it as criminals desperate for forgiveness. Abba Moses, for example, had been a murderer as well as a thief. The penitent experienced a conversion and chose the desert life as a path of expiation. He found reassurance in Luke: "He who humbles himself will be exalted."

The solitary life was one of constant vigilance. Would-be monks were warned about the need to control the sensual appetites. Only long, hard effort would produce the purity before God that they sought. They stayed awake at night in anticipation of the Second Coming, fasted because the word of God was food enough, and kept silent so that they could hear God's voice. A watchword was, "Sit in your cell and it will teach you everything." Antony summed it up with characteristic simplicity: "Just as fish die if they stay too long out of water, so the monks who loiter outside their cells or pass their time with men of the world lose the intensity of inner peace."

Antony's example drew both men and women by the thousands to the monastic life. As Athanasius noted, "The desert was made a city by monks." Indeed, near the end of the fourth century, one traveler

Starting in the deserts of Egypt, monasticism soon spread throughout the empire. By the fourth century, it had reached Cappadocia in Asia Minor, where monks hollowed out their cells in the rocky cliffs in the wilds of the Göreme Valley (present-day central Turkey).

Mary of Egypt, inspired by the Virgin Mary, repented her life of sin and went to live in the desert wilderness of Jordan. For 47 years, she lived alone. According to legend, she was clad only in her hair, as depicted here in this 14th-century statue.

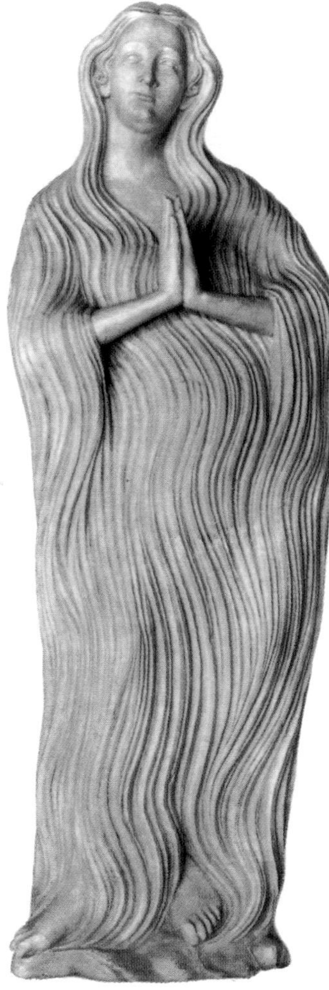

The First Saints

The Apostle Paul often referred to fellow Christians as "saints," in other words, holy ones. (The word comes from Latin *sanctus*, "holy.") In later times, however, the title "saint" was used increasingly to honor Christian martyrs. By the fourth century, this understanding of sainthood was also applied to many desert hermits. Paul of Thebes and Antony were among the first desert monks to be revered as saints. In time, very devout bishops and theologians also came to be called saints upon their deaths. Concerned that the requirements for sainthood were becoming too lax, in 1234 the Roman Catholic Church established the first official criteria for canonization. Since that time, sainthood can be conferred only upon those for whom documented proof of holiness can be provided.

quipped that the number of desert dwellers was about the same as the secular population of Palestine and Egypt. Not surprisingly, such a phenomenon provided an easy target for the satirist. The fourth-century pagan poet Palladas, a Greek of Alexandria, ridiculed the movement in an epigram:

If solitaries, why so many?
So many, how are they then sole?
O crowd of solitaries
feigning solitude!

Though the monks were not solitary, their lives were apparently as austere and difficult as in Antony's day. According to one chronicler: "Water is hard to find. . . . Here abide men perfect in holiness (for so terrible a place can be endured by none save those of absolute resolve and supreme constancy); yet is their chief concern the loving kindness which they show to one another and towards such as by chance may reach that spot." To believers, however, it seemed that the desert monks "lived the life of heaven in the world," and stories about them were avidly shared. Even among the pagans their holiness was recognized. Crowds of the sick and infirm made pilgrimages to the cell of one monk who had not spoken for 30 years, and many were said to have come away cured.

Women of the desert

Women also sought the sanctity and silence of the desert. Especially moving are the accounts of several of them who left a life of sin to seek God's forgiveness and mercy in the wilderness. One of the first was Mary of Egypt. When Mary was a young woman, probably in the fifth century, she ran away from her native village to Alexandria and lived as a prostitute for the next 17 years. Out of curiosity, she embarked one day on a journey to Jerusalem with a band of pilgrims, eager to celebrate the feast of the Holy Cross in the sacred city. Upon reaching the Church of the Holy Sepulcher, her companions entered to view a relic of the "true cross," but she was restrained by an invisible force. No matter how strenuously she tried to follow them, she could not pass into the church. Suddenly struck by the magnitude of her sins, she wept and prayed to the Virgin Mary, vowing a lifetime of penance. Then, with a lightened heart, she entered the church. On her way out, pausing to give thanks to the Virgin Mary, she heard the words, "Go over Jordan and thou shalt find rest."

Thenceforth, according to tradition, she lived alone in the punishing desert climate, suffering its extremes of heat and cold for 47 years, subsisting on dates and wild plants, while God instructed her in the mysteries of faith. One day, as the legend goes, she was accidentally discovered by a monk named Zosimus, who asked her to tell him her story. She agreed. At her request, Zosimus returned the following year during Lent to give her Holy Communion. She was on the other side of the Jordan River and, much to his amazement, walked across the water to meet him. A year later, when he came again, she was dead. Nearby, Mary had written in the sand: "Father Zosimus, bury the body of lowly Mary. Render earth to earth and pray for me. I died the night of the Lord's Passion, after receiving the divine and mystic Banquet."

Perhaps an even more moving example of contrition is Maria. An orphan since age seven, Maria was reared by her uncle, a desert monk named Abraham. For 20 years she led a devout life in a cell adjacent to his, sharing his distrust of worldly things. Then one day, she allowed herself to be seduced by a fellow monk. Utterly ashamed, Maria fled to the city, for she had not yet learned the central lesson of the desert: to rely solely on the mercy of God. Abraham asked a friend to search for her, and learned that she was living as a prostitute. Deeply saddened, Abraham rode off to bring back his niece.

At first Maria refused to go, saying that her sins were too great. But Abraham said: "To you, your sins seem like mountains, but God has spread his mercy over all that He has made. . . . It is not new to fall, my daughter; what is wrong is to lie down when you have fallen." Back in her desert cell Maria put on a hairshirt and wept and prayed daily for forgiveness. After three years of repentance, she was rewarded with the gift of healing, and throngs came to her for spiritual blessings and the restoration of health.

Legendary stories of the Apostles

The public appetite for wondrous stories was not confined to accounts of pious contemporaries, however. In the second and third centuries a number of books were written that revolved around the miraculous powers and supernatural adventures of the revered Apostles. Because the stories are not included in the New Testament, they are called the apocryphal Acts. (In this context, "apocryphal" refers to all early accounts of Jesus or his Apostles that have not been officially included in the New Testament.)

These tales of miraculous adventures were similar in both style and content to popular non-Christian novels of the time. They served not only to entertain but also to impart moral precepts. Some later writers thought several of these Acts were suspect. Early in the fourth century Eusebius of Caesarea pointed out that

The life of a desert monk was grueling and harsh. Food and water were scarce, and caves provided the main means of shelter. Temperatures in the Egyptian desert near Thebes could boil past 110° F during the summer, and fierce windstorms were frequent. For those who burned to prove their love of God, however, the desert provided an alternative to martyrdom.

they were heretical in style and teaching. In 787, the Second Council of Nicaea called the *Acts of John* "this abominable book" and judged it "worthy of being committed to the flames." Christians in the third century, however, loved the lively tales, which stressed the virtue of following in the Apostles' spiritual footsteps by living a chaste life. The Acts of Andrew, John, Peter, Paul, and Thomas abound with examples that illustrate the power of the spirit to fight evil.

In the *Acts of Peter,* believers could read about the renowned "Quo vadis" ("Where are you going?") story, a prelude to the execution of the Apostle. As related in the story, Peter had been convinced by worried friends to flee Rome because of Nero's persecutions, but along the way he encountered Jesus going in the opposite direction and asked, "Where are you going, Lord?" Jesus replied, "I am going to Rome to be crucified." The chastened Apostle turned on his heel and returned to be martyred on a cross, crucified head downward at his own request.

A well-known story in the *Acts of Paul* involves a baptized lion. While imprisoned in Ephesus, one night Paul was miraculously freed of his iron chains by angels so that he could go out and baptize new

One who emulated the desert fathers, but carried asceticism to an extreme, was Simeon Stylite (right), a fifth-century monk who lived atop a pillar for 37 years. Supplies were delivered to him by basket; the ladder was for visitors on special occasions. The base of his pillar, above, stands in the ruins of a Syrian church.

disciples. When finished, he returned to his fetters, leaving his guards none the wiser. Later, he was led to the stadium, where he was to face a wild beast for public amusement. A lion "of huge size and unmatched strength" was loosed, but the animal trotted over and lay down calmly at Paul's feet. (According to the narrative, the Apostle had encountered the lion in the wild some time before and preached to it. The creature had professed belief in Jesus and had thereupon been baptized.) At this juncture, a tremendous hailstorm peppered the stadium, killing many people and animals, and the pagan governor was converted. The lion then fled to his home in the hills.

A key episode from the same book tells of Paul's conversion of a young woman named Thecla, who lived in Iconium in Asia Minor. After hearing the words of Paul, Thecla refused to marry her betrothed, preferring instead to follow Paul. Deeply angered, Thecla's fiancé brought the matter before the Roman governor, who had Paul scourged and banished. Thecla too was arrested, and upon hearing that she had chosen a life of chastity and thus would never marry, her mother cried out, "Burn the lawless one." Thecla was placed on a pyre; when it was lit, rain and hail descended from heaven, quenching the fire. The governor spared Thecla, and six days later she overtook Paul. She then followed Paul on a missionary journey where more miracles saved her from death. Later, she returned to Iconium to convert her mother. Ever since late Roman times, Thecla has been venerated as a saint by Eastern Christians.

The *Acts of Andrew* recounts many of that Apostle's miraculous deeds, including exorcisms of devils, cures of the desperately ill, and the calming of a tempest. His martyrdom occurs after he persuades the wife of Aegeates, Roman governor of Achaia (Greece) to live in perfect chastity. The enraged governor threatens to torture the Apostle unless his wife returns to the marriage bed, but Andrew counsels her to be steadfast. Aegeates has Andrew scourged and then crucified. Yet Andrew preaches from the cross and wins the hearts of the townspeople. When Andrew dies, Aegeates commits suicide. Throughout this story, doctrines taught by the desert ascetics, for example, the renunciation of sex in marriage, are inculcated. Paradoxically, the Apostle is regarded nowadays in certain regions of Germany as the patron saint of girls who wish to get married.

The longest of the apocryphal works is the *Acts of Thomas,* which follows the famous "doubter" on his wanderings through India. When he is hired by King Gundaphorus to construct a great palace, Thomas instead distributes to the poor all of the moneys invested in the project. The monarch, infuriated, throws the Apostle in a dungeon, but Gundaphorus' deceased brother appears in a vision to explain that a royal palace has been built in the heavenly kingdom, and Thomas is released. In another tale, the Apostle raises a murdered girl from the dead, and she recounts her experiences in hell. In still later adventures, a sudden flood thwarts an attempt to torture Thomas with hot irons. After his death, the dust from outside his tomb is described as powerful enough to cure a young boy of demonic possession.

Perhaps the most skillfully written of the apocryphal tales is the *Acts of John,* which contains a strong narrative and a realistic grasp of character. In one episode, the Apostle prays to God to let the evil spirits flee from Ephesus, and parts of the Temple of Artemis fall down. As the temple collapses, the stones crush to death the priest serving the goddess, but he is brought back to life and becomes a believer in Jesus.

A note of humor

Ancient readers doubtless appreciated the story of the bedbugs, which even the author refers to as "a droll matter." When John and his fellow travelers stay at a deserted inn, the Apostle takes the only bed, which teems with insects. His followers laugh to themselves when they hear him cry out in the night,

"I say unto you, O bugs, behave yourselves, one and all, and leave your abode for this night and remain quiet in one place, and keep your distance from the servants of God." The next morning, John's companions discover a horde of bugs standing patiently outside the door. When John himself finally awakens, he says, "Since ye have well behaved yourselves in hearkening to my rebuke, come unto your place," at which the insects skitter back to the bed and quickly disappear. As is characteristic of these tales, even this amusing anecdote has a serious moral: "This creature hearkened unto the voice of a man, and abode by itself and was quiet and trespassed not," comments John; "but we which hear the voice and commandments of God disobey and are light-minded."

In the Acts of Andrew, *when an enormous serpent destroys a house, Andrew comes to the rescue. He bids the serpent to "hide thy head, foul one, which thou didst raise in the beginning for the hurt of mankind, and obey the servants of God, and die." With that, the serpent reared up and expired.*

Although rejected by some serious-minded believers as absurd, impious, and sometimes heretical, the apocryphal Acts were lodged in the popular tradition for centuries. They often reflect problems of the times, such as conflicts with the unconverted or the abiding mystery of incurable illnesses. Scattered throughout are early liturgies and hymns, including one hymn, recorded in the *Acts of John,* purportedly sung by Jesus and his disciples shortly before his arrest.

The legends were told everywhere from Persia to Spain, despite the objections of church leaders, and became so familiar that they have been portrayed in Christian art ever since.

Gregory the Wonderworker

Stories of Christians performing miracles abounded in the third century. One of the more beloved legends of that period concerned Gregory Thaumaturgus, or the "Wonderworker," bishop of Neocaesarea in Pontus (in present-day Turkey). He was born around 213 in Neocaesarea to aristocratic pagan parents, who had him educated in Roman law, philosophy, and rhetoric. About 233, Gregory met the great Christian scholar Origen in Palestine. For some five years he studied with the master, moving from a broad curriculum of secular subjects to the challenges of biblical texts and revelations of faith in Jesus. He later wrote that meeting Origen was "the first time the true Sun began to rise upon me."

Having become a deeply committed Christian, Gregory went home, but Origen wrote to him, urging that he use his spiritual gifts in service to the Lord. When he was offered the bishopric of Neocaesarea, he declined because he feared the responsibility, but was ordained in abstentia. Giving in finally, Gregory presided in a city with a mere 17 Christians; but by the time of his death, around the year 270, it was said that there were only 17 pagans remaining.

Revered for his wisdom and devotion to his flock, Gregory was enshrined in the popular imagination as a "second Moses" because of the many tales of his ability to work miracles. It is said, for example, that when the local river Lycus threatened to flood, he turned back the waters. When two brothers quarreled bitterly over the rights to their father's lake, he dried up the disputed property with a twitch of his cloak. He also vanquished demons and once saved some Christians from a terrible plague. After escaping the Decian persecutions in 250, he instituted a Christian version of pagan games, thus astutely competing with the entertainments of the heathens. His games were produced as festivals in honor of those martyrs who had died because of their faith in Christ.

The powers of Gregory still elicit awe today. Because he is credited with stopping the Lycus River from flooding, his name is invoked in some parts of Italy and Sicily when an earthquake is expected.

Under army rule

The world from which ascetics fled in the third century was suffering tremendous unrest. Invasions were frequent and destructive—Goths and other Germanic peoples were sweeping into the Western provinces of the empire, while the Persians were intent on recovering territories long held by Romans in the East. The empire desperately needed protection, but as the military grew in might, it demanded privileges and payments that bled the economy. From 260 to 284, Rome had nine different emperors, nearly all elected by the military. The senatorial class, which had long supplied leaders, was incapable of providing them during this period of almost constant warfare.

After Valerian was captured by the Persians in 260, his son, Gallienus, commander of the Western troops, became sole emperor. Unlike many of the soldier-emperors to follow, Gallienus surrounded himself with men of letters. Under his administration, the empire experienced a flowering of Greek philosophy, and persecutions of the Christians were suspended. Then Gallienus was murdered in 268, and the army chose as his successor Claudius II, a cavalry commander. He brought the army back to peak discipline and efficiency. More important, Claudius successfully drove back the Goths and for this victory was dubbed Claudius Gothicus. He was loved by the military and civilian population alike for his probity and fairness. Unfortunately, his reign ended after only two years, when he succumbed to the plague that repeatedly struck throughout the ill-fated century.

During this chaotic period, the death of an emperor easily triggered civil unrest. When Claudius II died in 270, his brother, Quintilius, raised an army and was proclaimed emperor. But the Roman Army, which was occupying the banks of the Danube, chose one of their own to be the next ruler. He was Aurelian, the

According to the Acts of Paul, *the Apostle Paul was once sentenced to be killed by wild beasts for preaching the gospel to the Ephesians. But when the animals were let loose in the stadium to attack Paul, a huge lion lay at his feet and did not harm the "holy body, standing like a statue in prayer."*

Two Favorite Saints

Portrayed in this 14th-century stained-glass window is a maiden, saved from destitution by a bag of gold given to her by Nicholas. (She is attempting to awaken her sleeping father.) For this generous act, Nicholas, a third-century bishop of Myra, came to be the patron saint of Christmas.

Though he never drove a sleigh pulled by reindeer through the sky, a real St. Nicholas is behind the story of Santa Claus. The facts about the life of Nicholas are few, but the legends that surround him are rich in detail. He was born in the late third century to prosperous Christian parents in Asia Minor. Later, he became bishop of the city of Myra (in present-day Turkey). Tradition credits Nicholas with several saintly deeds and miracles. In one story, he was on a voyage when a violent storm arose. All on board the ship feared they would be lost but not Nicholas. He calmed the winds with his prayers, enabling the vessel to sail safely to port. As a result he is venerated today as the patron saint of sailors.

On another occasion, Nicholas is said to have confronted an evil innkeeper, who had murdered three young brothers and hidden their corpses in a tub of brine. He prayed over the bodies until they rose from the dead, making him forevermore the protector of young children.

It was such legends that made Nicholas one of the most popular saints during the Middle Ages. As further evidence of his lasting appeal, more than 2,000 churches, including some 400 in England, were dedicated to him. He was also adopted as the patron saint of both Greece and Russia.

Nonetheless, it is for his association with Christmas that St. Nicholas has gained widespread recognition. As the story goes, Nicholas played the role of secret benefactor for three young women whose father was about to sell them into servitude because he had no money for their dowries. Nicholas stealthily threw three bags of gold through the window of the sisters' house, thus enabling them to marry as they wished. From this chivalrous good deed, his name has come to be inextricably associated with gift giving on Christmas.

St. Valentine

Less is known about the man who gave his name to St. Valentine's Day. Traditionally, February 14 is linked with the martyrdom of two Valentines. One may have been a Roman priest, beheaded by Claudius II about 270. The other, also beheaded about the same time, was bishop of a town some 60 miles from Rome. How these martyrs became associated with the celebration of love is unclear. According to one legend, Valentine of Rome was killed because he continued to perform marriages after Claudius, in an effort to encourage young men to join the army, had forbidden them.

Another story connects Valentine's Day with the Roman festival of Lupercalia. On February 14, the eve of this ancient fertility rite, young men perhaps chose the names of maidens to be their partners during the celebration. In fact, some have speculated that the beheading of St. Valentine possibly served as entertainment for the Lupercalia. The Valentine custom of exchanging love notes, which began in the late Middle Ages, might be based on a belief that birds begin mating at this time.

heroic commander in chief of the cavalry. Quintilius is reported to have committed suicide upon hearing the news, and thus civil war was averted.

Aurelian's reign lasted about five years; during this time he waged war almost continuously and won back the territories of Gaul, Spain, and Britain from a usurper. Adding to the military reforms of Claudius II, he prohibited gambling and drinking in the army and forbade soldiers to demand supplies from the citizens. He cruelly punished those foolish enough to disobey. Bowing to embarrassing necessity, Aurelian began construction of a 12-mile-long wall to defend Rome, a city that had once counted on the might of the Roman Empire as its bulwark.

Aurelian's conquests

One of Aurelian's strongest foes was Queen Zenobia, an athletic beauty who reigned in the desert kingdom of Palmyra (modern-day Syria) and had conquered Egypt and much of Asia Minor. Zenobia took Cleopatra as her model but surpassed the Egyptian queen by vigorously leading her own troops on horseback, even marching on foot for many miles at a time.

Zenobia won the first battle against Aurelian, but he soon defeated two of her armies and besieged her capital, Palmyra, a richly endowed oasis. He asked for her surrender; she answered him with insults. The emperor complained that "the Roman people speak with contempt of the war which I am waging against a woman," but he recognized her as a well-prepared, wily, and desperate adversary. Eventually, the city fell, and Zenobia, her neck chained in gold, became the centerpiece of Aurelian's triumphal parade in front of cheering crowds in Rome. Her defeat affected the

To defend the city of Rome from barbarians, Aurelian built a wall around it. Aurelian's Wall was 20 feet high (later doubled to 40) and extended 12 miles with 381 towers, most set at 100-foot intervals.

Zenobia, queen of Palmyra, was an astute leader and great warrior. Determined to rule the Roman Empire in the East, she fought alongside her garrisons and captured parts of Asia Minor. Alarmed by her growing ambition, Aurelian fought back and won. In 272 he captured the beautiful queen as she was fleeing to safety in Persia.

church, for her chief finance minister was the luxury-loving Paul of Samosata (see pages 196–197), bishop of Antioch. His version of the Trinity as a union of Father, Wisdom, and Word had made him a heretic in the eyes of mainstream Christians. But until Zenobia was defeated, they had been unable to remove him from office. Aurelian was merciful toward his enemy and married her off to a Roman senator. The "desert tigress" became a respectable matron in Tivoli, and her daughters married into Rome's noble families.

Despite this display of magnanimity toward Zenobia, Aurelian was a harsh disciplinarian. The Senate hated him and his staff feared him. In the end, it was his severity that led to his downfall. When he threatened one of his secretaries with punishment for extortion, the man forged a list of Aurelian's officers who were supposedly to be executed and showed it to them. Thus deceived, the officers plotted against their emperor. In 275 one of Aurelian's most trusted and beloved generals killed him. When the secretary's treachery was uncovered, he was immediately executed, but this action did little to undo the mischief. For more than eight months, an eerie calm fell over the leaderless state. Aware that its credibility was severely tarnished, the army refused to designate a new emperor and instead returned the honor to the Senate.

The senators warily accepted the responsibility and began to search for a suitable candidate. At last, in response to rumors of rebellions in Gaul and the East, the politicians prevailed upon the 75-year-old Tacitus, a descendant of the historian of the same name, to assume the robes of office. With Tacitus in power, the Senate enjoyed its last days of glory. As the 18th-century historian Edward Gibbon noted, the "senate displayed a sudden lustre, blazed for a moment, and was extinguished for ever."

A revolving door

Tacitus' six-month rule, though beneficent and skilled, ended with his natural death, perhaps hastened by quarrels with an insubordinate military. His Praetorian prefect, Florian, usurped the title but was killed by his own men three months later. By common consent, the imperial power was conferred upon Probus, a proven leader who had reconquered Egypt for Aurelian and had become commander in chief of all Eastern provinces under Tacitus.

After his acclamation by the military, Probus took pains to flatter the Senate. During the six years of his reign he concentrated on restoring peace and stability; he freed at least 60 cities in Gaul from the Germanic barbarians and constructed a line of frontier garrisons that stretched from the Rhine to the Danube. Tens of thousands of Germans were killed in the campaigns. Probus was magnanimous to the defeated survivors.

He was intent on rebuilding the internal structure of the empire, which had been neglected of late. Instead of sending the army on conquests, he put soldiers to work building temples, bridges, and palaces. To keep idleness at bay, Probus ordered men accustomed to warfare to plant vineyards on the hills of Gaul. They grudgingly obeyed, until the fatal day when Probus is said to have expressed the hope for universal peace and an end to the need for any military force. Exhausted from their labors, some of the soldiers threw down their tools, took up their arms, and rushed at their emperor, stabbing him to death.

Sons of war

The army was back in power. It elected Carus, a high-ranking officer, to wear the purple. Before he set off to wage war against the ever threatening Persians, Carus named his sons, Carinus and Numerian, as his political heirs. Carinus, the older but less capable of the two, was elevated to caesar (subordinate ruler), while Numerian went with his father on a drive to push the Persians back beyond the Tigris. Carus died in Mesopotamia, on the verge of victory. Rumors spread that he was killed by lightning. Because death by lightning was thought to be a sign of the gods' wrath, Numerian's superstitious troops believed that crossing the Tigris would mean certain defeat. The soldiers persuaded Numerian to retreat from the very brink of victory, bewildering the Persian enemy.

Numerian remained in the East. Meanwhile, back in Rome, Carinus reveled in his new-found privileges as co-emperor, abandoning himself to luxury and the abuse of his power. He put to death schoolfellows who had not sufficiently appreciated his latent greatness and filled the palace with singers, dancers, and prostitutes. While his actions stunned the Senate, he managed to appease the populace by funding costly and spectacular public entertainments. A forest was transplanted to the center of the circus arena and then stocked with ostriches, stags, and wild boars. In just one day, gladiators killed 100 lions, 100 lionesses, 200 leopards, and 300 bears. At various times the spectators were able to view zebras, Indian tigers, hyenas, elk, a rhinoceros, and, on one memorable occasion, 22 elephants. Nets to restrain the animals were made from gold wire; Carinus gloried in the pageantry and in the praises of his subsidized poets.

In the East, a very strange drama unfolded. Numerian, supposedly troubled by an affliction of the eyes, kept to the darkness of his tent and sent out orders through his father-in-law, Aper. But a strong odor coming from the imperial tent alarmed the soldiers. They broke in and discovered Numerian's rotting corpse. Had Aper killed his sovereign or merely concealed a natural death because of his own ambitions? The troops' candidate for emperor, Diocletian,

Many farmers were driven into bankruptcy by heavy taxes, which paid for the ever increasing needs of the army during the war-torn third century. In this relief, carved about 270, a goatherd sits in his wickerwork shelter, milking a goat.

gave a resounding answer. "This man is the murderer of Numerian," he shouted, as Aper stood before him in chains, and he quickly plunged a sword into the prisoner's chest. Diocletian prepared for civil war, though his army was weakened from campaigns in Persia. Indeed his troops were no match for Carinus' armies, but as matters turned out, the latter's own immorality led to a quick resolution—a tribune killed Carinus for seducing his wife.

In 284 Diocletian, the son of freed slaves from the province of Dalmatia, became sole ruler of the Roman Empire. He had his work cut out for him. The preceding years of military rule had wrecked the political and economic stability of the state.

The emperor Diocletian, top, came to power in 284. He ordered cruel persecutions of the Christians and then retired to tend a garden at his palace, above. This grand estate was at Split in Dalmatia (now part of Yugoslavia).

Diocletian and the tetrarchy

One thing was clear to Diocletian: the empire was too large a burden for one man. He formed the tetrarchy, or rule of four, designating his comrade-in-arms and friend Maximian as co-augustus in the West. Two subordinates, called caesars, were appointed to serve under them: Constantius was named to administer Gaul, Spain, and Britain; Galerius would manage the forces on the Danube. In a bold move, Diocletian sealed the loyalties of his colleagues by insisting they dismiss their wives and marry women of imperial families. Constantius abandoned Helena, the mother of his son Constantine (a future emperor), and married the daughter of Maximian. Galerius repudiated his wife to marry Diocletian's daughter.

Constantius brought Britain back into the empire after a 10-year separation, while Maximian subdued rebellious nomads in western Africa, and Diocletian crushed a revolt in Egypt. In the East, Galerius defeated the Persians. Meanwhile, Diocletian had every aspect of empire, civilian and military, divided into East and West, an administrative reform that eventually led to completely separate empires.

Peace reigned, at last; the tetrarchy was working. Now Diocletian could attend to economic reform. The economy was in shambles; excessive taxes and inflation had all but wiped out the middle and upper classes, the financial backbone of the empire. Many citizens chose to abandon their homes and farms rather than pay their oppressive tax bills. Two popular questions put to one Egyptian oracle were, "Am I to become a beggar?" and "Shall I flee?" Clearly, the tax base had to be reformed, especially since the recurring plague had caused an estimated decline in population from 70 million to 50 million.

But reforming the tax system proved an impossible task for Diocletian. Instead of reform, he planted the seeds of serfdom by forcing farmers to keep to their land and craftsmen to their jobs and then legally binding their sons to continue in their fathers' footsteps.

He issued a wage and price freeze in 301, hoping that it would spur production and cut inflation. The policy had exactly the opposite effect, calling a permanent halt to what little of a free market was still operating. The rights and labor of the individual had been completely subsumed to the needs of the state.

Forty years of Christian expansion

From about 260 to 300, Christians enjoyed relative peace and even a certain amount of prosperity. A half century later, the church historian Eusebius of Caesarea wrote that during this period there was "clemency of emperors toward our brethren." Indeed, Christians were becoming leaders in trade and government. The faith began to spread rapidly. Entire towns in Asia Minor, particularly in Phrygia, became Christian. Conversions were especially numerous in some communities where a large number of Jews lived or had long exercised cultural influence. Rome alone now numbered at least 20 churches, and the congregations had been organized into seven districts.

The empire itself was partly responsible for helping to spread the faith. While the soldier-emperors ruled, the state was too impoverished to offer assistance to citizens in need, such as the orphaned and elderly. Continuing the Jewish tradition of caring for the needy, Christians provided relief for them. Later, during the fourth century, the last pagan emperor, Julian, acknowledged that it was "benevolence to strangers, their care for the graves of the dead, and the pretended holiness of their lives that have done most to increase atheism [Christianity]."

In addition to doing good works, Christians strove to imitate the love of Jesus in their personal lives. Their piety made a striking contrast to the widespread corruption of the army and the oppressive greed of the emperors. The soldier-emperors were so intent on squeezing the last drachma in taxes out of the more prosperous cities that thousands of people fled to the countryside, where they converted to Christianity.

Divergent versions of the New Testament

By the time Diocletian had become emperor in 284, there were an estimated 5 million Christians throughout the empire. As their message spread to diverse ethnic groups, the text of what was called the *Novum Testamentum*, or the New Testament, began to take on distinct local characteristics. Year after year, as the original Greek texts were copied and recopied, hundreds of variations crept into the wording. Some were simply the errors inevitable in hand-copying—a line omitted, a misspelling, or a word written twice. Still others arose from faulty judgment by scribes, who perhaps attempted to correct what they thought were problems of grammar or poor style. A few efforts were made to harmonize similar passages in different Gospels, such as adding phrases to the Lord's Prayer in the Gospel of Luke in order to make it agree with the more well-known form of the prayer in Matthew.

In the third century there were two major versions of New Testament writings. One, usually called the Alexandrian Text, was most common around the eastern Mediterranean. The second, called the Western Text, was used widely in Italy, Gaul, and North Africa. Though most differences between the two were small, some major variations did arise. In the Western Text, for example, Acts is almost 10 percent longer than in the Alexandrian and includes interesting details that are missing in the other text. When Paul lectures in Ephesus, for instance, the Western Text notes the number of hours that he spoke, while the Alexandrian Text does not.

Near the end of the third century an attempt was made to overcome these differences. Lucian, a presbyter in the Antioch church, prepared a

Recognizing that the Roman Empire was far too large for any one man to rule, Diocletian devised the tetrarchy, or four-man rule. In this fourth-century statue from St. Mark's in Venice, Diocletian is the one standing second from right, clasping his co-augustus, Maximian; the caesars Constantius and Galerius stand on the left.

Gregory (right), known as the Illuminator of the Armenians, in about 301 converted the ruler of Armenia, who in turn made Christianity the country's official religion. To help spread the word, an Armenian alphabet was created; the example above is from the opening page of a 10th-century illuminated Gospel of Luke.

revision of the New Testament that smoothed out many variations in the texts available to him. Often when Lucian found two or more variant phrases, he did not try to decide which was original but included them both. Most scholars consider Lucian's revision further from the original wording of the New Testament than any of its predecessors. It quickly became popular because of its eloquent language and its harmonization of divergent passages. During the fourth century, Lucian's version, now known as the "Byzantine Text," or "Received Text," became the overwhelming favorite of the church. It provided the basis for such important modern translations as the King James version. Since the late 19th century, however, translations of the New Testament have been primarily based on a return to the earlier Alexandrian Text.

Armenia, the first Christian state

According to Armenian tradition, an infant named Gregory, who was born around 240, was spirited away to safety just before his Parthian family was massacred for involvement in the assassination of King Khosrov I of Armenia. Gregory was raised as a Christian in Cappadocia in Asia Minor. Later, he married a Christian woman and returned to Armenia to serve at the court of King Tiridates III.

Gregory's zealous espousal of Christian teaching and his refusal to sacrifice to a local goddess outraged the king. He ordered that Gregory be tortured and then hurled into the Khor Virap, a deep pit reeking with the noxious fumes of rotting corpses. Miraculously, Gregory survived inside the pit for some 13 years, and was released finally in the hope that he could cure the king of a grave illness. Gregory healed his sovereign and then converted him, along with his family and the entire army. Gregory went further, destroying major pagan shrines throughout Armenia and setting up crosses in their place.

Around 315, Gregory was ordained a bishop. As legend has it, he then baptized the whole Armenian nation. Thus, Armenia became the first Christian state in history. Under Gregory's guidance, numerous churches were built and monasteries established. When his work was done, he turned the bishopric over to his younger son and retired to the wilderness. He is remembered today as Gregory the Illuminator and is the patron saint of Armenia.

Paul of Samosata

While Christians were enjoying positions of importance within the empire, one man was attempting to combine worldly and ecclesiastical power. He was Paul of Samosata, bishop of Antioch from 260 to 268, when it was part of Queen Zenobia's kingdom. At the same time, he was also the queen's chief finance minister and was accused of having amassed a fortune in bribes. This bishop outraged people by encouraging applause during his sermons and by having choirs of women sing psalms of praise specifically to him. Worst of all, Paul preached that Jesus was "an ordinary man," though uniquely inspired and "anointed," when the divine Word came and rested on him. He would not allow his congregation to sing hymns to "our Lord Jesus Christ."

The church felt compelled to act against one of their own. A synod of bishops condemned Paul in 268, charging him with financial misconduct and heresy for teaching that Jesus was only man and not God. But the synod's request for Paul's removal went unheeded. Paul's protectress, Zenobia, refused to acknowledge the church's authority. Not until Aurelian finally defeated Zenobia in 272 were the synod's demands granted. The emperor's action proved the growing importance of the Christian church in Roman affairs. Aurelian banished Paul from Antioch and turned his church over to the orthodox bishops.

Plotinus, a pagan mystic

In the midst of the political upheavals and intellectual uncertainty of the third century, one man shone with such wisdom that many Romans considered him their spiritual director. He was Plotinus, a philosopher who reconciled the 600-year-old teachings of Plato with certain mystical ideas current in his own time. Plotinus' synthesis of these streams of thought is called Neoplatonism, a philosphy that became a source of inspiration to Christian philosophers for centuries to come. Plotinus believed that the highest principle is the One, which encompasses all being and nonbeing. It is an immaterial force that overflows into progressively lower levels of existence. The first level is the "world-mind," the second, the "world-soul," and the third, the level of individual souls.

In some ways his view of the One was similar to the Christian conception of the Trinity. He maintained that the ultimate goal of human souls is to reunite with the One by contemplation, a belief that was echoed throughout the ages by leading Christian thinkers, such as Augustine and Thomas Aquinas.

Born around 205, Plotinus studied for 11 years in Alexandria with the Platonist philosopher Ammonius

In Armenia many churches are dedicated to St. Gregory. The one shown here was built in the 13th century in the old Armenian capital of Ani (near the modern-day border of Turkey and the Soviet Union).

Devotion to Mithras

Mithras, originally a Persian god of light, embodied all the virtues a Roman soldier hoped to attain. He was an undefeated warrior, a keen hunter, and an able horseman. More important, he adhered to a code of self-discipline and honorable conduct.

Although earliest evidence of Mithraism in the Roman world dates to 67 B.C., it was during the first century A.D. that Mithras began to attract a large following among soldiers. A significant number of shrines in ports and commercial centers indicates that he also had devotees in the merchant and commercial classes. By the third century, Mithraism was probably the most widespread mystery religion in the empire.

Despite Mithraism's popularity, little is known about its rituals, for initiates were sworn to secrecy. The art and inscriptions found in numerous Mithraic shrines, however, do help to shed some light on the nature of this mysterious god.

According to the Mithraic myth, the sun god commanded Mithras to slay a great bull. Mithras hunted, captured, and then dragged the beast to a cave, where he reluctantly sacrificed it. From this feat, Mithras created the world; for when the blood of the dying bull spilled on the earth, life sprang forth. An inscription in a Mithraic shrine in Rome says: "You saved us by having shed the eternal blood."

Paintings and reliefs of the slaying depict grain sprouting from the bull's tail, symbolizing Mithras' bringing of life to the earth. The force of evil, however, is also present: a scorpion tries to drink the bull's blood. It does not succeed, and good is triumphant over evil. After this great deed, the sun god and Mithras shared a sacred meal consisting of the bull's meat and blood. Mithras then ascended to the heavens in the sun god's chariot. The two deities are often portrayed shaking hands.

In the third century, Mithraism was a leading pagan religion. Mithras is shown here in a marble relief surrounded by signs of the zodiac.

His worshipers believed that Mithras granted spiritual salvation and an eternal afterlife, but initiation was not easy or open to all. Women were excluded, while men who participated were perhaps subjected to some frightening experiences. It is thought that those being inducted were often blindfolded and possibly branded. Initiation took place in shrines that were constructed to resemble caves, recalling the place where Mithras slew the bull. Baptism was also a feature of the ritual, as was a ceremonial meal of bread and wine, in remembrance of the feast of meat and blood shared by Mithras and the sun god.

Once admitted, Mithras' followers worked on developing spiritual and moral discipline. All aspired to ascend through the seven ranks of spiritual growth. The highest rank was that of "father." If followers reached the top level, then they could enter paradise at their death.

Christian writers, such as Justin Martyr and Tertullian, were vehemently opposed to Mithraism. They viewed the Mithraic "eucharist" and baptism as diabolically inspired parodies of Christian practices.

In the fourth century, Mithraism faded. Like many pagan religions, it tended to absorb other deities. Moreover, Mithraism had no organization beyond the local level, and it became diluted by regional variations. Contributing to its demise also was competition with Christianity.

Saccas, who earlier had taught Origen, the Christian scholar and theologian (see pages 158–161). Little is known of Ammonius, who guided two of the best minds of the second and third centuries. However, it can be assumed that this great teacher strongly encouraged Plotinus' quest for spiritual truth. Plotinus had heard tell of the wisdom of Indian and Persian sages, and in 243 he used connections to travel with an imperial expedition on its way to invade Persia. The spiritual quest turned into a dangerous mission, and Plotinus barely escaped with his life.

A year later Plotinus settled in Rome, where his brilliance was attested to by all who heard him speak. He won the admiration of the emperor Gallienus and his wife, Salonina. Plotinus tried, without success, to persuade the emperor to construct a city whose inhabitants would live according to Plato's *Laws*.

A mystic by nature, Plotinus strove throughout his life to experience the unknowable One, which he also called the Good. To that end, he worked to keep himself spiritually pure, much as the desert fathers had done. According to Porphyry of Tyre, his student and biographer, Plotinus lived an ascetic life and went repeatedly without sleep in order to spend the night meditating. This was a practice that he called "the prayer of quiet." For his efforts, Porphyry reports in *The Life of Plotinus*, the philosopher was rewarded with a mystical union with the One, no less than four times. To achieve that union, Plotinus believed that the individual must exert both intellectual and moral effort. Reunion does not require the grace of God, as taught in Christian mysticism; rather it can be achieved by understanding and will.

During his mature years, Plotinus devoted energy to refuting what he saw as one of the biggest enemies of philosophy—namely dualism, which he believed impeded the understanding of the One. (Dualism is the name given to theories that incorporate two opposing principles of the universe, such as good and evil or light and darkness.) Plotinus wrote down his thoughts in a collection titled the *Enneads*. One of the essays in the *Enneads* is directed against the dualism of the Gnostics (see pages 129–131). Plotinus fervently believed that all of the universe emanated from God, and he disagreed with the Gnostics, who preached that the universe was divided into realms of light and dark. Moreover, Plotinus was against the Gnostics for reviling the body as evil, for such arguments make men hate what he considered to be a natural, albeit inferior, part of the universe.

Porphyry, a fierce critic of the church

When Plotinus died in 270, his mantle went to his most gifted pupil, Porphyry. A devoted student of Neoplatonism, Porphyry lacked Plotinus' creativity, but he was a remarkable scholar who became a forceful opponent of Christianity.

Porphyry was more prolific than his teacher and wrote a diatribe, *Against the Christians*, in which he pointed out inconsistencies between the New Testament books. He argued that their stories were mainly fantasy. How else could one explain such conflicting accounts as those of the death of Judas Iscariot given in Matthew and in Acts? (In Matthew, Judas hangs himself; in Acts, he falls down and bursts open.) Porphyry thought that to convert to faith in Jesus was a "barbarian adventure." He admitted, though, that trying to reconvert a Christian to paganism was more difficult than writing letters upon the surface of the water, where the liquid closed over each stroke.

Nonetheless, Porphyry impressed many Christians, for he was one of the few pagan intellectuals to demonstrate an interest in the Bible. His theological questions were straightforward and effective: What will the resurrected body actually be like? What about the souls of people who lived before Jesus and had no opportunity to believe? In the end, Porphyry and his philosophy receded from center stage, but his work had to be answered and refuted by educated Christians. It sparked responses in a number of Christian

Plotinus was a Neoplatonic philosopher who often spent entire nights in deep contemplation over the divine principle that he called the One. When he died at the age of 66, after a long, painful illness, his last words were to a close friend: "I was waiting for you, before the divine principle in me departs to unite itself with the divine in the universe."

apologists. His treatise, *Against the Christians*, was still considered so powerful 150 years later that a Christian emperor had his writings burned.

Lactantius, a staunch defender of the faith

Try as they might, pagan philosophers could not discredit Christianity, for Christian scholars were just as resolute in its defense. Lactantius, known as the Christian Cicero for his mastery of Latin rhetoric, was the first Latin author systematically to refute paganism in favor of Christianity. In 303, when Diocletian began his persecutions, Lactantius was dismissed from his post as teacher of rhetoric and began writing several commentaries and histories of the time. He lived in poverty until Constantine, the first Christian emperor, appointed him as tutor to his son Crispus. Lactantius' principal works eloquently attack pagan writing on morals and theology while explaining the Christian point of view.

Lactantius addressed issues, such as divine justice, that were widely discussed by pagan intellectuals. He asserted that all men have the right to make their own religious judgments and to inquire freely after the truth. One of his few surviving prose works, *On the Deaths of the Persecutors*, is a history showing God's wrath against tormentors of Christians. Beginning with Nero, who died by his own hand, Lactantius argued that all who had persecuted Jesus' followers had died a horrible death.

The apologist is also remembered for a remarkable and moving symbolic poem, "The Phoenix." The myth of the phoenix, which appeared in Egyptian as well as Greek and Latin literature, concerns an Eastern bird that lives for as long as a thousand years, dies in flames, then rises again from its own ashes. This symbol of rebirth was adopted by early Christians to stand for the Resurrection of Jesus and for their own. One writer cited the tale in relation to John 10:18: "I have power to lay it [my life] down, and . . . to take it again." In Jewish lore, the phoenix earned long life by refusing to eat the forbidden fruit in Eden. According to tradition, Eve had successfully tempted all of the other animals in the garden, except for the phoenix.

> *Her body, destroyed . . . grows warm, and*
> *the heat itself gives birth to a flame, and from*
> *the ethereal light afar off it conceives fire;*
> *it blazes, and, when scorched, it dissolves*
> *into ashes . . . nature stirs up, and it has*
> *effect like to that of seed. Hence an animal is*
> *said to arise. . . . and the phoenix sprouts*
> *forth when the shell has broken.*

Lactantius was the first one to write a poem devoted to the myth. His aim, as understood from the above fragment, was to portray the promise of Jesus.

Catacombs, early Christian cemeteries

From the middle of the second century onward, an increase in Christian converts is partly confirmed by the large number of Christian catacombs, or underground burial sites, they created. The dead entombed in 42 catacombs around Rome alone have been estimated at up to 750,000 laid in 60 to 90 miles of tunnels along the Appian Way and other major roads surrounding the city. They were located there because a law forbade burying the dead inside the city walls.

On the Italian peninsula such burial places existed as early as the sixth century B.C. and have been found throughout the Mediterranean area. But they became especially popular in the second and third centuries A.D., when suburban land prices were costly. A certain type of rock in the vicinity of Rome lent itself to fairly easy tunneling, yet it was sturdy enough to support multiple layers, which, of course, could accommodate more burial sites per acre.

Cremation had been practiced since the beginning of imperial times, but Christians, like many Jews, preferred burial because they hoped for resurrection after death. In fact, *cemetery* comes from the Christian use of the Greek word *koimeterion*, which means "bedchamber." So that even the poor could have a proper burial, wealthy Christians began to share family crypts with their brethren during the second century. A number of catacombs are named for these generous patrons, who often had their vaults richly decorated. The church took on the responsibility for burials in the third century, making the land available and specifying that costs be kept nominal. Professionals, called diggers, usually did the tunneling and decorating. An ideal site was a low, wide hill, which could be entered from the base. If the excavations began at ground level, a long stairway had to be dug.

As the burial sites of favorite martyrs drew large crowds to certain catacombs for memorial services, vents were provided to let in light and air from the surface. People vied for the prestige of being buried near a martyr's tomb, probably hoping to share in the bliss of the martyr in the next life. By the ninth century, most of the martyrs' remains had been moved to churches in Rome because of repeated raids of the tombs by barbarian invaders. The catacombs were then forgotten until rediscovered in the 16th century.

Diocletian the despot

By 300, Diocletian had succeeded in restoring the peace, as well as Rome's reputation. To awaken a reverence for authority in a government riddled with corruption, he adopted an imperious, semidivine style of governing. He ignored the Senate, began wearing a diadem set with pearls, and ordered all visitors to prostrate themselves on the floor in his presence.

Diocletian had always venerated the state's traditional gods, choosing Jupiter, chief god of Rome's pantheon, as his own personal protector. The emperor was so resolute in his paganism that he issued an edict in 295 stating, "The Roman empire has attained its present greatness by the favor of all deities only because it has protected all its laws with wise religious observance and concern for morality." Those that he considered to be acting immorally, such as the followers of the prophet Mani (see pages 167–169), were arrested and sentenced to hard labor in the mines.

In the beginning of his reign, Diocletian was somewhat tolerant of Christians. From his palace in his new capital of Nicomedia (modern Izmit, Turkey), he looked out upon a Christian basilica on the adjacent hill. Reportedly, his wife and daughter, along with many of his personal retinue, sympathized with those who professed belief in Jesus. Perhaps also the large numbers of Christians serving in the government and

Continued on page 204

The phoenix, a mythical bird that rose from its ashes, was considered a Christian symbol of resurrection. The magnificent sixth-century mosaic of the phoenix, above, adorns the apse of the Church of SS. Cosmas and Damian in Rome.

The Roman catacombs consisted of long, narrow galleries, or tunnels, with rectangular niches carved on both sides. A typical example is the Catacomb of Priscilla, above. Mourners traditionally placed vases of perfume and terra-cotta lamps above the crypts of the deceased.

Geometric patterns and floral garlands, painted by diggers, mark the entrance to a funeral chamber in the Catacomb of Pamphilus. The figure of the Good Shepherd, a favorite representation of Jesus, is shown (upside down) at the top of the vault.

This third-century fresco of a basket of bread and fish graces the crypt of Lucina in the Catacomb of Callistus. The bread and fish probably represent the miracle of the loaves and fishes, a precursor of the eucharistic meal.

The Art of the Catacombs

Surrounding Rome are 42 catacombs in which Christians buried their dead from about A.D. 150 to 410. Discovered within these labyrinthine tunnels was a wealth of murals, sculptured sarcophagi, and small artifacts. Rich in symbolism, many catacomb paintings are the earliest surviving examples of Christian art.

In the Catacomb of Via Latina, a scene from the book of Numbers in the Old Testament is painted on the arch of a burial chamber. Balaam (on the donkey) is admonished by the angel of the Lord, who brandishes a sword at the renowned diviner for not wholeheartedly following the will of God.

The cemetery of Via Anapo, just discovered in 1921, contains five funeral chambers with spectacular third-century frescoes. The ceiling vault of the third chamber is decorated with a stunning scene of Jesus and the twelve Apostles. All the figures were first incised in the fresh plaster, then painted.

Christian crypts in the catacombs were often decorated with pictures like this one of Jesus performing the miracle of the loaves. He is shown here using a special rod. The scene was painted sometime in the late third century.

military stayed his hand. Diocletian's tolerance, however, was not shared by the other members of his tetrarchy. His caesar in the East, Galerius, was fiercely anti-Christian. In 297 Galerius had won a decisive victory over the Persians and subsequently had declared himself a son of Mars, the god of war. He believed that the enemy would never have gained strength in the first place if the gods had not been angry because they were not being universally worshiped throughout the Roman Empire. Because Christians refused to pay homage to the state gods, he concluded that they were hostile to the empire.

Galerius' notions finally hit their mark during a sacrifice in 298. Both he and Diocletian were watching as the priests ritually killed the animals and examined their livers for marks that would interpret the future. Much to Diocletian's embarrassment, the priests failed to find any signs. The augurs blamed it on the presence of nonbelievers. According to Lactantius, who recorded the fateful event, some in the court had noticed that Christians in attendance had made the sign of the cross. Upon hearing this, Diocletian was so infuriated, he ordered all present to make a sacrifice to the gods or be flogged. Moreover, he demanded that every soldier do the same or be discharged.

An even greater test of faith

Diocletian managed to put the troubling incident behind him but not Galerius. He began to insist that Christians be vigorously suppressed. Diocletian believed that violence, however well meant, would only harm the empire. Nonetheless, he sent an augur to ask the oracle of Apollo at Didyma for guidance. The oracle's enigmatic reply was, "The just upon earth stand in the way of his speaking the truth." A priest at court told Diocletian that "the just" meant Christians. Diocletian was assured that the oracle approved of the suppression of Christianity; he sided with Galerius and issued the first of a series of edicts that would shatter the Christian community for the next decade.

On February 23, 303, Diocletian ordered that the church he had viewed for so many years be razed and its copies of sacred writings burned. An official edict, posted the next day, stated that churches were to be demolished throughout the empire and all Christian books burned. Those followers of the faith who held power were no longer protected, for the edict also dismissed all Christians from public office.

Some of the faithful attempted to protest but were brutally silenced. When one bold Christian ripped down a copy of the edict posted in the forum of Nicomedia, he was captured and tortured. An unexplained fire in Diocletian's palace gave Galerius cause to blame Christians, but Diocletian held back until a second fire broke out two weeks later. Apparently feeling pushed to the extreme, he ordered the entire imperial court, including his wife and daughter, to offer sacrifice. Some Christian chamberlains refused and were martyred.

More horrors were to come. A second edict, issued several months later, condemned all Christian clergy to prison. The jails became so full that a third edict followed shortly thereafter ordering Christian prisoners to make sacrifice and then be freed.

According to Eusebius, some church leaders did lapse, "hiding disgracefully in one place or another." Others, however, proved so stubborn that frustrated officials physically coerced them to act out the letter of the law and make a sacrifice. In his *Martyrs of Palestine,* Eusebius recorded the lengths to which the government went to have the ordinance carried out: "Thus, in the case of one man, others held him fast by both hands, brought him to the altar, and let fall on it out of his right hand the polluted and accursed sacrifice: then he was dismissed."

Those Christians who handed over copies of Scripture were branded *traditores* (Latin for "traitors.") In North Africa, 47 church members, who insisted upon worshiping despite the ban, were imprisoned. Their bishop, however, was considered a traitor for allowing church Scriptures to be burned. All 47 died of starvation but not before agreeing that all ecclesiastics who allowed secular authorities to destroy the Bible would be condemned to eternal damnation.

Council of Elvira

In the West, where many Christians were spared, the issue of Christian discipline burned intensely. A council of 45 Spanish clergy met probably sometime around 310 in Elvira, a town in southern Spain. This small group set down the church's first known rules of discipline. The canons from the Council of Elvira list the offense and the ensuing punishment. One of the few means of punishment open to the church at that time was excommunication, or denying a member the right to partake of the Eucharist. For example, the council determined that the sin of heresy barred a reformed penitent from sharing the Eucharist for 10 years. The graver sins of adultery, incest, and false accusation that caused the accused's death, however, called for sterner punishment—permanent excommunication. The Spanish clergy ruled that the sinner was not allowed to take communion, "even at the last." For the first time, the last rites, which invoke God to confer everlasting life, were used as a threat.

The threat of explusion was also wielded. The Council of Elvira was the first on record to order members of the clergy "to abstain completely from their wives and not to have children." Those who disobeyed this rule were deposed from their office.

Zealots for paganism

In the winter of 303, Diocletian fell ill. Some historians believe that he suffered a nervous breakdown; others speculate that he had a lingering infection. Whatever the ailment, Diocletian left many imperial duties in the hands of Galerius, who took the opportunity to issue the harshest edict of all against the Christians. Written in 304, it commanded all men, women, and children to sacrifice to the pagan gods, on pain of death. Many lives were lost. In the East, particularly, thousands of Christians were killed. In Phrygia, an entire Christian town was destroyed and its inhabitants burned to death for refusing to deny their faith and sacrifice to pagan idols.

Diocletian did recover from his malady, but for reasons that still mystify historians, he decided to retire. After ruling the empire for two decades, he now became the first emperor to abdicate voluntarily. At his urging, Maximian retired with him in 305.

While the persecutions continued for another seven years, Diocletian lived peacefully in his retirement palace on the Adriatic, in present-day Split, Yugoslavia (much of the building is still standing). According to a famous anecdote, Diocletian was once urged by Maximian to return to power, but he replied that he had

In 303 the emperor Diocletian unleashed his campaign of terror against the Christians. He issued an edict to confiscate all church property. In a typical incident, soldiers forced open church doors during a service and, with the help of local pagan leaders, ransacked the place for valuables, such as gold chalices, silver lamps, and glass altar vessels. The most prized items of booty, however, were Christian texts. Scriptures not hidden in time were seized and burned. "Bring out what you have," was the order of the day. Presbyters who refused to hand over their sacred books were arrested.

succeeded in growing very good cabbages in his garden and did not wish to forgo his pleasure in them for the demands of the imperial court.

Despite Diocletian's retirement, his edicts continued to inflict widespread harm and misery. Galerius was now master of the state and, more important, the military commander in the East. His first act was to overrule the old tetrarchy by refusing to permit the sons of Constantius and Maximian (Constantine and Maxentius) to become a part of the new tetrarchy. Instead, Galerius chose his nephew, Maximinus Daia, and a fellow officer, named Severus, as his caesars. Constantius, who had been promoted to augustus in the West, reluctantly approved.

According to Eusebius, who recorded much of the persecution, Maximinus Daia proved to be as zealous a pagan as his uncle Galerius. His first order was to repair pagan temples and appoint priests to serve in them. He went so far as to offer tax exemptions to cities that helped persecute Christians in their midst.

In 306 Maximinus Daia extended the reign of terror to the provinces. Everyone, regardless of age or sex, was ordered to sacrifice at the temples. Those who refused were to be killed. The emperor was intent on bringing Christians back to the pagan fold. But their resistance was so firm that he commuted the death penalty to mutilation and forced labor in mines and quarries. Soon the stone quarries of Egypt were so crowded with Christian convicts that many were sent along to the copper mines of southern Palestine.

The crumbling tetrarchy

The tetrarchy, Diocletian's creation to ensure political stability, was weakening from within. Mistrustful of Constantius in the West, Galerius had kept Constantius' son and heir, the ambitious Constantine, more or less under house arrest in his court in the East. But the wily young man gave the slip to the emperor's guards and rode night and day to Gaul, joining his father before a military foray into Britain. The armies of the West were devoted to Constantius, for he was upright and humane. His brave son, Constantine, earned his own share of their loyalty. When Constantius died in 306, the army urged the title of augustus, or full emperor, upon his son, but Constantine knew that would mean war with Galerius; he chose the lesser title of caesar, for the time being.

Severus had been promoted to augustus; when he died in 307, Maximinus Daia no doubt assumed that Galerius would now promote him to augustus in the West, but instead Galerius appointed Licinius, his old friend and brother-in-law. At news of this slight, both Constantine and Maximinus Daia proclaimed themselves augusti in the West. Galerius could no longer contain the ambitions of his colleagues.

Maximinus Daia continued his fanatic paganism, ordering that all food sold in the markets be sprinkled with blood from the sacrifices and that everyone, including babes in arms, be forced to taste the sacrificed meat. From this, even the pagans shrank in disgust.

In the spring of 311, fate took an unexpected turn. Galerius developed a painful malady. He began to fear that he had angered the God of the Christians. At his wife's urging, he issued in April 311 an edict of toleration. It granted "henceforth that Christians should exist and restore their assemblies, provided they do nothing against good order." In return, Galerius hoped, "they will be bound to entreat their god for our well-being." At last there was peace and all Christian prisoners were freed. The proclamation closed with yet another request for Christian prayers for the emperor. Galerius died within a week after issuing his decree. With his death, the empire would now go to the man who could claim it first.

Constantine was in the north warring against the Franks. Maxentius, the son of Maximian, took control of Italy, while Maximinus Daia raced to the prize territory, Asia Minor, and claimed its capital, Nicomedia, thus ousting Licinius, who subsequently teamed up with Constantine. By 312, the Roman

When Constantine defeated Maxentius at the Battle of the Milvian Bridge in 312, he turned the tide of history. In this ninth-century illumination, Constantine is crossing the historic bridge toward Rome. A cross hovers in the background, a testament to Constantine's vision of Christ's support and power that insured his victory. Four of the original arches of the Ponte Milvio *(as the bridge is known in Italian) still stand today, as seen below.*

Empire was poised on the brink of civil war. The two great hallmarks of Diocletian's reign, the tetrarchy and the persecution, had failed. Four men were now fighting to rule the empire. To better their individual chances, Maximinus Daia and Maxentius conspired against Constantine and Licinius.

"In this sign, conquer"

Anticipating his rivals, Constantine crossed the Alps in 312 and sped his troops toward Rome with such disciplined rigor that one historian compared his advance with Julius Caesar's momentous march after crossing the Rubicon River. Heavily outnumbered, the forces of Constantine charged the imperial army of Maxentius on October 28 at Saxa Rubra ("Red Rocks"), a site some nine miles north of Rome. Maxentius was forced to fight with his back to the Tiber River, where the only retreat possible was over the

Ancient "Christograms"

In Constantine's hands the magical Chi-Rho monogram, which he had perceived in a vision at a turning point in his life, became an emblem of Christianity's triumph over paganism. Constantine believed that this symbol, formed from the first two letters (X and P) in the Greek spelling of the name Christ (ΧΡΙΣΤΟΣ), had the power both to inspire and protect.

The Chi-Rho emblem became popular among Christians during the fourth and fifth centuries. It was carved into the walls of the catacombs and figured in wall paintings, floor mosaics, lamps, goblets, vases, wedding rings, coins, and amulets. As an abbreviation for "Christ," it was also used in manuscripts and inscriptions. By the late Middle Ages, the Chi-Rho was being replaced by the Latin letters IHS, a partial transliteration of the first three letters of Jesus' name in Greek (ΙΗΣΟΥΣ).

The letters IHS have been thought to stand for a number of other names and phrases as well. Drawing on the Constantine legend, many people have believed the letters were an abbreviation for the words occurring in Latin-language accounts of the emperor's vision on the eve of the battle of the Milvian Bridge: *"In hoc signo [vinces],"* or "In this sign, [you will conquer]." Some others have thought that the IHS stands for the Latin phrase *Iesus Hominum Salvator*, "Jesus, savior of mankind." IHS has been a dominant Christogram in the church from the 15th century to the present; it frequently appears in religious art.

The Chi-Rho sign, with the Greek letters alpha and omega, is a symbol for Christ.

narrow Milvian Bridge. Before committing himself to battle, Maxentius consulted the Sibylline books, oracular texts that were said to predict the future. The entry for October 28 read: "On this day, the enemy of Rome shall perish." Maxentius declared this a good omen and prepared to fight, certain that the gods were granting him victory.

As Constantine made ready for battle, according to various reports he had a dream, or possibly a vision, in which he saw an unusual sign in the heavens and heard the Greek words *En toutoi nika* ("in this [sign], conquer"). The sign incorporated the first two letters of the name Christ in Greek: chi (X) and rho (P). On the eve of battle, Constantine made a new imperial standard, or labarum, bearing the sign of a P fixed in the center of an X, and ordered his men to emblazon the same symbol on their shields. Constantine carried the new standard during the fight and was victorious. His men routed Maxentius' armies, forcing them to retreat across the Milvian Bridge into Rome. Thousands of the soldiers, including Maxentius himself, perished in the waters of the Tiber.

Constantine's victory over Maxentius changed the course of history, for while Christianity was still a minority religion, it had symbolically triumphed over paganism. Property confiscated from churches during the persecution was ordered returned to them. When Maximinus Daia died later that year, Constantine consolidated the peace with Licinius, now augustus in the East, by giving him Constantine's half-sister in marriage. One of the first actions of the new master of the West was to join Licinius in issuing the Edict of Milan in 313, which not only confirmed the religious toleration of Christians announced by Galerius but also extended it to include adherents of all faiths. A new era of Western civilization was dawning.

Mary
Wilshire

Chapter Seven

THY KINGDOM COME

The unthinkable had happened. Rome's new co-emperor Constantine supported Christianity! Soon the church, under his patronage, would forge a lasting creed. Pagans would fight back but in vain. Meanwhile, a New Rome would arise in the East.

With the peace of Constantine, many Christians no doubt hoped, as their imperial champion did, that a golden age was at hand. In keeping with such longings, Constantine came to feel, in the second decade of his rule, that his new Christian empire should have a new capital city. He chose the small Greek seaport of Byzantium (present-day Istanbul, Turkey) for its site. It was one of the most ambitious urban renewal projects in history. In a span of about six years, from 324 to 330, little Byzantium underwent major changes in its transformation from modest seaport to metropolis. Under Constantine's direction an army of artisans descended on the city to work on scores of projects, from a basilica to an imperial palace to a newly enlarged hippodrome. On the triangle of land that served as the crossroads of Europe and Asia, *Nova Roma* ("New Rome") took shape. Posterity commonly referred to it as Constantinople ("City of Constantine"). The glittering jewel on the Bosporus eventually supplanted Rome as the center of the empire. This story of the shift of power to the East dates from the days of Constantine's rise as emperor.

Constantinople, dedicated in 330, was rich with colonnades and statuary. Its main street, the Mese, is shown here leading toward the Forum of Constantine, where a statue of the great emperor himself stands astride a column of porphyry (a purple stone).

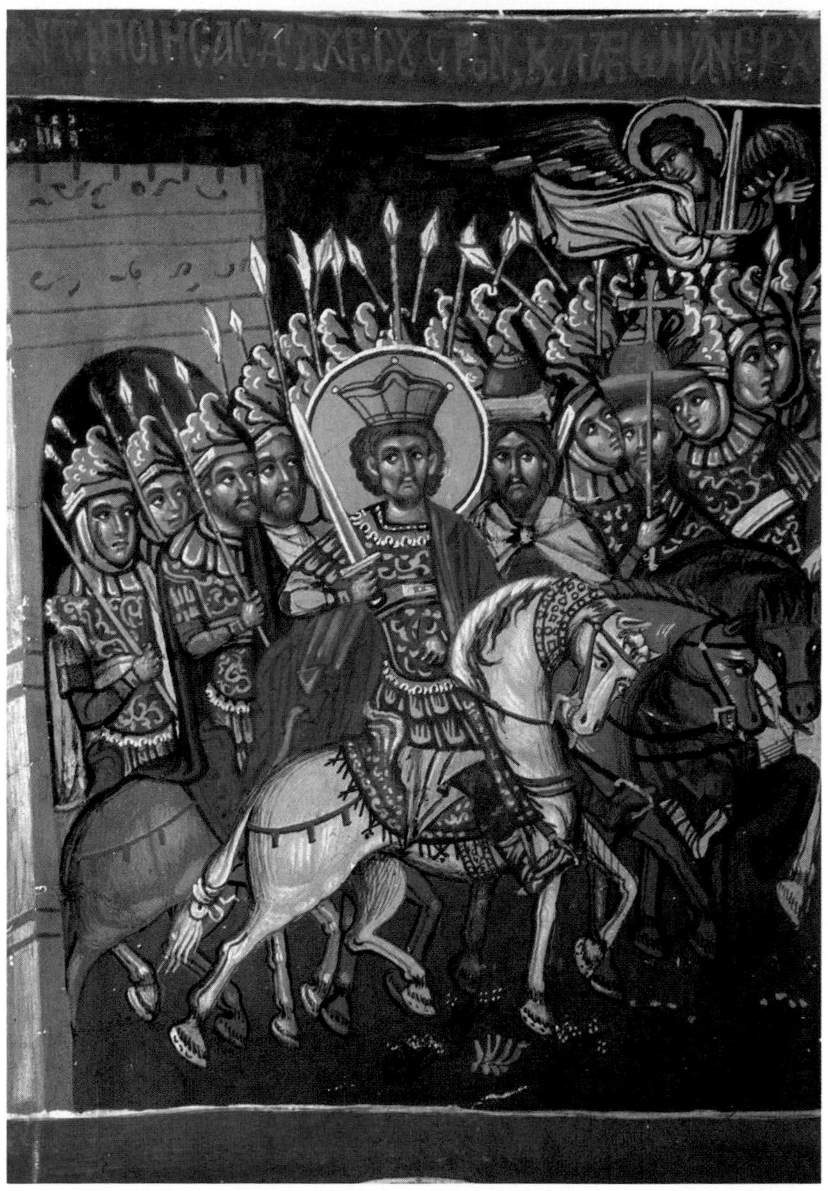

In this Byzantine painting of Constantine's triumphal entrance into Rome in 312, he wears a saint's halo and is accompanied by a guardian angel with a sword. The cross is an anachronism; it did not come into use until later.

After his victory at the Milvian Bridge, Constantine marched triumphantly into Rome on October 29, 312. The procession most likely wound through the city, giving the crowds a chance to catch a rare glimpse of their new ruler. One source says that his nickname among the people was "Bullneck." Surviving likenesses confirm this; he was built like a wrestler. As in other official processions, Constantine would have been flanked by a guard of honor in gilt or silver armor and accompanied by silk banners that floated balloonlike in the autumn air. That day, after passing through the Porta Triumphalis, along the Via Sacra, and into the Forum Romanum, Constantine met with the Senate, which confirmed him in the rank of augustus, or senior emperor.

Although Constantine had acknowledged God's help in his battle against Maxentius, apparently at first he had no exclusive commitment to Christianity. He seemed to pick and choose from Christian and pagan beliefs. While he no doubt approved when the Senate commissioned a statue of him with a Christian symbol in one hand, he also authorized a medallion that attributed his liberation of Rome to the sun god Sol Invictus ("Unconquered Sun"). And he retained the title of *pontifex maximus*, or chief priest of the state religion. (The popes later adopted the same title.)

Why did Constantine champion Christianity? The vision he claimed to have had before the battle at the Milvian Bridge possibly made an impression that deepened with the telling. Perhaps his mother, Helena, a Christian convert, had influenced him. It is even more likely that Constantine looked on Christianity from the standpoint of a pragmatist. He had seen Christians defy the odds and survive major persecutions in his lifetime. Though they were a numerically weak minority, Christians had evolved into a strong faction throughout the empire. Constantine most likely perceived that the church's extensive network could prove an invaluable aid to unifying, and subsequently ruling, a far-flung empire.

The Edict of Milan

In February 313 Constantine met with his co-emperor, Licinius, in Milan. Much of their meeting seems to have been taken up with the issue of Christianity and marks a turning point in the history of church-state relations. The two emperors dispatched a letter, which has come to be known as the Edict of Milan, to governors throughout the empire. It ordered that the state should give "complete toleration" to anyone who had "given up his mind either to the cult of the Christians" or one "which he personally feels best for himself." With a stroke of the pen all anti-Christian decrees had been revoked, and the era of persecutions had come to an end. Now Christians were not only free to worship, but their places of worship and other church property were to be returned to them.

Not everyone welcomed the Edict of Milan. Maximinus Daia, an enemy of Christianity who shared command of the East with Licinius, said Christians "were to be borne with in a long-suffering and moderate spirit" and that he valued worship of the pagan gods far above the "superstition" of the Christians.

Angered at Constantine's promotion to augustus and alarmed by the alliance between Constantine and Licinius, Maximinus Daia moved against Licinius. According to legend, on the eve of an important battle, Licinius dreamed that an angel dictated to him a prayer for victory. Transcripts of the prayer, which could be construed as either Christian or pagan, were duly distributed. The soldiers recited the prayer before the battle and, though outnumbered, emerged victorious.

The Donatist controversy

Ever since the great persecution under Diocletian the African church had been torn by undercurrents of dissension. At issue was the status of Christians who had weakened during the persecution—and behind that, the notion that only people who led blameless lives had a right to belong to the church. A powerful faction of Christians in North Africa, some of them actually eager for martyrdom, branded as "traitors" those church members who under duress had handed over Scriptures to state authorities to be destroyed. More moderate members, often the more well-to-do, declared themselves content with clergy who had gone into hiding instead of openly defying the state authorities. Denunciations and mutual recriminations flew back and forth, until things finally came to a head in 311 with the election of the moderate clergyman Caecilian as bishop of Carthage.

Measuring about 9 feet high, this huge head is one of the few remaining fragments from a colossal statue of Constantine, which may have been a seated figure. The statue once stood in the Basilica of Constantine in Rome. On a coin issued by the emperor (above), Constantine holds in his right hand the labarum, a standard that was his victory sign.

Constantine had this triumphal arch built in Rome to commemorate his victory at the Milvian Bridge. The arch contains sculpture from several earlier monuments, possibly an indication of the haste with which it was constructed.

Opponents of Caecilian, known as Donatists, claimed that his election was invalid, since he himself had been consecrated by "traitors." The Donatists, mostly from Numidia (in modern Algeria), called a synod of 70 bishops and announced that Caecilian had been deposed. In his place they ordained Majorinus, who died shortly thereafter and was replaced by Donatus, after whom the movement is named. Caecilian and his supporters did not recognize the authority of the synod. Thus, Carthage had two bishops, and the church was threatened with a full-blown schism.

Alarmed that Constantine apparently recognized Caecilian (in an official letter circulated at the time, the emperor referred to "the catholic church over which Caecilian presides"), the Donatists took their case to the emperor himself. On April 15, 313, they delivered a petition that read: "We pray you, most excellent emperor . . . whereas there are disputes between us and the other bishops in Africa, we pray that your piety may order judges to be given to us."

Constantine did intervene. "In those provinces which divine providence has voluntarily entrusted to my devoted self," the emperor declared, any division was unacceptable. He instructed Caecilian to come to Rome with 10 bishops who supported him and 10 Donatist bishops. They could present their case before Bishop Miltiades of Rome, himself a native of Roman Africa, and three bishops from the province of Gaul. Miltiades added 15 Italian bishops to the court, transforming it into a synod that ruled on matters of doctrine. After several days of testimony, the synod recognized Caecilian and ruled against Donatus. The Donatists did not accept the decision; they asked for a new judgment from Constantine. He was dismayed by the growing rift but agreed to another hearing. This time 33 bishops met in a synod at Arles and again ruled against the Donatists.

Controversy continued to rage as the Donatists refused to accept the verdict. Riots broke out in North Africa, and Donatists who were killed as a result of

The left-hand figure is Sol Invictus, or the Unconquered Sun, the god of the principal imperial cult during the century preceding Constantine's reign. The similar image to the right represents Christ Helios, or Jesus as the Sun of Righteousness. The latter, also dating from before Constantine, is in a mausoleum located under St. Peter's in Rome. The church succeeded in defeating the cult of the sun god while at the same time assimilating both his image and his birthday, December 25th. That date came to be celebrated as the birthday of Jesus some time between 274 and 336.

governmental repression were hailed by their brethren as martyrs. "I shall come to Africa," Constantine announced, "and shall most fully demonstrate . . . as much to Caecilian as to those who seem to be against him just how the Supreme Deity should be worshiped." As these words indicate, the emperor now saw himself as more than a secular ruler; he was also God's emissary, empowered to unify his church.

Constantine never went to Africa. He continued to vacillate between the urges to tolerate Donatism and to quash it. But in 316 he ruled in favor of Caecilian; the following year he not only ordered the confiscation of Donatist church property but also exiled the sect's leaders. Only three years after the Edict of Milan, the Roman state found itself once again the persecutor but this time in the name of Christian orthodoxy. Always the voice of the more humble classes, the Donatist movement held its ground. Carthage continued to be the scene of violent strife as Donatists tenaciously resisted, many choosing torture, imprisonment, and even death rather than submission to the "traitors."

Eventually, Constantine gave up in disgust and in 321 revoked his anti-Donatist edict. He had learned a lesson. Abrogating his own Edict of Milan had proved futile. Never again would he attempt to squash a movement within the church, though, as the

In this early book illustration, orthodox Christians flee in a boat that their Arian persecutors have set on fire. The fourth-century controversy over the teachings of Arius caused violence and disruption in the church for many years.

Arian conflict would soon demonstrate, he was always prone to underestimate the scope of sectarian disagreements. Constantine had failed in his first attempt to unify the church, but he had established his right as emperor to mediate ecclesiastical disputes.

The Arian controversy

While the Donatist controversy was raging in the West, another storm was brewing in Alexandria and elsewhere in the East. Like Donatism, it threatened to split the church; unlike Donatism, it involved a basic theological issue—the divinity of Christ. Once again, Constantine found himself embroiled in a heated debate within the church.

At the center of this debate was Arius, an intelligent, independent, and popular presbyter in Alexandria. Like his predecessor Origen and other Christian theologians, Arius differed with numerous believers over the nature of the Son of God and his relation to God the Father. He taught that there was "One God who is alone unbegotten, alone eternal and alone without beginning." The Son of God, Arius said, was himself created and therefore must be subordinate to the Father. ("There was a time when he [the Son] was not," is how many summed up the Arian doctrine.) In effect, Arius was denying, if not the divinity, at least the coeternity of the Son of God, Jesus Christ, in order to maintain a basic monotheism.

Other theologians held that the Son of God comes from "God himself," not "from the nonexistent," as Arius claimed. The Son of God is divine, and not only eternal, but eternally begotten, they explained. Alexander, bishop of Alexandria, ordered Arius to stcp preaching his views. It was too late. The tall, ascetic Arius, whose skills in philosophical debate were formidable, had won some strong support among the Christians of Alexandria, including the clergy. In 318, or a little later, a synod of nearly 100 Egyptian and Libyan bishops examined Arius' teachings, condemned him as a heretic, and excommunicated him.

Arius was undaunted. He gained support for his views from Eusebius, bishop of Caesarea, Eusebius, bishop of Nicomedia, and others. Just as Donatism had split the Western church, Arianism threatened to divide the East into two theological camps.

Constantine's showdown with Licinius

Divisions within the church were not Constantine's only worry. The alliance between him and Licinius had been tarnished by mutual distrust and even outright warring. As early as 314 the two had clashed over control of Italy. That dispute settled by arms, there followed five or six years of amicable relations. But Licinius' growing mistreatment of Christians drove a wedge into the alliance. Licinius in 320 withdrew his favor from the Christians, who, he suspected, owed their loyalty to Constantine rather than to himself. Throughout the empire's Eastern territories, he prohibited church synods (only at such gatherings could new bishops be consecrated), forbade women and men to worship together, and, for what he said were public health reasons, decreed that Christians could not meet in churches within a city; they must worship outdoors, beyond the walls. Bishops were imprisoned; church buildings were closed and even destroyed. Licinius also mandated a pagan sacrifice to qualify for civil service, effectively barring Christians.

Licinius' persecution of Christians gave Constantine an excuse to move against his co-emperor and to realize a long-cherished goal, total domination of the empire. When Constantine marched into Thrace to attack bands of marauding Goths in January 323, Licinius accused him of violating his territory. The die was cast; civil war was declared. Constantine treated it more like a holy war than a civil war. He enlisted the aid of Christian bishops and brought with him a private chapel for use during the campaign. An elite guard of 50 soldiers was entrusted with Constantine's Christian military standard, the labarum. They were instructed to bring it wherever danger threatened. According to Eusebius, no soldier who ever carried it during a battle was killed.

Constantine marshaled 130,000 troops, Licinius, 165,000. The war began in 324, when the two armies clashed at Adrianople (modern Edirne, Turkey). Although outnumbered, Constantine's troops fought valiantly and defeated their opponents. Byzantium fell to Constantine, and at Chrysopolis, on September 18, the war was decided after Licinius' troops were decimated. Constantine spared his brother-in-law at first but later ordered his execution.

Arius' doctrine of Christ's relation to God the Father holds that Christ was at once less than God but more than man. This early painting of Jesus' baptism represents the Father, Son, and Holy Spirit.

Part of an ancient wall still stands in Nicaea, capital of the Roman province of Bithynia in what is now northwest Turkey. Shaped in a square, the city was built by Greeks about the time of Alexander the Great. In Roman times Nicaea was a major commercial center at the junction of several important roads.

The road to Nicaea

Constantine had won his civil war, but religious unity would prove to be a more elusive goal. Chief among the troubles was the Arian controversy. Constantine was determined to end it as fast as he could. At first he accused Arius and Alexander of arguing merely for the sake of arguing. In a letter to them he called the controversy "perfectly inconsequential and quite unworthy." Obviously, Constantine did not grasp the complexity of the theological issues. He did wish that they could be speedily resolved, however. "Give me back peaceful nights and days without care," he wrote, "that I too may keep some pleasure in the pure light and the joy of a tranquil life henceforth."

Constantine dispatched his letter to Alexander and Arius in the care of his ecclesiastical counselor, Ossius, the bishop of Cordoba. In 312, after suffering in the persecution under Maximian, Ossius had joined Constantine's court and reportedly played a major role in his conversion to Christianity.

After delivering the emperor's somewhat condescending letter and investigating the matter firsthand, Ossius decided to ally himself with Bishop Alexander against Arius. He attended, and perhaps presided over, a synod in Antioch that issued a declaration condemning Arius and his followers. At the same meeting Eusebius of Caesarea was excommunicated for his qualified support of Arius; the dispute showed no signs of abating. It had spread from Alexandria into Palestine, Syria, and Asia Minor. No longer could Constantine term it "inconsequential."

To settle the controversy, in 325 Constantine summoned bishops and their representatives to join him at what would be the first—and most famous—general council in the history of the Christian church, the Council of Nicaea. Messengers were dispatched from Rome to bishops in every corner of the empire with Constantine's summons to "assemble . . . without delay in anything" at a small city in Bithynia with an agreeable climate (modern Iznik in northwestern Turkey). This choice of venue would enable Constantine to "be near to watch and take part in the proceedings," as he put it in his summons. The message was one of urgency, and envoys were offered free use of public conveyances to go to the council (a privilege that soon became common practice).

More than 200 answered the call. Only a scattering of representatives came from the West. (For the next several centuries, controversies in which the nature of Christ was at issue proved to be a peculiarly Eastern, in other words, Greek, preoccupation.) Pleading poor health, Bishop Sylvester of Rome sent two envoys to represent him. Besides Ossius of Cordoba and Caecilian of Carthage, the two or three other Westerners who came were outnumbered by the delegation from Egypt, by the 100 or so from Asia Minor, and by some 20 from Palestine; but they were sufficient to make the Council of Nicaea the first true ecumenical council of the Christian church.

All leading scholars and theologians of the Eastern Empire came, including Eusebius of Caesarea (the future church historian), Eusebius of Nicomedia (the powerful Arian bishop who occasionally served as Constantine's adviser), Alexander of Alexandria, and Marcellus of Ancyra (modern Ankara). Some, such as Eusebius of Nicomedia, were, and would remain in spite of the way they voted in Nicaea, sympathetic to Arius' views. However, most of the delegates were simple servants of the church, conservative and perhaps anti-intellectual, or at least mistrustful of change. Some bore the title of "confessor," bestowed upon them for their sufferings under persecution.

The Council of Nicaea

On a late spring morning in 325 the bishops filled the great hall of Nicaea's imperial residence. Waiting for the emperor, they took their places, which were assigned according to rank, on benches that ran down both sides of the hall. At a sign, all rose, and Constantine, now about 45 years old, entered, wrapped in his imperial robes. He must have cut an impressive fig-

The Council of Nicaea in 325 laid the groundwork for the Nicene Creed, a statement of belief still accepted by members of the Roman Catholic, Eastern Orthodox, and some Protestant churches. The figure reclining in the foreground and holding his ears is Arius. Over his shoulder is a scroll identifying him as one who fought against God.

This page from an Ethiopian Bible depicts the nativity of Jesus, whose divinity was debated at the Council of Nicaea. The Ethiopian (Abyssinian) Church was founded by Frumentius, a foe of Arianism, early in the fourth century.

ure, with his broad shoulders, firm jaw, and manly bearing. Without guards, he walked to a small gilded chair in the middle of the hall and invited the bishops to be seated. With equal deference, the bishops indicated that the emperor should have precedence in sitting down. To resolve the predicament, everyone sat down simultaneously.

There are no surviving contemporary descriptions of the proceedings at the Council of Nicaea. According to later accounts, however, feelings over the Arian question ran high, and debate was acrimonious. Some bishops held their hands over their ears when Arius spoke. Constantine himself reportedly referred later to Arius as "that shameless servant of the Devil" and to the theology of his own adviser and Arian sympathizer, Eusebius of Nicomedia, as "drunken railing." Did the emperor lose his temper during the actual sessions at Nicaea? It is easy to imagine him absenting himself, yet the sources say that he stuck out all two months of meetings to the end.

At this distance in time, the theological issue in the Arian controversy may seem to have been merely a matter of semantics. But in fact it touched the very heart of Christianity at a moment when the church was struggling to satisfy two distinct needs. On the one hand, the church had given the world a monotheistic religion available to everybody; on the other hand, it distinguished itself clearly from Judaism by its belief in the divinity of Christ. How divine was he? If he was fully divine, were there not two Gods? Or, counting the Holy Spirit, three Gods?

Arius was so much a monotheist that, in his eagerness to preserve the singularity of God the Father, he felt he had to deny something—not divinity exactly, but coeternity—to Christ the Son. The classic Arian formula was: "If the Father begat the Son, he that was begotten had a beginning of existence; hence it is clear that there was a time when the Son was not. It follows then of necessity that he had his existence from the non-existent." That is, Christ, unlike God, came from nothing; hence, the Son was subordinate to the Father. To many church members who, like Arius himself, had embraced the notion of a Jesus born of the Virgin Mary, resurrected from the dead, and risen to sit at the right hand of the Father, this view seemed both reasonable and scriptural, while to others it was not just wrongheaded, it was outright heresy.

In an attempt to walk a middle line between factions, Eusebius of Caesarea offered a baptismal creed that had long been traditional in Palestine and Syria. This creed went in part as follows:

We believe in one God, the Father, almighty, the maker of all things visible and invisible. And in one Lord Jesus Christ, the Word of God, God from God, light from light, life from life, only-begotten Son, first-born of all creation, begotten from the Father before all the ages, by whom also all things were made, who for our salvation was made flesh and lived among men, and suffered, and rose again the third day, and ascended to the Father, and will come again in glory to judge the living and the dead. And we believe also in one Holy Spirit.

While Constantine approved of this profession of faith, many bishops who had come to Nicaea for the express purpose of condemning Arianism complained that it seemed to incorporate both the orthodox and Arian views. Indeed, the Arian bishops found nothing in it they could not subscribe to. So the conservative side demanded a creed that clearly excluded Arius' ideas. The solution came from an unexpected quarter.

Constantine's decisive intervention

Could not the creed be amended to include the word *homoousios* ("consubstantial," or "of the same substance"), Constantine suggested, when describing the relationship of the Father to the Son? It was a loaded (and already much debated) word, which had been used by certain third-century Christians who were condemned for denying the Trinity. There was also widespread popular opposition to the term because it was not in the Scriptures. Putting it forward in this way was not only audacious on Constantine's part but a deft political move, for no matter what else Arians were ready to tolerate in a conciliar creed, this term, in particular, Arius himself had rejected in his recent formal declaration of faith. So the great advantage of this word, from the standpoint of anti-Arians, the majority at Nicaea, was that it was absolutely unacceptable to Arians.

Eventually, no doubt due to the emperor's prestige and powers of persuasion as well as the threat of excommunication, all but Arius and two of the council's bishops went along with Constantine's suggestion. The final version read:

We believe in one God, the Father, almighty, maker of all things visible and invisible;

And in one Lord Jesus Christ, the Son of God, only-begotten from the Father, that is, from the substance of the Father, God from God, light from light, true God from true God, begotten not made, of one substance [homoousios] *with the Father, through whom all things came into being, things in heaven and things on earth, who for us men and for our salvation came down and became flesh, becoming man, suffered and rose again on the third day, ascended into heaven, and will come to judge the living and the dead;*

And in the Holy Spirit. But as for those who say, "There was when he was not," and "Before being born he was not," and that he came into existence out of nothing, or who assert that the Son of God is of a different reality or substance, or is subject to alteration or change—these the catholic and apostolic church anathematizes.

This last sentence contains four anathemas, or ecclesiastical condemnations, against four of the major Arian tenets. It was for this kind of statement that the anti-Arian bishops had been holding out. Even if they had doubts about Constantine's *homoousios,* they must have been pleased with the anathemas.

Though the Arian controversy continued to fester, the Council of Nicaea had set a historic precedent as

Battle over an *i: Homoousios* or *Homoiousios?*

Are God the Father and God the Son "identical" or only "similar?" This question so vexed the conscience of fourth-century Christians that it became a burning political issue and remained so for the next several hundred years. Bishop Gregory of Nyssa described the situation in Constantinople in 378: "In this city if you ask anyone for change, he will discuss with you whether the Son is begotten or unbegotten. If you ask about the quality of bread, you will receive the answer that 'the Father is greater, the Son is less.' " The Council of Constantinople, convened by Emperor Theodosius I in 381 in order to unite the church, was destined to set the course for Christian orthodoxy down to modern times. For it was there that the Nicene Creed took its present form, thus resolving a struggle among four contending parties. Here is a thumbnail sketch of the contenders at Constantinople and their respective positions.

Arians

Watchword: "dissimilar" (*anomoios*)

Beliefs: God the Father and God the Son are dissimilar in essence. The Son is divine but not fully divine. Because the Son was begotten by the Father, there must have been a time when the Son did not exist. The Son is subject to the Father, and the Holy Spirit is subject to the Son.

Advocates: Arius himself and a powerful group of Eastern bishops, including Constantine's Arian adviser, Eusebius of Nicomedia, all of whom were opposed to the Nicaean doctrine of identical substance because, in their view, it obliterated the distinction between God the Father and God the Son.

Developments: Arianism flourished in the East until Theodosius I presided over its demise at the Council of Constantinople in 381. By that time it had been transmitted to the Goths north of the Danube by their first bishop, Wulfila, an Arian. Goths later brought Arianism to the West, where it remained an obstacle to religious unity for the next 400 years.

Semi-Arians

Watchword: "similar" (*homoios*)

Beliefs: The Son is similar to the Father but not in all things. He is not a "creature" of God in the way that angels and mankind are defined as "creatures." The word *homoousios* ("of identical substance") used by the Nicaeans is wrong because it is not in the Bible. The word *homoios* ("similar") is in the Bible and therefore acceptable. Semi-Arians also used the term *homoiousios* ("of like substance") for Father and Son.

Advocates: Emperor Constantius (reigned 353–361) and several prominent bishops led by Basil of Ancyra.

Developments: Synods in Sirmium (357), Ariminum (359), and Selencia (also 359) put this party in a controlling position in both East and West for a few years. This was the fateful period of which Jerome was to comment retrospectively that "the whole world groaned in astonishment to find itself Arian." The semi-Arians remained influential until 381, although the victory of orthodoxy at the Council of Constantinople was partly thanks to Semi-Arian backing of the Cappadocians, who were on the winning side.

Nicaeans

Watchword: "of identical substance" (*homoousious*)

Beliefs: The Father and the Son are of identical substance with each other. The Son must have full divinity in order to vanquish evil and save sinners.

Advocates: Bishop Athanasius of Alexandria, Bishop Hilary of Poitiers, and others, especially in the West. The Nicaean party enjoyed strong popular support in many places. Constantine endorsed the Nicaean side during the Council of Nicaea (325) and for a while afterward but seems to have spent his later years endeavoring to accommodate and reconcile all sides.

Developments: The Nicaean party was vindicated at Constantinople in 381, thanks in part to the backing of Theodosius I, and then again in 451 at the Council of Chalcedon. Eastern and Western churches remained divided on some issues, but the Nicene Creed, as put forth by the Nicaeans and their neo-Nicaean allies, the Cappadocians, has remained a basic article of faith for Christians East and West ever since.

Cappadocians

Watchword: "of like substance" (*homoiousios*)

Beliefs: Like the Nicaeans, the Cappadocians believed that God the Father and God the Son were of identical substance; but they also emphasized that the Father and the Son were distinct, though equally divine—hence their term *homoiousios*, "of like substance."

Advocates: Bishop Basil of Caesarea, Bishop Gregory of Nyssa, and Bishop Gregory of Nazianzus, who were all from the province of Cappadocia (in present-day Turkey).

Developments: Cappadocians joined forces with Nicaeans in 381 and were instrumental in winning over enough Eastern bishops to condemn Arian and Semi-Arian hold-outs. *Homoousios* was confirmed, but henceforth it was understood to mean *homoiousious*. In other words, "of identical substance" meant the same as "of like substance." Athanasius' watchword stuck, but it was Eastern theology—holding to the separateness of the Son and the Father—that really won out in the end.

the first ecumenical Christian council. Its decisions became church orthodoxy, upon which future generations would base their worship. Christianity had, in its triumph over paganism, found its voice, and Constantine as its official spokesman was more committed now than ever to Christianizing the empire.

How today's Nicene Creed evolved

Today's version of the Nicene Creed, the only Christian creed accepted as authoritative by the Roman Catholic, Eastern Orthodox, Anglican, and major Protestant churches, bears a general resemblance to the original. Subsequent to the meeting in Nicaea, however, it underwent some changes.

Two other councils were apparently vital to the development of the Nicene Creed as we know it today, though details are blurred by the passage of centuries. The official proceedings of a council called in 451 at Chalcedon refer not only to the fathers who met in Nicaea but also to the "150 who met at a later date." Scholars believe the latter is a reference to a council that met in Constantinople in 381 to deal with new questions that had arisen in the 56 years since Nicaea. No one can say if the creed was simply reaffirmed at Constantinople or significantly revised, but we do know that by 451, when it was promulgated at Chalcedon, the creed was recognizably the one we know today. (This version, called the Nicene Creed by most people, is referred to by some historians as the Niceno-Constantinopolitan Creed.)

The anti-Arian anathemas were gone from the new version, so that the creed was unspoiled by any note of discord. It had been rewritten to begin with the creation and end with the life of the world to come. Also there was now a paragraph on the Holy Spirit. The only thing added to the creed after Chalcedon was the so-called *Filioque* clause (Latin for "and [from] the Son") to the effect that the Holy Spirit proceeds from the Father "and the Son." This clause represented yet another effort to claim full divinity for Christ. The clause never took hold in the Eastern churches, where it was considered theologically incorrect; but otherwise, the version since Chalcedon is identical with what is now known as the Nicene Creed.

We believe in one God, the Father, almighty, maker of heaven and earth, of all things visible and invisible;

And in one Lord Jesus Christ, the only Son of God, begotten from the Father before all ages, light from light, true God from true God, begotten not made, of one substance [homoousios] *with the Father, through whom all things came into being, who for us men and for our salvation came down from heaven, and became flesh from the Holy Spirit and the Virgin Mary and became man, and was crucified for our sake under Pontius Pilate, and suffered and was buried, and rose again on the third day according to the Scriptures, and ascended into the heavens, and sits on the right hand of the Father, and will come again with glory to judge the living and the dead, of whose kingdom there will be no end;*

And in the Holy Spirit, the Lord and life-giver, who proceeds from the Father [and the Son (Filioque)*], who with the Father and the Son is worshiped and glorified, who spoke through the prophets; and in one, holy, catholic and apostolic church. We confess one baptism for the remission of sins; we look forward to the resurrection of the dead and the life of the world to come. Amen.*

The creed is used by Western churches in the eucharistic liturgy and for both baptism and the Eucharist in Eastern churches. Its concise, elegant phrases have echoed Christian faith throughout the ages.

After Nicaea

"For the decision of three hundred bishops must be considered no other than the judgment of God," is the way Constantine grandly described the resolutions made at the Council of Nicaea. Before long, though, he realized that not everyone agreed with his estimation of the recently concluded council. A month or so after the council, he learned that Eusebius, bishop of Nicomedia, had served communion to the excommu-

The combative Athanasius was bishop of Alexandria for many of the years between 328 and 373. He was reportedly once asked, "How is the Son equal to the Father?" He replied, "Like the sight of two eyes."

nicated Arius and was conspiring with Theognis of Nicaea and other Arians. Enraged, Constantine exiled both bishops, then, for reasons unknown, reconsidered and decided to make up with the very men who had opposed him at Nicaea.

Some historians believe that the emperor was influenced by his mother, half-sister, and sister-in-law, all of whom were pro-Arian. Whatever the reason, in an attempt to bring Arius back into the fold, Constantine gave him a chance to repent. In a letter to the bishop of Alexandria, Constantine explained how Arius had agreed. "I tell you that Arius, *the* Arius, came to me, the Augustus, on the recommendation of many persons, promising that he believed about our Catholic Faith what was decided and confirmed at the Council of Nicaea." Satisfied that Arius was truly sincere, Constantine reassembled the Council of Nicaea in 327, readmitted him, and, for good measure, restored Eusebius and Theognis to their bishoprics.

Eusebius of Nicomedia

Not to be confused with his colleague Eusebius of Caesarea, Eusebius of Nicomedia played a pivotal role in events surrounding the Council of Nicaea. His influence with Constantine's family made him a power behind the throne. It was he who nearly singlehandedly turned what had been an Egyptian dispute over Arius into a worldwide controversy, and it was he who set in motion the political machinery that led Constantine to summon the bishops to Nicaea. His actions were to reverberate for centuries.

Born in Syria to an upper-class family, Eusebius had studied in Antioch, where he was a classmate of Arius. The two youths were star pupils of Lucian, the school's founder and a Bible scholar whose extensive editing of the New Testament formed a major base of the text that has come down to us today. Theologically, Lucian was a follower of Origen, and like Origen he held that the Son was subordinate to the Father. Lucian suffered martyrdom in Nicomedia in 312.

This image from a medieval book of hours illustrates the orthodox Trinitarian concept of God in three persons, associated with Athanasius and the creed once attributed to him. The Athanasian Creed is still used by some Western Christians.

Six years after Lucian died, Eusebius was made the bishop of Nicomedia (present-day Izmit, Turkey). He enjoyed high favor in the entourage of Licinius at this time. Licinius' wife, Constantia, a half-sister of Constantine, was his particular friend and protector. When Licinius was defeated by Constantine in 324, Eusebius owed his own survival to the protection of Constantia. He soon won Constantine's confidence, and one of the first matters he took up with him was the plight of his friend Arius. The Council of Nicaea the following year was in part the result of Eusebius' lobbying with the emperor.

At Nicaea Eusebius campaigned aggressively on behalf of Arius and signed the creedal statement only under coercion from Constantine himself. Within three months he had repudiated his signature and been exiled to Gaul. Three years later, he offered a retraction and was restored to his see in Nicomedia and to his influential position in the imperial court.

When in 337 Constantine realized he was dying, it was Eusebius of Nicomedia who baptized him. In 339 Eusebius was made bishop of Constantinople, a big promotion that made him, an avowed Arian, one of the most powerful church leaders alive. Eusebius survived his emperor by only four years. In 341, the year of his death, Eusebius consecrated the 30-year-old Wulfila, a missionary to the Goths of Dacia, north of the Danube, as first bishop of the Goths. This act had far-reaching consequences, for when the descendants of Wulfila's followers invaded the West three generations later, they took Wulfila's Arianism with them, and it constituted a major stumbling block to Christian unity until the time of Charlemagne.

Athanasius, pillar of Nicene orthodoxy

While Constantine wishfully imagined that he had at last united the Eastern church and quieted the controversy over Arianism, there was no evidence to support this. Indeed, in spite of the agreements reached at the two Councils of Nicaea, the church was racked by feuding, recriminations, and downright treachery. Arianism divided the Eastern church as bishops turned against one another, often mounting intricate intrigues to promote their theological viewpoints. To win the day, or just to survive, churchmen needed both a theologian's wisdom and a politician's savvy. One man who possessed both qualities was Athanasius, a passionate native of Alexandria and a staunch anti-Arian. Athanasius entered the clergy at about 17, was ordained a deacon some six years later, and served as secretary to Bishop Alexander. Like Alexander, Athanasius criticized the Arians for their attack on the full divinity of Christ and was a firm backer of the creed of Nicaea. Shortly after Alexander's death, Athanasius was installed as bishop of Alexandria. While his appointment was opposed by the Arians, Athanasius' supporters hailed him as "an upright man, and a virtuous, a good Christian, an ascetic."

Over the many years of his episcopate Athanasius displayed a single-mindedness that earned him much opposition. He was incapable of compromise and believed that anyone who disagreed with him was not only wrong but also evil. In his lifelong battle against Arianism, he never shied away from conflict with anyone who sided with Arius, even the emperor himself. Constantine wrote threatening to depose and exile him if he did not agree to readmit Arius to the church. But the stalwart Athanasius never wavered in his defense of the full divinity of Christ. Mankind had no chance for redemption, he believed, if Christ was less than fully divine.

The position of Athanasius and his supporters on the nature of Christ did not permit any compromise; they steadfastly upheld the "faith of Nicaea." But their opponents' views were not so simply stated. Outside Egypt most bishops in the Eastern church believed in the divinity of the Son but rejected Nicaea's "of the same substance," or "consubstantial" (*homoousios*) concept, claiming that this term erased all distinction between the Father and the Son. Others, such as Eusebius of Nicomedia, rejected it in favor of the term "of like substance" (*homoiousios*) and held that there was a definite separation between God and Christ. (The two Greek words were so similar, even though they had dissimilar meanings, that the 18th-century historian Edward Gibbon commented that "the profane of every age have derided the furious contests which the difference of a single diphthong excited between the Homoousians and the Homoiousians.")

In an attempt to topple Athanasius, Eusebius and his supporters allied themselves with the Melitians (a splinter group who believed they had been victimized by Athanasius) and even went so far as to accuse him of murdering a Melitian bishop and using the corpse for black magic. Even when Athanasius produced the "victim" alive and well in court, the Melitians said "he had used his magic arts to fool men's eyes." Unfazed, they produced other charges: that he had tried to levy a tax on Egyptians to buy his priests linen vestments; that he had defiled a Melitian church by smashing the eucharistic chalice; even that he had raped a woman. The woman was unable to recognize him in court, so her testimony was discounted. No doubt the charges were made because Athanasius had been autocratic in his dealings with dissenters in his church. Constantine called for a full ecclesiastical council in 335 at Tyre, where the pro-Arian faction succeeded in having Athanasius deposed. His fortunes rose and fell over the next several decades—he endured, for example, five periods of exile—but for his courage in standing against Arianism he is considered one of the Fathers of the Church.

Eusebius of Caesarea

Eusebius of Caesarea, who signed the Council of Nicaea's creed in 325 but then wrote to his own church apologizing for it, is remembered more as the "father of church history" than for his role in the Arian controversy. His *Ecclesiastical History* is one of our most important sources of information about the church.

Born about 260 in Palestine, Eusebius was baptized in Caesarea, where he studied under Pamphilus, a scholar-priest who trained him in the tradition of Origen. During the persecutions that began in 303, Eusebius saw his beloved teacher martyred, churches razed, and holy books burned. The violence of the persecutions moved him to begin work on his first book, the *Chronicle*, a summary of universal history beginning with the creation.

Much of Eusebius' writing was intended to defend Christianity. In his *Preparation for the Gospel,* he explained the nature of Christianity for "those who know not what it means," in other words, pagans. A principal object of the book was to show why Christians accept the Hebrew religious tradition while, at the same time, rejecting the Greek.

About 315 Eusebius became bishop of Caesarea. Over the decade prior to the Council of Nicaea, he had supported Arius and was eventually summoned to Antioch on charges of Arianism. Perhaps to clear his name he later accepted, though with reluctance, the emperor's insertion of the term *homoousios,* or "consubstantial," into the revision of a creed formulated at Nicaea. (The reason for Eusebius' reluctance to endorse the term was that it appears nowhere in the Bible; he strongly doubted the propriety of using non-Scriptural language, especially language tainted by previous heretical usage, in a formal statement of faith concerning the nature of the Deity.) Subsequently Eusebius was prominent as a leader of the moderate party in the debate on the full divinity of Christ.

Over the 12 years following the Council of Nicaea, Eusebius apparently enjoyed Constantine's favor. In 331 he was offered the bishopric of Antioch, where some six years earlier he had been summoned on charges of heresy, but he refused the appointment. In 335 he attended the Council of Tyre. Soon after this, he was summoned by Constantine to assist in the adjudication of the charges against Athanasius. In several of his writings Eusebius provides a sort of outline of the Constantinian state, especially as regards the relationship between church and state. The emperor, he explains, can claim God as his source of strength and can rule on earth as the representative of God.

None of Eusebius' works rival in importance his *Ecclesiastical History*. The book's scope is very ambitious. As he noted, "I am the first to venture on such a project. . . . I have failed to find any clear footprints of those who have gone this way before me; only faint traces." Eusebius' history of Christianity is an uncritical chronicle of the church's triumph over conflict. Like all his writings, the *Ecclesiastical History* is heavy going. He is verbose and relies heavily on quotations from earlier writers. But this fault has made his work all the more important to modern historians, as his citations are the sole source for many otherwise vanished authors. In all, Eusebius' work endures as an invaluable view of Christianity's first footsteps.

Division of East and West

Constantine's decision to move the capital from Rome to Byzantium (Constantinople) was based on a variety of factors. First, Rome itself was no longer the administrative capital of the empire; administration moved with the emperor. Nicomedia, for example, had served as headquarters for Diocletian, Galerius, and Licinius. Constantine himself had settled for a while in Serdica (present-day Sofia, Bulgaria) and was even reputed to have claimed, "Serdica is my Rome." Furthermore, Rome's role as the economic hub of the empire was being usurped by such Eastern cities as Sirmium, Aquileia, Nicomedia, and Thessalonica, which had prospered from bustling trade routes.

Religion also influenced his decision. Constantine was disgusted with the pagan sacrifices that Romans had made at his 20th-anniversary celebrations in 326. By building a new imperial city, he could create a predominantly Christian capital, something pagan Rome would seemingly never become. After considering and rejecting several Eastern cities, including Jerusalem and Nicomedia, the emperor traveled to Troy, the ancient city immortalized by Homer. According to legend, after Constantine had laid out the city's boundaries and work had begun, God spoke to him and bade him choose another site for *Nova Roma*. Constantine later explained that he chose Byzantium for his new capital "on the command of God."

Byzantium's location also made it a natural choice. Set on a promontory at the southwestern outlet of the Black Sea, this triangle of land dominated the sea route to the Mediterranean. It also served as a transit point for the land routes between Asia and the Eastern Empire. Ivory, silk, cotton, jewels, spices, and other such

Continued on page 231

The prolific Bishop Eusebius of Caesarea is remembered mainly for his Ecclesiastical History, *his* Life of Constantine, *and his* Preparation for the Gospel. *Eusebius also drew up a set of charts, the* Canon Tables, *that cross-reference corresponding passages in the four Gospels. On the fragment of a canon table, left, the face near the top represents an unidentified Apostle. This manuscript was probably made for an imperial collection in Constantinople sometime between 600 and 700.*

In this fourth-century relief from Constantinople, the empty throne awaits the Second Coming of Christ, while two lambs, symbolic of the Apostles, suggest that the "peaceable kingdom" of the millennium is at hand.

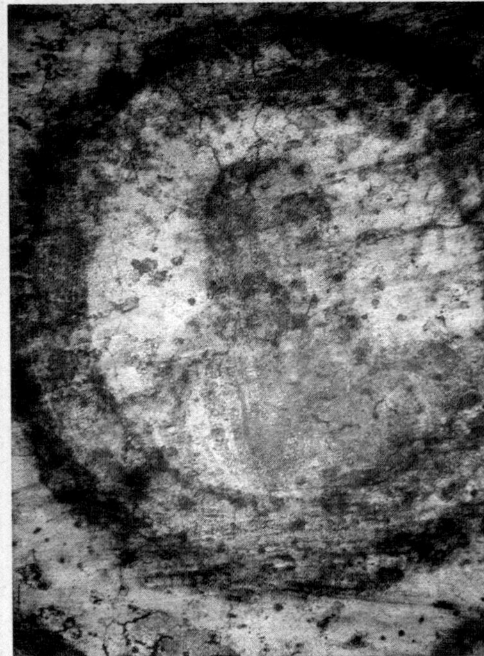

The portrait above, said to be the earliest known image of Jesus, was done in a Greco-Roman style no later than the third century; on the gilded glass, right, the martyr Agnes appears, praying with outstretched hands. Both painting and glass are from the Roman catacombs.

On this Roman sarcophagus lid of about the fourth century is represented the Last Judgment: "Before him [Christ] will be gathered all the nations, and he will separate them one from another as a shepherd separates the sheep from the goats, and he will place the sheep at his right hand, but the goats at the left." Matthew 25:32–33.

"As a bride adorns herself"

Christian art had its modest beginnings in the second century, but from Constantine's reign on, artists of the faith indulged in richly eye-catching representations. At the same time, their art reflected the pagan traditions of the surrounding society.

A mosaic of wine making, probably dating from Constantine's time, is one of several agricultural scenes related to the mystery of the Eucharist that embellish the ceilings of the vaulted aisles in St. Constance' Church, Rome.

Built by Constantine over the traditional burial place of Peter, the original Basilica of St. Peter in Rome presumably looked much as it does in this painting. Early basilicas included courtyards for pagans who wished to come and listen to the Gospel reading at church services.

The above Byzantine oil lamp is decorated with Christian symbols. Lamps often stand for divine guidance in many well-known Bible passages.

This votive leaf, overlaid with silver, is from Roman Britain. It combines the Chi-Rho monogram with the letters alpha and omega.

This small, garnet-adorned piece from a necklace is decorated with the Chi-Rho monogram of Christ's name; it comes from Constantinople.

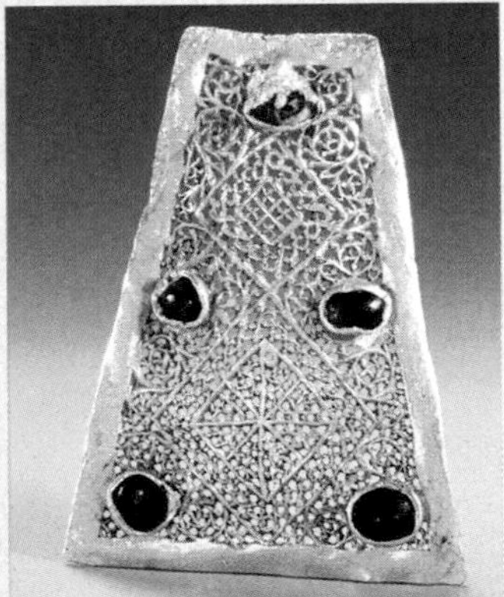

In this Coptic funerary slab the jackal (in the upper left-hand corner) is Anubis, who, according to ancient Egyptian belief, led the dead to judgment. Gnostics identified him with Christ, who, they believed, led the souls of the elect to the light.

This wooden door from St. Sabina's in Rome, dating from the early fifth century, is the oldest sculptural representation of the Crucifixion. It is probable that realistic depictions of the Crucifixion would have been distasteful to Christians of the first four centuries.

This six-sided, mold-blown glass pitcher, probably from Syria, is adorned with the Christian cross and dates from late Roman to early Byzantine times.

In a textile from Coptic Egypt, woven during Roman times, the figure of an equilateral cross within a circle is adapted from a very ancient non-Christian sign that some think originally symbolized the four winds or the sun.

goods enriched the city's merchants. It was also a natural fortress, protected on three sides by water and approachable by sea only after passing through outer defenses in the straits of the Bosporus and the Hellespont. Its protected harbor, the Golden Horn (named for its shape and the riches that regularly stood on its docks), offered a safe haven to war fleets as well as trading ships and could easily be defended in case of attack. Unlike Rome, the city was also convenient to two of the empire's major fronts—the Persian frontier to the east and the Danube to the north.

It may have been shortly after his victory over Licinius in late 324 that Constantine and his engineers visited Byzantium and laid out the boundaries for the new capital. He moved the city's walls a mile and a half farther to the west, more than quadrupling the urban area. Architects, smiths, cabinetmakers, marble workers, mosaicists, masons, gilders, glaziers, and others were enticed—and in some cases ordered—to Byzantium to carry out the emperor's plan. No expense was spared in the construction. On Constantine's orders, statues and other works of art, bronze doors, and marble columns were removed from pagan temples throughout the empire and shipped to Constantinople. The streets were decorated with fountains and porticoes; the massive public baths were adorned with scores of marble and bronze statues. All but a few of Byzantium's temples were razed, and statues of the gods were recarved or used to ornament a new building or plaza. A temple to Aphrodite was torn down and replaced with the Church of the Holy Apostles, a basilica that contained effigies of the Twelve Apostles and a sarcophagus for Constantine, who was represented as the "the thirteenth Apostle."

Other churches rose throughout the city. Symbols and relics associated with biblical and church history multiplied on all sides. In the Forum of Constantine, at the base of a column supporting a statue of himself portrayed as the sun god, Constantine buried an object purported to be the ax Noah used to build the ark

For almost 1,000 years, until its capture by Turks in 1453, Constantinople was the economic, political, and intellectual hub of the late Roman and Byzantine world. This intriguing overview of the ancient city was painted early in the 16th century.

and the jar supposed to have held the ointment with which Mary Magdalene anointed the feet of Christ. Further, to confer upon the New Rome some of the apostolic sanctity that Old Rome derived from the tombs of Peter and Paul, Constantine ordered that relics of Andrew (legendary Apostle to the Black Sea region including Byzantium), Timothy, and Luke be brought to Constantinople.

To populate his new imperial city, Constantine offered various enticements. Senators who left Rome for Byzantium were rewarded with state-supplied mansions. Citizens of lower rank who built houses for themselves in the new capital were entitled to free food distributions. A law required those who held crown lands in Asia Minor to build a second home in the city. Thousands of others needed no prodding; the city quickly bustled with bureaucrats, soldiers, shopkeepers, tradesmen, and others drawn to the new seat of the empire. In 337 some 50,000 people lived in Constantinople; by 400 the population would double, and a century later it would reach nearly a million. Constantinople was dedicated on May 11, 330. Forty days of festivities marked the transformation of Byzantium into the hub of a new Christian empire.

With the center of the empire now 1,000 miles east of Rome, the Western portion was deprived of much revenue and manpower that it had previously demanded from the East. Soon it would be vulnerable to attacks from its enemies on the upper Danube and the Rhine. While the relocation led to more imperial control of the Eastern church, it also increased the prominence of Rome's bishop. Eventually, the Roman church would become the most powerful institution in the West. At the same time, Constantinople was preserving the fruits of Greco-Roman civilization; for many centuries the city withstood attacks from nearly every front. Long after Rome had been vanquished by barbarians, Constantinople was flourishing as the center of the Byzantine Empire. (Historians often refer to the Roman Empire in the centuries after the building of Constantinople as the Byzantine Empire.)

While Constantine labored hard to promote Christianity, he never lost sight of his role as ruler of all his subjects. He once told a group of clerics, "You are the bishops of those within the Church, but I would be a bishop established by God of those outside it." Yet his alliance with Christianity and the founding of Constantinople overshadow his other accomplishments. He also reorganized the army, made changes in the empire's awkward bureaucracy, and stabilized the currency. Given the range of his achievements, there is little doubt that he deserves the title posterity has bestowed on him, Constantine the Great. He did have shortcomings, however. He was extravagant, vulnerable to flattery, and often ruthless. He showed the dark side of his nature in 326 when he had his wife, Fausta, and his eldest son, Crispus, killed for reasons that remain obscure. His greatest political mistake also involved family. In 335, instead of naming a sole heir, he bequeathed the empire to his three remaining sons, thus opening the way for jealousy and intrigue.

Shortly after Easter in 337, Constantine became seriously ill. Convinced that his illness was fatal, he received baptism from Eusebius of Nicomedia, the

Continued on page 236

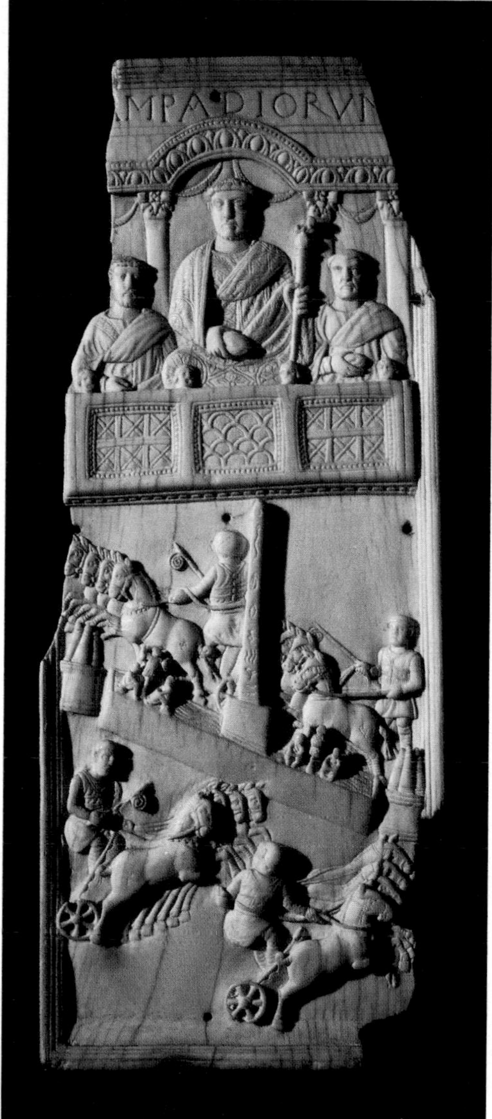

Measuring 1,509 by 502 feet, the hippodrome in Constantinople had an imperial box that formed a miniature palace communicating directly with the main palace. At right is an ivory horn probably used for the sort of races held in the gigantic stadium. It is carved with scenes typical of the hippodrome—chariots, horsemen, jugglers, circus animals.

The Quest for Holy Relics

The belief that a possession or the bones of a holy person can bring special protection or effect a miraculous cure is an ancient one. Traditions abound of miracles associated with the remains of saintly persons. In the church, the cult of relics goes back to the ministry of Paul; objects touched by the Apostle reportedly cured the sick. From the second century onward, Christians held services at martyrs' graves, in the belief that these venerated ones would take special care of those who worshiped there. During Constantine's reign, the custom began of building churches over martyrs' graves and of placing relics beneath a church's altar.

So great became the desire to possess relics that graves were opened and saints' remains were parceled out to churches far and wide. In 386 Theodosius I put a ban on the disinterment, dismemberment, or transporting of any human remains, but the prohibition had almost no effect on the spread of relics throughout Christendom. In 787 the Second Council of Nicaea, in fact, ruled that no new church could be dedicated unless it contained consecrated relics.

Not only did relics confer a special sanctity on a church, they frequently provided income by attracting a steady stream of pilgrims. Competition for relics eventually led to some decidedly un-Christian behavior, including relic-napping and trade in fake relics. More than one church claimed to possess St. Patrick's bones and John the Baptist's head.

Commerce in relics was intense during the Middle Ages. The catacombs of Rome were an especially rich source of remains. Not only saints' bones were sold but also dust from their tombs and bits of cloth brought in contact with the tombs. People wore such relic fragments inside amulets, rings, and crosses. Another not uncommon practice was to seek political or military support from a powerful person by presenting him with the bones of a much venerated saint.

Many objections to and justifications for relic veneration have been expressed over the years. In Constantine's time, some church leaders deemed the practice too much like pagan idolatry. Yet, the theologian Gregory of Nazianzus and others justified reverence for relics by the miracles that God was working

This fresco depicts the emperor Constantine and his mother, Helena, holding the cross of Jesus after Helena's discovery of the cross in Jerusalem. Constantine himself never actually visited the Holy Land.

through them. During the century following Constantine's death, further endorsement was made by such church leaders as Ambrose and Augustine.

The invention of the cross

Closely associated with Constantine in the promotion of holy objects to a rank of major importance was his mother, Helena, a zealous supporter of Christianity. In 326, already in her 70's, Helena went to Jerusalem. During her sojourn there, she founded churches on some of the presumed sites of major events in the life of Jesus. It was she who discovered the cave in which Jesus was supposedly buried. A basilica was dedicated there in 335, but only a few portions of it remain. (The present-day Church of the Holy Sepulcher dates to the mid-12th century.) This and Helena's other grand buildings established the Holy Land as a main center of Christian pilgrimage from that time onward.

According to legend, Helena discovered inside the cave something even more important than the place itself. She found the cross of Jesus. Her "invention" (from Latin *inventio*, "discovery") of the cross is traditionally dated May 3, 326. According to one version of the story, all three crosses were there. To determine which one had held Jesus, Helena had the body of a dead man brought and laid on one of the crosses. Nothing happened. He was then brought into contact with the second one, again to no avail. At the touch of the third cross, he came to life.

She had portions of the "true cross," and nails from it also, sent to Constantine. As a charm to protect his new city from harm, Constantine enclosed a fragment of the cross inside a statue of himself, and he had the nails used in the making of bridle bits and a helmet. By 350 other fragments of the cross had found their way to churches throughout the Roman world.

Behind these traditions looms a major historical development. For more than a century, perhaps even since Christ's death, Christians had been crossing themselves on the forehead with the thumb or index finger and attributing miraculous power to the sign. Now the cross became Constantine's victory emblem. Though his vision before the Milvian Bridge battle seems to have been of the Chi-Rho (see page 209), the Chi-Rho was blended later with the cross. Eusebius the historian links "the victory-granting cross" with Constantine's military successes. But it appears that full use of the cross symbol as we know it may not have come into use until about a decade after Constantine's death in 337. (Significantly, it was Constantine who abolished crucifixion as a form of capital punishment because of its association with the death of Christ.)

Whether or not Constantine lived to see the cross used in all the now familiar ways, posterity has rightly credited the innovation of its use as a symbol to him and his mother. Behind this use was a perception of Christ as king of the universe, whose cross was the instrument of his cosmic victory over the power of Satan.

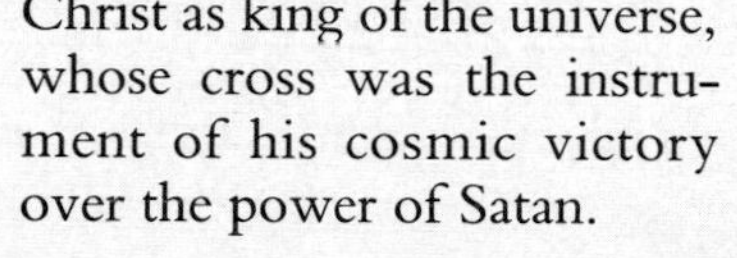

Reliquaries, special containers for relics, have often taken elaborate forms and been lavishly decorated. The center medallion of this sixth-century jeweled cross reliquary contains a splinter purported to come from the cross of Jesus. Next to it is a box reliquary that features on its lid an icon of the Crucifixion.

longtime spiritual adviser with whom he had clashed more than once over doctrine and politics. (Like many Christians of that time, Constantine had delayed baptism to the end, since he feared he could not avoid mortal sin during his lifetime, and such sin after baptism was widely held to be unforgivable.)

The emperor, now about 57, traded his purple robes for the austere white garments of a Christian neophyte. He died on May 22, 337, during the festival of Pentecost. First he was laid in state in the imperial palace, where the citizens of Constantinople filed by to do him honor. Then, as he had requested, his body was entombed in Constantinople's Church of the Holy Apostles. In Rome, there was also an intense response. According to Eusebius, "The Roman senate and people felt the announcement as the heaviest and most afflictive of all calamities, and gave themselves up to an excess of grief. The baths and markets were closed, the public spectacles, and all other recreations in which men of leisure are accustomed to indulge, were interrupted." Even the heavens seemed moved at his passing—a comet was said to have announced (or appeared at the time of) his death.

Though he had, in effect, been the first Christian ruler, he was still revered by pagan subjects. Coins were issued that referred to him as "the deified Constantine," and the fourth-century historian Eutropius noted, "He was deservedly enrolled among the divine [that is, deified pagan] emperors."

Dividing the empire in three

To Constantine II, the emperor's eldest living son, went Britain, Gaul, and Spain. Constantius II received the East, while Constans, the youngest, inherited the middle region, including Illyricum (modern Yugoslavia), Italy, and North Africa. Among the issues that faced them was the familiar Arian controversy.

Constantine II and Constans supported the Nicene Creed, while Constantius followed the Arian views of Eusebius of Nicomedia. One of the first official acts of Constantine II was to permit exiled anti-Arian bishops, including Athanasius, to return to their sees. While this move pleased the Western churches, which supported the Nicene Creed, it angered the Eastern bishops, who were dissatisfied with the council's formula. The Eastern faction, led by Eusebius of Nicomedia, claimed that Athanasius had forfeited his see, and they forced him to flee from Alexandria. Athanasius enlisted the aid of Bishop Julius of Rome, who in 340 called a synod and ruled that Athanasius and the other exiled anti-Arians were innocent of all charges that had been brought against them. The Eastern bishops met in 341 and, ignoring the Western synod, denied the Roman bishop's right to mediate for the Eastern churches. A major split between the Latin and Greek churches seemed imminent.

To remedy the situation another synod was called in the autumn of 343. It was a fiasco. Both sides still refused to alter their views. Athanasius was restored to his bishopric at Alexandria, but after Constans was murdered and Constantius became the sole emperor in 353 (Constantine II had been killed while invading northern Italy in 340), Athanasius was again deposed and exiled. Like his father, Constantius struggled to develop a creed acceptable to both sides—a seemingly impossible task, since both sides considered matters of eternal life and death to be at stake in their beliefs.

Western bishops criticized Constantius for his support of the Eastern anti-Nicene faction. "You distribute episcopal sees to your partisans and substitute bad bishops for good," wrote Bishop Hilary of Poitiers. "You imprison priests and use your army to terrorize the Church." (Hilary, a Neoplatonist until his conversion to Christianity, is remembered as the author of a treatise on the Trinity and as the first known writer of Christian hymns.) Even Ossius, once an adviser to Constantine I and now reentering church politics at the astonishing age of 101, attacked Constantius for his meddling: "Do not intrude yourself into church matters, nor give commands to us concerning them,"

The death of Constantine was acknowledged with the pomp and reverence fully befitting so great a man. According to Eusebius, the emperor was laid out in diadem and purple robes atop a golden coffin, centered in the main chamber of the imperial palace. Here he was "surrounded by candles burning in candlesticks of gold . . . and encircled by a numerous retinue of attendants, who watched around it incessantly night and day," as the people of Constantinople filed by to pay him homage.

Treasures in an Ancient Monastery

Located at the foot of Mount Sinai, the Greek Orthodox Monastery of St. Catherine is one of the world's oldest. Constantine's mother, Helena, reportedly had a chapel and tower built on this site, where, according to tradition, Moses saw the burning bush. Today's visitors see the larger, fortified compound and basilica erected here in the sixth century to protect desert monks from marauders. Among its treasures are early icons and ancient manuscripts.

In 1844 a German student named Constantine Tischendorf visited St. Catherine's, accessible then only by a rope tow. In the great hall, he found pages of a timeworn manuscript, which were about to be burned to provide warmth for the monks. What Tischendorf had discovered was a portion of the Codex Sinaiticus, *a fourth-century Bible in Greek, one of the oldest in existence! On a return visit to St. Catherine's in 1859, Tischendorf located additional folios; several more sections were found in 1975. The codex, which contains the earliest known complete text of the New Testament, is shown below.*

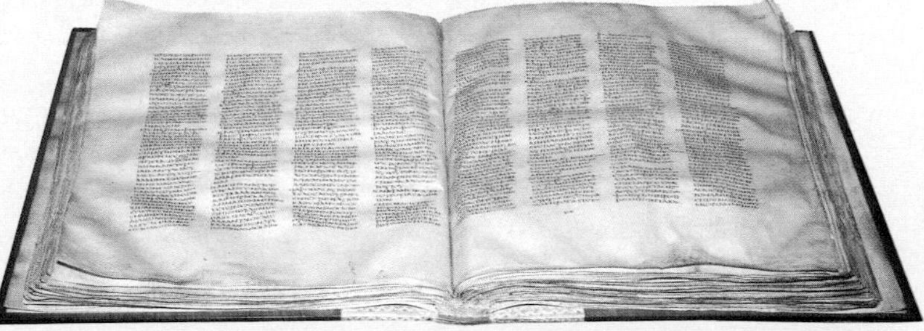

he wrote. "God has put into your hands the kingdom; to us he has entrusted the affairs of his church."

The controversy, which Constantine I had once called "perfectly inconsequential," would continue to confound emperors and bishops alike. The warring sides did agree on one issue, however, that paganism was an affront to Christianity. An assault on the pagan cults had begun under Constantine, when he ordered the looting of temples to embellish his new imperial city. He even had some torn down and replaced with churches. His sons went several steps further. In 341 major anti-pagan legislation was enacted. Firmicus Maternus, a Christian senator, expressed the feeling of many during that decade. "These practices must be completely excised, destroyed and reformed," he said. "Away with the Temple treasures! Let the fire of your mind and the flame of your smelting-works roast these gods!" Over the next several years, pagan temples were closed and sacrifices were prohibited.

The church as an official institution

As pagan temples were shut, it became apparent that something would have to be done to care for the poor and destitute who had depended on the largesse of wealthy temples. The church came forward to fill the void. Freed from oppression and enriched by donations from wealthy converts, the church could now minister to the general public. Constantine himself had sponsored the founding of the first network of hospitals throughout the empire. At the Council of Nicaea it was decided that every city should have separate facilities for the sick, the poor, and pilgrims. Clergy were given the authority to distribute food to orphans and widows. When famine struck Asia Minor in 368, Bishop Basil of Caesarea fed the region's hungry for an entire year. Such open-handed charity drew many to the church and offered a much needed boost to its reputation, which had been tarnished by the recent internal quarrels. Even Christianity's critics could not deny the church's good deeds.

Charity also played a role in the development of Christian monastic life. By the middle of the fourth century, monasteries had evolved from loosely associated groups of hermits living in the desert to organized communities, like those begun by Pachomius near the River Nile. Basil of Caesarea (see page 247) believed that monastic communities should be less isolated, more closely linked with the church and the community. He encouraged monasteries that, in addition to fostering a strict ascetic life, would provide relief for the poor and offer medical treatment for the sick. As a bishop and an ascetic, he urged others to

Sunday: A Legal Day of Rest

When Constantine came to power, Christian worship was still rather loosely structured, though there were general guidelines. About the only thing all Christian churches had held in common since the first century, however, was the Sunday gathering for worship; on that day (called the first day of the week) Christians commemorated the Resurrection.

In 321 Constantine made Sunday a public holiday and put into effect what might be called the world's first "blue laws." The edict proclaimed, "All judges, city-people, and craftsmen shall rest on the venerable day of the Sun. But countrymen may without hindrance attend to agriculture, since it often happens that this is the most suitable day for sowing grain or planting vines." Despite the edict, many Christians continued the long-standing practice of observing the Jewish Sabbath (Saturday) as well, until the mid-360's, when the church forbade it.

locate their monasteries on the outskirts of cities, where they could provide these services to a large population. He set forth his ideas in two sets of monastic instructions, which have survived and are used in Greek and Russian monasteries to this day.

Julian the Apostate

His critics labeled him "the Apostate." To his supporters he was a "saint," a "philosopher-king," a "veritable god, under the appearance of a man." Historians have been more balanced in their estimation of Flavius Claudius Iulianus, or Julian, successor of Constantius. He is best remembered as the emperor who tried to topple Christianity and restore paganism as the official religion of the Roman Empire.

A nephew of Constantine, Julian was only five years old in 337, when he saw soldiers kill his father to make way for the reign of Constantine's sons. After the murder, Julian was sent to Nicomedia, where he remained under the guardianship of Eusebius, the bishop of that city, until the latter was made bishop of Constantinople. In 342 he went to a remote estate in Cappadocia, where, under the watchful eyes of household eunuchs, he spent six years studying Christian theology. But his real love was the classics, and over the next decade or so—first in the capital, then in Pergamum and Ephesus—he explored the world of Greek poetry, mythology, and philosophy.

Julian had a brush with death in 354. He and his brother, Gallus, were summoned to Milan, where Constantius, angered that Gallus had abused his role as caesar, had him tried and ordered his execution. Julian managed to convince the emperor that he himself had no interest in politics and posed no threat. He was spared and allowed to visit Athens, where he sharpened his philosophical skills.

Influenced by his teachers, especially the Neoplatonist philosopher Maximus of Ephesus, he had become an ardent (but secret) pagan. He threw aside the Bible and sought inspiration from Homer. He called Christians, especially those responsible for the slaughter of his family, "superstitious atheists" who worshiped "a new-fangled Galilean god." Julian was convinced that Constantine had destroyed the empire's traditional religious values. Until he inherited the imperial robes in 361, Julian concealed his paganism from all but a small circle of friends and teachers. He called his form of paganism Hellenism and drew from various philosophical streams in his attempt to establish a new organized religion. From Plato he adapted the concept of an unknowable "Supreme Being," from whom there emanated a creator-god. By various stages, or steps, the human soul could rise to bliss.

There were striking parallels in the terminology of fourth-century Neoplatonism and that of Christian theology of the same period. The revered Church Father Augustine discovered a quarter-century later that Neoplatonism could serve as an excellent bridge for those like himself who were on their way toward Christianity. Neoplatonism had a different effect on Julian. As one historian put it: "Julian went across the bridge but in the opposite direction."

Julian's attempt to reestablish paganism

In 355 Constantius made Julian caesar and shipped him off to Gaul with orders to govern that prefecture, which had recently been invaded by Germanic tribes. After crossing the Alps with 360 men, Julian wintered at Vienne on the Rhone, where he studied the art of war. In the spring he gathered an army and managed to defeat the invaders. For the next five years he remained in Gaul upgrading the economy, defenses, and administration of the region. Everyone was amazed that he had so successfully transformed himself from a schoolboy into a military commander and able administrator.

With the war going badly on the Persian front, in 360 Constantius ordered Julian to send his best troops to help defend the empire's eastern border. The army refused to go, and then hailed Julian as augustus. He

Rome's last pagan emperor was Julian the Apostate. Julian dreamt of conquering Persia and India. Here he stands at the gates of the Persian capital, Ctesiphon. Although his augurs warned him of inauspicious signs, Julian abandoned his siege of Ctesiphon in order to penetrate farther inland and fight the enemy's main army, commanded by Shapur II. Julian died in action shortly afterwards. Shapur had launched a great persecution of Christians in 339, perhaps in response to the adoption of Christianity as the religion of the Roman Empire, yet within another century or so Ctesiphon itself became a Christian center.

accepted their call and led his troops to the imperial city of Constantinople. Civil war was averted when Constantius died of a fever in November 361.

The new emperor wasted no time in declaring his paganism. Even before arriving in Constantinople, he had written his former tutor Maximus, "We now publicly adore the gods, and all the army that followed me is devoted to their worship." After clearing the court of Christian hangers-on, he organized a pagan church. It had a hierarchy modeled on that of the Christian church, with himself at its head as *pontifex maximus*. He ordered temples reopened and his uncle Constantine's Christian emblem removed from the legions' standards. Temple lands were restored and public worship of the gods was revived. Pagan schools were established again in towns throughout the empire.

Julian did not outlaw Christianity, but he did strip the church of many privileges it had received under Constantius. Christian clergy were no longer exempt from taxation and could not use the state transport or postal system without cost. Christians were barred from governmental office, and Christian professors were forbidden to teach the classics. Of all Julian's anti-Christian measures, this one provoked the loudest and most sustained outcry.

For all his enthusiasm and passionate belief in paganism, Julian never managed to restore worship of the ancient gods to the dominant religion of the empire. Some converted to paganism; for most it held little allure. To many, the pagan rites seemed anachronistic. Even before "the Apostate," as Christians called him, was killed on the Persian front on June 26, 363, it was obvious that his plan to resurrect paganism had failed. Athanasius said it best. After Julian ordered him into exile in the summer of 362, he told his congregation, "It is but a little cloud and it will soon pass."

Chapter Eight

DECLINE OF THE EMPIRE

Nothing had been mightier than the Roman Empire; now nothing was weaker, or so believed the Church Father Jerome, as he saw the church grow ever stronger. Barbarians deposed the last Western emperor in 476, but in the end, Christianity triumphed.

By the close of the fourth century, Christian tolerance for paganism, still practiced by many, if not most, in the empire, was wearing thin. In 391, about 80 years after Constantine had legalized all religions, anti-pagan sentiments led to riots between pagans and Christians in the streets of Alexandria. An important victim of the mob's rage was the statue of the god Serapis. As part of the tale goes, a Christian mob was set on raiding the Temple of Serapis, at that time, possibly the largest place of worship in the world. A tense crowd watched as a trembling soldier, armed with an ax, approached the huge statue of the god. No doubt many of the spectators feared for their lives, because it had been prophesied that the mere touch of the gleaming idol by a mortal would bring about the immediate destruction of the world. The soldier struck the idol's cheek with sufficient force to send the head crashing to the ground. Much to the relief of onlookers, the earth stood firm. When the god's massive head came off, the story continues, mice scurried out. Later, Christians carried the god's head through the streets in raucous triumph.

In a move aimed at "the very head of idolatry," a throng of soldiers and Christians, encouraged by the militant bishop Theophilus, smashed the colossal statue of the great god Serapis in his temple in Alexandria in 391. It was a mortal blow to paganism.

Despite earlier attempts to stamp out paganism, many cults were still active when Theodosius I issued new anti-pagan edicts in 391 and 392. Two groups that held on were the devotees of Serapis, whose altar at Delos is shown above, and the Vestal Virgins (priestesses of Vesta, goddess of the hearth). The Vestals, right, depicted making a sacrifice, were granted honors and rewards that Bishop Ambrose of Milan thought inappropriate. He believed that, like Christian virgins, they should be virtuous with no expectation of gain.

The destruction of the Serapeum

The fall of Serapis was the handiwork of one of the most powerful men in the Roman East, Theophilus, the bishop of Alexandria. Whether for love of God or love of power, the bishop was determined to establish the church's supremacy in Alexandria, and he was prepared to use any means to reach that goal.

Theophilus had long been keen to confiscate the treasure of wealthier pagan temples, but the Serapeum had seemed beyond his reach. One of the wonders of the ancient world, the Serapeum was a veritable city within a city, an enormous complex of meeting halls, treasuries, arsenals, kitchens, lodges, and storage rooms. Inside the compound were the Halls of Books, surviving annexes of the great Library of Alexandria (the main library had been destroyed in a fire hundreds of years earlier). At one time, these halls may have housed as many as 300,000 scrolls.

The temple stood atop a raised platform covered by white stone. To reach it, a worshiper had to climb 100 marble steps, lined with statues of sphinxes. The vast Temple Hall was richly decorated with tapestries and murals, its stone-vaulted roof upheld by massive columns. At the farthest reach shone the huge statue of Serapis, studded with precious stones.

A few days before the attack on the Serapeum, Theophilus had ordered secret ritual objects used in the worship of Dionysus to be derisively paraded through the city streets. Incensed at this sacrilege, Olympius, a philosopher, had led a group of pagans to barricade the Serapeum against possible attack. It was rumored that these zealots had also taken Christian captives and tortured them. When Theodosius, the Christian emperor of the East, got word of these alleged outrages, he ordered the prefect of Alexandria to demolish all pagan houses of worship.

The end was drawing near. The day before the Christians stormed the Serapeum, it was said that Olympius heard a disembodied voice singing "Hallelujah," a hymn he must have recognized as Christian. Shaken by what he thought to be a harbinger of defeat, he fled the Serapeum and later escaped to Italy. The next day, as the story was told, when the mob stormed the temple, intent on destroying the idol of Serapis, they found stones with crosses engraved on them. Nearby, hieroglyphics were discovered that read: "When the cross appears, the Temple of Serapis will be destroyed." Reportedly, many pagans converted after this revelation, but even greater numbers joined the faith the following summer, when the Nile flooded with unusual vigor and assured a rich harvest. Clearly there would be no divinely sent famine or flood to punish mankind for the desecration of the Serapeum. To many this must have seemed final proof that the old gods had lost their power. Busts of Serapis were removed from doorways and windows, and in their place the sign of the cross was painted.

Further upheavals

The death knell for paganism had already sounded in 341, when Constantius II prohibited sacrifices to the traditional gods. About 354, a sterner edict was issued, ordering the closing of the old temples and prescribing death for those who sacrificed in public places. Julian the Apostate tried but failed to return the empire to paganism over his 20-month reign, from 361 to 363; and the late-fourth-century emperors who succeeded him were influenced by powerful churchmen who viewed paganism as an enterprise of the Devil. Nonetheless, a number of pagan rites were permitted to survive. The Vestal Virgins still guarded the eternal flame in Rome, and many traditional festivals continued to be observed.

In aristocratic circles, Christian converts mingled freely with pagans, each group respecting the other. Even more remarkable, perhaps, is that many people entertained Christian sympathies while still clinging to old beliefs. Husbands and wives, parents and children, were not necessarily split by religious differences. Even the Bible translator and theologian Jerome related benignly the story of a white-haired pagan priest smiling as his granddaughter sat on his lap and sang a hymn learned from her Christian mother.

In the late 370's the Christian emperor Gratian declined the pagan title of *pontifex maximus*, or "high priest," which had been held traditionally by Roman emperors. More important, he ended government subsidies for the Roman cults and had the hallowed Altar of Victory removed from the Senate house sometime in 382. Pagan leaders were horrified.

The winged goddess of victory was the cause of controversy in the late fourth century, when her altar and possibly her statue, which had resided in the Roman Senate since 29 B.C., were ordered removed by Gratian in 382. The respected patrician Symmachus argued eloquently for the altar's restoration, but to no avail.

The fall of the Winged Victory

For more than 400 years the Senate proceedings had opened with a sacrifice to Victoria, the winged goddess of victory, also known by her Greek name, Nike. Her statue and altar commemorated the beginning of the Roman Empire with Octavian's victory at Actium in 31 B.C. In 383, when Gratian was assassinated and a famine laid waste the land, many raised the old cry that the gods were manifesting their displeasure.

With Gratian's death, the empire came into the hands of his coruler, Theodosius I, a devout Christian. When Gratian had appointed him emperor of the East in 379, Theodosius had immediately begun to consolidate the role of Christianity as the official religion. Later, he became the first ruler to bow to the will of a Christian bishop, the powerful Ambrose of Milan, a man who was vehemently opposed to the state sanction of pagan rites and especially to the restoration of the Altar of Victory.

Honoring the 10th anniversary of Theodosius' imperial rule is this magnificent silver platter, which shows the emperor receiving gifts from his subjects. He is flanked by his two sons, Honorius and Arcadius, each of whom is attended by Gothic (Germanic) members of the Imperial Guard. Theodosius had made a treaty with the Visigoths in 382, confirming their right to settle on the lands between the lower Danube River and the Balkan Mountains. They, in turn, were pledged to help protect the Roman Empire.

A bitter debate over the Victory began. The Senate's position was argued by Symmachus, Ambrose's relative, then the prefect of Rome. He pleaded for religious toleration: "Each nation has its own gods and peculiar rites. . . . Leave us the symbol on which our oaths of allegiance have been sworn for so many generations. Leave us the system which has so long given prosperity to the State." He added, "What matters it by what method each of us reaches the truth? We cannot by a single road arrive at so great a secret."

Although Symmachus was greatly respected, even by his Christian adversaries, his request was repeatedly denied. It appeared that Ambrose had won. But the pagans were not so easily routed. When the emperor in the West, Valentinian II, was murdered, a usurper named Eugenius was elevated in 392. Though he was a Christian in name, Eugenius was in fact a pagan sympathizer, who sanctioned a brief pagan revival in the West. Pagan rites were celebrated anew and their expenses were once again borne by the state. More significantly, about 393, the Altar of Victory was returned to the Senate. Angered by the blatant display of such pro-pagan policies and goaded by the ever vigilant Ambrose, Theodosius brought his armies west in 394 to engage the forces of Eugenius.

Like Constantine and Licinius before them, Theodosius and Eugenius were vying for the spiritual as well as the political control of the empire. As one version of the story goes, the day before the battle, Theodosius flung himself on the ground in prayer, in full view of both armies. According to another account, during the night, he had a vision: John the Evangelist and Philip the Apostle appeared on white horses and promised victory. The next day, at a critical moment in the battle, a great storm rose up; as the wind blew savagely, Eugenius' soldiers lost heart, believing that the Christian God himself must be against them. Eugenius himself was killed.

Theodosius' baptism

Who was this man Theodosius I (also known as Theodosius the Great), who had so profound an impact on the demise of paganism? Born to well-to-do parents near Toledo, Spain, about 346, he was probably brought up as a Christian. His father, who was connected to the court, was suddenly put to death in 376. Before his execution, he was baptized. At the news of his father's death, Theodosius quit his post as an army general and retired to the family estate in Spain. He might have remained there had Gratian not prevailed upon him to become co-emperor in 379. His reign was turbulent, yet Theodosius managed to stay in power for 16 years, while many a political rival rose and fell.

He was a devout Christian and a firm believer in the Nicene Creed, having been reared in the anti-Arian West. During his second year of rule, he became gravely ill in Thessalonica. Undoubtedly thinking that death was near, the emperor, then about 34, accepted baptism. When he recovered, he believed, as did most devout Christians at the time, that baptism had irrevocably committed him to a blameless life, in which further sins could lead to eternal punishment after death. (The church had not yet formulated a mechanism for regularly granting forgiveness and imposing penance.) The emperor's dread of falling into unforgivable sin might help explain his zeal for the orthodox faith as well as his continuing submission to the demands of the extraordinary Bishop Ambrose.

Soon after recovering, Theodosius showed his pro-Nicene stance by summoning Demophilus, the Arian bishop of Constantinople, and offering him the choice of embracing Nicene orthodoxy or being deposed. The bishop chose defiance and was replaced. Subsequently, Theodosius declared Christianity, as practiced by the pro-Nicene bishops of Alexandria and Rome, to be the official religion of the empire. The following year the emperor ruled that all property of nonorthodox churches, such as the Arian, the Meletian, and the Donatist, should be handed over to the orthodox church. He also forbade such congregations to hold any worship services. Persecution and bloodshed followed. Heretics, or those on the losing side, were hunted down. Many were tortured and some were even executed.

Theodosius was intent on crushing paganism as well. About 392 he made it a crime to engage in any form of public or private worship of the pagan deities. Throughout the latter part of the fourth century, pagan temples in Gaul and elsewhere were destroyed. However, like Constantine, Theodosius insisted that some buildings be saved and converted for Christian use. Thus, the Parthenon in Athens became, for a time, a church of the Virgin Mary.

The Council of Constantinople

In keeping with his pro-Nicene stance, Theodosius summoned a council of bishops in Constantinople in 381. Its sole purpose was to stamp out the Arian movement once and for all. What we now call the Nicene Creed (see page 223) was adopted at that historic meeting. This version also became the creed in the Western church. Among other decisions coming out of the council was a condemnation of Arians.

The triumph of the Nicene faith in Constantinople owed much to the brilliance of Gregory of Nazianzus. He pursued the Nicene cause valiantly, even after being threatened by pro-Arian mobs prior to the council. Sensitive and quick-tempered, Gregory was remembered by churchmen in the East as "the Christian Demosthenes" for his powerful eloquence.

The Cappadocian fathers

Gregory was one of three Christian intellectual leaders known as the Cappadocian fathers, for all three were natives of Cappadocia, in what is today eastern Turkey. The other two in the group were the brothers Basil the Great and Gregory of Nyssa.

Basil, a classmate of Gregory of Nazianzus at the University of Athens, was devoted to the Nicene Creed. He studied rhetoric and then, influenced by his elder sister, Macrina, called the Teacher, gave up a promising administrative career to become a monk.

With the help of his friend Gregory of Nazianzus, Basil created a community for religious contemplation on one of his family estates. Over the next five years or so, aided by fellow monks, he drew up rules

Aelia Flacilla, the first wife of Theodosius the Great, is immortalized in this lovely statuette. About a year after Aelia Flacilla died in 386, Theodosius married Galla, a sister of Valentinian II, who was emperor of the West from 375 to 392.

Until an unfortunate incident in 372 marred their friendship, Gregory of Nazianzus (top) and Basil of Caesarea were close collaborators in composing monastic rules and compiling excerpts from Origen's writings.

During a general council of bishops in Constantinople in 381, Gregory of Nazianzus was consecrated bishop of that city. The gathering was rent with controversy, however, and when bishops from Egypt and Macedonia challenged his installation, Gregory relinquished the prestigious post to avoid further discord in the church.

on the theory and practice of monasticism. Then he accepted an appointment as bishop of Caesarea and built hospitals and hostels, using some of his family's great wealth. Basil was concerned about the material disparity between different classes of society, and he urged the rich to share their property with the poor. To this day, his genius for administration is reflected in the strict discipline of religious communities throughout the East, as well as in specific prayers and parts of the liturgy in the Eastern Orthodox Church. He is known as the father of Eastern monasticism.

Basil died before the Council of Constantinople convened, but at the gathering, Gregory of Nyssa fervently argued his late brother's pro-Nicene position. Afterward, Gregory became a theological adviser to Theodosius. His writings, many of which survive, reflect a deeply mystical spirituality. Though he was married in his youth, Gregory became a monk after his wife died. In his writings he explored such wide-ranging topics as the natural sciences, medicine, and the spiritual significance of virginity. He also wrote two touching works on the life of his sister Macrina, who with their mother founded one of the earliest communities of Christian women dedicated to the search for spiritual perfection. In *The Soul and Its Resurrection*, Gregory recreates a dialogue in which he and Macrina, serene on her deathbed, discuss the Christian hope for immortality and the nature of the afterlife. Most significantly, however, he is remembered for his full development of several fundamental mystical and philosophical themes, first introduced by Origen some 150 years earlier (see pages 158–161).

Theodosius' conflicts with Ambrose

From 388 to 391, Emperor Theodosius resided mostly in Milan, where Ambrose was bishop. Many of Theodosius' political acts during this period created friction between the militant churchman and himself. For example, in 388, after Christians burned down a Jewish synagogue in a small town in Mesopotamia, Theodosius wanted the synagogue rebuilt at the local bishop's expense. But Ambrose argued that church money could not be used to support non-Christian beliefs. In a letter to the emperor, Ambrose asked, "Which is more important, the idea of law and order or the cause of religion?" Theodosius held his ground. The bishop then refused to offer communion during a worship service until the emperor, who was in attendance, promised to revoke his orders. Theodosius relented, but from then on, he tried to keep Ambrose uninformed of his imperial actions.

Little escaped Ambrose's watchful eye, however. In Thessalonica in 390, a Roman garrison commander imprisoned a popular charioteer for gross immorality. The champion's loyal fans gathered in a lynch mob and brutally killed the commander. Theodosius was enraged by the death of his officer. Soldiers went to the stadium and killed spectators. It is said that 7,000 civilians died in the rampage.

Ambrose was appalled by what looked like an act of officially sanctioned violence. He wrote a letter to Theodosius explaining that "the emperor also is a man, and may fall into temptation," and like King David before him, must repent his sins. If he did not, then Ambrose dared not celebrate the Eucharist in the imperial presence. "Pardon me for what I do—I must give honor to God!" wrote the bishop. Theodosius was deeply shaken at what amounted to a threat of

Basil of Caesarea and his brother Gregory of Nyssa wrote homilies on a martyrdom that had taken place in 320. It involved 40 Christian soldiers, left naked on a frozen pond, while steaming baths on the shore tempted them to give up their faith.

John Chrysostom, who was the bishop of Constantinople from 398 to about 403, is remembered for his vivid sermons and eccentric ways. He championed care for the poor and locked horns with Empress Eudoxia over her many extravagances.

excommunication. He doffed his purple robes, appeared before the bishop in the cathedral, and publicly begged for forgiveness. Ambrose was not swayed by such a calculated display of contrition. Before he would offer Theodosius communion, Ambrose had the emperor undergo several months of penance.

Theodosius died in Milan in 395 and the empire passed to his two sons. The 18-year-old Arcadius was granted sole control of the East, while the West went to the 11-year-old Honorius.

John Chrysostom versus Theophilus

Ambrose's long career underscored his political acumen, but such statesmanship was lost on an equally famous bishop of Constantinople, John Chrysostom. Consecrated in 398, John, later dubbed *Chrysostomos*, or "golden-tongued," was an inspiring preacher. He brought the austerity of a long-time ascetic to bear on every aspect of his office, railing against material wealth and working tirelessly to persuade the rich that their money ought to be spent alleviating the plight of the poor. Moreover, he condemned brutal treatment of slaves, argued that wife and husband are equal in marriage, and attacked the greed of the clergy.

While such sermons earned John a popular hearing, they made the rich and powerful of Constantinople uneasy. He even took it upon himself to criticize Eudoxia, wife of the emperor of the East, Arcadius. In 401 John went so far as to depose at least 13 bishops for buying their offices. Such a move evoked the wrath of Theophilus, who deeply resented any expansion of John's influence. (This was the same bishop of Alexandria who had engineered the destruction of the Serapeum 10 years earlier.)

These two men were fated to clash. When Theophilus condemned four monks as heretics because of their devotion to Origen's precepts, the monks went to Constantinople and appealed to John Chrysostom. Theophilus hastened to the capital and, rather than be judged by John, ingratiated himself with high-ranking people, spending money lavishly to procure their influence. His bribes worked. Theophilus became the accuser instead of the accused. Thanks to the empress Eudoxia, Theophilus obtained permission to call a synod to try John on trumped-up charges of heresy. Fearful of John's spellbinding power over the populace, the Alexandrian gathered 36 bishops, all enemies of John, at the Palace of the Oak, outside city limits. The list of charges against John included eating alone, stinginess, intriguing against another cleric, and visiting women with no one else in the room.

John refused to appear before this so-called Synod of the Oak. When the synod ruled that he be deposed, citizens gathered at John's church in Constantinople and for three days managed to protect him from the Imperial Guard. Hoping to restore order, the government at last had John taken away.

Church versus state

The people were so upset at the loss of their spiritual leader that Eudoxia had him reinstated. But a few months later, the unveiling of a silver statue of Eudoxia caused such commotion that John halted his church service in order to inveigh against the vain empress. Eudoxia was now determined to rid herself of this troublesome man, but a provisional synod, called at Chrysostom's request, overturned his previous condemnation. The bishop's enemies were unsure how to proceed against him. Finally, Eudoxia took action. On Easter Eve 404, when thousands of converts appeared for baptismal rites, soldiers routed the worshipers, injuring many.

The situation was intolerable. Arcadius, fearing insurrection, exiled the bishop from the capital. On the night that John was secretly ferried across the Black Sea, a fire sprang up beneath the bishop's ceremonial chair, destroying both the church in which it stood and the nearby Senate house. The actual cause was never determined, but suspicions ran high against John's supporters, and persecutions followed.

For three years, John conducted a voluminous correspondence with supporters throughout the empire, until vengeful enemies had him removed even farther from the capital. In 407, on a forced march to his new exile, John Chrysostom died of exhaustion at about age 60. His fate reveals how seriously the church stood in want of a single center of authority. Each crisis forced the ecclesiastical leadership to call a synod; yet, the ruling of one synod could always be challenged by another. When consensus was impossible, the imperial government often stepped in.

The photograph above shows one of the many remarkable churches that were carved out of volcanic rock in the Göreme Valley of Cappadocia. The faces of these structures are vertical stone, and the interiors follow traditional church forms such as the cruciform. Typically, the walls are covered with paintings.

The politics of theology

The church of the fourth century was on its way to becoming a powerful and rich institution. It became a practice at this time for wealthy Christians to leave one-third of their estates to the church. Some clerics did not welcome the new prosperity. Jerome was one who deplored the displays of wealth. "Our walls glitter with gold," he complained, "yet Christ is dying at our doors in the person of his poor, naked and hungry." In fact, church wealth was spilling over onto the clergy. Pope Damasus, for example, spent lavishly on enlarging basilicas to hold thousands and hiring the best architects, artisans, sculptors, and calligraphers.

If they seemed extravagant to some, the activities of Damasus and other bishops had a very serious aim: to establish orthodox Christianity as the unchallenged religion of the empire. Its truth was universal, they believed, and was open to all, hence the term *catholic* (from *katholikos*, "universal") church. So it happened that about this time the word *catholic* became synonymous with Western orthodox Christianity. By the end of the fifth century, the church in the West would be referred to as the Catholic Church.

If accumulating wealth and gaining upper-class support were deemed essential, so was the uprooting of nonorthodox variants of Christian belief. In 380 Theodosius issued a law specifically forbidding religious arguments due to heresy; he believed civil and religious order were equally threatened by heretics.

Still theological controversies continued to erupt, as the church struggled to define its tenets. In extreme cases, bishops used excommunication (the refusal to administer the sacraments) to condemn those who

At the first Council of Toledo in 400, all bishops who professed Priscillianism were condemned but then reconciled to the church. This 10th-century illustration depicts, from top to bottom, Toledo, churches, clerics, and a tent city, probably standard living quarters for participants in such councils.

refused to recant. But without one central authority, punishments were difficult to enforce. Nevertheless, the orthodox church was determined to suppress all nonorthodox forms of Christianity. By the end of the fourth century, its efforts had escalated into virtual war. An early casualty was the bishop Priscillian.

A condemned bishop

Priscillian, bishop of Avila in Spain, was a fiercely antipagan patrician, whose ascetic beliefs and practices had attracted a large following. Priscillianists struggled for the highest spiritual perfection by eschewing marriage, meat eating, and all pleasures of the senses. Somewhat like the Gnostics before him, Priscillian taught that the spirit is good and all matter, including the human form, is evil. In this notion detractors discerned an implication that Jesus could not have been truly human.

Priscillian's growing influence and reforming zeal proved too much for two rival Spanish bishops. Around 380 they convened at Saragossa a synod of his enemies, who condemned him as a heretic. Priscillian went to Italy and won from the civil authorities a reversal of their judgment, which Pope Damasus and Ambrose refused to support. When Emperor Gratian died in 383 and was replaced by Maximus, Priscillian's fate was once more open to debate.

Maximus called a synod at Bordeaux to denounce Priscillian. Perhaps he wanted to prove himself the protector of the orthodox church, or perhaps he desired only to seize the goods of wealthy Priscillianists. Whatever his reasons, the synod met his demands and found Priscillian guilty of heresy and witchcraft. Priscillian refused to plead before the synod. He was then forcibly transported to Trier (in present-day Germany) for trial on the clearly false charge of sorcery, a capital crime under Roman law, and tortured until he confessed. The state ordered his execution.

Martin of Tours, today revered as the patron saint of France, went to Trier. He was horrified that Maximus would dare to execute a bishop. Martin, who

Martin of Tours, a patron saint of France, was born of pagan parents in Hungary but was baptized at 18. He began his career as a soldier, then became a monk, and is believed to have established the first monastery in Gaul. He continued the monastic way of life even after his consecration as bishop of Tours about 371. Martin tried, unsuccessfully, to prevent the execution of the Spanish bishop Priscillian for heresy in 386, but he did induce other bishops at least to withdraw their charges against the Priscillianists.

The First Popes

In the third and fourth centuries the title *pope* (meaning "papa") designated any bishop in the church. Gradually, it came to refer exclusively to the bishop of Rome, and along with the title went the recognition of Rome as the center of authority in the Western church.

In 382 Pope Damasus underscored Rome's claim to supremacy by referring to the city as the Apostolic See, with its authority handed down from the Apostle Peter, believed to be buried there. The oldest known papal decree is in a letter written in 385 by Pope Siricius. With the election of Pope Leo I in 440, the papacy became more firmly established. Leo considered all bishops equal but guided by "Peter in the person of Peter's successor."

had sometimes been consulted by the emperor, made him promise to spare Priscillian. Just to appease Maximus, Martin shared communion with the bishops who had condemned Priscillian. But in 386 Maximus ordered that Priscillian and six of his followers be executed anyway. Appalled, Martin blamed himself in part. Later, he complained that this experience of treachery had diminished his spiritual powers.

The episode was traumatic for the church; it had permitted the state to interfere dramatically in ecclesiastical affairs. After Priscillian's death, the bishops who had accused him were excommunicated. Soon afterward, Theodosius overthrew Maximus, rescinded all the former emperor's orders, and deposed the guilty Spanish prelates. Galicia (in northwest Spain) remained Priscillianist until 400, when most Priscillianist bishops in that province were reconciled to the church at the first ecclesiastical Council of Toledo.

The Christological controversy

In 325, at the Council of Nicaea, the church had struggled to come to terms with the nature of Christ's divinity. Barely 100 years later, it was wrestling with the other side of the same issue, namely the nature of Christ's humanity. The Gospels told of Jesus the man, who had suffered hunger and thirst and died on the cross. But they also said that with his coming, "the Word became flesh and dwelt among us."

The problem confronting theologians of the fourth and fifth centuries was extraordinarily difficult: how to determine the nature of Christ's humanity and his divinity. This area of inquiry is referred to as Christology, the study of Christ's person, or the relationship of the divine and human in Christ. The Scriptures were perused for any light they could shed on this subject. A passage in Luke, for example, stated that "Jesus increased in wisdom and in stature, and in favor with God and man." Did that mean that as a child he was lacking in wisdom? How could Jesus increase in wisdom if he was divinely all-knowing? Was his divinity separate from his humanity or a part of it?

Answering such questions would test the mettle of the orthodox church and require at least five ecumenical councils. There were two main schools of thought: one held that Christ had a single nature that was divine, for his humanity had been subordinated to his Godhood; the other insisted that Christ was both man and God, whose two natures—the human and divine—were distinct but not separate.

Those who stressed the singleness, or unity, of Christ's nature believed that when Christ became flesh, a divine spirit had replaced his human spirit. One who espoused this doctrine was Bishop Apollinaris of Laodicea. He envisioned that the Logos and human flesh were perfectly melded in Christ, just as the human soul and human body are one in man.

Theologians who defended the other view believed, as Pope Leo later put it, that while the union was indeed perfect, the natures remained perfectly distinct. To them, the issue was the salvation of man. Christ had to be divine to provide this salvation, but he had to be fully human for others to be saved by his death and Resurrection. The words of Gregory of Nazianzus uphold this point: "Whatever the Logos did not assume in the incarnation," wrote Gregory, "he did not heal, he did not cure."

Both groups had their moderate advocates, whose formulas were eventually brought together in the orthodox consensus that favored the distinctness. There were also extreme factions—the Eutychians, who seemed to have fused the divine and the human into a third kind of reality, and the Nestorians, who were accused of separating Christ's divinity and humanity. The designation *Theotokos* ("God Bearer," or "Mother of God"), a devotional title for Mary that had long been used by Greek-speaking Christians, became a symbol for those who feared a separation of natures.

Theodore of Mopsuestia and Nestorius

Although his surviving doctrinal writings are fragmentary, we know that Theodore of Mopsuestia was a leading Eastern theologian of the early fifth century. His conception of Christ was based on two realities: the "divine nature" of the Logos, or Divine Word, that was Christ and the "human nature" of the man who was Jesus. But he took it one step further when he insisted that Jesus had not only a human soul but also free will and was even subject to sin. The Incarnation, he said, was a special indwelling in which God abided within the man "by good pleasure . . . as in a son." Theodore died in 428, the year his student Nestorius, who also believed in the distinct natures of Christ's humanity and divinity, was ordained the bishop of Constantinople.

Nestorius and his followers carried the teachings of Theodore to new lengths. In his first year as bishop, he revealed that he was opposed to the orthodox designation of Christ as both God and man when he refused to designate the Virgin Mary as *Theotokos*. To Nestorius' mind, this would have been the same as calling her a goddess. Also, how could a human baby be God? Nestorius asked rhetorically. "That which was formed in the womb is not . . . God," he said, adding that "God is not a baby two or three months old." In line with the view of two natures of Christ, he preferred the designations *Theodokos,* meaning "God receiving," and *Christotokos*, meaning "Christ Bearer," to describe the Virgin Mary. Staunchly opposed to this concept set forth by Nestorius was Cyril, the bishop of Alexandria.

The ruthless zeal of Cyril

No one defended the orthodoxy concerning Christ's person more zealously than Cyril. He vehemently upheld the term *Theotokos* and was a ruthless enemy of all who opposed this view. Cyril had been elected bishop in 412, despite widespread opposition; he ruled with an iron hand for 32 years, making Alexandria "the city of the orthodox."

When Cyril heard of the Nestorian sermons on the Virgin Mary, he flew into a rage. How dared they suggest that the infant Jesus was not divine! At the Council of Nicaea Christ's divinity had been determined to be timeless. As far as Cyril was concerned, Nestorius had proved himself a heretic who deserved the full wrath of the orthodox church.

Cyril based his scriptural interpretations upon the teachings of early Church Fathers as well as the Bible itself. Later theologians referred to him "as the guardian of accuracy." The "royal way" of theology, he wrote, is "to inquire into the beliefs of the holy Fathers, which came about through the inspiration of the Holy Spirit; and to keep firmly in mind the train

Cyril of Alexandria, right, opposed Nestorius of Constantinople on the issue of whether the Virgin Mary should be called Theotokos *("God Bearer") or* Christotokos *("Christ Bearer").*

of their thoughts." He cautioned against new interpretations. The Fathers, he contended, had "not left out or overlooked anything vital."

A man of unbending will, Cyril proved a brutal adversary. Like his uncle, Theophilus, who had brought about the destruction of the Serapeum in 391, Cyril was intent on giving orthodoxy the force of law. He closed the churches of nonorthodox Christians and was involved in the expulsion of Jews from Alexandria. Worst of all, Cyril may have instigated, or at least tacitly approved, the bestial murder, in 415, of one of the most admired of pagan thinkers—the beautiful and talented Hypatia.

Daughter of the respected mathematician Theon, Hypatia was so advanced in mathematics and Platonic philosophy that she was appointed to the chair of phi-

During Lent in 415, the philosopher Hypatia was accosted by the parabolani, *a disreputable band of lay monks. They dragged her from her carriage and into a church, where they brutally murdered her. This shocking, violent event underscored the danger facing prominent pagans of the day. Hypatia held a public position of importance (rare for a woman in her time); her influence would have caused many to envy her.*

losophy at the prestigious Museum (or university) of Alexandria. The historian Socrates Scholasticus tells us that she "was so eminent in learning as to surpass all the philosophers of her own time." (None of her published works have survived, however.) Cyril may have envied her popularity, for according to Socrates, not only did students travel from afar to learn from this remarkable woman, but churchmen were drawn to her as well. Bishop Synesius of Ptolemaïs was among her pupils and was said to bring his manuscripts to her for criticism. Cyril must have resented also Hypatia's friendship with Orestes, Roman prefect of Alexandria. Orestes, who apparently consulted Hypatia on civil matters, had, on occasion, complained to the court in Constantinople when Cyril had overstepped his prerogatives. But it seems that neither Orestes nor Hypatia realized just how determined Cyril was to rid the city of anti-Christian influences.

Under Cyril's personal command was a small army of lay monks, the *parabolani*, or "reckless ones," who acted as attendants to the sick in times of plague and were sworn to stay on the job, whatever the risk—hence their name of "reckless ones." At this time, however, the *parabolani* under Cyril's command were no angels of mercy but a private militia used by the bishop to intimidate and terrorize pagans, Jews, and nonorthodox Christians.

During Lent in 415, for reasons that remain obscure, the *parabolani* set upon Hypatia and dragged her from her carriage into a church. There they stripped her naked and beat her to death with tiles. Then, according to Socrates, they tore Hypatia's body limb from limb and carried the remains away for burning.

There was an investigation. Many felt that Cyril was responsible, but horrified officials in Constantinople were unable to clearly determine responsibility. The monks, judged dangerous to the public welfare, were placed under the prefect's authority. Eventually, however, Cyril not only regained control of his band but also increased their number from 500 to 600.

The Council of Ephesus

Cyril was aware that the fate of orthodoxy lay in the hands of those who were well connected with high-ranking members of both the church and the state. Perhaps part of his opposition to Nestorius lay in his fear that this bishop was consolidating too powerful a position at the court of Theodosius II (ruler of the East who was the grandson of Theodosius the Great). Cyril's cry of heresy against Nestorius finally led Pope Celestine I, in 430, to threaten Nestorius with excommunication unless he recanted his doctrine.

To settle the matter, the emperor called a council in Ephesus in 431. The pope agreed to send his representatives, even though he still regarded Nestorius as "the denier of God's birth." The emperor, however, did not reckon on the cunning tactics of Cyril, who raced to Ephesus and opened the council before the papal legates or the Eastern bishops loyal to Nestorius had time to get there. Nestorius, not surprisingly, declined to appear. Cyril then presided over the council's decision to condemn his rival as a heretic and affirm the Virgin Mary's status as *Theotokos*. These actions were reported to Nestorius in a letter that began with the greeting, "To Nestorius, the new Judas."

Within the week, the Eastern clerics arrived and convened a new council. They announced their support of Nestorius and deposed Cyril. Not long after, however, Pope Celestine's deputies appeared on the scene and approved Cyril's ouster of Nestorius.

Following these suits and countersuits, Theodosius had Nestorius and Cyril, as well as the bishop of Ephesus, jailed. Cyril dispensed bribes and thus managed to escape from custody. Nestorius subsequently was allowed to retire to Antioch.

John of Antioch, one of the bishops at the Ephesian council, was in a particularly difficult position. As the leader of the so-called Orientals, bishops of the Eastern provinces, he disagreed with Cyril's theological stance, particularly with the definitions of heresy that Cyril had provocatively set down in a public letter as

Above are the ruins of St. Mary's Church in Ephesus, where a council met in 431 to settle controversies on the Virgin Mary and the divinity of Christ. Principal protagonists were Cyril of Alexandria and Nestorius of Constantinople. The result was a deadlock that could be broken only by Theodosius II, who had both parties arrested. Cyril bribed his way free and Nestorius was allowed to retire.

12 anathemas. These were 12 ideas that Cyril considered so unorthodox that anyone who dared to confirm them was to be cursed, or anathematized.

The new orthodoxy

In 433 both sides finally compromised and articulated their agreement in a letter known as the Symbol of Union. John of Antioch reluctantly agreed to recommend that Nestorius be deposed as bishop of Constantinople, while the obstinate Cyril moderated the harsh language of his 12 anathemas. Such phrases as "one nature" and "hypostatic union" (meaning joining of essences in a single individual) were dropped, and other language, such as "union of two natures," was adopted. Nestorius lost much of his important support and was sent into exile in the Libyan Desert. He died about 450 in Egypt.

The controversial designation *Theotokos* was at last affirmed as orthodox by both John and Cyril. But a large number of the Oriental bishops refused to accept the condemnation of Nestorius. In spite of Cyril's powerful opposition, Nestorius' beliefs gave rise to a new movement called Nestorianism. It became the professed teaching of the church in the Persian Empire, in large part because its communicants could seek the protection of Persian rulers by claiming that their kind of Christianity differed from that of Persia's traditional enemies, the Romans. Full of missionary zeal, the Nestorians evangelized in India and made converts as far away as China. (Centuries later, Marco Polo noted their churches all along the route from Baghdad to Beijing.) Their communities survived in Mesopotamia until 1400, when the Mongols sacked Baghdad and drove the Nestorians into the mountains of Kurdistan. One of their liturgies is perhaps the oldest in use in any Christian church today.

The road to Chalcedon

Cyril adhered to the compromise that was set forth in the Symbol of Union, but with his death in 444, controversy erupted once more. The trouble started in Constantinople, where Eutyches, the head of a monastery, taught that Christ's humanity was absorbed by his divinity; while he had two natures before the Incarnation, afterward his divinity alone remained.

To Flavian, bishop of Constantinople from 446, this teaching was heresy, for it denied the full humanity of Jesus. Flavian sided with those churchmen who believed that the divine and human natures of Christ coexisted after the Incarnation. Politics once again muddied the waters. Eutyches was influential at the court of Theodosius II. Flavian was not. Eutyches' political status no doubt attracted Dioscoros, bishop of Alexandria, who hoped to step up the power of Alexandria relative to that of Constantinople. Theodosius convened a new council in 449. Again, both sides met in Ephesus, but this time Pope Leo I entered the fray at the request of Flavian, who hoped that Leo would refute Eutyches' errors.

In his *Tome,* or doctrinal letter, Leo upheld the ideas in the Symbol of Union and passed over the excesses of both sides. Where Flavian had stressed two distinct natures, Leo described two natures "coalescing into one person." To counter Eutyches' extreme position that Christ was of one divine nature, Leo asserted that God as incarnated was "whole in his own nature, whole in ours." Each nature acted in harmony with the other. "To hunger, thirst and to sleep were manifestly human," he wrote, "but the satisfaction of the five thousand with five loaves [of bread] and walking on the sea were manifestly divine."

The *Tome*, though masterly and authoritative, was not immediately influential. While Leo stayed in Rome, Dioscoros, arch-defender of Eutyches and an expert at packing the house, made sure that a majority of the 130 bishops who met in Ephesus were in his party; he also brought along an army of lay monks, the same street fighters that murdered Hypatia.

Presiding over the council, Dioscoros refused to have any papers that disagreed with his position read aloud. Flavian's intentions were reversed. The accused, Eutyches, now became the accuser. Flavian saw his supporters give ground. Shouts went up from the angry Alexandrians, and one Antiochene heard threats against Flavian: "Burn him alive! Cut him in two this man who divides the Christ!" The assembly became so tumultuous that imperial commissioners had to be summoned to restore order. The emperor sided with Eutyches. As militant monks bellowed threats and soldiers backed them up, reluctant bishops agreed to depose Flavian as the bishop of Constantinople. The Egyptian clerics handled Flavian so roughly that he died of the injuries.

At the Council of Ephesus in 431 rival groups met separately and deposed both Cyril and Nestorius. In the end, eight canons were passed, some of which favored Cyril's position; still the controversy raged.

Since glorification of the Virgin Mary began in the late fifth century, icons of her have graced churches throughout the world. The one above is a sixth-century tapestry, probably from Egypt. Archangels Michael and Gabriel appear on either side of Mary; Christ looks down on her. The statue, left, is from 13th-century Strasbourg.

For one brief moment, Dioscoros, strongly supported by Theodosius II, had established the doctrine of one divine nature in Christ as the dominant position. Leo was furious at what he called the synod of thieves, but he was powerless to repair the damage wrought by Dioscoros, whose position was protected by the emperor himself. The church was teetering on the verge of a permanent schism.

Then in 450 Theodosius fell off his horse and died. His death changed the course of theology once more, for his successor, his sister Pulcheria, opposed the crafty Dioscoros. She chose as her consort Marcian, who became emperor of the East. The new emperor sided with his wife in favoring Leo's position. In 451 Marcian called a new council to decide the issue. Much to the dismay of Leo, who feared the intrigue of Oriental bishops, Marcian demanded that it be held in the East. Perhaps as many as 520 bishops met at St. Euphemia's Church in Chalcedon, just across the Bosporus from Constantinople.

The Council of Chalcedon

The tables had been turned again. Dioscoros found himself seated in the assembly as one of the accused. This time Eutyches was condemned, and Dioscoros and five of his colleagues were deposed. More than half of the bishops signed a definition of the Incarnation of Christ that closely followed the definition formulated in Leo's *Tome.* It stated that Christ had two natures "without confusion, without change, without division, without separation," a statement that ruled out the extreme ends of the theological spectrum and affirmed the central points of both positions.

The agreement reached by the bishops at Chalcedon had added a new chapter to the Christological controversies. For many Christians, the language adopted there, "a single Person in two Natures," was at least workable. Indeed, it became the standard of orthodoxy. But the issue was far from settled, and Leo's theological victory was marred by a political de-

During the fourth century, when Christian bishops sought to gain the upper hand in theological disputes and Christian emperors strove to stamp out paganism, many people were apparently unaffected by either enterprise. It was business as usual in the workshop that produced these two glass bowls: The one on the left depicts Adam and Eve with the words, "Rejoice in God, drink, and may you live." The one on the right features the deities Apollo and Artemis and bears the words, "Take the pleasing bowl."

feat. Echoing language used at the Council of Constantinople in 381, the churchmen at Chalcedon declared, in Canon 28, that Constantinople was now the "New Rome" and its power would extend over such additional areas as Thrace (in the Balkans) and parts of Asia Minor. Still, Rome remained first in rank. Moreover, the council elevated Jerusalem to a partriarchate, making it the fifth one along with Constantinople, Rome, Alexandria, and Antioch. The pope's representatives protested, but to no avail.

The theological compromise of the council created a furor in Egypt and Palestine, where the common people joined with fanatical monks in a violent rejection of the council's actions. In 457 a mob lynched Dioscoros' successor. Jerusalem remained in turmoil for years. Those who could not accept the definition that was set forth at Chalcedon eventually left the orthodox church and became known as Monophysites, or believers in one divine nature in Christ. This first permanent schism resulted in three independent churches—the Armenian Church, the Coptic Church of Egypt, and the Jacobite Church of Syria.

Pagan resistance

Around 400, pagans probably made up the majority still of the empire's population; nonetheless they had learned to avoid attracting attention lest they be forced to convert. The sincerity of many such conversions may be evaluated from one surviving quotation: "I therefore am thinking of the danger to my life, and so off I go now to the church, to evade the death that otherwise awaits me."

Educated pagans did their best to ignore Christianity's assaults on paganism. A number endeavored to create new and original literary works in the classical mold. The historian Ammianus Marcellinus was a scrupulous chronicler and sober stylist whose works are often compared with those of his illustrious prede-

Continued on page 264

The Pilgrimage of Etheria

Few tourists have ever been as indefatigable as Etheria (also known as Egeria), a Christian pilgrim of boundless energy who traversed the Holy Land and other places more than 1,500 years ago. To Etheria, who may have been a nun, the Bible was more than a book of religious inspiration; it was also the perfect travel guide. With God's word to direct her, Etheria visited religious landmarks the way modern tourists rush to the Statue of Liberty. She scaled Mount Sinai, explaining that it was "straight [and seemed] as if you were going up a wall." At the top, she could not resist, like tourists in every age, marveling at the panoramic view: "We were able to see Egypt and Palestine, the Red Sea and the Parthenian Sea . . . as well as the vast lands of the Saracens—all unbelievably far below us."

In her journal she recounted a visit to the place where the people of Israel had worshiped the Golden Calf. But when she went to see the pillar of salt, which was said to be all that remained of Lot's wife, she found "the pillar itself . . . has been submerged in the Dead Sea." Etheria observed the celebration of Holy Week in Jerusalem, where on Palm Sunday "everyone is carrying branches, either palm or olive, and they accompany the bishop in the very way the people did when once they went down with the Lord."

Etheria's caravan trod the shores of the Red Sea, clambered over mountains, and crossed sandy deserts with "no road whatsoever." No hardship, however, was great enough to dull her enthusiasm. When a local presbyter asked if she had the stamina for an unscheduled side excursion "to see the water that flows from the rock, which Moses gave to the children of Israel when they were thirsty," Etheria's reply was instantaneous: "At this we were eager to go."

When Etheria had to consider bringing her journey to an end, she conveniently remembered the bones of additional martyrs she should visit: "My present plan is . . . to travel to Asia, since I want to make a pilgrimage to Ephesus, and the martyrium of the holy and blessed Apostle John," she writes. To the sisters, for whom she described all her wanderings, Etheria added, I will "write to you . . . if my plans change."

The journal of Etheria's colorful travels was lost for almost 800 years, until a single copy was rediscovered in an Italian monastery in 1884. Sadly, much of her original document had by then disappeared; only the middle portion remained. Perhaps at the beginning or end of her book, Etheria gave details about herself that are now frustratingly absent. Some scholars believe she came from a convent in Spain and that she journeyed from 380 to 384. Her life is a mystery, but her adventurous spirit is summed up in the greeting the bishop of Edessa extended to her: "Since I see, my daughter, that from a spirit of religion you have gone to such great efforts to journey here from distant places, we shall, if you desire it, show you all the places here which Christians like to see."

As more pilgrims made their way to the Holy Land, flasks such as this one were filled with holy oil or Jordan water, which were sold to travelers as souvenirs.

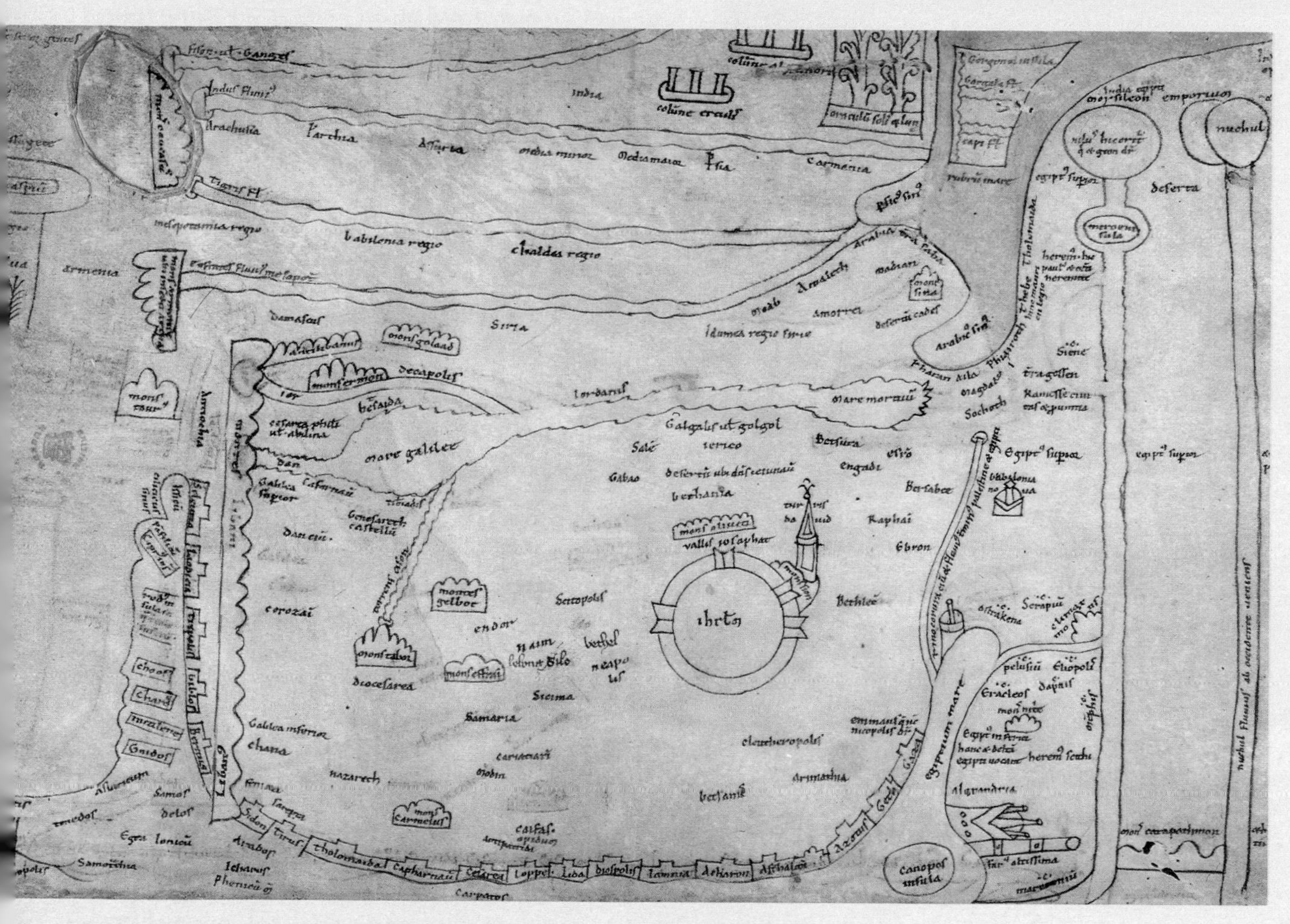

This map of the Holy Land is a 12th-century copy of the original made by Jerome in 385. The Church Father is known mainly for his Latin translation of the Bible, but he was also a cartographer who explored Palestine for 35 years. His map was made a year or so after the pilgrim Etheria is believed to have visited the area; her descriptions and his have provided us with much of what we know about the Holy Land in the late fourth century. The map includes territory from Constantinople to Alexandria (lower right) and from the Mediterranean coast (bottom) to the Ganges River (top). Jerusalem is represented by the large circle with a tower.

Begun in the year 379, this church in Milan was dedicated to Ambrose, then bishop of the imperial city. Ambrose had accepted the post reluctantly, but during his 25 years of service, he wielded more power than any churchman who had preceded him.

cessors Livy and Tacitus. Macrobius, from whose books we have the clearest picture of the intellectual life during the sunset of paganism, was widely read by philosophers throughout the Middle Ages. His reference to the theory that the earth revolves around the sun may have inspired Christopher Columbus. Another impressive defender of late paganism was the celebrated Libanius, who assumed the chair of rhetoric in Antioch in 354 and taught or corresponded with such notable Christians as Theodore of Mopsuestia, John Chrysostom, and Basil the Great.

Ambrose of Milan

One who opposed paganism and, at the same time, withstood the wills of emperors and empresses was Bishop Ambrose of Milan. Born in Trier, around 340, to aristocratic Christian parents, he was well educated and well connected. In his 30's Ambrose was serving as governor of Upper Italy, when the death of the Arian bishop of Milan about 373 created a bitter election stalemate between Arians and champions of the Nicene faith. Milan was on the verge of civil strife, and Ambrose stepped in to restore order. Legend says that as he made his way through a tumultuous assembly, a small child cried out, "Ambrose for bishop!" Whereupon, the crowd took up the cry.

A devout Christian by belief but as yet unbaptized, Ambrose accepted the nomination and resigned his government post. In just eight days, he underwent instruction, was baptized, and was ordained through successive ecclesiastical ranks.

As bishop, Ambrose dealt directly with a number of rulers. With each, he strove to ensure that the universal, or catholic, church was recognized as the only legitimate religion of the empire. He championed the church's alliance with the state on an equal footing yet struggled to keep it free from state interference. To this end, he embroiled himself in countless political battles. For example, in 383, he agreed to act as ambassador to Maximus, the usurper of the Western Empire. The bishop convinced Maximus not to attack Italy and to spare the lives of the legitimate Western emperor, the 12-year-old Valentinian II, and his mother, the regent Justina. Maximus complied. Two years or so later, Justina, an Arian, repaid the favor by demanding that Ambrose turn over a Milanese church to a congregation of Arians. Nothing would induce him to grant her request. Meanwhile, throngs of Ambrose's supporters massed around the disputed church.

When the Imperial Guard came to claim the building, Ambrose turned them away saying, "The palaces belong to the Emperor, the churches to the Bishop."

The court relented, but a year later, it again asked Ambrose to relinquish a church. Once more he refused. Crowds flocked around. All Milan was caught up in the crisis between the church and the state. Augustine, the future bishop of Hippo, was in Milan at the time and was deeply impressed with the popular outpouring of support for Bishop Ambrose.

The courage of his convictions

Justina had Ambrose summoned to appear before a court of arbitration. The resolute bishop declined, writing that "in matters of faith, and in any problems of the ecclesiastical constitution . . . bishops can be tried only by bishops." With the stroke of his pen, Ambrose had just placed the church outside the jurisdiction of the state! Justina was incensed and ordered Ambrose to leave Milan. He refused.

About that time, two skeletons were unearthed near a church in Milan. Ambrose wrote to his sister that surely these were martyrs' bones, for when they were being removed "a blind man was healed." After the discovery of these holy relics, Justina admitted defeat. Ambrose had prevailed. The incident gave great impetus to the cult of relics (see box page 234).

Ambrose remained one of the church's staunchest advocates. Even Theodosius I was unable to withstand the bishop's resolute convictions. However, this astute churchman was also a pastor who carefully tended his flock. Some of his accomplishments are taken for granted today. For example, in the worship service, he is credited with having borrowed the Eastern church's style of antiphonal chanting, in which separate choruses answer each other, musical phrase for musical phrase. Reportedly, when the bishop and his supporters occupied a church to prevent its seizure by forces loyal to Justina, Ambrose introduced the chanting to uphold morale during the anxious vigil.

In his sermons, Ambrose proved an accomplished theologian. He often made symbolic, or allegorical, interpretations of the Old Testament. This approach,

The carved panel, above, from the altarpiece in the Church of St. Ambrose, depicts scenes from the life of the powerful bishop, who has been named one of the doctors, or authoritative teachers, of the church. Ambrose is remembered especially for giving eloquent sermons, championing morality, zealously defending orthodoxy and the church's independence, and generously donating his personal wealth to the poor. The mosaic, left, made in the early fifth century, is probably a true likeness.

inspired by earlier Greek theologians, helped convert many educated Romans and was instrumental in the conversion of Augustine.

On his deathbed in 397, this man of steadfast faith prayed silently until the end, extending his arms to form the sign of the cross. His faith was expressed in the plainest of terms: "I am . . . not afraid of death, for we have a good Lord."

Jerome, Bible scholar and translator

The early church had many scholars, but none was so learned or prolific as Jerome. Born about 345 near the Italian-Dalmatian border to Christian parents, he was given a fine classical education. Jerome studied under an eminent grammarian and was introduced to the works of Virgil and Cicero, which had a lifelong influence on him. He also delighted in oratory, later recalling the vanity of his school days when he went about "wearing the specially donned toga, spouting petty forensic exercises before the professor."

Assisting Jerome in the mammoth task of translating the entire Bible into Latin were two of his devoted followers, Paula and her daughter Eustochium. At last, all of the Scriptures would be available to people who spoke and wrote only the common language of the Roman West.

About 372, the young Jerome made a pilgrimage to Antioch, where he learned Greek and pursued Bible studies. Longing for the ascetic life, he took to the desert but kept up a voluminous correspondence.

Though a devout Christian, Jerome worried that his passion for Cicero was distracting him from the truth of the Scriptures. (Many Christians during this period felt the need to denounce pagan literature.) His anxiety expressed itself in a nightmare in which he was accused by a tribunal of being a Ciceronian, not a Christian. He was then scourged, and while suffering the beating, vowed never again to possess secular books. When Jerome awoke, his shoulders were black and blue. Still, he could not keep his promise. For the rest of his life he worried about his inability to forgo the pleasures of the pagan classics.

After more than two years in the desert, Jerome returned to Antioch, where he was ordained a priest. In 382 he became secretary to Pope Damasus, who wanted to encourage Latin theological works. The church in the West needed a new Latin translation of the Greek New Testament; Damasus selected Jerome for the job. The assignment, which he expanded by translating the Old Testament, largely from the Hebrew, took him about 23 years to complete.

A confirmed ascetic, Jerome earned a reputation for being an obstinate and exacting priest. He was spiritual counselor to a group of devout Roman women, who followed his disciplined routines of fasting and all-night vigils. Rumors spread that when Blaesilla, a young noblewoman, died in 384 or 385, it was due to her adherence to Jerome's strict asceticism. Her death may have marred his ecclesiastical career, for he left Rome, eventually settling in Bethlehem. Blaesilla's mother, Paula, and another daughter, Eustochium, faithfully followed him. These two women served Jerome until their deaths. (It was not unusual, at this time, for patrician women to serve the church without taking vows or living in an ascetic community.)

While in Bethlehem, Jerome worked fervently on the interpretation of Scripture and studied Hebrew with several Jewish teachers. Some are said to have so feared the disapproval of fellow Jews for teaching a Gentile that they visited Jerome under cover of night. He was a meticulous scholar, familiarizing himself with both the Greek and Hebrew texts. Borrowing from the methods of Origen, he sought out the spiritual message of each passage, decoding any allegorical meaning and noting pertinent historical details. The legacy of Jerome's scholarship is staggering. When he died at about 75, he had written 63 volumes of Latin commentaries and more than 100 homilies on the meaning of the Scriptures. But his most lasting monument was the first comprehensive Latin Bible, which came to be known as the Vulgate.

The brilliant Augustine

"Can any praise be worthy of the Lord's majesty? How magnificent his strength! How inscrutable his wisdom! Man is one of your creatures, Lord, and his instinct is to praise you. He bears about him the mark of death, the sign of his own sin, to remind him that you thwart the proud. But still, . . . he wishes to praise you. The thought of you stirs him so deeply that he cannot be content unless he praises you, because you made us for yourself and our hearts find no peace until they rest in you." So begins Augustine's moving autobiography and dialogue with God, the *Confessions*, written when he was about 45.

Possessed of a deep spirituality and enormous intellect, Augustine left a stronger mark on the Western church than any other theologian. Much of what we know about his life comes from his *Confessions*. He was born in 354 in Tagaste, Numidia (in present-day Algeria), to a pagan father and a Christian mother.

In a magnificent example of ninth-century calligraphy, this copy of a preface, from Jerome's New Testament translation, has been artfully shaped like a cross. Using colored inks on stained parchment was a popular technique in the early Middle Ages for producing deluxe copies of books.

His parents were middle class and gave him a good education that would prepare him for teaching or the civil service. At age 17, he went to Carthage to study rhetoric and there became enthralled with Manichaeism. Augustine's love of philosophy found a perfect fit in Manichaeism, which promised its believers "the open, undiluted truth." Looking back on those youthful days in the *Confessions,* Augustine wrote: "What crooked paths I trod! What dangers threatened my soul when it rashly hoped that by abandoning you [God] it would find something better!"

In 375 Augustine returned home to teach rhetoric. His mother, Monica, heartsick at his conversion to Manichaeism, barred him from the house. She prayed to God to make her son see the error of his ways and implored the local bishop to intervene. "It cannot be

This detail from a Roman fresco, painted probably in the sixth century, is an early portrait of Augustine. From his death in 430 to the end of the Middle Ages, Augustine was the most popular and influential of the Church Fathers. His ideas continue to have a powerful hold over Western theology to this day. Some consider his influence second only to that of Paul.

that the son of these tears should be lost," he replied.

Still Augustine would not be swayed. In 383 he left for Rome. There he met Symmachus, the pagan prefect who was leading a campaign to induce the government to restore the Altar of Victory to the Senate. With Symmachus' help, Augustine was appointed professor of rhetoric and public orator in Milan.

Life in Milan brought Augustine conflicts. He heard the riveting sermons of Bishop Ambrose, whose allegorical interpretations of the Old Testament removed many objections raised against this text by the Manichaeans. He wrestled with his Manichaean faith and finally, at the age of 32, renounced it. In 386 a marriage to a Milanese heiress was arranged but was put off while Augustine disengaged himself from his mistress of more than 13 years. She had borne him a son, whom Augustine loved dearly but referred to as the "child of my sin." His famous cry, "Lord, give me continence and chastity but not now," springs from those youthful years when, though he espoused the Manichaean ideal of chastity, he did not practice it. His strong sexual appetite had always been a torment to him.

The conversion of Augustine

During the summer of 386, however, the sermons of Bishop Ambrose and the prayers of Monica, who had followed her son to Milan, began to work their way into his soul. Augustine came to recognize that imitation of Christ would be possible only if his pride and sensuality were defeated. To Augustine, such an ascetic Christianity held the promise of uniting the aims of classical philosophy and his own personal ideals. But while "convicted by the truth," as he later expressed it, his will still resisted.

In spiritual torment, he went into a garden late one summer day and heard a child's voice chanting, "Take and read; take and read." He took up his Bible, and his eyes fell upon two lines of Romans 13:13–14: "Not in reveling and drunkenness, not in debauchery and licentiousness, not in quarreling and jealousy. But put on the Lord Jesus Christ, and make no provision for the flesh, to gratify its desires." Those two lines seemed spoken to him from heaven above. As he described the experience in the *Confessions:* "For in an instant, as I came to the end of the sentence, it was as though the light of confidence flooded my heart and all the darkness of doubt was dispelled."

Augustine called off the wedding and resigned his posts. Much to his mother's joy, he and his son were baptized in 387. Tradition says Ambrose performed the ceremony. Then they left Italy to found a monastery in Augustine's hometown of Tagaste. "I desire to know God and my own soul. Nothing else; nothing whatever," wrote the new convert.

The bishop of Hippo

Augustine's many talents were called into service in 391, when the bishop of Hippo, a thriving seacoast city, demanded that Augustine be ordained a priest. Four years later, Augustine himself became bishop of Hippo. He used the might of his pen and office to check the growing Donatist movement (see pages 245–248). While Donatism had been trounced in the East, it had found renewed strength in North Africa. Donatist clergy were accusing orthodox Christians of impurity and insisting that the Donatist church was the only true one. Those who wished to join it, moreover, had to be rebaptized.

At first Augustine used magnanimity. He wrote that the universal church had to be inclusive of all, or the promise made by God that Abraham would be "a father of a multitude of nations" would never be fulfilled. Like a net that captures a variety of fish in the sea, the catholic church welcomes the "unclean" as well as the "clean," who will be sorted out finally on Judgment Day. The Donatists, in Augustine's view, were being uncharitable when they excluded others. They were "erring brethren" and should be corrected for the sake of their own salvation.

As the acrimony increased, Augustine's position hardened. From a parable in Luke, Augustine found justification to use force. In that parable, a man gives a banquet that is poorly attended. He tells his servants to "go out . . . and compel people to come in, that my house may be filled." Augustine urged a policy of physical coercion, in the hope that it would help to correct the Donatists' false beliefs. Thus, he sanctioned the use of physical force against Christians by Christians. (Centuries later, Augustine's support of

In Confessions *Augustine describes an incident in his youth, wherein he and a few friends stole some fruit. "Our pleasure," he said, "consisted in doing something that was forbidden."*

such "corrective measures" would be used to justify the use of torture in the Spanish Inquisition.) Then in 411 a conference was held in Carthage at which the Donatists were condemned. The emperor subsequently banned the Donatist church and confiscated all of its property.

Pelagius and divine grace

At the turn of the fifth century, as the empire in the West teetered toward collapse, a new ascetic movement began to spread. Its leader was Pelagius, a British monk, who had already inspired a number of wealthy citizens to forsake their material possessions and take up the ascetic life of Christ. Brilliant and devout, this strong-minded Briton had been horrified by the venal excesses, materialism, and sensuality of many orthodox Christians in Rome.

But in leading believers back to basics, he had expressed what, to Augustine, were some alarming new ideas. For instance, Pelagius believed that Adam and

Augustine was guided in Christian ways by his mother, Monica, shown in this fresco taking him to school. He abandoned the faith while he studied and taught rhetoric but was drawn back to it by Bishop Ambrose of Milan.

Eve did not infect the human race with sin; they only led it astray. Thus, babies were born free of sin. The implications of Pelagian theology disturbed Augustine deeply. If man was born without sin, then what need did he have of God's grace? What need was there for salvation, if man could attain moral perfection through his own human efforts?

Pelagius arrived in Africa in 410, accompanied by Celestius, a disputatious follower. After his mentor had departed for Jerusalem, Celestius caused a sensation in Carthage. At issue was man's free will and the Pelagian belief that man can choose whether or not to take the pathway offered by Christ. God had provided the Old Testament and the Gospels, all that man needed for moral direction. The choice to follow was man's; those who refused would face the terrors of the Last Judgment. To this view, Augustine replied, "A man who is afraid of sinning because of Hell-fire, is afraid, not of sinning, but of burning."

The Pelagian definition of free will disturbed a number of churchmen. When the Briton moved on to Palestine, Jerome was soon referring to him as a "corpulent dog . . . weighed down with . . . porridge." But it was Augustine who pursued the debate. In refuting Pelagius, Augustine defined the orthodox view on free will and divine grace. Pelagius' idea that man had the freedom to determine his own life was ridiculous to Augustine, who believed that human activity was determined by God. Being a Christian meant more than emulating Christ's behavior; it meant experiencing God's grace, which heals the soul. In his work *On Nature and Grace*, Augustine insisted that only the gift of grace allows man to achieve anything worthy. Freedom stems from God's grace, not from human nature, which is so prone to sin.

The aging Augustine worked fervently to stop the spread of Pelagianism. At synods held in Jerusalem and Diospolis, Pelagius defended himself so deftly from charges of heresy that the bishops of Palestine exonerated him. But when the bishops at two synods

Monica, Mother of Augustine

Most of what we know about Monica, the determined, pious woman who patiently nurtured Christian faith in her son, Augustine, comes from Augustine's descriptions of her in his *Confessions*. She was born in Tagaste, a city in Numidia that is now the town of Souk-Ahras in Algeria. Though she came from a family of devout Christians, her husband, Patricius, remained a pagan until near the end of his life.

Perhaps in imitation of his father, Monica's brilliant son flouted her greatest wish for years by refusing to be baptized. He wrote, "I have no words to express the love she had for me, and with how much more anguish she was now suffering the pangs of child-birth for my spiritual state than when she had given birth to me physically." To escape his mother's domination, Augustine, at the age of 29, fled to Rome without warning Monica. Undeterred, Monica followed, but by the time she arrived in Rome, Augustine had taken up residence in Milan, and she followed him there.

In Milan, Monica found herself in a quandary. Both in her native land and in Rome, Christians had fasted on the traditional Jewish Sabbath, Saturday. But the Saturday fast was not observed in Milan. This so troubled Monica that Augustine consulted Bishop Ambrose of Milan about what his mother should do: fast on both days or just on Sunday. Ambrose's answer gave rise to the familiar saying, "When in Rome, do as the Romans do."

In Milan Monica's dream was finally realized. Augustine was baptized, and soon afterward, he and his mother prepared to return to North Africa. But in the Italian seaport of Ostia, Monica fell ill. She told Augustine that she had hoped only to live long enough to see him become a Christian. "God has granted my wish. . . . What is left for me to do in this world?" Nine days later she died at the age of 56.

in Africa condemned his views, the matter was referred to Pope Innocent I, and Pelagius was subsequently excommunicated in 417. On this occasion, Augustine remarked: "The case is finished. Would that the error were finished also."

But the case was far from closed. Pelagius professed his ideas so convincingly that a new pope, Zosimus, restored him to the church. Not long afterward in Rome, Celestius provoked so much controversy over Pelagian teachings that Honorius, the emperor of the West, pressured Zosimus to expel the troublemaker. In 418 the pope wrote a letter condemning Pelagian ideas. Honorius banished Celestius from Rome. Pelagius, driven out of Palestine, disappeared from history. (The problem of free will and divine will surfaced again many centuries later when both Martin Luther and John Calvin, inspired by the works of Augustine, redefined the concept of predestination.)

In the later years of his life, Augustine witnessed the beginning of the final days of the Western Roman Empire. From refugees who fled to North Africa, he heard the news that Alaric, king of the Visigoths, had sacked Rome in 410. Pagans argued that the old gods were wreaking revenge on the "blasphemous" Christian state. Augustine answered with his famous book, the *City of God*. In this magnum opus, which took some 15 years to write, he attempted to demonstrate that the "city of man" (of which the crumbling ramparts of Rome were an apt symbol) could not endure because it was the product of a misdirected love for material things. The kingdom of God was the "eternal city." The true movement of history was the unseen conflict between sin and salvation.

The demise of the Western Empire

Since 476, the official date of the fall of the Roman Empire in the West, thoughtful people have sought to understand what brought about the collapse of one of the world's most powerful civilizations. Edward Gibbon, the 18th-century historian who devoted years to writing the classic *Decline and Fall of the Roman Empire*, concluded that the empire was undermined by moral decadence. Other historians have since noted that relentless war, famine, and taxation took an enormous toll. By the fifth century, the population was greatly reduced, thinning the empire of soldiers and leaders. Meanwhile, the warlike peoples of northern and eastern Europe had greatly increased in number. Their populations, hungry for fertile land, were beginning to move south.

Rome was ill prepared for the invaders. Corruption and bureaucracy had weakened the empire's ability to defend its far-flung borders. In several instances, Roman emperors had to pay tribute in land or money to stop the invaders from pillaging. Though the warriors came from various regions and had different tribal names and languages, Romans called them all "barbarians." (The word is from Greek *barbaros*, a non-Greek; in Roman usage, it meant anyone other than a Roman or Greek. *Barbaros* was an onomatopoeic word, standing for the meaningless speech of foreigners).

Among these peoples were two Germanic groups: the Vandals, who hailed from Scandinavia, and the Goths, who were originally from the same region but had moved across what is now Poland and Russia as far as the Crimea and the Black Sea. The Goths split into two groups, the Visigoths (Western Goths) and the Ostrogoths (Eastern Goths). They were all Arian Christians, and their growing militancy was putting both the empire and the orthodox church in peril.

Defending the frontiers

One man who successfully defended Roman frontiers in the 360's and 370's was Valentinian I. The son of a peasant rope seller, this emperor rose to power through the army and was dedicated to refortifying the borders of Italy and Gaul. In 375 Valentinian signed a peace treaty with the Quadis, who had migrated from Germany to Gaul. But several months later, when barbarian envoys remonstrated with him, he flew into a rage, suffered a stroke, and died. His four-year-old son, Valentinian II, was designated a co-emperor with Gratian, an older half brother. A devout Christian, Gratian protected the younger ruler.

Meanwhile, a new disaster was brewing that threatened to shatter the empire. Around 377, Goths were driven from their lands just outside its northeastern frontiers by the advance of the Huns, warlike nomads from Mongolia. It was at this time that the Goths divided into two groups. The Ostrogoths eventually settled in what is now the Balkans. As the homeless Visigoths approached the empire's borders, Valens, brother of Valentinian I and emperor of the East, set conditions for their entry. They could cross the Danube River if they gave up their arms and surrendered

In 364 Valentinian I became Roman emperor in the West and shortly afterward, appointed his younger brother Valens as emperor in the East. Both brothers, depicted on the above coin, devoted much of their energy to defending the empire against Germanic barbarians; Valens was killed in 378 during a major confrontation with the Visigoths.

their children as hostages. The Visigoths accepted the pact, but the Romans were slow to grant entry and provisions. Rebellion was inevitable. Promising loot, the Visigoths persuaded other barbarians, including the Huns, to join them. Valens underestimated their strength; instead of waiting for reinforcements from Gratian, he took on the barbarians in 378 on the fields of Adrianople (present-day Edirne, Turkey) near the western shore of the Black Sea. When the battle was over, some two-thirds of the Roman army had been killed, including Valens.

Gratian had no time to deal with this stunning defeat, for word came that other Germanic forces had invaded Thrace. To defend the East, he appointed Theodosius, who succeeded so well that Gratian later made him co-augustus. Theodosius proved a masterful commander, who inspired a new discipline in the army. While Theodosius was bringing peace, Gratian made a truce with the Visigoths, whereby Rome would give them provisions and they, in turn, would supply the Roman Army with fresh recruits.

Meanwhile, resentment toward Gratian was growing, because some felt he showed too much regard for his German troops. Sometime in 383, a general named Maximus gathered an army of disgruntled Roman soldiers and confronted Gratian near present-day Paris. Maximus prevailed, forcing Gratian to flee with only 300 loyal horsemen at his side. Finally captured, Gratian was assured that he would be spared, but in the end, he was stabbed to death.

Maximus pressured Valentinian II to abdicate. Though the child's mother, the regent Justina, was the pro-Arian who opposed the orthodox Ambrose, the bishop came to Valentinian's defense. He managed to stall the usurper until the Italian frontier could be secured by troops loyal to the boy-emperor. In 388 Theodosius successfully fought Maximus, and his victory secured the rule of the West for Valentinian II. After Justina died, the young emperor chose catholic over Arian Christianity.

Once again barbarians in high places shook the empire. In the 390's the top military commander in Rome was Arbogast, a Frank (a Germanic barbarian). When Valentinian II was murdered in 392, possibly at Arbogast's behest, the Frankish strongman took charge of the government and appointed Eugenius, a former rhetorician and secretary in the imperial service, as emperor. This was the first time a barbarian had been powerful enough to designate a Roman emperor. Theodosius defeated both Eugenius and Arbogast in 394 but never recovered from the battle. He died four months later. The Eastern Empire passed to his older son, Arcadius, the Western went to his younger son, the 11-year-old Honorius.

The sack of Rome

The real power in the West lay with Stilicho, a remarkable general whose lineage was half Vandal and half Roman. It was he who saved the empire from conquest by Alaric, king of the Visigoths. The teenage Honorius celebrated the victory by treating the citizens of Rome to magnificent public games. Chariot races and wild beast fights delighted the weary populace. Gladiatorial contests were included, but for

Valentinian III ruled mainly in name only. He was six when he became emperor of the West in 425. His mother, Galla Placidia, acted as regent until 437, after which power rested largely with the patrician general Aëtius. Valentinian's tenure was marked by the passing in 444 of Novel 17, granting the bishop of Rome supremacy over provincial churches.

Valentinian II, the son of Valentinian I, was a child-emperor who nominally ruled Italy, North Africa, and Illyricum until he was deposed by the usurper Maximus in 387. (His mother, Justina, was the Arian regent who tried to force Bishop Ambrose of Milan to relinquish some orthodox churches.) After Theodosius I overthrew Maximus in 388, Valentinian regained his dominion but was murdered just four years later.

the last time; Honorius would soon outlaw them. Over the years, jealous enemies at court plotted against the powerful Stilicho. Honorius, now in his early 20's, was easily swayed by the accusations and ordered Stilicho's execution, leaving Alaric free to attack. While Honorius and his feckless advisers remained safe in Ravenna, to which he had transferred the Roman capital, Alaric marched on Rome in 410.

Twice Alaric neared the gates of the Eternal City, the nerve center of the crumbling Western Empire, but withdrew after accepting huge bribes: 5,000 pounds of gold, 30,000 pounds of silver, 4,000 tunics, 3,000 skins, and 3,000 pounds of pepper. The third time, a traitor within the walls opened a gate. For three days, the Visigoths pillaged, killed, and burned at will. But because they were Arians and respected Christian institutions, several churches were spared. The news of the disaster shook the world.

In his monastery, in faraway Bethlehem, Jerome exclaimed, "The city which has taken the whole world is itself taken!" Pagans declared that Christians were at last being punished by the traditional gods of ancient Rome. Augustine answered their charges with his masterpiece, the *City of God*.

Alaric moved to southern Italy with his booty, which included some very high-ranking prisoners, such as Galla Placidia, a sister of Honorius. The Visigothic king savored his victory only briefly. He died that same year. Slaves were forced to divert the course of the Busento River, bury his body in the river bed, and then return the waters to their natural pathway. To ensure that the secret of the grave would never be revealed, the hapless slaves themselves were killed.

Four years later, the captive Galla Placidia married Alaric's successor. When he died, she returned to the Roman court at Ravenna, where she married the Roman general Constantius in 417. A few years later Constantius was named emperor, only to die within the first year of his reign. His and Galla Placidia's six-year-old son, Valentinian III, was named emperor in 425. Galla Placidia, who had become her son's regent, was the only woman to reach the pinnacle of power among both the Goths and the Romans.

Wulfila, apostle of the Goths

Arian Christianity predominated among the Goths, thanks to the work of Wulfila (also known as Ulfilas), or "Little Wolf," who was born to Christian parents in Gothic territory north of the Danube around 311. He was descended from Roman citizens, who some years before had been taken prisoner by the Goths, but Wulfila considered himself a Goth in spirit. He went to Constantinople as a young man, became an Arian, was consecrated a bishop there about 341, and soon afterward returned to his homeland as a missionary. After seven years, persecutions of his converts by the heathen chieftain Athanaric forced Wulfila to apply for permission to settle in Roman territory. When it was granted, he crossed the Danube with a throng of followers and settled in Moesia (in present-day Bulgaria), where he worked for more than 30 years. He died about 383.

The fifth-century church historian Sozomen states that the Goths believed Wulfila incapable of doing or saying anything wrong. Their descendants remained true to his Arian faith for centuries.

Wulfila also translated both the Old and New Testaments into Gothic, omitting only the books of Kings, it is believed, because he felt that his war-loving Goths "needed the bridle," not the spur. Wulfila's Gothic Bible is the earliest extant document of any Germanic language. A sizable fragment of one translation survives in a sixth-century manuscript written in silver letters on purple parchment.

The marauding Vandals

Around 406, the Vandals forced their way across the Rhine and pillaged Gaul before settling in Spain. The devastation was immense. Then in 416, the Visigoths invaded the Spanish territory of the Vandals, who

After pillaging Gaul and Spain in the early fifth century, the Vandals crossed to North Africa in 429 and made Carthage their capital. From this vantage point they could control the Roman grain trade and pirate merchant vessels. By the late fifth century, many prosperous Vandals, such as the nobleman shown next to his villa in this mosaic, had given up plundering and settled on large estates.

along with their allies, the Alani and the Suevi, fled into southern Spain. At the southernmost tip they looked hungrily across to the fertile lands of North Africa. In 429, inspired by their new king, Gaiseric, the Vandals went after this great prize.

Gaiseric's army plundered their way across the region. They attempted to lay siege to Hippo, where Augustine was bishop, but were unsuccessful. In 431, when a Roman army tried to thwart the barbarian menace, it was beaten. Rome had little choice but to sign a treaty that gave the Vandals huge portions of corn-rich North Africa. Gaiseric took to the seas as a pirate. Despite the treaty of 439, he laid siege to Carthage. Able but unscrupulous, Gaiseric was greatly feared even by his own people. As an Arian, he was hostile to the catholic clergy and turned important churches in Carthage over to the Arians.

After the death of Valentinian III, Gaiseric lost no time in rallying his Vandals to strike at Rome. It has been said that his attack in 455 was partially deflected by the courageous intervention of Pope Leo I, who came unarmed to meet the invaders. Lives as well as churches were spared but pillaging continued for two weeks. Church relics and holy objects, along with golden ritual objects that the Romans had brought from the Temple in Jerusalem centuries before, were carried back to Carthage. The empress and her two daughters were taken hostage with the spoils.

The Eastern and Western Empires cooperated in raising a great navy to punish Gaiseric, but he destroyed at least half their fleet. Gaiseric's kingdom grew so strong that the powerful Visigothic king, Theodoric I, sought an alliance by offering his daughter in marriage to Gaiseric's son, Huneric. Neither the marriage nor the alliance lasted long. Gaiseric, claiming that his new daughter-in-law was poisoning him, cut off her ears and nose and sent her back to her father. Gaiseric reigned without opposition until his death in 477. His Arian Christian kingdom would not be conquered by orthodox Christian forces from Constantinople for more than half a century.

Pope Leo the Great

Throughout the years of barbarian invasions, the orthodox church stood firm, and the prestige and power of the papacy grew. Catholic Christians continued to regard the city of Rome as holy. It was during this unsettled century, in fact, that Pope Leo I served as expert administrator of the church there. Faced with a crumbling empire and a corrupt, ineffectual imperial court, he stepped in to stem the tide of chaos, twice saving Rome from massive destruction.

Ordained in 440, Leo preached that the pope stands in the place of Peter, who was charged by Jesus with presiding over all believers. The pope is, therefore, the "primate of all the bishops." Although Leo would not accept the controversial ruling that had made Constantinople the "New Rome" for the Eastern Empire, he did approve the doctrinal decisions of the Council of Chalcedon (see page 260). Urging that the church be forgiving, he stressed the spiritual life in his dealings with his flock.

Leo was well known too for his personal courage. When Attila the Hun planned to attack Rome in 452, Leo was sent to negotiate with this allegedly implacable conqueror from the East. According to legend, Leo and a small delegation went unarmed to speak with Attila and somehow convinced him to retire and accept an annual tribute. Three years later, the intrepid Leo managed to mitigate the destruction made by the more determined Vandal, Gaiseric. Leo the Great, as posterity has fittingly called him, presided over the church of Rome for 21 years, leaving the populace and clergy deeply bereaved upon his death in 461.

"The Scourge of God"

To many, the very name of Attila the Hun suggests a mass-murdering barbarian. But history has not been entirely fair to this masterful military leader. Attila (his name means "Little Father" in Gothic—his Hunnish name is unknown) was the charismatic king of Mongolian nomads known as Huns. They were fierce warriors and expert horsemen, who rode into battle with incredible speed and intimidated their enemies with wild howls. Indeed, they lived on horseback. According to one fourth-century historian, "On horseback they buy and sell, they take their meat and drink, and there they recline . . . and yield to sleep."

Moving westward from their native Asian steppes in the fourth century, the Huns made their first hostile contact with the Germanic peoples who were inhabiting regions outside the Roman Empire's northeastern borders. These encounters are believed to have precipitated successive Germanic invasions of the empire.

In 434 Attila was sharing the rule of the Huns with his brother, Bleda. They crossed the Danube, raiding at will and exacting huge payments from the terrified Roman populations. After his brother was slain about 445, Attila took sole control of his people. He was a cunning adversary, equally adept at negotiating and using terror to get what he wanted. Short and ungainly, he no doubt bore on his cheeks the scars from slashes customarily given to Hunnish boys at birth.

Attila never tried to set up a permanent capital. He maintained instead a rugged headquarters in a village on the Hungarian plain. His residence was a large house made of polished logs and lavishly furnished with skins and furs. One Roman emissary left us this description of Attila: "A luxurious meal, served on silver plate, had been made ready for us and the barbarian guests, but Attila ate nothing but meat on a wooden trencher. In everything else, too, he showed himself temperate; his cup was of wood, while to the guests were given goblets of gold and silver. His dress, too, was quite simple, affecting only to be

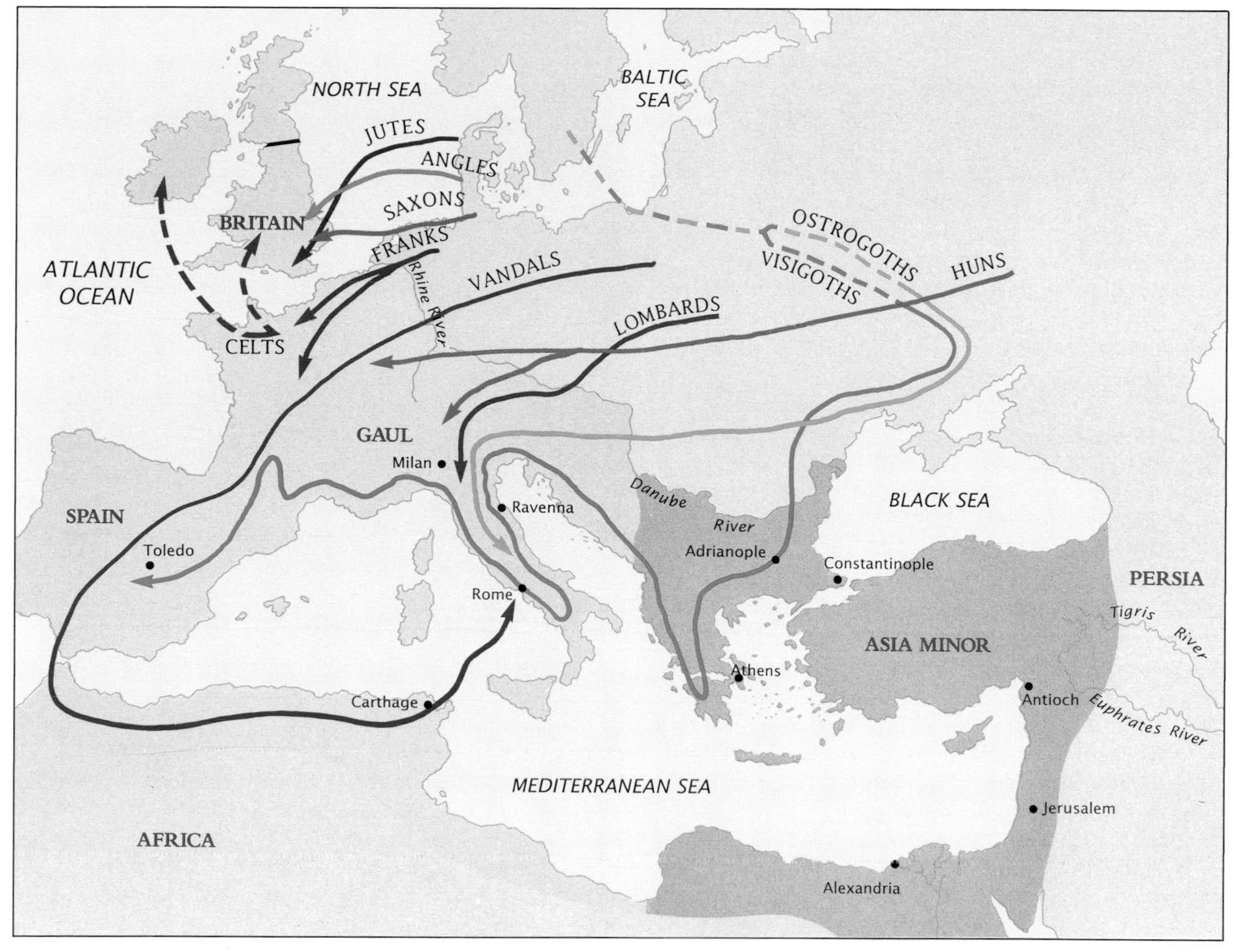

Long before the Roman Empire was formed, movements of barbarian peoples were taking place. Dotted lines trace the migrations of early Celts and Goths; the filled lines show how pervasive the barbarians became after the fourth century. By 400, neither the Western Empire (depicted in yellow) nor the Eastern Empire (in pink) was safe from the land-hungry invaders. The Visigoths sacked Rome in 410. The Vandals moved into Spain, then invaded Africa in 429. Their conduct was so savage it gave rise to the term vandalism. The Huns were even worse, laying waste to much of northern Gaul and northern Italy during the 450's. Up north, the Angles, Saxons, and Jutes took over southeast Britain. During the sixth century, the Franks became the masters of western Gaul and the Lombards gained control of northern Italy. By 600, the Western Empire was almost entirely in the hands of barbarians.

clean." The freedom enjoyed by his horsemen, and the absence of any form of taxation, induced many Romans to settle in the Hunnish territories.

Attila's policy was not to conquer but to sap the Roman strength through bargains and payment of tribute. At the peak of his power, the Hunnish leader had under his sway a vast area, comprising modern Austria, Hungary, Rumania, and southern Russia. For reasons that still puzzle historians, Attila finally decided to invade the Western Empire. He easily forced his way into Gaul but in 451 was checked by General Aëtius, who was sent by Valentinian III to stop the Mongol invaders. A year later the Hunnish leader invaded Italy, but he was seriously overextended, and famine and plague were beginning to take their toll on his army. It was in 452 that Pope Leo, armed with a promise of tribute, succeeded in turning back "the scourge of God," as Attila had come to be called.

This unforgettable profile of Attila the Hun, the "scourge of God," appears on a medallion from a building facade in Pavia, Italy. Having driven the Visigoths and Vandals out of most of the Western Roman Empire, Attila for a time controlled territory from the Caspian Sea to Gaul. Thanks to the adroit diplomacy and the offer of a money settlement by Pope Leo the Great, Attila abandoned his plan to sack Rome.

In 453 Attila died of a burst artery on his wedding night with a young Gothic woman. His followers soon scattered throughout the empire.

What had Attila achieved? He had neither established a Mongol state nor managed to destroy Rome. But he had slowed the fall of the empire, for his invading hordes forced the Romans and the Goths to come to some kind of peace. With the death of their leader, the Huns retreated to the Russian plains. The Germanic tribes were now free to act. A full-scale invasion of the empire was inevitable.

The last emperor of the West

The death of Valentinian III in 455 was the beginning of the end for the Western Empire. Nine weak emperors followed in the next 20 years. The real power lay with whoever held the post of master of the troops. Imperial armies, now drawn from Germanic barbarians, reported to him. In 475 the job was given to Orestes, a Roman who had served as Attila's secretary, because the Mongolian leader had needed someone to read and write state correspondence in Latin. This ambitious politician, who had married into the Roman aristocracy, contrived to have his son named emperor at Ravenna in 475. The boy, Romulus, was to be the last emperor in the West.

Though supported by Germanic troops, Orestes made the fatal mistake of refusing to honor their request to be granted a third of Italy. Unused to the restriction of Roman barracks life, these soldiers wanted to settle as farmers, a tradition for Germanic people, and to serve in the ranks only when the nation was threatened. Having already lost much of southwestern Gaul to the Visigoths, Orestes was unwilling to surrender more of the ancestral Roman lands. The troops consequently elected a certain Odoacer as king in 476. Orestes was summarily beheaded.

Sympathetic to the handsome young Augustulus, the new German ruler pensioned the boy off with a pleasant villa and 6,000 pieces of gold a year; then he

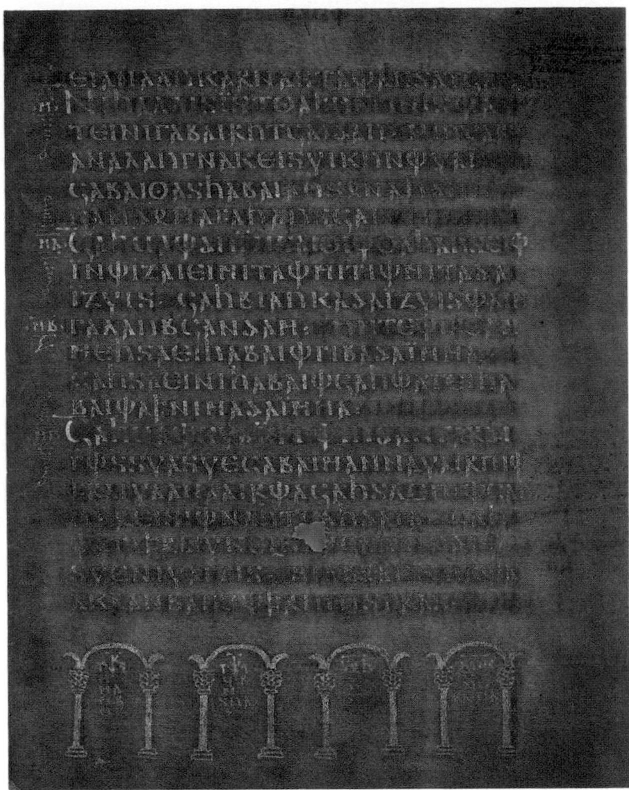

The Goths, who became Christians in the fourth century, had their own Bible. It was translated by Bishop Wulfila, who created Gothic writing so that converts could read Scripture.

vigorously began his own reign. He was recognized neither as emperor nor as king of Italy, however, and the date of his accession is generally viewed as the "fall" of the Western Empire. Indeed, there would be no emperor again in the West until centuries later. During Odoacer's time, the emperor of the East, Zeno, was legally the sovereign of a unified empire.

Christianity has often been implicated in the collapse of the Roman Empire, charged with being an internally divisive force. In fact, the church played a role in efforts to preserve the realm. Augustine himself had written persuasively that the faith of Jesus does not condemn all wars. It was the common view that a believer could fight to defend his country against aggressors. Though Leo the Great and other prelates sued some invaders for peace, it was not so much because these bishops were pacifists but that resistance had become futile. More likely, the gradual dissolution of the empire was chiefly the result of the state's coming to depend on barbarian generals and troops for its security. Only thus could an Odoacer have been acclaimed king.

The rise of Clovis

With the empire in ruins, how could the orthodox church survive the assault of barbarians intent on its destruction? A new champion and protector was called for. Some would say that Clovis, the pagan ruler of the Franks, was one who met this need. According to legend, in 496 Clovis made a promise to his orthodox Christian wife, Clotilda, on the eve of a battle. He said that he would convert to Christianity if he won. The Franks, who held much of Gaul, were about to fight Alamanni invaders from Swabia (in present-day Germany). Clovis did win, and he and 3,000 of his people evidently were baptized on Christmas Day in 496. "Henceforward," commanded the bishop of Reims, who baptized Clovis, "burn what thou hast worshiped, and worship what thou hast burned."

Clovis' conversion politically strengthened orthodox Christianity. His actions led to an alliance between the Franks and orthodox Gallic bishops. Among the Frankish people, conversion to Christianity did not become immediately widespread, but the Frankish state began a complex relationship with Rome that was destined to influence centuries of church and secular history in Western Europe.

On the one hand, Clovis and the papacy were bound together in the affirmation of orthodoxy. On the other, Clovis cleverly took administrative control of the church within his borders. (Conflict between the popes of Rome and the kings of France provoked many crises in the Middle Ages.) In addition, Clovis encouraged the Germans to convert to orthodoxy. Germany, too, for hundreds of years, witnessed power struggles between church and state of the same sort that had divided Ambrose of Milan and Theodosius the Great in the fourth century.

As the ancient empire in the West continued to crumble, the East grew in strength. New states were established by descendants of the barbarian invaders. Rome's loss in political prominence was offset by its rising role as the seat of orthodox Christianity.

Clovis, the first Christian king of the Franks, is shown in the above painting being miraculously cured by touching the robe of St. Severin. It was often the accounts of such miracles that convinced barbarians to convert to Christianity.

Animals were a favorite motif of barbarian craftsmen. This eagle, made of gold and garnets, appears on the shield of an Anglo-Saxon warrior. Made before the seventh century, it shows superb metal craftmanship. Such fanciful animal designs were used also in early medieval illuminated manuscripts.

An artisan used nearly a pound of gold to make this belt buckle, no doubt the prized possession of an Anglo-Saxon chieftain. Buckles were important accessories, for warriors commonly wore sword belts.

Gold jewelry set with semi-precious stones was popular in the Byzantine era. This necklace, made of 10 garnets encased in gold, perhaps belonged to a Gothic princess. Found in south Russia, it was made in the fifth century.

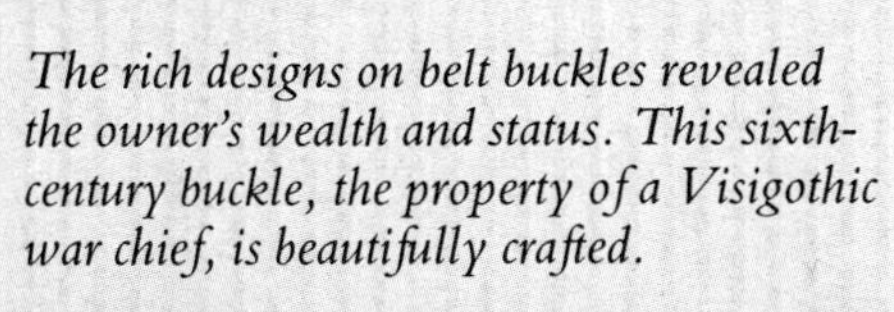

The rich designs on belt buckles revealed the owner's wealth and status. This sixth-century buckle, the property of a Visigothic war chief, is beautifully crafted.

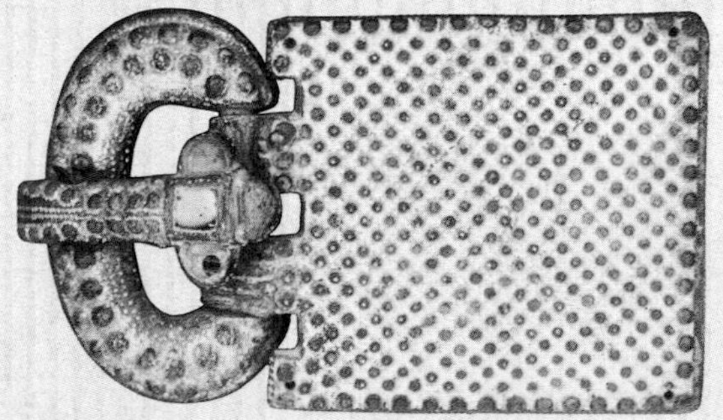

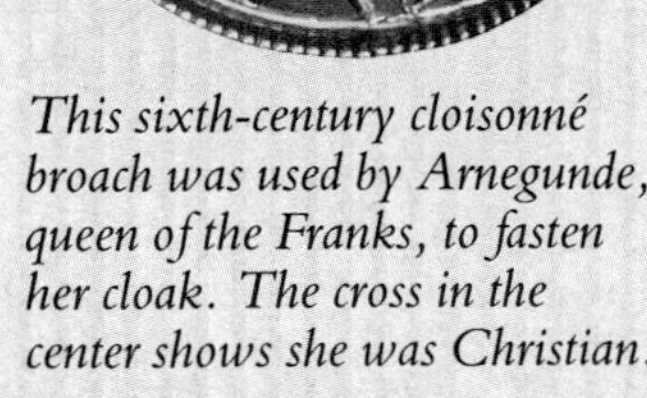

This sixth-century cloisonné broach was used by Arnegunde, queen of the Franks, to fasten her cloak. The cross in the center shows she was Christian.

Among the riches found inside the burial mound of an Anglo-Saxon chieftain is this plaque taken from a purse lid. Using gold and blood-red garnets, the artisan captures a bird of prey as it hooks its claws into a duck.

Barbarian Treasures

The art of personal adornment was elevated to great heights by barbarian artisans, as it was one of the few ways for these unsettled peoples to exhibit their wealth and status. Here, then, is a dazzling assortment of some of their treasured objects.

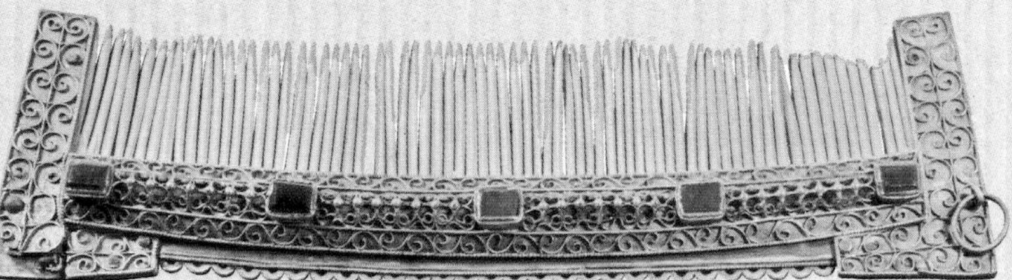

This lovely comb of ivory and silver belonged to Theodolinda, queen of the Lombards, a Germanic tribe that invaded Italy in 568. Theodolinda helped to convert her people from Arianism to orthodox Christianity.

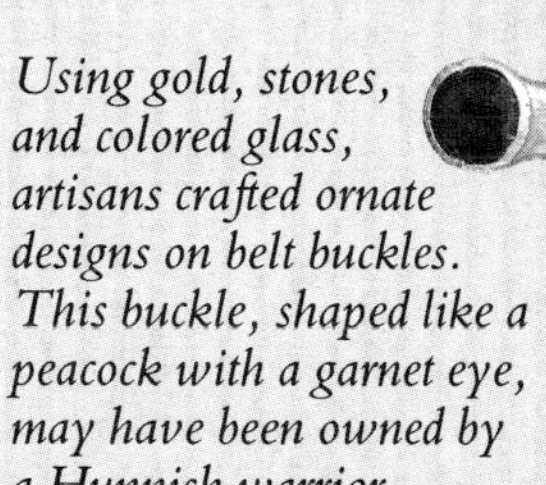

Using gold, stones, and colored glass, artisans crafted ornate designs on belt buckles. This buckle, shaped like a peacock with a garnet eye, may have been owned by a Hunnish warrior.

The elaborate curvilinear designs on the back of this bronze mirror from first-century Britain illustrate Celtic craftmanship at its finest.

The S-shaped stem of this sixth-century Celtic bronze dress fastener was designed to slip through slits in a garment. The spiral designs have been deeply etched into the bronze. Coils turn into bird heads with eyes, combs, and beaks.

One of the treasures of the Lombards is this gold crown inlaid with stones, worn by Queen Theodolinda during her reign, which began in 590. The Lombards then controlled most of northern Italy, a region now called Lombardy.

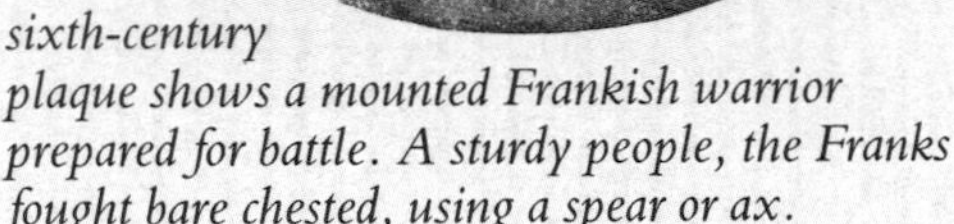

This sixth-century plaque shows a mounted Frankish warrior prepared for battle. A sturdy people, the Franks fought bare chested, using a spear or ax.

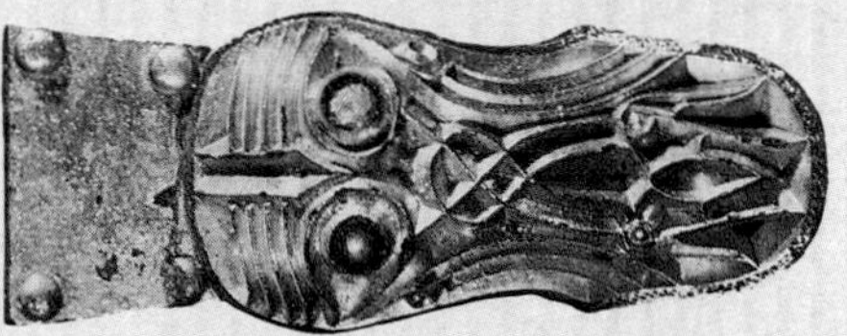

Fierce Norse sea rovers, known as Vikings, also had a love of craftsmanship and display that is apparent in this gold buckle, which resembles a fanciful animal head. Found in a Viking burial site in Uppland, Sweden, it dates sometime after the mid-sixth century.

Caldrons were sacred vessels to the Celts, whose Druid priests perhaps used them to hold magical potions during religious rites. The Gundestrup caldron, below, is considered the most magnificent one ever found. The silversmithing is so ornate that it is hard to believe it was made in the first century B.C. *On the right, a panel from the caldron shows a Celtic god, whose eyes were once filled with glass; sacrificial stags appear on either side of his face.*

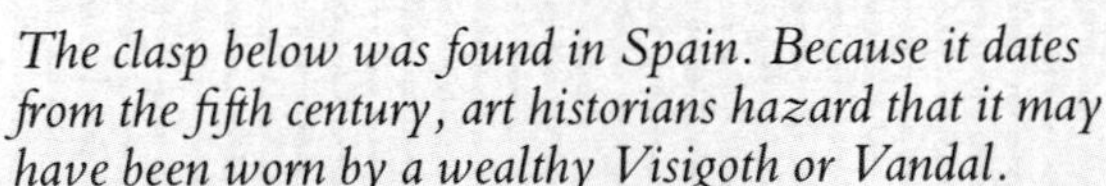

The clasp below was found in Spain. Because it dates from the fifth century, art historians hazard that it may have been worn by a wealthy Visigoth or Vandal.

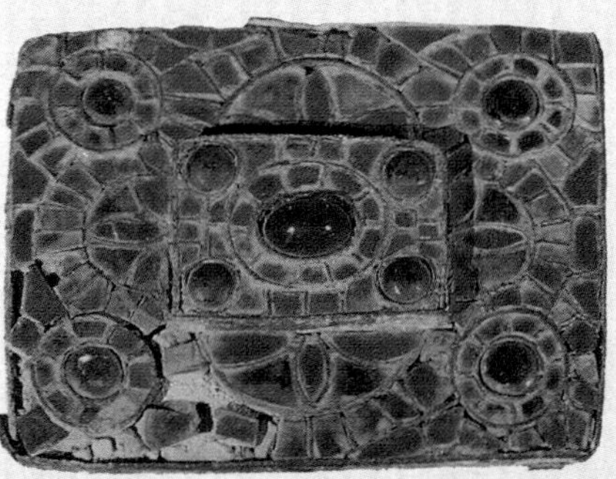

The Celts were famous for their metal craftsmanship. This beautifully enameled bronze shield was apparently thrown into the Thames River in Britain as an offering to the river god. Though the shield dates from the first century, many pieces of colored enamel inlay are still visible today.

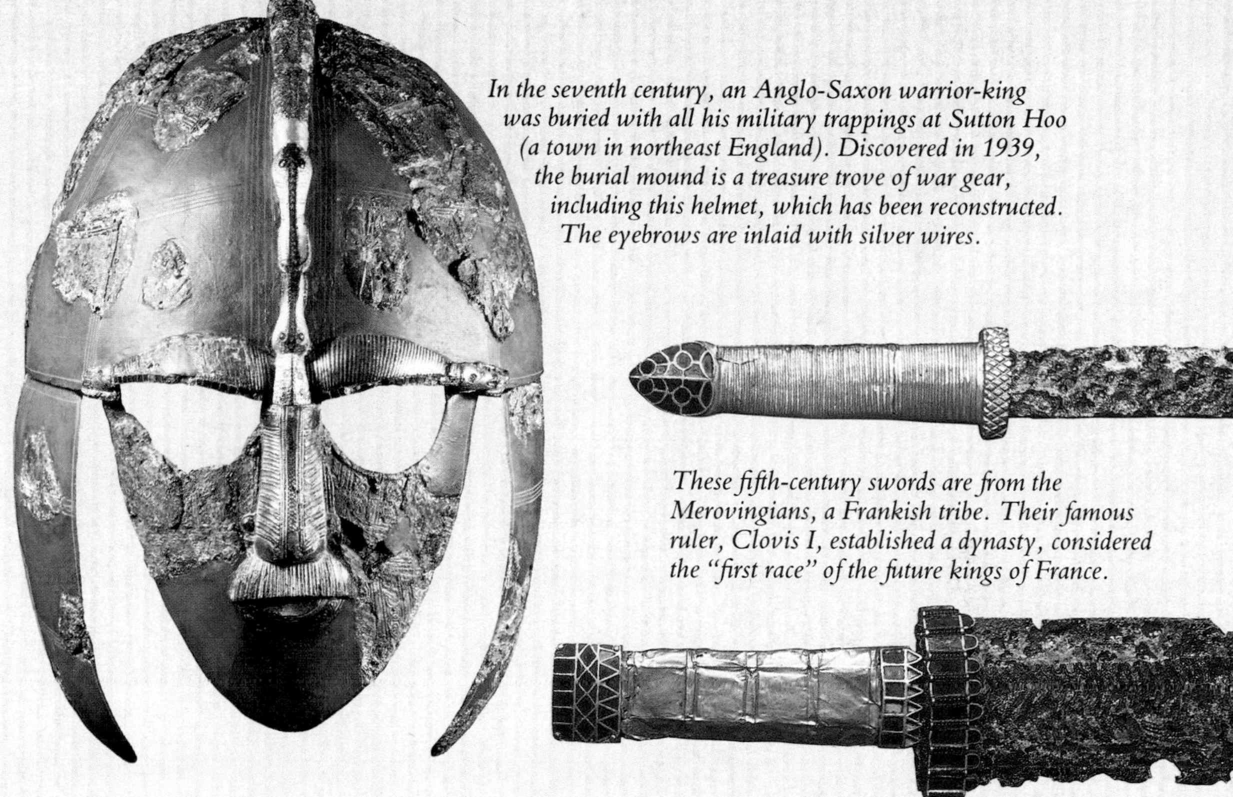

In the seventh century, an Anglo-Saxon warrior-king was buried with all his military trappings at Sutton Hoo (a town in northeast England). Discovered in 1939, the burial mound is a treasure trove of war gear, including this helmet, which has been reconstructed. The eyebrows are inlaid with silver wires.

These fifth-century swords are from the Merovingians, a Frankish tribe. Their famous ruler, Clovis I, established a dynasty, considered the "first race" of the future kings of France.

Made from gilded copper, this part of a unique helmet decoration shows Agilulf, the king of the Lombards (and husband of Theodolinda), holding court surrounded by his comitatus, *or picked comrades in arms. On either side, winged victories carry signs saying* Victuria, *or "victory," and usher in figures paying tribute to the king.*

Chapter Nine

DAWNING OF THE MIDDLE AGES

"Byzantium the golden" glowed with vigor in the East, and the emperor Justinian sought to return the empire to its earlier glory. But in the West, war and plague struck. Pope Gregory saved Italy, sent missionaries to the Angles and Saxons, and ensured the continuance of Roman civilization into the Middle Ages.

On December 27, 537, the emperor Justinian walked alone to the pulpit of the newly completed Church of Holy Wisdom in Constantinople, also known as St. Sophia, or Hagia Sophia (Greek for "holy wisdom"). Legend relates that upon reaching the pulpit, the emperor stretched up his arms toward the magnificent dome and exclaimed, "Glory be to God, who has thought me worthy to finish this work! Solomon, I have surpassed thee!" Indeed, never before had so grand a design on so large a scale been attempted. The nave alone was an enormous oblong, 250 feet by 107 feet; suspended high above the central section was the dazzling dome measuring 107 feet in diameter. The stupendous construction of Hagia Sophia, along with its lavish interior decoration, made it the wonder of the Byzantine Empire. A courtier poet enthused: "Once anyone sets foot in this holy enclosure, he's unwilling ever to leave, but with eyes enchanted turns to and fro, craning his neck in every direction."

The emperor Justinian considered the building of Hagia Sophia, or the Church of Holy Wisdom, his greatest architectural triumph. He spared no expense in materials and paid each worker a piece of silver every day.

Hagia Sophia, now a museum, remains a jewel in the heart of present-day Istanbul. For centuries it was the center of the Eastern Orthodox Church, but in 1453, when the city fell to the Turks, Hagia Sophia was converted into a mosque. Minarets were added from which the faithful were called to prayer five times a day.

More than any other accomplishment of Justinian, Hagia Sophia was a testament to the might of Christianity and the imperial power in the East. A great builder, Justinian poured much of the wealth of the Byzantine Empire into construction, even in areas as far away as Syria and Africa. During his reign, from 527 to 565, he built fortifications, monasteries, hospitals, aqueducts, bridges, and churches, some 25 churches in the vicinity of Constantinople alone.

It was Hagia Sophia, however, that truly marked the splendor of Justinian's long reign. The altar was made of gold and inlaid with precious stones. The bishop's chair was of gilded silver. The walls, floor, and pillars of the church were created from many different marbles brought from far and wide, black marble from the Bosporus region, for instance, green from Greece, and rose from Phrygia. The marble and silver fairly gleamed at all hours of the day, for a ring of arched windows around the base of the dome flooded the church with natural light. At night, hundreds of oil lamps set in numerous silver chandeliers illuminated the evening services.

But it was the unprecedented ribbed dome, which seemed to float high above the nave, that amazed and delighted the eye. It rested on four enormous arches, 128 feet tall, bringing the total height of the dome to 180 feet. In the words of Procopius, the historian who chronicled the construction of Hagia Sophia, the lofty ceiling "seems not to rest on solid masonry, but to cover the space with its golden dome suspended from Heaven." Actually, the magnificent dome was secured to the nave not so much by the four arches, but by the four pendentives, or triangular vaults, which filled the spaces between the arches and the rim of the dome. Never before had pendentives been used on such a large scale—architects would not again make the attempt until the Renaissance.

The basilica was somewhat plain on the outside; its facade was a monotone of gray marble. But inside was another matter: more than four acres of gold mosaics covered the dome, arches, and vaults. The columns were reportedly sanctified with such relics as a fragment of the true cross, a veil worn by the Virgin Mary, and a piece of the basket used when Jesus performed the miracle of the loaves and fishes.

The worshipers entered Hagia Sophia through the atrium, provided with a fountain in which they could wash. An inscription on the fountain read: "Do not wash only your face, but also your sins." Thousands of worshipers could offer their prayers within the church, which was open for daily prayer services. When the full liturgy was celebrated on Sundays and feast days, the faithful filled the nave, broad flanking aisles, and upstairs galleries. To see the reenactment of the Eucharist (performed behind a screen), the laity crowded around the sanctuary.

Hagia Sophia proved a costly endeavor; it required the labor of some 10,000 workmen, and the sanctuary alone was adorned with 40,000 pounds of silver. Justinian, who had spent so lavishly to build his "eye of faith," was equally generous at its dedication. Legend has it that some 1,000 oxen, 6,000 sheep, 600 stags, and 10,000 birds were slaughtered, and 30,000 bushels of meal were distributed to the poor people of Constantinople. The cost of maintaining Hagia Sophia took the income from 365 farms scattered from East to West. Worship services on holy days consumed, according to one writer, "1,000 measures of oil, 300 measures of wine, and 1,000 sacramental loaves."

The Nika revolt

Ironically, this enduring monument to Christianity might never have been built if the emperor had not almost lost his throne in a civil rebellion. The population of Constantinople avidly followed two sports factions, the Blues and the Greens, so named for the colors worn by their charioteers in the races at the hippodrome. Rowdy and uncontrollable, the Greens and Blues were known to instigate mob violence.

In January of 532, widespread discontent with the administration of the government led to a massive demonstration in the hippodrome. Fights broke out in the street. Two instigators—one Green and one Blue—were arrested and sentenced to death. While the crowd watched, a nervous hangman bungled the job, and the accused fell unharmed to the ground.

The crowd demanded the release of the miscreants, who viewers believed had been graced by heaven. When Justinian refused, the enraged Blues and Greens joined forces, looting and rioting wildly. They went after the city's hated prefect and burned his office. "Nika!" the mob screamed, meaning "vanquish!" Their madness increased as they set fire to the imperial palace. The blaze spread to the old Hagia Sophia, built by Constantine. Justinian gave in to their demands and removed the prefect, but it was too late; the mob had tasted power. The Nika revolt, as it came to be called, continued. Soon Constantinople was convulsed by a revolution; the mob now sought to replace the emperor. Most of the senators fled. For nearly a week, an indecisive Justinian remained in his palace while his capital fell into chaos.

Several of Justinian's advisers implored him to flee for safety, but his wife, Theodora, who had heard their pleas, silenced them: "Every man born to see the light

"Who could speak of the beauty of the columns and stones with which the church is adorned?" marveled the sixth-century historian Procopius about Hagia Sophia. The large discs, added during its Muslim era, are inscribed with texts from the Koran.

of day must die. But that one who has been emperor should become an exile I cannot bear. May I never be without the purple I wear, nor live to see the day when men do not call me 'Your Majesty.' " The emperor stayed and gave orders to his able general, Belisarius, to attack the mob. Belisarius recruited a troop of Gothic mercenaries, and in less than one week, some 30,000 people had been killed.

Justinian and the rise of the Byzantine Empire

With the suppression of the Nika revolt, Justinian had confirmed his position as emperor. He had come a long way from his lowly station as the son of peasants. A fine education had been made possible by his uncle Justin, commander of the palace guard. When Justin usurped the title of emperor in 518, Justinian proved so capable that in time the childless emperor made him heir apparent. After Justin died in 527, his 44-year-old nephew assumed the purple. Perhaps because of his humble lineage, Justinian was eager to display the pomp and circumstance of his new office. All who came before him were instructed to kiss the hem of his robe. Money was spent lavishly.

An orthodox Christian, Justinian ordered pagans to attend church and be baptized or suffer exile and the confiscation of their property. "Hope in God is our sole recourse for the existence of the monarchy," he explained. He was reasonably tolerant of the Jews, but he made certain that laws were passed against alien religions, such as Manichaeism, and against heresies,

Churches erected during Justinian's long reign were enriched by the Byzantine art of mosaics. Shown here, in the Church of San Vitale in Ravenna, Justinian and his retinue are memorialized in dazzling colors. Justinian, center, wears the royal purple and a diadem, complete with a nimbus. He carries a golden paten, the sacred vessel used to hold the bread of the Eucharist. To his immediate left, is the archbishop Maximian.

such as Nestorianism. "It is right that those who do not worship God correctly should be deprived of worldly advantages too," he said.

Just 40 days after the end of the Nika crisis, the new Hagia Sophia started to rise on the site of the burned one. To speed construction, the emperor cleverly set his workmen in competition: one half worked on the left, the other half on the right. The emperor himself laid the foundation stone. Wearing a simple white robe and a kerchief over his head, he was often at the site, measuring the progress of each team. The church was completed in less than six years.

Many believed that the plan of the church had come to Justinian in a dream. Actually, it was designed by two brilliantly talented natives of Asia Minor. The principal architect was Anthemius of Tralles, whom Procopius described as "the most learned man in the skilled craft which is known as the art of building."

In fact, the plan was not likely to have come to Justinian in a dream, for this abstemious ruler was known as "the emperor who never slept." Seemingly tireless, he read and worked far into the night. By nature a solitary man, he often prayed and fasted, and he was happiest when studying religious books and debating doctrinal issues with priests and scholars. He was also fond of music and may have composed a hymn, "Christ the Only-Begotten Son."

One of Justinian's most acclaimed accomplishments was the codification of Roman law. Although some earlier emperors, including Antoninus Pius and

At San Vitale, on the wall opposite her husband, Justinian, resides the empress Theodora, surrounded by her attendants. The location is fitting, for in real life Theodora sometimes countermanded her husband's imperial orders. Working during the 540's, Byzantine artisans captured their empress' regal bearing and with mother-of-pearl created highlights and shadows on her face, crown, and halo. She holds a jeweled gold chalice used for the Eucharistic wine.

In 530 Belisarius, commander in chief of the Byzantine Army, outwitted the larger Persian Army to win a glorious victory. To commemorate the triumph, Justinian had this gold medallion struck. Though hardly a soldier (Justinian rarely left Constantinople), he nonetheless had himself depicted on the coin astride a horse and in full battle dress.

Hadrian, had worked to codify Roman law, by Justinian's time, the laws were an unwieldy mass of decrees, with expert opinions appended to specific cases. No one could read through them all, much less master them. Justinian was eager "to cut short the prolixity of lawsuits by pruning the multitude of enactments"; and he decreed in 528 that 10 jurists act as a commission to set down systematically a clear, reformed code.

In five years' time, the commission had created a number of legal works that were to make a tremendous impact on the law, one that is still felt today. This new legislation defended the rights of the slave against the master, the debtor against the creditor, the wife against the husband. The disadvantaged were finally beginning to gain the protection of the law.

As was her custom, the empress Theodora made her mark upon her husband's work. She saw to it that laws were enacted to outlaw the flourishing trade in prostitution and banish procurers.

In addition to providing more equity before the law, Justinian's commissioners, by skillful editing, succeeded in cutting down the total legislation from some 3 million lines to about 150,000 lines. This legal digest, or code, was published in 533. Thenceforth, court decisions were bound by it. A second version of the original code, published in 534, is the one that has endured. It was revived by jurists during the Middle Ages, giving the legal systems of Western Europe a direct line back to what Justinian called the "holy temple of Roman justice."

With Justinian as head of the empire, the orthodox church triumphed, for not only did several of his new laws make heresy a crime, but he insisted on closing those schools that still taught the pagan classics. By 529 nearly all pagan schools had been suppressed, including the Academy in Athens—the famous intellectual home of philosophy for a thousand years. Forced into retirement, the great teachers of Athens were nonetheless treated politely and may have been given a pension from the imperial treasury.

Theodora, empress extraordinaire

Justinian's cautious, intellectual character was complemented by that of his wife. Where he was unduly hesitant, she urged decisive action; where he mandated an orthodox theology, she wanted compromise that made political sense. Though vain and vindictive, Theodora's personal courage, common sense, and love for her husband made her his ideal companion.

Like Justinian, Theodora came from poor circumstances. Her father was a bear keeper for the Greens. When he died, Theodora's mother remarried and hoped that her new husband would receive her former husband's job, but another man had bribed his way into it. The family was faced with destitution when Theodora, though a young girl, walked courageously into the hippodrome and pleaded, along with her two sisters, for the Greens to give her stepfather the post. They refused, but the Blues, who had the post vacant, were moved to hire her stepfather.

Theodora grew up to be a strikingly attractive woman. She reportedly made her living as an actress, became a concubine, and had an illegitimate child. When Justinian met her, she had given up the stage and was earning her living by spinning wool. He was immediately captivated by the beautiful brunette with large black eyes. Love's course did not run smoothly, however, for Justinian's aunt, the empress, protested the match. Moreover, the law forbade marriage between a patrician and a member of the theatrical class. But Justinian was already powerful enough to have the law amended. In 525, with the blessings of Emperor Justin, Theodora and Justinian were married. In 527, when Justin elevated Justinian to co-augustus, Theodora was crowned alongside him in Hagia Sophia. With the death of Justin several months later, Justinian made Theodora his coruler. Provincial governors had to swear oaths of allegiance to both of them.

The new empress avidly enjoyed the pleasures of wealth—rich food, fine wines, ostentatious dress and jewelry, palaces by the sea. She wielded her authority with sharp wit and decisiveness. Justinian consulted her in all things. On several occasions she overruled him. She was particularly influential in matters of religion. Although her husband was a devout follower of orthodox Christianity, Theodora was a firm believer in the one divine nature of Christ, or Monophysitism (see pages 293–294). Though Monophysitism had been discredited at Chalcedon some 80 years before, many in the Eastern churches still adhered to it.

Theodora went so far as to shelter Monophysite bishops in her own chambers and to manipulate the appointment of a pope she thought would be pro-Monophysite. She wanted religious toleration for the sake of the empire, while her husband seemed more interested in writing theological doctrine.

Despite their differences, their marriage was a successful one. Ever loyal to her husband, Theodora was quick to punish his enemies. When she died from cancer in 548, Justinian was inconsolable.

General Belisarius

Justinian's political goals were far-reaching—he wanted all of the old Roman Empire united again. This entailed recapturing Africa from the Vandals, Italy from the Ostrogoths, Spain from the Visigoths, Gaul from the Franks, and Britain from the Saxons. The fact that any part of this noble plan was achieved was due to one man, the great general Belisarius. For his resourcefulness and tactical genius against his enemies, Belisarius has been likened to Julius Caesar.

Tall and dashing, Belisarius was a young cavalry officer when Justinian appointed him to the imperial staff. Though some 20 years younger than Justinian, Belisarius proved so capable that Justinian commissioned him to command the Roman Army against the Persians. After his victory in Persia, Belisarius married the comely Antonina, who like her good friend, the empress Theodora, was a former actress. Belisarius defeated the Persians, but to stave off full-blown

Portions of mosaic flooring that depict scenes from mythology and country life are among the few remaining splendors of the emperor's Great Palace in Constantinople. Here a farmer attempts to feed his obstinate donkey.

Another mosaic from the Great Palace shows a boy chasing geese. The art of mosaic was elevated to extraordinary heights in the Byzantine Empire. What sculpture had been to the West, mosaics now were to the East.

Egyptian Christians who believed in Monophysitism, the doctrine that Christ had one nature, formed the Coptic Church in the fifth century. Egypt, which grew most of the cotton for the empire, was the center for textiles. This lovely Coptic Christian rondel of linen embroidered in brightly colored silk depicts the Annunciation and Visitation. It dates from the sixth century.

war, Justinian recalled his general and agreed to buy off the enemy with 11,000 pounds of gold.

Belisarius' loyalty was given the ultimate test by the Nika revolt. His quick thinking and masterly moves saved Justinian's throne. In 533 Justinian was ready to launch his master plan. He sent Belisarius with about 16,000 troops and 92 warships to reclaim North Africa from the Vandals. Accompanied by his wife, Belisarius sailed there and took city after city, finally entering Carthage, where he was hailed by joyous Roman Africans. The war was over. The Vandals were utterly defeated; the surviving members of the once fierce tribe dispersed, never to fight again.

Belisarius returned to Constantinople loaded with spoils. Among them was the great golden menorah taken from the Temple in Jerusalem by Titus in 71. (The Vandals had taken it as booty when they sacked Rome in 455.) An official triumph was held in his honor. Justinian was so pleased with his young general that he named him consul. Not only had Belisarius recaptured a former Roman province, he had also made possible the reestablishment of the Catholic Church in Africa to replace Arianism.

Justinian then ordered Belisarius to undertake the next phase of his grand design—reconquest of Italy from the Ostrogoths. With only 8,000 men, the gifted general took Ravenna and Rome. But Justinian had heard rumors that during the Italian campaigns the Ostrogoths had offered to make Belisarius their emperor; he began to suspect his general of unbridled personal ambition. Justinian sent him quickly off to the eastern borders, where the Persians were restive. By 542, Belisarius had put an end to this new threat.

The plague

In May 542, as Constantinople commemorated its founding, ships from all over the Mediterranean docked in its great harbor. Vessels from Egypt were carrying rats infected with the bubonic plague. No one could have predicted the horrors that were to follow. Fleas from the rats soon transmitted the disease to man. At first only a few people fell ill. Symptoms began with a sudden high fever, followed by painful swellings in the groin or armpits. Some experienced a violent delirium. In most cases, death followed soon afterward. Doctors watched helplessly as hundreds, then thousands, died. Only those whose swellings turned to boils that burst and released the poison, had any chance of survival.

The city was gripped with terror. Rival Blues and Greens jointly buried the dead. Bodies in one suburb were piled so high that "an evil stench pervaded the city and distressed the inhabitants still more."

Justinian came down with the disease, but the news was kept secret. Theodora made social appearances to give the impression that all was well. During these dark hours, a spy reported to Theodora that Belisarius would not support an heir of her choosing. The empress was insulted. Always a woman of quick action, she ordered the general back to the capital, confiscated much of his fortune, and made certain that he was ostracized. Her vengeance might have been even more brutal, except for the war hero's popularity.

Justinian recovered and though still weak, exonerated Belisarius and inspired the people by walking about the city, dressed in his official robes. He visited many of Constantinople's churches, in which relief hospices were set up. The Christians' nursing of the sick inspired many a survivor to convert.

After four months the pestilence abated. As many as 300,000 had died—more than a third of Constantinople's population. The plague then spread across much of the known world. "The whole human race came near to being annihilated," wrote a contemporary. Successive waves of the disease occurred for some 50 years and then died out. But it struck again in the 14th century and killed perhaps one fourth the population of Europe—earning the name Black Death.

News soon arrived that the Ostrogoths had retaken the Italian peninsula. The ever stalwart Belisarius went back into the fray. The Gothic War, as the campaign came to be called, dragged on, largely because he did not have enough men, and Justinian was not sending sufficient supplies.

Antonina usually followed her husband into the thick of his military adventures, enduring the hardships of camp life and supporting his aims. Older and more worldly than her husband, she often tried to use her influence with her friend, the empress Theodora In 548, as the situation in Italy turned desperate, she headed back toward Constantinople, hoping to convince Theodora to intervene and send reinforcements. But she arrived too late. On June 28, 548, the empress succumbed to cancer. Belisarius, no doubt exhausted by the uphill struggles of field and finance, returned home and went into retirement.

An empire divided by Monophysitism

During Justinian's reign the prevailing orthodox belief was the one confirmed at Chalcedon in 451: that Christ was both man and God; he had two natures, one human, one divine (see pages 260–261). Those who continued to believe that Christ had a single nature, namely the Monophysites, were anathematized. The word *monophysitism* is a combination of the Greek

Images of Christ on his throne were a favorite theme among Coptic Christians. In this painting, Christ holds a book with the triple acclamation "Holy, holy, holy."

words *monos*, "one," and *physis*, "nature." While the Western clergy took up the orthodox position, those in the East continued to believe that Jesus was of one nature; in other words, his divinity had absorbed his human nature, as the sea swallows up a drop of water.

The Monophysites had a strong ally in the empress Theodora. Justinian was an orthodox Christian, but his wife never wavered in her support for these Monophysites, who, reportedly, had offered her shelter at a time of need in her youth. Though Justinian may have privately sided with Theodora, he was eager to unite the empire under one religious doctrine. The Western Empire, which had long been without an emperor, was dominated by the clergy, who were staunchly pro-Chalcedon. However, by the time of Justinian, Monophysitism was dominant in Egypt as well as in much of Syria and Palestine.

Justinian, at times, actively persecuted Monophysites, but for the most part he waited passively for their decline. When a Monophysite bishop died, he replaced him with an orthodox churchman. Theodora, too, was biding her time, but not for her husband's cause. A woman of action, she gave sanctuary to persecuted Monophysites in a monastery she had built within the Great Palace. When the king of an Arab state on Syria's border begged the empress to allow a Monophysite bishop to be consecrated for Edessa, Theodora saw her chance.

Thanks to Theodora's manipulations, an energetic bishop named Jacob Baradaeus was consecrated about 542. He singlehandedly started a Monophysite revival. Disguised as a beggar, he toured Palestine and Syria, convincing his followers that Monophysitism gave the true picture of the nature of Christ.

The failure of Justinian's ploy

Upset by the Monophysite revival, Justinian came up with an idea to unify his empire behind one religious doctrine. He reasoned that the best way to unite the Monophysites and the Chalcedonians was to renew a condemnation against an old common enemy, namely the Nestorians (see pages 255, 257–258). Justinian seized on the fact that at the Council of Chalcedon in 451, writings by three men accused of Nestorianism had been overlooked by the attending clerics. In an edict that was published in 544, Justinian condemned the three men and their works, which came to be called the *Three Chapters*.

His decree stirred up resentment on both sides. In the West, the clergy were exasperated with Justinian for tampering with ecclesiastical affairs. They saw his actions as an attack on the Council of Chalcedon and Pope Leo I, who had provided its doctrinal content. Moreover, though the writings of the three men in question had been previously condemned, the men themselves had not. All three had, in fact, received the last sacraments and the blessing of the church when they died. How could they now be condemned? Meanwhile, in the East, the Monophysites scarcely acknowledged the edict at all.

Justinian persisted in his scheme. He expected from the Western clerics immediate support. But the West's independence became apparent when Pope Vigilius ordered his representative in Constantinople to excommunicate Menas, the patriarch of Constantinople, who had sided with Justinian. No doubt Vigilius' bold move shocked Theodora, who had managed to have him elected to the papacy on the secret understanding that he would compromise on the issue of Monophysitism. Vigilius, however, had no intention of being a pawn of the empress. He faithfully upheld the canons of Chalcedon and insisted that Rome, not Constantinople, was the final arbiter of orthodoxy.

For almost 10 years, Justinian tried everything he could to bend Vigilius to his will. Still the Pope would not relent. In January 553 Justinian made yet another effort to force the clergy to bow to his theology by calling for an ecumenical council—the fifth one in church history. When proceedings of the Second Council of Constantinople began in Hagia Sophia on

May 5, 553, only a few Westerners were present. The vast majority were Eastern bishops ready to confirm the emperor's theological pronouncements. The emperor was not present at the council, nor was Vigilius.

As a compromise, the pope issued a statement that condemned the *Three Chapters* but not its authors. Justinian, however, whose forces had defeated the Ostrogoths, no longer needed the West's political support. He had in hand secret declarations in support of his position that the pope had made earlier, including a written oath taken in 550. The documents were shown to the shocked assembly.

The conclave agreed to condemn not only the *Three Chapters* but also its authors. Pope Vigilius was humiliated by the emperor's revelation and in 554 he consented to publish a new statement, which agreed with the council's denunciation of the *Three Chapters* and its authors. For a reward, he was allowed to return home to Rome, but he died en route.

For the first time, an emperor had called an ecumenical council to settle an issue that he himself had raised. Though his goal was to settle the differences between the Monophysites and pro-Chalcedonians, he insisted that his theological stance on the *Three Chapters* and its authors be affirmed. Never before had an emperor ruled so completely over the church.

The Second Synod of Orange

Aside from Monophysitism, debates over the works of Augustine captivated the minds of sixth-century Western theologians. Some thought that his doctrine of original sin meant that only the gift of grace redeems man and inspires him to do good works. The question they pondered was whether those who resist

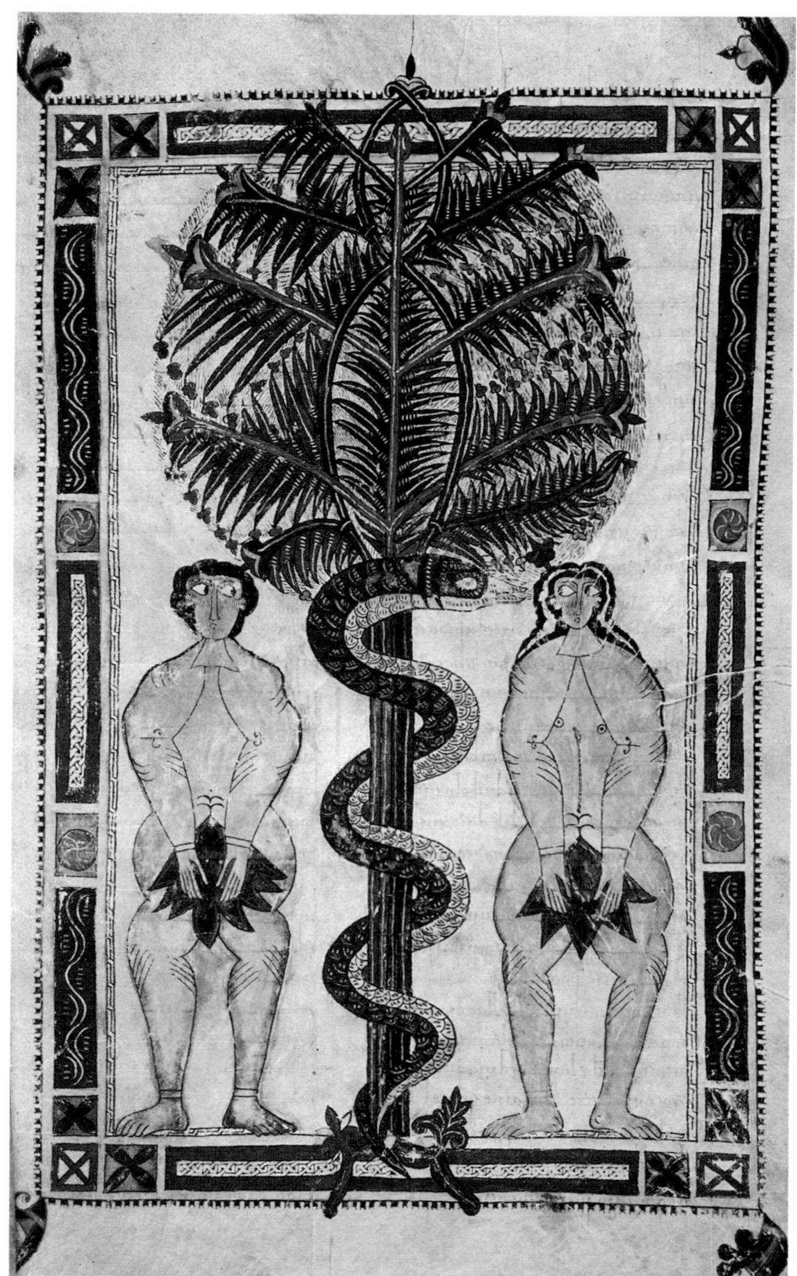

A few sixth-century theologians, who had misread Augustine's works on predestination, held that the fall of Adam and Eve (shown in this 10th-century manuscript) meant man had no free will.

God do so of their own free will or because they are predestined to sin. A synod was convened to settle the matter. Held in southern Gaul in 529, this Second Synod of Orange established doctrine for the church regarding grace, free will, and predestination. Some 15 bishops wrestled with the nature of grace.

The conclusion of the synod affirmed Augustine's position on the need for divine grace. "God loves us as being such as we are about to become by his gift," the participants agreed, "not as we are by our own merit." But at the same time, the conclave rejected the predestination to sin that a number of Augustine's followers had found in his work. Those who sin, agreed the assembled bishops, do so of their own free will. God predestines those who are saved, but those who are lost, perish by their own volition. These views, which made Augustine's ideas on divine grace part of orthodoxy in the Western church, remain dominant today in both Roman Catholicism and much of mainstream Protestantism.

On the mystical path

The sixth century witnessed a powerful new flowering of theological thought in the East. Two major works of the period were *Mystical Theology* and *On the Divine Names*. These caused a sensation, because the

Above, the kindly monk Romanus, who delivered food to Benedict during his three-year hermitage, gives him his hard-earned monastic habit. Benedict went on to found the famed monastery at Monte Cassino (right), near Naples, Italy.

The Halo: Symbol of Holiness

The halo, also called nimbus, is a glorious light that encircles the head of a holy person. It is usually represented in painting and sculpture by a circle, a disc, or rays of light. The Greeks portrayed some of their deities, especially the sun god, and even some of their kings, with halos. Borrowing from Greek tradition, Roman emperors were portrayed also with a halo-like crown, to emphasize the godlike nature of imperial rulers. Although its previous association with paganism made the halo an unattractive symbol to early Christians, by the fourth century, Christ was usually portrayed with a halo; by the sixth century, halos were used regularly in representations of saints and the Virgin Mary.

During the Middle Ages, Christians developed a variety of symbolic meanings in their use of halos. For example, a square halo was used for a living subject, usually a person being honored for donating a substantial amount of money for a religious painting or stained-glass window. A triangular halo symbolized the Trinity, and a simple circular halo was the mark of a saint. The Virgin Mary's halo, though circular, was often more elaborately decorated.

The Holy Trinity, Jesus, and Mary were sometimes depicted with light streaming from the entire body, an emanation known as an aureole. The aureole itself might be enclosed by an oval border called a mandorla (from the Italian for "almond"). In addition, Jesus was shown often with a halo that contained a cross or the Greek letters alpha and omega. These letters, the first and last in the Greek alphabet, were used to indicate that Christ was both the beginning and the end of the world.

From the 6th century to the 12th, many artists painted halos as shimmering circles of transparent light. By the 14th century, they were rendering them more often as solid discs (usually golden), sometimes inscribed with a saint's name or initials. Painters of the 15th century, striving for more realism in their art, deemphasized use of the halo, while Titian and Michelangelo, two of the greatest artists of the Renaissance, abandoned its use entirely.

author had combined Neoplatonism and Christianity in such a way as to produce a unique blend of mystical theology. The new "Christian mystagogy" revealed mysteries that could lead to the union of the human soul with the divine, resulting in a progressive deification of man. This process, the author wrote, would require going beyond rational thought. The author's premise was that to be brought closer to God, a believer must enter a state of "unknowing" and thus leave behind the physical senses and intellect.

The authorship of these books was a mystery. They were published as the works of Dionysius, a convert of the Apostle Paul. (In Acts, Paul converted Dionysius the Areopagite in Athens.) When these works first appeared, their authenticity was briefly questioned, but at least one pope accepted them as writings from the first century. Later devotees included Thomas Aquinas, the 13th-century theologian, who cited one of the works some 143 times; Meister Eckhart, a German mystic of the 14th century; and the anonymous author of a Middle English mystical text, *The Cloud of Unknowing.*

Not until the 1800's did scholars begin to surmise that the works were actually composed by a Syrian monk in the early sixth century. This man, nowadays referred to as Pseudo-Dionysius, was a well-schooled student of classical philosophy. In an effort to support the cause of Monophysitism, he had tried to reconcile orthodox Christianity with Neoplatonism in order to create a new Christian mysticism.

Benedict's monastic Rule

In the sixth century, while armies fought for control of war-torn Italy, one man created a haven of peace and order. He was a monk named Benedict. The rules he laid down for his monastery stressed obedience and humilty; in due time his ideas provided a blueprint for Christian culture in the Middle Ages.

Continued on page 300

Glorious Christian Art

During the sixth century, the church became increasingly rich and powerful. Precious materials, such as gold, silver, and silk—once lavished on pagan and imperial art—were now used to glorify Christ and his church.

Ornate liturgical vessels were often donated to the church by wealthy Christian patrons. This sixth-century paten, made of gilded silver, shows two figures of Christ giving communion to the Apostles (in Eastern tradition, both the priest and deacon serve the Eucharist).

Christ said to his Apostles, "I am the true vine," John 15:1. That statement is beautifully captured on the Antioch chalice, a famous liturgical cup from the sixth century. Standing 7½ inches high, it is made of gilded silver. In the center is Christ enthroned.

Silk making came to the West during Justinian's reign, thanks to some enterprising monks who had traveled to China and learned how to cultivate silkworms. This piece of a silken tapestry depicts the Annunciation.

This enamel portrait depicts a noblewoman and her two children. It dates about the fifth century and is part of a silver cross that belonged to Galla Placidia, a devout Christian and daughter of Theodosius the Great.

The words "Lord help the wearer" are inscribed in Greek on the small medallion of this necklace. The large medallion shows a seated Virgin Mary. Though found in Egypt, the necklace was probably made in Constantinople in the seventh century.

This pair of almost identical gilded silver book covers dates about 570. Each cover bears a cross, fanned by two palm branches. Spiral columns support an arch beautifully etched in a shell pattern.

Christian icons were first created in the fifth century. They frequently depicted martyrs and confessors of the early church. This Coptic icon (from the Monastery of St. Catherine on Mt. Sinai) shows Christ on the right, with his arm around the shoulder of St. Menas, an Egyptian martyr.

The Mysterious Pagan Rites of the Druids

In 1984 a British workman, slicing peat in the Lindow Moss bog near Manchester, England, made a momentous discovery: buried in the rich, mossy earth was a body so well preserved that at first he thought he had unearthed a recent murder victim. The body, that of a stocky man under 30 years old, was indeed a victim—but one who had been killed more than 2,000 years before in a religious ritual. Experts believe the Lindow man was a Druid, a member of the Celtic priesthood, who willingly submitted to having his head smashed in and his throat cut as a sacrifice to the gods.

The discovery of his body was especially interesting because so little is known about the role of Druids in Celtic society. Romantic legend usually portrays Druids as white-robed elders conducting secret rites in groves of oak trees, which were sacred in Celtic lore. Other sources tell us that Druids were not only priests but also judges, philosophers, and teachers for perhaps 200 years or more before Julius Caesar and his invading Roman legions defeated the Britons in 55 B.C. So important was the role of the Druids, whom Caesar considered the backbone of resistance to Roman rule, that he was determined to exterminate them.

Apparently, Druids were not a hereditary caste: Any young man (and there is some evidence that a young woman also) could become a Druid after a rigorous training period, which might have lasted as long as 20 years. The time was spent in memorizing a vast number of verses by which traditions were passed on. Unfortunately for posterity, none were ever put in writing. As a result, much of what we know about Druids is based on often unreliable accounts from Romans and Greeks, most of whom were writing secondhand. Even the firsthand chronicles of Caesar may have been influenced by his eagerness to make the Druids seem forbidding, in order to emphasize the scope and worthiness of his victory. In his *Commentaries*, he writes that they wove enormous wicker baskets in the form of human beings and filled them with men, often condemned criminals, before setting the baskets aflame as a sacrifice to the gods.

Roman occupation (and to some degree, later Christianity) successfully crushed the power and influence of the Druids in Gaul and Britain; however, they continued to hold sway in Ireland until Patrick converted the island to Christianity in the fifth century. Patrick forbade Druids to practice their religion, but he permitted them to keep alive their oral traditions as wandering bards, and their poetic tales of Irish glory have become part of the literature and tradition of the Emerald Isle.

Though the mysteries of ancient Druidic faith have almost all been forgotten, at least one of their traditions, the high-spirited revelry of Samain on the eve of November first, lives on as Halloween.

Born in Italy to a noble family about 480, Benedict went to Rome as a young man to study the classics. Sometime in his 20's, apparently he became disgusted with the city's immorality and fled to a cave near Subiaco, 30 miles outside Rome. There, he lived alone for three years. Each day a friendly monk would drop a basket of bread to him on a rope. Like Antony, the Egyptian monk of two centuries before, Benedict soon attracted other ascetics, who wished to become his disciples.

He established a number of monasteries and after several years moved his headquarters to Monte Cassino, a rocky hill some 85 miles southeast of Rome. In the 520's, near a temple of Apollo where pagans may still have been worshiping, Benedict built a self-sustaining community, complete with a garden, a flour mill, and a bakery. Unlike the austere asceticism of Eastern monasteries, Benedict's way was balanced. Monks lived together in family-style groups, under an abbot. They were expected to stay in the community for the rest of their lives. The black monks, so called because of their simple black robes, came from every level of society. All experienced a "conversion of life" and adopted poverty, chastity, and obedience to the authority of the abbot, who was elected for life by his brother monks.

Within the walls of Monte Cassino, Benedict wrote his famous *Rule*. This masterpiece of common sense and piety was only some 13,000 words long, but it covered all areas of a monk's life, from how many hours a day to pray, to what type of bedding should be assigned to each man. Eastern monks had often vied with one another in contests of austerity, but under Benedict, cooperation and moderation prevailed. The Western monk's life was orderly and purposeful.

"Idleness is the enemy of the soul," wrote Benedict. The day was devoted to prayer, work, and sleep. A monk's daily diet consisted of two cooked dishes, a pound of bread, and a pint of wine, with fruits and vegetables added in season. Reading and copying of devotional books were allowed but not advocated. Though well educated himself, Benedict favored spiritual pursuits, singing of psalms, and outdoor work over scholarly endeavors.

Benedictine monks inaugurated new agricultural techniques, wove cloth, cared for the sick, established libraries, taught in monastery schools, and extended hospitality to guests. "Let no one follow what he thinks most profitable to himself, but rather what is best for another," wrote Benedict.

During the next 600 years, the Benedictines set up hundreds of monasteries, which brought intellectual, social, and agricultural enrichment to much of Europe. The real strength of the order, however, was in its missionary work. In fact, converting the heathen had been one of Benedict's most cherished goals.

Spreading the word

Missionary work often called for arduous and sometimes lengthy journeys. The Apostle Thomas may have ventured the farthest. Syrian tradition says that Thomas proselytized in India, but many people deemed the story unlikely until 1498. That year missionaries from Portugal reached Malabar, on India's southwest coast, and found a group of Indians who called themselves Thomas Christians.

A sixth-century writer, Cosmas Indicopleustes, had noted the presence of Christians in India and Ceylon. Cosmas was not a missionary but a merchant from Egypt who became a monk. He combined theology and geography in his *Christian Topography*. In this work, written about 547, he tried to correct presumed errors of the second-century astronomer Ptolemy, who had taught that the universe was a sphere. Cosmas' own topography was based on the Scriptures. He claimed that the universe looked something like a house. The earth, a flat rectangle, formed the ground floor; beyond the oceans was a land that humanity had inhabited before the flood. Upstairs was heaven.

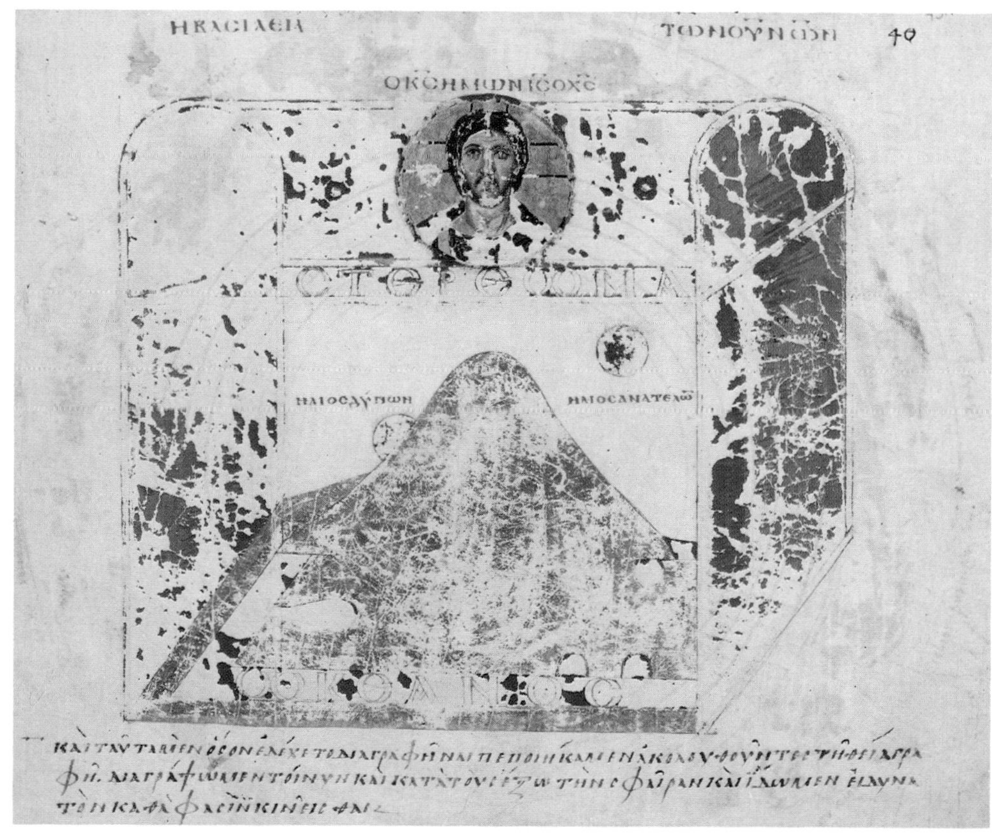

A page from a ninth-century manuscript of Christian Topography, *written by the monk Cosmas Indicopleustes, illustrates his view of the cosmos. God is in heaven, above; the earthly world is seen as a mountain, with waters flowing beneath it.*

Patrick, patron saint of Ireland

During a wave of missionary activity in the fifth and sixth centuries, monks traversed mountains and seas to reach those who had not heard the word of Christ. Wandering abroad for Christ was held by some to be a greater sacrifice than dying for him. One who responded fervently to the missionary calling was Patrick, who greatly altered the religious life of Ireland. Patrick was born in Britain, the son of a Christian deacon. When he was 16, Irish raiders stormed his village, took him as a captive to Ireland, and sold him as a slave. Paganism was practiced on the rugged island by the Celts, members of a great barbarian tribe, some of whom had migrated from Gaul to the British Isles a number of centuries before the birth of Christ. Forced to herd pigs, Patrick took comfort in Christian prayer, and his faith grew. After six years of captivity, he escaped and walked some 200 miles to reach the coast, where a ship took him to Gaul. From there he managed to work his way back to the home of his parents in Britain. But Ireland had made an indelible impression upon Patrick. One night, he dreamed that the Irish were begging him to return.

He began studying at a monastery and spent 14 years there, until his education was considered complete. In 432, Patrick, then about 43, was made a bishop and he set sail for Ireland. The church had sent missionaries there before, but they had realized little

At a Celtic Christian site, on White Island in Northern Ireland, stand these 3-foot-high stone figures, which may represent Patrick and his abbots. They were carved into the wall of a Romanesque church sometime in the 10th century. Below is an ancient iron bell, dipped in bronze, which tradition says might have been used by Patrick.

success with the warring Irish clans. Stories were soon circulating of miraculous feats Patrick performed to combat the magic of the Druids (see box, page 300). He was so successful, legend credits him with introducing Christianity to Ireland, and he is regarded as one of its patron saints. Patrick died about 460; a new generation of Irish monks carried on his work.

Other Irish saints

One monk especially took to heart Patrick's urging to wander for Christ. He was Brendan, who during the sixth century founded several monasteries in Ireland. Brendan is known best, however, for his legendary travels in search of the "promised land." Tradition holds that he sailed with a crew of followers in a curragh (a wooden-frame boat covered with animal skins) to western Scotland, the Hebrides, Wales, and the coast of Gaul. The *Voyage*, written at least two centuries after Brendan's death about 583, has many delightful elements of the fantastic. Some students of the work have gone so far as to speculate that the saint may have found his "promised land" on the coast of North America, perhaps at the Newfoundland Banks.

Monastic life was open to women, too. One of the most popular Irish saints was Brigid, the pioneering woman who founded the first nunnery in Kildare, eastern Ireland. She most likely lived in the late fifth or early sixth century. According to legend, her parents had been baptized by Patrick.

Another renowned Irish missionary was Columba, an aristocrat passionately devoted to monastic life. About 563 he took 12 followers with him to Iona, a tiny island off the west coast of Scotland. There, Columba, whose name is Latin for "dove," was asked to act as peacemaker between warring Pictish chiefs on at least two occasions, perhaps using skillfully a voice famed for being "so loud and melodious it could be heard a mile off." Over a nine-year period, he inspired the conversion of the northern Picts, a unifying feat that helped form the nation of Scotland.

Irish missionaries became "pilgrims for Christ," sailing across chilly Western seas to spread the word to distant lands. One of the most renowned of the wandering monks was Brendan, whose travels later became popularized in a work called the Voyage. *Here, an illustration of this fascinating medieval work shows Brendan (carrying the shepherd's staff of an Irish missionary) and his monks being held aloft by a sea monster.*

Gregory of Tours

When Gregory of Tours was consecrated bishop of that Gallic city in 573, the wealth and duties of his office were extensive. As bishop, he was responsible in his diocese for the church's gold plate, care of the tombs and relics of saints, repair of churches, supervision of the church dining halls, maintenance of the monasteries and nunneries, and the administration of

The Franks were a fierce Germanic people who, by the sixth century, ruled over most of Gaul. Above is a Frankish tombstone showing Jesus as a warrior, carrying a spear.

church properties. Even more important, as the representative of the church in a land dominated by the Franks, Gregory played a key role in upholding Christian morals as well as Roman civic and cultural values in an era of tumultuous change.

After he became bishop, Gregory began keeping a chronicle of life in Gaul. He recorded church history, stories of miracles, and intrigues of Frankish rulers. This fascinating narrative, the *History of the Franks*, is one of the few extant records of the period.

This ornately embellished folding throne may have belonged to a Frankish king. During the early Middle Ages, such easily transportable chairs were used by kings and bishops.

Filled with amazing stories and unusual characters, Gregory's work often reads more like a novel than a history book. In one passage, he relates how two spoiled Frankish princesses, who had joined the nunnery in Poitiers, started a revolt against their abbess. Gregory was asked to look into the matter and noted their complaints: "poor food, the lack of clothing and . . . that other people shared their bathroom." They were also accusing the abbess of an illicit sexual liaison. The charges proved to be false; the abbess was acquitted and reinstated, and the princesses were "cut off from communion." Though the Franks ruled with an iron hand, the church sometimes managed to triumph over willful royalty.

Gregory recorded many miracles, including some cures effected by holy relics. Once, when ill with dysentery, he himself resorted to a potion containing dust from the tomb of the revered Martin of Tours (later named a patron saint of France) and immediately recovered. His powerful faith and pragmatic sense of justice are evident throughout his writings. On one occasion, when some citizens of Tours were involved in a particularly bloody feud, Gregory intervened, urging the disputants to "stop this riotous behavior and not let the wrong which has been done spread any wider." The exhortation was not enough. But when he offered church funds to help one side pay the required blood money, peace was restored.

Gregory also records movingly the terrible effects of disease: "The epidemic [an outbreak of dysentery] began in the month of August. It attacked young children first of all and to them it was fatal: and so we lost our little ones, who were so dear to us and sweet, whom we had cherished in our bosoms and dandled in our arms, whom we had fed and nurtured with such loving care. As I write I wipe away my tears and I repeat once more the words of Job the blessed: 'The Lord gave, and the Lord hath taken away.' " Gregory's chronicle ends in 591, just three years before his death at the age of 55.

Britain occupied by barbarians

A hundred years passed before the church produced another historian to match Gregory. This time the hand holding the pen belonged to an English monk, later known as the Venerable Bede, who lived in the late seventh and early eighth centuries.

Bede's celebrated *History of the English Church and People* is renowned for its accuracy and careful attention to detail. He noted that since 55 B.C., when Roman soldiers had first set foot on British soil, Britain had been contending with hostile invaders. Raids by the Scots and the Picts (Celtic people from the north and northwest) posed a constant threat. Rome offered some protection until the mid-fifth century, but then Roman soldiers were called home to help save the empire from barbarians. The Picts and Scots took advantage of the opportunity to begin a full-scale attack.

In 449 the Britons appealed to the Angles, Saxons, and Jutes for protection. These Germanic tribes, from across the North Sea, saved the day. But that same year, they suddenly turned on their allies. Led by the brothers Hengist and Horsa, who were said to be Jutes, they attacked the defenseless Britons. Horsa was killed, but his brother was victorious and founded a kingdom in Kent. According to Bede, within a short time, the barbarians "established a stranglehold over nearly all the doomed island." Needing land for their teeming population, boatloads of Angles, Saxons, and Jutes came and took further control. They brought with them their love of warfare and their Norse beliefs. Their invasion, or migration, as some scholars call it, was so successful that in due time, Britain came to be called Angle-land, or England.

The epic of Beowulf

Nothing captures the spirit of Britain's barbarian invaders so vividly as the epic poem *Beowulf.* It is a haunting story of good and evil, in which a murderous monster, Grendel ("kindred of Cain"), is finally killed by the hero Beowulf.

The Christian Calendar

About 532 a monk in Rome invented the dating system by which we now refer to events of this era. Dionysius, who called himself Exiguus ("the Little"), was a gifted mathematician, astronomer, and theological scholar. He intended only to set down rules for working out the correct date of Easter. In fact, he created the Christian calendar and started the practice of dating events as A.D., or *anno domini nostri Jesu Christi,* meaning, "in the year of our Lord." (In 1627 the scholar Petavius invented the parallel system of dating events B.C., or "before Christ.") However, because of a lack of historical data, Dionysius miscalculated the probable date of Jesus' birth by as much as seven years. The Nativity, according to scholars today, took place between 7 and 4 B.C.

Many a brave nobleman, while sleeping in Heorot, the great hall of Hrothgar, king of the Danes, has been eaten by Grendel. It falls to Beowulf, a powerful young warrior from the coast of Sweden, to put a stop to the carnage. "With bare hands shall I grapple with the fiend, fight to the death here, hater and hated!" promises Beowulf. Indeed, when Grendel attacks the hall, Beowulf fights him and inflicts fatal wounds upon the monster. The great hall rings with rejoicing, but the next night, Grendel's mother, a mighty ogress, kills the king's favorite warrior. She then steals off to her underwater lair. Undaunted, Beowulf dives after the ogress, fights off "throngs of sea-beasts," and kills her with a sword. Peace reigns at last. Fifty years later, Beowulf, now a king in Sweden, slays a fire-breathing dragon. That feat costs him his life.

About 450, boats bringing the Angles, Saxons, and Jutes began to arrive on Britain's shores, as depicted in this 12th-century illumination. By the seventh century, the eastern half of the island was theirs.

In the poem, bits from the Bible are incongruously mixed with Norse paganism. The anonymous bard was obviously familiar with stories from the Old Testament, for he refers to the creation of the Garden of Eden and the slaying of Abel by Cain. An almighty God is mentioned, but there is no reference to Christ. In spite of its biblical overtones, the poem is essentially pagan. When Beowulf dies, he is given a pagan burial. His body and war gear are burned on a funeral pyre, then walled up inside a barrow, or burial mound, no doubt much like the one discovered in 1939 at Sutton Hoo, England. The bard describes it thus:

"*What remained from the fire*
they cast a wall around, of workmanship
as fine as their wisest men could frame for it.
They placed in the tomb both the torques and the jewels,
all the magnificence that the men had earlier
taken from the hoard in hostile mood.
They left the earls' wealth in the earth's keeping,
the gold in the dirt. It dwells there yet,
of no more use to men than in ages before.
Then the warriors rode around the barrow,
twelve of them in all, athelings' sons.
They recited a dirge to declare their grief,
spoke of the man, mourned their King . . .
they said that he was of all the world's kings
the gentlest of men, and the most gracious,
the kindest to his people, the keenest for fame."

Combining ancient legends with actual events in Danish history, *Beowulf* gives vivid glimpses of the way of life of the northern barbarians.

The history of the church in Britain

Bede recorded that Christianity first came to Britain in 156, when "Lucius, a British king, sent him [the bishop of Rome] a letter, asking to be made a Christian by his direction." In the fourth century, Jerome reported that "Britain in common with Rome, Gaul, Africa, Persia, the East, and India, adores one Christ, observes one rule of faith." But there, similarities with the church of the later Roman Empire ended. British delegates did manage to attend the Synod of Ariminum, held in northern Italy in 359, but only thanks to the charity of the emperor, who paid their way. In time, geographic distance, coupled with the steady withdrawal of the Roman legions, lessened further contact between the long impoverished British church and the West.

The coming of the Angles, Saxons, and Jutes altered radically the history of Britain and its church. These fierce warriors pillaged town and countryside, slaughtering all who attempted to fight back. In a short time, their Germanic language, the ancestor of English, had replaced the Latin used in Britain. The invaders also introduced the religion of the Norse gods, supplanting Christianity with it in many British localities. All Anglo-Saxon chieftains claimed descent from Woden (Odin), the chief god of the Norse pantheon. (The names of Norse gods survive today in the English designations for several days of the week: Tuesday, for example, means "the day of Tiu," the war god. Wednesday stands for "Woden's Day." Thursday is named for Thor, the god of thunder, and Friday is "the day of Frigg," goddess of love.)

Converting England's new rulers

By the sixth century, the Angles, Saxons, and Jutes were firmly entrenched in Britain, or England. They had divided their newly won territory into a federation of four kingdoms: the Jutes took up residence in Kent, while the Saxons dispersed to the south, east, and west. Their three kingdoms were called Sussex (Southern Saxon), Essex (Eastern Saxon), and Wessex (Western Saxon).

It was clear the invaders were there to stay; nonetheless, British clergy would not obey the new pagan conquerors. Moreover, they refused to try to convert their rulers. A few of these clergy left for Wales, while others fled to Gaul.

This fresco of a Christian in prayer, painted about 350, graces the wall of a small chapel in Kent, England. The Celts, a barbarian people who had long lived in Britain, were first introduced to Christianity in the second century. Roman protection kept the Celtic natives safe from invasion and indirectly allowed Celtic Christianity, an independent form of the faith, to grow.

One man, far away in Rome, was deeply concerned about the religious life of England's new rulers. As legend has it, about 595 Pope Gregory chanced to see a group of blond, fair-skinned boys at a slave auction in Rome. When told they were Angles, he retorted, "Not Angles but Angels!" Keen to convert this handsome Nordic race, Gregory instituted a powerful missionary effort in England. In 597 he sent a Roman prior, Augustine, and 40 missionaries to win the favor of the Jute ruler, Ethelbert, king of Kent. Augustine had reason to hope for success because Ethelbert was married to Bertha, a Christian Frankish princess. As part of the prenuptial agreement, Bertha had brought along a bishop as her personal chaplain. Ethelbert had gone so far as to restore a chapel, built outside Canterbury during Roman times, for his new queen.

Stamped at Frankish mints, these gold coins were issued sometime after 625. They were among the artifacts found in the famous burial mound of a seventh-century Anglo-Saxon king in Sutton Hoo, England. The coins and other objects were to aid the pagan king in the afterworld. Christian and pagan motifs were often blended in Anglo-Saxon art. On this whalebone casket from the eighth century, the Adoration of the Magi is carved next to a scene from a Germanic myth.

Ethelbert agreed to meet with Augustine, but fearful that the prior and his entourage would try to work their magic under his roof, he insisted on holding the meeting outdoors. Later, Ethelbert agreed to give Augustine a residence in Canterbury. The ascetic and devout lifestyle of the missionaries impressed the king; within months he had converted. As Bede notes: "Thenceforward great numbers gathered each day to hear the word of God. While the king was pleased with their faith and conversion, it is said that he would not compel anyone to accept Christianity; for he had learned . . . that the service of Christ must be accepted freely and not under compulsion."

The first archbishop of Canterbury

Hearing that Augustine "had a rich harvest but few to help him gather it," Pope Gregory sent a second group of missionaries to England. These men came bearing the authority to make Augustine the first archbishop of Canterbury and also to create 12 new bishoprics in England. In addition, Pope Gregory sent along gifts and a letter of praise to the man who had become the church's champion, King Ethelbert.

Augustine had converted thousands of Angles, Jutes, and Saxons. But the more people he brought into the church, the greater became the acrimony among the British clergy. Native Britons, or Celts, who despised the invaders, felt betrayed by Rome's proselytizing efforts. They refused to accept Augustine as archbishop or preach to the Anglo-Saxons. "We will never, never, preach the faith to this cruel race of foreigners who have so treacherously robbed us of our native soil," declared one British abbot.

The British clergy were fiercely independent and refused to comply with Roman observances. They celebrated Easter on a different day because they would not adopt Rome's calendar. Moreover, the tonsure in England was different from that in Rome. In the West, the crown of the head was shaved, leaving a ring of hair, which was supposed to symbolize the crown of thorns. The Celtic custom called for the entire front half of a cleric's head to be shaved.

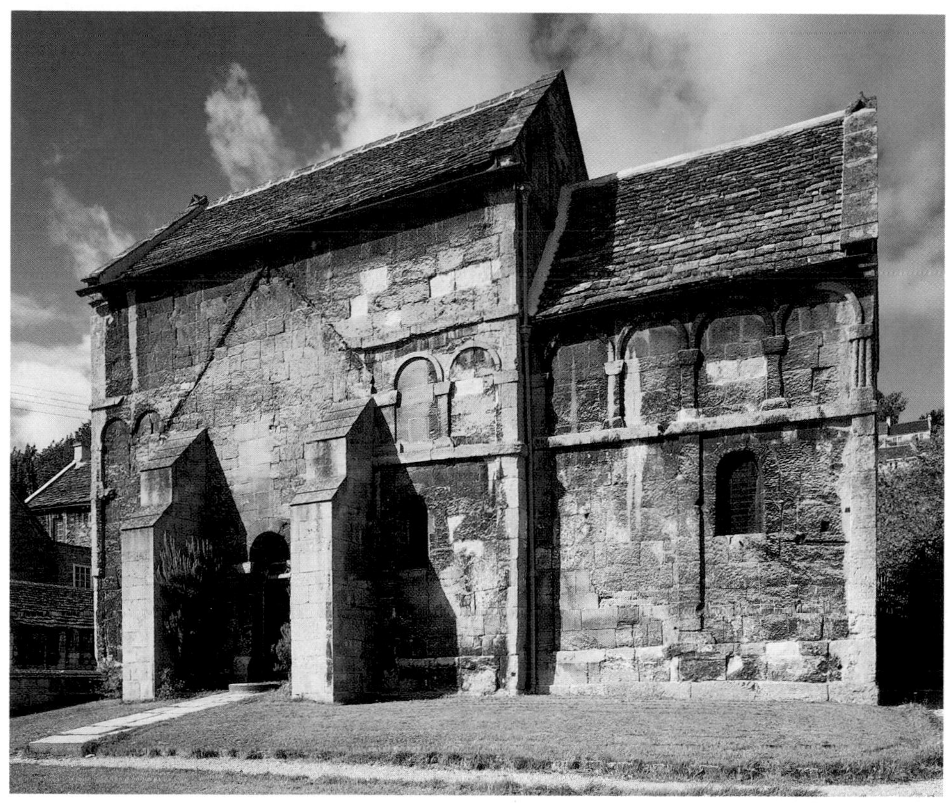

While Irish churches in the sixth and seventh centuries were built mostly of timber and sod, Anglo-Saxon churches, such as this one at Bradford-on-Avon, were made of stone. A great monument of Anglo-Saxon Christianity is the Ruthwell Cross, right, which stands in the church of Ruthwell in Dumfriesshire, Scotland. This eighth-century cross is embellished with carvings of biblical scenes and runes, or old Germanic writing. The runes spell out passages of a poem in which the cross itself speaks of the Crucifixion: "I held the High King, Heaven's Lord. I dared not bend. . . . Christ was on the Cross."

Thanks to Rome's missionary zeal, most of southern England accepted the Roman practices, while many British churches in the North and West refused to conform. Finally, the Anglo-Saxon king Oswy called a synod in 664 to settle the matter. After hearing both sides, he decided in favor of Rome: "Peter is guardian of the gates of heaven, and I shall not contradict him." The issue of the tonsure was settled also. Oswy decreed that all priests adopt the Roman tonsure. (In the Roman Catholic Church, the tonsure was worn by monks until 1972, when it was abolished.) Though the Celtic church was now formally aligned with Rome, in Wales and Ireland, it retained for years a certain measure of independence.

The rise of Theodoric

By 476, the Western Empire was officially without an emperor. Rome was in the hands of a Germanic barbarian king, Odoacer, but Italy was about to suffer yet another upheaval. Eyeing Odoacer's kingdom was Theodoric the Ostrogoth. Theodoric had grown up at the imperial court in Constantinople, where, as a young boy, he had become the prize pawn in a treaty between the Ostrogoths and Romans. As part of the treaty, the emperor Leo had agreed to pay 300 pounds of gold to the barbarians; and to make sure that they kept all their promises, Leo demanded as a hostage Theodoric, the son of the Ostrogothic king. For some 10 years, Theodoric remained in Constantinople,

A Legendary King of Britain

In the late fifth or early sixth century, a group of Britons led by an intrepid warrior successfully fought off Saxon onslaughts. Though the place and leader of those encounters have never been identified, out of them possibly evolved one of the great legendary heroes of all time—King Arthur.

Some historians believe Ambrosius Aurelanius, a soldier, was the man we now know as King Arthur; others think the real Arthur might have been a northern prince credited with a decisive victory. Still others say that Arthur was a prince from Dalraida, a Celtic Irish colony in Scotland.

Nennius, a Welsh chronicler of the ninth century, claimed that Arthur not only defeated the Saxons in 12 battles but during the climactic encounter, single-handedly killed 960 men! Although Nennius was the first author to refer directly to these exploits, some 250 years earlier a Welsh poet named Aneurin had dismissed a famous man-at-arms with the comment that though he was brave, "he was no Arthur." And the name *Arthur,* seldom used in England before the sixth century, appears to have become more popular from that time on. Presumably then, as now, parents liked to name their sons after great men.

In the 15th century, Sir Thomas Malory, in *Le Morte d'Arthur*, immortalized Arthurian legend in English literature, transforming it into an epic of romantic chivalry. Malory entwined the story with legends concerning the Holy Grail, sometimes identified as the chalice Christ used at the Last Supper. In Malory's version, instead of merely battling Saxon foes, Arthur and his knights of the Round Table performed heroic deeds and searched unceasingly for the Holy Grail. After this time, however, Arthur and his court became background for the deeds of other heroic characters.

Malory's embroidery on Arthurian lore was further embellished by the Victorian poet Alfred, Lord Tennyson in his epic *Idylls of the King*. Tennyson's poetry, in turn, inspired such retellings of the story as T.H. White's *The Once and Future King* and its adaptation as the Broadway musical and later movie *Camelot*.

King Arthur, the subject of countless stories of heroic deeds, is depicted with his legendary knights of the Round Table in this 15th-century French woodcut.

learning how to wage military campaigns but not how to read or write. He led a patrician life with the wealth bestowed upon him by the emperor.

Upon his father's death, Theodoric became king of the Ostrogoths. In 488, backed by the new Eastern emperor, Zeno, Theodoric led a large army into Italy. Within five years, he had not only captured Ravenna but had killed Odoacer treacherously with his own hands, during the peace banquet to which he had invited his defeated opponent. It was an ominous beginning; nonetheless, Theodoric's 33-year rule was marked by peace and stability.

Keen to repair damages from earlier invasions, Theodoric salvaged materials from crumbled ramparts to restore aqueducts and city walls. A contemporary recorded that "he rejuvenated Rome and Italy in their hideous old age by amputating their mutilated members." He drained marshes and stabilized the price of grain. To secure political alliances with barbarians outside the empire, he married his three daughters and two sisters to the chieftains of leading tribes. He also conquered Sicily and made inroads into present-day Yugoslavia, Hungary, and Germany.

Theodoric deeply respected the Roman way of life. "An able Goth wants to be like a Roman: only a poor Roman would want to be like a Goth," he is said to have remarked. Court life was Roman in character, with the nobility vying for favors at the palace in Ravenna. The Goths of Italy, however, retained their own laws and officials, whereas native Italians were ruled by Roman officials appointed by Theodoric.

Like most Goths, Theodoric was an Arian, yet he was tolerant of both orthodox Christianity and Judaism. Initially, he had enjoyed the backing of the Catholic bishops. But he angered many of them by issuing decrees that sternly enforced tolerance of the Jews. Church Fathers had long been trying to separate Christianity from the influence of Judaism, for fear that Jewish rites and rituals would lure Christians away. About 523, Christians in Ravenna had gone so far as to force Jews to be dunked in baptismal water and had even burned synagogues. Theodoric made many enemies when he ordered the intolerant Christians to rebuild the Jewish houses of worship. At the same time, the Arianism of the Ostrogoths was under attack in Constantinople, where the emperor Justin had dictated heresy laws against the Arians. Theodoric commissioned Pope John I to travel to Constantinople to plead the Arian cause. Reluctantly, the pope met with the emperor, but to no avail. Justin refused to change his anti-Arian position. When the pope returned to Ravenna with the bad news, Theodoric had him jailed. The ailing prelate died soon afterward and was popularly viewed as a martyr.

Theodoric came to suspect key people in the court at Constantinople of plotting against him. Possibly the church was involved, perhaps even the Senate. Fear worked insidiously on the aging king. When a scheming courtier went to Theodoric in 523 and accused the senator Albinus of writing letters to the emperor Justin that were highly critical of Theodoric's governing, Theodoric took the bait and had Albinus jailed. Shocked at such action, another senator, Boethius, rushed to Albinus' aid and pleaded his innocence before the wary king.

Boethius the scholar

If any man could have swayed the king, it would have been Boethius. A virtuous and intelligent person, he was one of the king's most trusted advisers. Boethius had been orphaned at an early age and adopted by Symmachus, a former prefect and now a senator. The senator's patrician forefather had been a standard-bearer of paganism, but Symmachus the younger was a Christian. A wise and gentle man, he had Boethius educated in Athens. When Boethius returned home, he married his adoptive father's daughter and entered the Senate. Theodoric appointed him consul in 510. Boethius, however, was more of a scholar than a statesman. One of the few sixth-century men in the

Graceful, curvilinear designs, which became the hallmark of much Celtic metalwork, were also used on stone. This seventh-century Celtic Christian slab, from County Donegal in Ireland, features a cross of interlaced bands.

Boethius, the sixth-century Roman scholar, assured the continuance of liberal arts education into the Middle Ages. This medieval frontispiece to his work On Music *shows the threefold manifestations of music in the cosmos. In the top panel, Music, personified as a Muse, points to the harmonic movements of the universe and its elements—earth, air, fire, and water. In the middle, she directs attention to four men who represent the four humors, or temperaments, whose harmony governs human life. The bottom panel shows the lowest of Music's guises: instrumental music. She shakes her finger at the fiddle player.*

West quite familiar with Greek thought, he translated many of Aristotle's and Plato's works into Latin.

Theodoric listened to Boethius' pleas on behalf of Albinus but was not moved, for the letters written to Justin (undoubtedly forged) incriminated Boethius also. Theodoric threw Boethius in jail for treason. Sorcery was then added to the charge. Boethius, who had a superior knowledge of engineering, had designed a water-operated clock, for which few understood the mechanical principles. Its wonders caused some people to suspect that Boethius was under the power of "the Evil One." Symmachus pleaded clemency for Boethius but was himself imprisoned.

Boethius was kept in the tower of Pavia, some 450 miles north of Rome. Meanwhile, the Senate set about the ugly business of trying his case. Assuming he would be found guilty and executed, Boethius wrestled with the problem of evil and the suffering of the innocent. The result was a philosophical memoir, *Consolation of Philosophy*, which became one of the most influential books of the Middle Ages.

The work begins with Boethius lamenting his fate in mournful verses, when suddenly the Muse of philosophy appears in his cell. " 'But it is rather time,' saith she, 'to apply remedies, than to make complaints.' " The Muse engages him in debates in which she proves that the pleasures of wealth, fame, and political influence are only transitory. True happiness, she tells him, lies in seeking God in all things. She assures Boethius that God sees all and that the deeds of evil men are punished and those of the just, rewarded. Boethius' inner peace is restored, and he is ready to face his fate. The *Consolation* ends with Boethius reminding his readers to "embrace virtues, possess your minds with worthy hopes. . . . There is, if you will not dissemble, a great necessity of doing well imposed upon you, since you live in the sight of your Judge, who beholdeth all things."

About 524 the executioner arrived; Boethius was strangled and his property confiscated. Symmachus, who had stood by his noble son-in-law, was also sentenced to death and executed in Ravenna.

Theodoric did not long survive his victims. In 526, according to tradition, he was dining one night on a large fish when he suddenly cried out that the dish had turned into the angry ghost of Symmachus, whose eyes were glaring and whose teeth were growing long and needle-sharp to devour him. Theodoric took to his bed, shivering in terror, mumbling his remorse. Three days later, he died.

The Ostrogothic succession

What followed proved disastrous for the Ostrogoths. After the death of Theodoric, his widowed daughter Amalasuntha became regent to her 10-year-old son, Athalaric. Beautiful, well-educated, and intelligent, this princess sought a political reconciliation with the imperial court at Constantinople, but her ambitions were considered unnatural in a warlike and male-dominated society. Concerned that she would make Athalaric into a Roman puppet, a group of Ostrogothic nobles demanded that she give him over to their tutelage. The young prince, accordingly, took up life with his hard-drinking and spirited kinsmen.

The loss of her son drove Amalasuntha into a secret correspondence with the new emperor, Justinian. In danger from intrigues by her kinsmen, she appealed to Justinian for protection in 532 but thought twice about going to Constantinople and living under Theodora's unfriendly scrutiny.

When her 17-year-old son died from drink in 534, Amalasuntha lost her regency. She asked her cousin Theodahad to join her as coruler, but instead he seized the throne and had her imprisoned. A horrified Justinian sent an ambassador to tell the Ostrogoths that if Amalasuntha were not released, his troops would enter Italy. Theodora, however, countermanded her husband's order; the ambassor was to tell Theodahad instead not to fear getting rid of Amalasuntha, for the emperor would do nothing. Historians continue to debate this act of treachery. Did Theodora act out of jealousy or astute policy? With the death of Amalasuntha, Justinian would now have a justifiable cause to invade Italy, long his dearest wish.

Amalasuntha was strangled in her bath. This murder shocked Romans and Ostrogoths alike, for her impeccable personal life and her many virtues were admired, no matter how ambitious her pursuit of the throne might have been. Justinian declared that this slaying was justification for war. With these events, the 20-year Gothic War began in Italy.

This section of a sixth-century ivory diptych may be a carving of Amalasuntha, daughter of King Theodoric the Great. When she became regent of the Ostrogoths, her reign was marred by a succession of crises, for her noblemen opposed her pro-Roman sympathies. In 535 she was murdered, and her death led to the Gothic War in Italy.

Justinian's last years

On May 7, 558, Justinian was shocked to hear that the great golden dome of his Hagia Sophia had collapsed, weakened by earth tremors. The ruin of Justinian's beloved church seemed to mirror the collapse of his empire. Costly military campaigns and huge building projects had all but bankrupted the treasury. Then, in 559, came the terrifying news that an army of Huns had advanced to within 30 miles of Constantinople.

General Belisarius was called out of retirement to fight off the invaders. To do the job he had only a militia of volunteers in the city. But his legendary mental agility saved the day; in an ingenious move he tricked the Huns into thinking that his ragtag force was far larger than it actually was. Somehow, the stratagem worked, and Belisarius was the victor. Unfortunately, the 76-year-old emperor saw fit to intervene, perhaps due to long-smoldering jealousy of his general. For the first and only time in his life, Justinian went onto the battlefield. There, he relieved his old comrade of his command and paid the Huns a ransom for their prisoners.

The above gold coin, which bears the image of Theodoric the Great, Ostrogothic king of Italy, was minted during his reign from 493 to 526. Theodoric built a large Arian church, which later became the property of the Catholic Church and was named St. Apollinare Nuovo. Beautiful Byzantine mosaics cover the walls of its nave. Represented on the wall shown here are the facade of Theodoric's palace in Ravenna and a procession of 26 martyrs. On the panel above are portraits of 16 biblical prophets.

In a pathetic attempt to recapture the days of imperial omnipotence and splendor, Justinian celebrated his "victory" with a grand triumphal march through the streets of his capital in 559. The procession halted only once, so that Justinian could enter the Church of the Holy Apostles and pray before the tomb of Theodora, dead now for more than a decade.

In his 80th year, Justinian presided over several days of festivities to celebrate the opening of a restored Hagia Sophia that boasted a new, even higher dome. Though the dome was now secure, the same could not be said of Justinian's empire. For more than 35 years, he had sought to unify the Roman Empire and usher in a new era. But the coming of the barbarians proved unstoppable. When Justinian died in 565, his passing marked the end of a great age.

The revenge of Procopius

Despite Justinian's many accomplishments, the pen of a court historian named Procopius would leave a lasting mark upon the emperor's reputation. Procopius was Belisarius' legal adviser during the general's war years in Persia, Africa, and Italy. His *History of the Wars* records these campaigns so objectively and accurately that it is considered a masterwork of historical writing. But in 550, the loyal adviser underwent a change of heart and began writing a vindictive account of the private lives of Constantinople's leaders.

His *Secret History* reveals scandal upon scandal. In an age when Christians and pagans alike believed that evil spirits worked wickedness in the world, Procopius charged that Justinian—just like Domitian and Nero—was a "demon-emperor," who was dedicated to destroying humanity. His fellow demon, Theodora, helped or directed him. Among their alleged crimes were murder, plunder of the wealthy, oppressive taxation of the poor, and destruction of time-honored Roman customs. Procopius paints a portrait of the empress as a woman motivated exclusively by vanity. Any who dared cross her suffered untold horrors. He describes the youthful years of Theodora in nasty and, no doubt, exaggerated detail, asserting that she was, among other things, a prostitute who eagerly engaged in obscene performances in theaters.

Why would so conscientious a historian write so scurrilous an attack upon those whose favor he had enjoyed for years? In his introduction, Procopius justifies his work by saying that it is the duty of historians to report the misdeeds of those in power, even though he envisaged "the probability that what I am now about to write will appear incredible and unconvincing to future generations." Some modern-day historians posit that Procopius may have been angry that he was not appointed to a powerful court position after years of service to the influential Belisarius. By the year 550, when the *Secret History* was composed, the government was in dire straits. Countless wars and massive building projects had left the empire nearly bankrupt. Years of financial mismanagement and court intrigues had taken their toll.

The *Secret History* was destined for publication after both the emperor and the historian were dead. In fact, the lively work was not discovered until the 17th century, when a copy turned up in the Vatican Library in Rome. Historians continue to debate its accuracy. Though obviously motivated by spite, Procopius' stories have nonetheless left an indelible mark upon one of history's more remarkable couples.

The ravages of the Gothic War in Italy

Two decades of war had completely devastated Italy, leaving its cities and towns empty of all life. One clergyman wrote of that time: "The whole world seemed brought to its ancient stillness: no voice in the field, no whistling of shepherds. The harvests were untouched." Exhausted from war, famine, and disease, Italy was now powerless to defend itself.

Chaos reigned. A leader was desperately needed to restore civil order. The man who eventually filled this need was Gregory. Born about 540 to a noble Roman family, he rose to the high office of prefect of Rome. When the Lombards began menacing the city in the 570's, Gregory organized Rome's defenses against them. Though a born leader, Gregory yearned for the contemplative, ascetic life of a monk. About 574 he gave away most of his inheritance and founded six monasteries on his family estates in Sicily and a seventh one in Rome. Retiring, then, from civic life, he settled in St. Andrew's Monastery in Rome.

The Lombards swept through northern Italy. Refugees, including a group of Benedictine monks, poured into Rome about 577. The monks carried with them a copy of Benedict's *Rule* for monastic life and gave it to Gregory, who was deeply impressed by its wisdom. Gregory himself would have been content to remain a monk, but the pope ordained him a deacon and sent him as papal ambassador to Constantinople in 579, to entreat the emperor to send troops against the encroaching Lombards. Gregory proved the ideal candidate, for he had a number of influential Roman friends at the imperial court. Despite his great powers of persuasion, however, no troops were forthcoming—the Eastern Empire had none to spare. The best that Constantinople could do was bribe the Franks in Gaul to attack the Lombards.

Pope Gregory, "God's consul"

In 589 devastating floods swept the Italian countryside, destroying crops. Worse still, a new outbreak of plague had struck. Pope Pelagius was taken ill and died in 590. The church, practically the only remaining source of order in the West, acted quickly; it unanimously elected Gregory as pope—the first monk elevated to the papacy. Gregory felt unworthy of the task. Unassuming and suffering from poor health, he referred to himself as "an ape forced to play the lion."

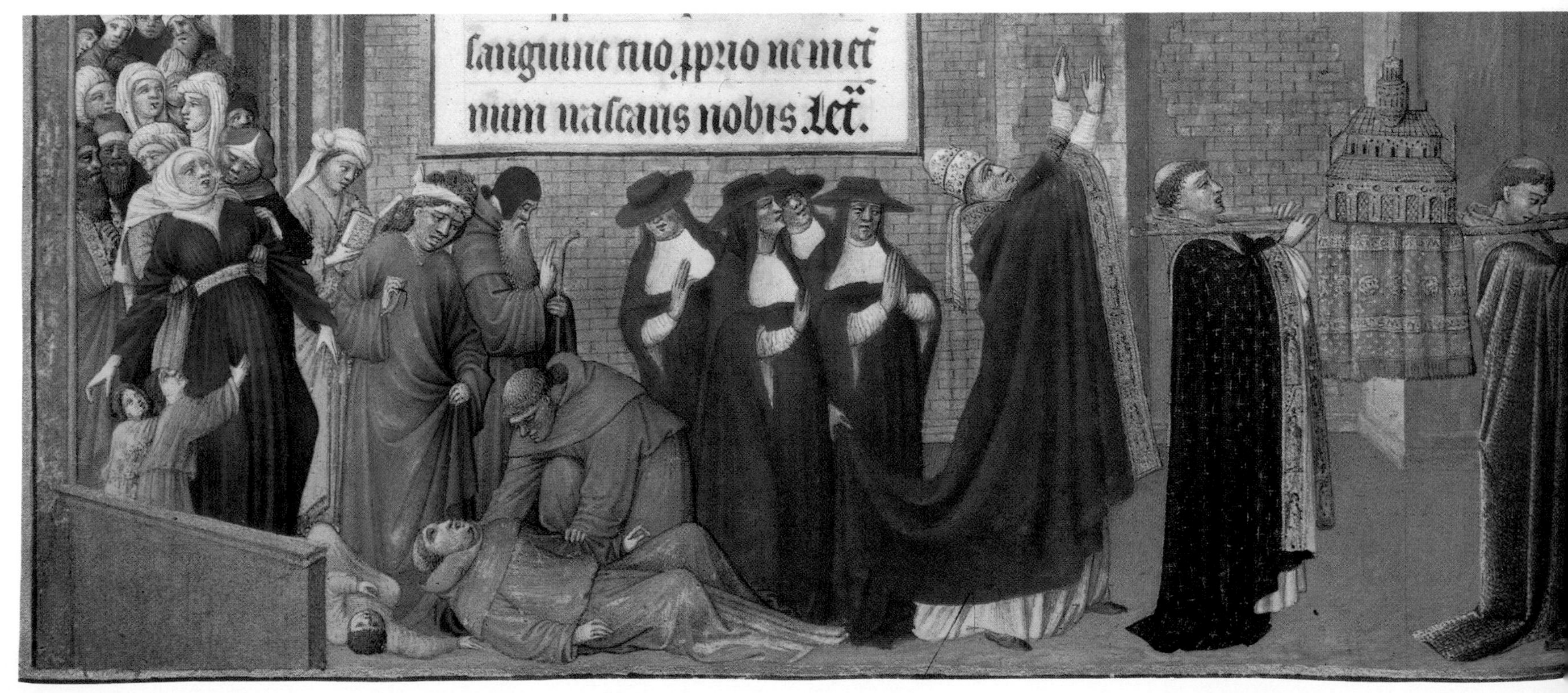

Gregory the Great was immediately canonized after his death in 604 and became the focus of several legends. This 15th-century illustration reenacts one of the more popular traditions: Pope Gregory stopping a plague in Rome in 590 by leading a procession of the faithful for a prayer service. Though some 80 people died en route, it was said that the pestilence vanished just as the archangel Michael appeared over the emperor Hadrian's monumental tomb.

Nevertheless, he was an indefatigable leader whose administrative brilliance saved Italy from ruin.

Gregory immediately set about providing relief for the hungry and sick. A prolific letter writer, he at once dispatched a letter to the magistrate of Sicily, requesting more grain for Rome. Gregory's true genius lay in his ability to solve difficult administrative problems. Many of his surviving 854 letters reveal a man with a keen eye for details and solutions. Intent on ridding the papal estates of corrupt laymen, Gregory wrote detailed instructions to a new cleric on how best to safeguard the "patrimony of St. Peter." There was to be no more squandering and waste of precious resources. He instructed his administrator to settle property disputes and sell unprofitable herds. To encourage conversions, Gregory reduced the taxes of converted Jews. Typically, Gregory signed all his letters, "Servant of the servants of God."

The pope's holdings included hundreds of square miles of land, revenues from which paid clerical salaries, maintained church buildings, and supported charities. The papal estates were soon so efficiently reorganized that they provided food for much of Italy. Gregory was the first pope to develop a filing system to keep track of letters and charitable donations.

Gregory also turned his attention to spiritual matters. Despite poor health, he continued to fast and hold nightly prayer vigils, as he had done as a monk. He insisted that his clergy adhere to strict laws of obedience and chastity. To guide future bishops, he wrote a handbook, *Pastoral Rule*. Gregory thought of the ideal bishop as someone "who disregards worldly prosperity; who fears no adversity." He could easily have been writing about himself. Gregory also wrote one book, *Dialogues,* that is filled with stories about the miracles of saints. *Dialogues* and another work,

Homilies, mark a clear break from the densely theological works of his predecessors. Unlike Augustine or Jerome, Gregory wrote for the ordinary, often uneducated Christian. His simple style of folk preaching served as a model throughout the Middle Ages. The plainsong known as Gregorian chant is also credited to Gregory, though some believe it was probably not developed until a century after his death.

As Rome continued to founder, and no help from Constantinople arrived, Gregory was forced to defend his city. In the absence of any civic government, he paid, fed, and housed Roman soldiers, appointed temporary commanders, and, when possible, negotiated treaties with the Lombards. Gregory died in 604; his epitaph read "God's consul." Indeed, no other pope before him had wielded such secular power. By becoming the supreme ruler of church and state, Gregory the Great, as he is now known, redefined the role of the pope and paved the way for the powerful papacies of the Middle Ages.

The rise of Islam

While Gregory was struggling to save the Western Empire and uphold the Catholic Church, a charismatic Arab named Muhammad was founding a new religion that would transform the Arab world. Born in Arabia about 570, Muhammad was orphaned in early childhood. Apparently, he earned his living as a caravan guide and traveled with a Bedouin tribe. As a young man, his wisdom was already evident and many came to him for advice. At about age 25 he married a rich widow, Khadija, some 15 years his senior.

Muhammad began to grow disillusioned with the polytheistic Arabic religion, which paid homage to some 300 deities. He was more impressed with the monotheism of Judaism and Christianity and the fact that these religions had a sacred text.

Many Arabs had long believed that they were descended from Ishmael, the son of Abraham and his Egyptian slave, Hagar. Muhammad wanted to bring back "the religion of Abraham," which he believed had been practiced in ancient times in Mecca. To ponder the problem, he went to the mountains to pray and meditate. In 610, when he was about age 40, Muhammad was meditating in a cave, when he had the first of a series of visionary experiences. He later wrote that the archangel Gabriel had appeared and revealed to him the word of God.

After much inner struggle, Muhammad understood himself to be God's chosen messenger, whose mission was to recite the word of God to his people. More divine revelations followed, and Muhammad began preaching. *Qur'an*, the Arabic word for "recite," became the title for the written collection of his revelations. In the Qur'an, or Koran, Muhammad tells of the nature of Allah, or God: "There is nothing in heaven or earth beyond the power of Allah. Mighty is He and all-knowing."

The religion Muhammad founded is called Islam, an Arabic word meaning "absolute submission" to the will of God. According to Islam, both Judaism and Christianity are earlier versions of God's divine plan, which is now completed with Islam. Muhammad considered himself the last prophet in a line that included Abraham, Moses, and Jesus.

The polytheistic Meccans began to persecute the followers of Muhammad, who were called Muslims, meaning those "who submit to God." A number of them fled to Ethiopia, where they were taken for Christians and given refuge. His life at Mecca in peril, Muhammad accepted a secret offer to mediate an Arab blood feud in Medina. He began his journey to Medina on July 16, 622, a date that is revered by his followers as the Hegira, or "emigration," and chosen as the start of the Islamic calendar.

Muhammad settled the feud and soon became the leading political, military, *and* religious authority in Medina. The lack of separation between church and state has been characteristic of Islamic society ever since. In time Muhammad conquered Mecca and

By 554, Emperor Justinian had recaptured Italy from the Ostrogoths, but the country was still wracked with famine and plague and was nearly destitute. Due to Pope Gregory's efforts, Italy was spared from total ruin. He used the resources of the vast papal estates and instituted a massive relief program to feed the thousands who were starving.

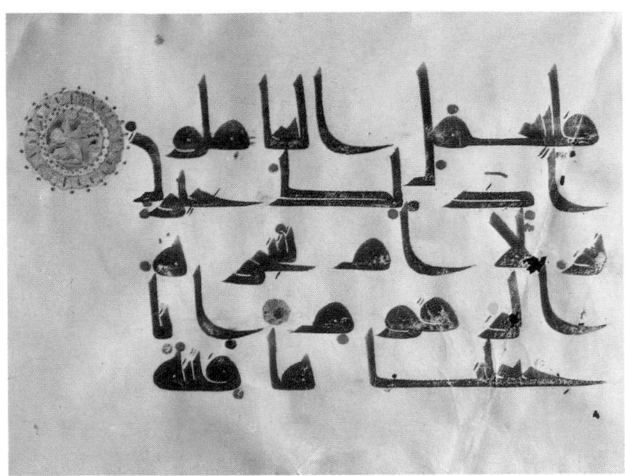

Since Islam forbade most representational art, calligraphy grew into an ornate art form. Here is a leaf from a ninth-century Koran, written in Kufic script, one of the oldest Arabic styles.

ruled Arabia, forcing Arab pagans to convert. By the time of his death in 632, the whole Arabian peninsula espoused the new faith.

The first and only major schism in Islam occurred shortly after Muhammad's death. Though he had a number of children, he left no sons to carry on his work. A dispute over who was the rightful *caliph*, or successor to Muhammad, led to the formation of two religious parties, the Sunnis and the Shi'ites. Despite this setback, Islam soon swept over Persia, Syria, and Egypt. Within 100 years the Islamic Empire stretched from Spain to central Asia.

Thousands upon thousands embraced Islam and its obligatory religious duties, known as "the Five Pillars of Islam." The first pillar requires a profession of faith: "I bear witness that there is no God but Allah and that Muhammad is the Messenger of Allah." The second pillar demands that all adult Muslims pray five times a day, bowing in the direction of Mecca. The third pillar calls for a pilgrimage, for everyone who can afford it, to the sacred city of Mecca. A daily fast, required during the entire month of Ramadan (the month in which the prophet first heard God's revelations), is the fourth pillar. And the last pillar is the payment of an obligatory tax, which goes to charity.

The triumph of Christianity

Throughout the first seven centuries of Christianity, passionate debates over theology sometimes threatened to split the church. But it was geography and politics that planted the most powerful seeds of schism. When Constantine moved the capital of the empire from Rome to Constantinople, he inadvertently drove the first wedge between Western and Eastern churches. Politics exacerbated the effects of distance. With the coming of barbarians, the empire's unity was severely shaken. By the end of the seventh century, much of the Byzantine Empire was overrun by Islam, and the East was cut off from the West.

In their isolation, during the Middle Ages, churchmen in the East carried on some practices that were different from those in the West. For example, they allowed their lower clergy to marry. They also revered icons—sacred pictures of Christ, the Virgin Mary, and the saints. "The icon is a song of triumph, and a revelation, and an enduring monument to the victory of the saints and the disgrace of demons," wrote John of Damascus in the eighth century.

Meanwhile, in the West, the Catholic Church took over where the crumbling Roman Empire had left off. It became the leading power and the pope its undisputed leader, not only in the church, but oftentimes in the court. Though the Eastern bishops looked upon the pope as first bishop of the church, they considered him first among equals and did not accept his sovereignty over the entire church.

Tensions between the Eastern and Western churches continued to mount. In 863 Pope Nicholas I put the matter to the test. He contested the election of the new bishop of Constantinople and demanded the right to appoint one of his own choosing.

The bishop of Constantinople added fuel to the fire by denouncing the West's formal inclusion in 794 of *Filioque* ("and from the Son") in the Nicene Creed to indicate that the Holy Spirit comes from both the Father and the Son. The East believed (and still does) that the Holy Spirit proceeds from the Father alone.

Discord between East and West came to a head in 1054, when a papal bull of excommunication was laid upon the altar of Hagia Sophia just as the bishop of Constantinople was about to begin services. Mutual anathemas were exchanged; schism was inevitable. The Roman Catholic Church and the Eastern Orthodox Church began to go their own ways.

Both in the East and the West during this period, Christianity touched almost every facet of life, from education to medical care. For example, the Christian tradition of caring for the sick was elevated to new heights during the Middle Ages, when a number of nursing orders were founded. One of the earliest, the Order of the Holy Spirit, was established about 1180. Backed by the pope, this order founded numerous hospitals throughout Christendom.

Medieval monasteries also assured the survival of ancient works that might otherwise have been lost, thanks to their tradition of copying manuscripts. (For instance, the West might never have heard of Hippocrates, the fourth-century B.C. physician, if a monk, Constantine the African, had not translated his works from Arabic into Latin.) Survival of the seven liberal arts of the Middle Ages was due also to monasteries, which instructed both monks and laymen in music, arithmetic, geometry, logic, astronomy, grammar, and rhetoric. Such scholastic training became the standard of excellence, and many medieval universities incorporated the liberal arts into their curricula.

In the 16th century, the growing tensions between church and state finally sparked a major political and religious crisis that led to the Reformation. Religious reformers, such as Martin Luther in Germany and John Calvin in Switzerland, protested the concept of the supreme authority of the church in both spiritual and political affairs. Was not the Bible, rather than the church, the voice of authority? they asked.

For centuries, the church had faced countless crises and survived. Would the Protestant Reformation signal its demise? Apparently not. As had happened in the past, theological differences ultimately served to spur the church's growth. In a little more than 100 years, both Protestant and Catholic churches were sending missionaries into the New World.

In the 20th century, the ecumenical movement has explored ways to unite different Christian groups. And in 1964 Pope Paul VI met with Athenagoras I, patriarch of Constantinople. In the following year, they lifted the mutual anathemas that had separated their respective flocks for more than 900 years.

This 13th-century illumination of a manuscript depicts a scene from an early medieval hospital. During the Middle Ages, religious orders did much to improve medical treatment. The Order of the Holy Spirit, for example, founded schools of surgery and pharmacology. Thanks to the support of the church and wealthy patrons, medical care was free.

KEY PEOPLE

Alaric (c.370–410) king of the Visigoths; sacked Rome in 410

Alexander (c.250–328) consecrated bishop of Alexandria in 313; enemy of Arius and Arianism

Amalasuntha (498–535) daughter of Theodoric the Great; regent of the Ostrogoths 526–534

Ambrose (c.340–397) consecrated bishop of Milan c.373; challenged several of Emperor Theodosius' policies; influenced Augustine's conversion

Antoninus Pius (86–161) emperor 138–161; able leader who maintained peace and prosperity

Antony of Egypt (c.250–356) one of the first holy hermits; a model for other desert monks

Antoninus Pius

Arcadius (c.377–408) emperor of the East 383–408; the elder son of Theodosius the Great

Arius (c.250–336) ordained a priest in Alexandria c.312; taught doctrine that Christ the Son is subordinate to God the Father; excommunicated c.318; condemned at Council of Nicaea in 325

Athanasius (c.296–373) consecrated bishop of Alexandria in 328; the most prominent of the anti-Arian Church Fathers; wrote biography of Antony of Egypt

Athenagoras (2nd cent.) Christian apologist, author of a defense of Christianity addressed to Marcus Aurelius and Commodus

Attila (c.406–453) king of the Huns 434–453; invaded Gaul and Italy; turned back by Pope Leo I

Augustine of Canterbury (?- c.604) first archbishop of Canterbury; sent to Britain by Pope Gregory in 597 to convert the Angles, Saxons, and Jutes

Augustine of Hippo (354–430) bishop of Hippo in North Africa 395–430; wrote *Confessions,* a spiritual autobiography, and *City of God*; his theological teachings on grace and predestination influential in both Catholicism and Protestantism to this day

Aurelian (c.215–275) emperor 270–75; waged war and won back Gaul, Spain, Britain, Egypt, Syria, and Mesopotamia

Bar Kokhba (?–c.135) leader of the Jewish war (132–135) for independence from Roman rule

Basil of Caesarea (c.330–379) Cappadocian father; consecrated bishop of Caesarea in 370; founded a monastic community in Cappadocia

Belisarius (c.505–565) Byzantine general appointed by Justinian I to command the army against the Persians in 530; stopped the Nika revolt, defeated the Vandals, and fought in Italy in the Gothic War

Benedict (c.480–c.550) monk who founded a monastery in Monte Cassino in Italy c.520; wrote the *Rule*, a guide for the monastic life

Boethius (c.480–c.524) Roman senator and philosopher; accused of treason by Theodoric; while awaiting execution wrote the *Consolation of Philosophy*

Caecilian (?–c.345) consecrated bishop of Carthage in 311; played an important role in the early stages of the Donatist controversy

Caligula (12–41) emperor 37–41; insane; proclaimed himself a living god; caused great unrest among the Jews

Caracalla (188–217) emperor 211–217; granted citizenship to virtually all free men, perhaps to increase the tax base

Carinus (?–285) emperor 283–285; reign marked by abuses and extravagant spectacles

Cassiodorus (c.485–c.580) Roman statesman, monk, and author; encouraged monastic scholarship

Celsus (2nd cent.) pagan philosopher; c.178 wrote the first important polemic against Christians, whom he accused of being traitors to the Roman Empire

Claudius I (10 B.C.–54 A.D.) emperor 41–54; expelled Jews from Rome in 49

Claudius II (214–270) emperor 268–270; restored discipline in the army and checked the invasions of the Goths

Clement of Alexandria (c.150–c.215) Greek theologian whose writings emphasized both intellectual and mystical aspects of Christianity

Clovis (c.466–511) king of the Franks 481–511; extended the Frankish kingdom; was baptized an orthodox Christian in 496

Columba (c.521–597) Irish missionary who founded a mission c.563 on Iona, an island off the western coast of Scotland

Commodus (161–192) emperor 180–192; son of Marcus Aurelius; reign marked by economic decline and tyrannical abuses

Constans I (c.323–350) emperor in the West 337–350; youngest son of Constantine the Great

Constantine I the Great (c.280–337) emperor 307–337; won the Battle of the Milvian Bridge in 312; in 313 issued with his co-emperor Licinius the Edict of Milan legalizing all religions; convened the Council of Nicaea in 325 and dedicated Constantinople as an imperial city in 330

Constantine II (317–340) emperor in the West 337–340; son of Constantine the Great

Constantius I (250–306) emperor 305–306; became a member of Diocletian's tetrarchy in 293; father of Constantine the Great

Constantius II (324–361) emperor in the East 337–361; son of Constantine the Great

Constantius I

Cyril (c.375–444) consecrated bishop of Alexandria in 412; opposed Bishop Nestorius, thus provoking the Christological controversy; writings used at the Council of Ephesus in 431

Damasus (c.304–384) pope 366–384; the first Roman bishop to term the See of Rome the Apostolic See; commissioned Jerome to revise the Latin translations of the Greek New Testament

Decius (c.201–251) emperor 249–251; persecuted Christians in an attempt to restore the preeminent status of traditional state cults

Dio Cassius (c.155–235) Roman historian and politician; wrote a *History of Rome*, which was a chronicle of the city, the republic, and the empire, from Rome's origins to the year 229

Diocletian (245–313) emperor 284–305; created the tetrarchy (four-man rule), officially dividing the empire into East and West; attempted economic reform but failed; began persecutions against Christians in 303; retired voluntarily in 305

Diocletian

Dionysius the Areopagite (1st cent.) converted by the Apostle Paul in Athens; his name later associated with several sixth-century mystical writings

Dionysius the Great (c.200–c.264) consecrated bishop of Alexandria in 247; student of Origen, later head of Origen's Catechetical School

Dioscoros (?–454) bishop of Alexandria 444–451; deposed and banished by Council of Chalcedon in 451 for defending the heretic Eutyches

Domitian (51–96) emperor 81–96; proclaimed himself "lord and god" and persecuted those who would not worship him

Donatus (?–c.355) one of two rival bishops in Carthage c.312; started a schismatic movement (later called Donatism) that was intolerant of lapsed Christians

Elagabalus (c.204–222) emperor 218–222; educated as a high priest of the Syrian sun god, whose cult he brought to Rome

Epictetus (?–c.130) Greek philosopher of the Stoic school

Ethelbert of Kent (c.560–616) first Christian English king; converted by Augustine of Canterbury c.597

Eudoxia (?–404) empress of the Eastern Empire 395–404; wife of Arcadius; instrumental in forcing John Chrysostom into exile

Eugenius (?–394) usurper of the Western Empire in 392; a pagan sympathizer; defeated and killed in 394 by Theodosius the Great

Eusebius (c.260–c.340) consecrated bishop of Caesarea c.315; prolific author best known for his *Ecclesiastical History*, which chronicles the first three centuries of Christianity

Eusebius (?–c.341) bishop of Nicomedia, later made bishop of Constantinople in 339; Arian sympathizer who instructed Wulfila; religious adviser to Constantine the Great, whom he baptized in 337

Eutyches (c.378–454) head of a Constantinople monastery and imperial favorite; condemned at Council of Chalcedon for his Monophysite teachings concerning the nature of Christ

Flavian (?–449) consecrated bishop of Constantinople in 446; attempted but failed to depose Eutyches; died of injuries sustained at the Council of Ephesus of 449

Gaiseric (?–477) king of the Vandals 428–477; conquered northern Africa; captured Rome in 455

Galerius (c.250–311) emperor of the East 305–311; member of Diocletian's tetrachy; carried on persecutions against the Christians from 303 until 311, when he issued an edict of toleration

Galla Placidia (c.390–450) empress 421; regent 425–c.440; daughter of Theodosius the Great; captured by the Goths, then later was returned to her brother Honorius and eventually ruled as regent for her son, Valentinian III

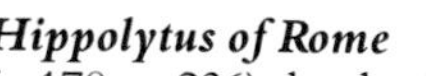

Gallienus (?–268) emperor 253–268; stopped barbarian invasions and persecutions against Christians; supported the views of philospher Plotinus

Gallus (203–253) emperor 251–253

Gamaliel (1st cent.) an illustrious rabbi who advocated leniency for the Apostles brought before the Sanhedrin

Gratian (359–383) emperor 367–383; as a Christian, ended government subsidies to several Roman pagan cults and removed the Altar of Victory from the Senate House

Gregory I the Great (c.540-604) pope 590-604; organized Italy's defenses against the invading Lombards and strengthened the church

Gregory of Nazianzus (c.329–c.389) Cappadocian father who helped develop the theology of the Trinity; in his writings affirmed the Nicene Creed

Gregory of Nyssa (c.330–395) Cappadocian father; younger brother of Basil; consecrated bishop of Nyssa c.371; championed Nicene cause

Gregory the Illuminator (c.240–332) founder of the Armenian Church and patron saint of Armenia

Gregory Thaumaturgus (c.213–270) consecrated bishop of Neocaesarea c.238; credited with performing many miracles, which earned him the the name *Thaumaturgus* ("Wonderworker")

Gregory of Tours (c.539–594) consecrated bishop of Tours in 573; author of *History of the Franks*

Hadrian (76–138) emperor 117–138; suppressed Jewish rebellion of 135

Helena (c.255–c.330) mother of Constantine the Great; according to legend, found the cross of Jesus in Jerusalem; instrumental in popularizing pilgrimages to the Holy Land

Hadrian

Hippolytus of Rome (c.170–c.236) theologian and martyr; chronicled much of third-century church practices and heresies; subject of disputed election as bishop of Rome

Honorius (384–423) emperor of the West 395–423; son of Theodosius the Great; ended gladiatorial contests

Hypatia (c.370–415) Neoplatonic philosopher, mathematician; taught at the Museum of Alexandria; murdered by a band of militant lay monks

Ignatius (c.35–c.107) bishop of Antioch who wrote seven letters to Christians while being taken to martyrdom in Rome

Innocent I (?–417) pope 402–417; pope during the Pelagian controversy

Irenaeus (c.130–202) theologian and bishop of Lyons; opposed Gnosticism and Marcionism

Jerome (c.345–c.420) biblical scholar; his Latin translation of the Bible, the Vulgate, used by Roman Catholics up until the 20th century

Johanan ben Zakkai (1st cent.) rabbi; escaped during siege of Jerusalem in 70 and started a rabbinical school at Jamnia, 30 miles west of Jerusalem

John of Antioch (?–c.441) consecrated bishop of Antioch in 428; after the Council of Ephesus, agreed to depose Bishop Nestorius, in order to avert schism

John Chrysostom (c.347–407) consecrated bishop of Constantinople in 398; a brilliant orator; was falsely accused of heresy at the Synod of the Oak in 403 and exiled

Josephus (c.37–c.100) Jewish priest, military commander, and historian who, under Roman patronage, wrote a history of the Jewish War of 66–70

Judah ha-Nasi (c.135–220) rabbi and sage; directed the compilation of the Mishnah, the first written record of the oral law

Julia Domna (c.167–217) empress, wife of Septimius Severus; known as Julia the Philosopher

Julian the Apostate

Julian the Apostate (332–363) emperor 361–363; ardently promoted a return to paganism at expense of Christianity

Justin (c.450–527) emperor 518–527; usurped throne when head of palace guard; anti-Arian in his policies; bequeathed rule to his nephew Justinian

Justin Martyr (c.100–165) Christian apologist and theologian who was martyred for his faith

Justina (?–c.389) regent for her son, Valentinian II; as an Arian, opposed Bishop Ambrose of Milan

Justinian I (483–565) Byzantine emperor 527–565; codified Roman law; extended borders of Byzantine Empire; as an orthodox Christian, built Hagia Sophia and many other churches

Lactantius (c.240–c.320) Christian apologist and historian celebrated for his poem *The Phoenix*

Leo I the Great (c.400–461) pope 440–461; wrote the *Tome*, which helped settle the debate at the Council of Chalcedon about the nature of Christ; later, bribed the Huns to spare Rome and mitigated destruction in Rome by the Vandals

Licinius (270–325) emperor 308–324; co-emperor with Constantine the Great, with whom he signed Edict of Milan legalizing Christianity; later carried out his own persecutions until Constantine defeated him

Lucian of Antioch (c.240–312) theologian and martyr; a follower of Origen; founded a school in Antioch, where he taught Arius

Mani (216–c.276) Persian prophet from Babylonia who founded Manichaeism

Marcellus (?–c.374) bishop of Ancyra; strong supporter of orthodoxy at the Council of Nicaea

Marcion (c.85–c.160) Christian reformer who founded Marcionite heresy

Marcus Aurelius (121–180) emperor 161–180; Stoic philosopher; author of *Meditations*

Martin of Tours (c.316–397) consecrated bishop of Tours c.371; patron saint of France

Maxentius (?–312) usurper of the empire in the West 306–312; defended pagan cults; was defeated by Constantine the Great in 312 at Milvian Bridge

Maximian (c.240–310) emperor 286–305, 306–308; member of Diocletian's tetrarchy and father of Maxentius

Maximinus Daia (?–313) emperor of the East 307–313; nephew of Galerius; a merciless persecutor of Christians; finally defeated by Licinius

Maximus (?–388) usurper of the Western Empire 383–388; ordered the execution of Priscillian, the bishop of Avila, the first heretic executed by the state

Menas (?–552) bishop of Constantinople who sided with Justinian in the *Three Chapters* controversy

Miltiades (?–314) pope c.310–314; convened a conference at which Donatism was condemned

Monica (c.331–c.387) mother of Augustine

Muhammad (c.570–632) founder of Islam

Nero (37–68) emperor 54–68; blamed Christians for the burning of Rome in 64; committed suicide after the Senate declared him an enemy of the state

Nerva (c.30–98) emperor 96–98; restored order to empire after the disastrous reign of Domitian

Nero

Nestorius (c.381–c.450) consecrated bishop of Constantinople in 428; preached an unorthodox view of Christ's nature; was denounced as a heretic

Novatian (c.200–c.257) Roman presbyter; strictly opposed readmittance of lapsed Christians to the church; died a martyr

Odoacer (c.433–493) first barbarian king of Italy 476–493; murdered by Theodoric

Origen (c.185–c.254) leading theologian of the early Greek church; developed first systematic theology

Ossius (or Hosius) (c.256–357) consecrated bishop of Cordoba c.296; anti-Arian adviser to Constantine I

Papias (c.60–130) bishop of Hierapolis in Asia Minor; gathered oral traditions about the life and teachings of Jesus

Patrick (c.390-c.460) British missionary who Christianized Ireland; patron saint of Ireland

Paul of Samosata (3rd cent.) heretical bishop of Antioch 260–268; finance minister for Queen Zenobia

Paul of Thebes (c.228–c.341) early Christian hermit who lived in the Egyptian desert

Pelagius (c.354–c.418) British monk and theologian who championed free will and rejected Augustine's views on predestination; denounced as a heretic

Perpetua (c.180–c.202) Christian catechumen whose dreams just before her martyrdom were set down in *The Passion of Perpetua and Felicitas*

Philip (224–249) emperor 244–249; known as "the Arabian"; presided over celebration of the 1,000th anniversary of Rome's founding; sympathetic to Christians; killed while fighting Decius

Pliny the Elder (c.23–79) Roman historian and naturalist

Pliny the Younger (c.61–c.112) Roman nobleman and administrator; wrote a famous letter to Trajan in 112 asking about the legal status of Christians

Plotinus (c.205–270) philosopher and mystic; father of Neoplatonism

Polycarp (c.69–c.155) revered early bishop of Smyrna; died a martyr

Porphyry of Tyre (c.232–c.303) Neoplatonic philosopher; student and biographer of Plotinus; opposed Christianity and wrote *Against the Christians*

Priscillian (c.340–386) bishop of Avila; led an ascetic movement; denounced, perhaps unjustly, as a heretic and executed

Probus (232–282) emperor 276–282; vanquished barbarians and restored peace but was killed by his own soldiers

Procopius (mid-6th century) Byzantine historian who recorded many of Belisarius' military campaigns; later wrote the *Secret History*, a scathing insider's account of Justinian's government

Romulus Augustulus

Pulcheria (399–453) sister of and regent for Theodosius II 414–416; empress of the East 450–453

Romulus Augustulus (c.461–?) emperor 475–476; considered the last Roman emperor of the West

Septimius Severus (145–211) emperor 193–211; established a military dictatorship

Shapur I, II (3rd and 4th cent.) Sassanian kings of Persia

Simeon Stylites (c.390–459) the first pillar saint; lived atop a pillar for 37 years

Sixtus II (?–258) elected pope in 257; martyred during the persecution by emperor Valerian

Stilicho (c.365–408) Roman general, though son of a Vandal chieftain; defeated Alaric, the Visigothic king; later, beheaded by Emperor Honorius

Sylvester (?–335) pope 314–335; sent two envoys to the Council of Nicaea

Symmachus (c.340–c.402) Roman senator and orator; in 384 made a celebrated speech in defense of paganism; repeatedly sought to have the Altar of Victory returned to the Senate

Tacitus (c.55–c.120) Roman historian; one of the first pagan writers to mention the Crucifixion

Tacitus (200–276) emperor 275–276; senator and descendent of Tacitus the historian; made emperor after the murder of Aurelian

Tertullian (c.163–c.230) Christian apologist; the first important Christian writer to write in Latin

Theodora (c.495–548) Byzantine empress 527–548; wife of Justinian I; sided with the Monophysites, though her husband was a supporter of orthodoxy

Theodore of Mopsuestia (c.350–428) Eastern theologian; teacher of Nestorius

Theodoric the Great (c.455-526) Ostrogothic king of Italy 493–526, who adopted Roman style of governing; executed Boethius for treason

Theodosius I the Great (c.346–395) emperor 379–395; as an orthodox Christian issued laws against heretics; in two notable instances submitted to the will of Ambrose, bishop of Milan

Theodosius II (401-450) emperor of the East 408–450; grandson of Theodosius I

Theophilus (?–412) bishop of Alexandria 385–412; may have instigated destruction of the great pagan Temple of Serapis in 391

Titus (39–81) emperor 79–81; Roman commander during the fall of Jerusalem in 70; as emperor, completed the Colosseum c.80

Trajan (53–117) emperor 98–117; took office in 99; born in Spain, first non-Italian emperor; expanded empire, conquering Dacia (present-day Romania)

Titus

Valens (c.328–378) Eastern emperor 364–378; killed by Visigoths at the Battle of Adrianople in 378

Valentinian I, II, III Western emperors: 364–375; 375–392; 425–455

Valentinus (2nd cent.) Gnostic leader; probable author of one of the texts found at Nag Hammadi

Valerian (?–c.269) emperor 253–260; the only emperor taken prisoner by an enemy, the Persians

Vespasian (9–79) emperor 69–79; doubled taxes to rebuild Rome after Nero's gross abuses; began the construction of the Colosseum

Victor I (?–198) pope 189–198; bid churches in Asia Minor to keep the same date for Easter as Rome

Vigilius (?–555) pope 537–555; coerced by the emperor Justinian in 553 to support his edict against the *Three Chapters*

Wulfila (or Ulphilas) (c.311–383) Arian bishop to the Goths; translated the Bible into Gothic

Zeno (c.450- 491) Eastern emperor 474–491; helped put the barbarian Theodoric in charge of Italy

Zenobia (?–c.274) queen of Palmyra (Syria); conquered Syria, Egypt, and much of Asia Minor; captured by Emperor Aurelian and taken to Rome

Zosimus (?–418) pope 417–418; briefly restored the controversial monk Pelagius to the church, until Augustine convinced him to denounce Pelagius

KEY TERMS

agape love of God or neighbor (the traditional, now somewhat old-fashioned, synonym in this sense is "charity"); also, the early Christians' love feast commemorating the Last Supper

agrapha sayings attributed to Jesus that do not appear in the four Gospels of the New Testament

anathema someone or something banned or cut off from a religious body; also, an ecclesiastical condemnation or excommunication

Apocrypha a group of Old Testament books that are wholly or partially accepted as Scripture in Roman Catholic and Greek Orthodox churches but not included in the Hebrew Scriptures and thus rejected by most Protestants; also, early Christian writings composd in forms similar to New Testament writings but not included in the Christian Scriptures

apologists defenders of the faith whose writings aimed to win over educated nonbelievers by a reasoned defense of Christianity

apostate one who repudiates his religious faith

Apostles the 12 disciples commissioned by Christ to proclaim the gospel, also including Matthias, who replaced Judas Iscariot, and Paul; term also applied to the earliest Christian missionaries, as well as some notable later ones—Patrick, for instance, sometimes known as the Apostle of Ireland

Apostles' Creed one of the earliest creeds, which begins, "I believe in God, the Father almighty"; used only in the Western church

apostolic age the period from the death of Jesus Christ until the reign of Trajan, during which the Apostles lived and worked

apostolic succession the concept that the authority for the ministry of the Christian church goes back in a continuous succession of bishops to the Apostles and from there to Christ himself

Aramaic the widely used Semitic language that was the vernacular spoken and written by Jews of Palestine in the time of Christ

Arianism Arius' teaching that Jesus was not co-eternal with God and that therefore the Son was inferior to the Father; declared a heresy by the orthodox church

Ascension Jesus' ascent into heaven after his resurrection from the dead

Athanasian Creed a statement of faith that like the Apostles' Creed and the Nicene Creed emphasized belief in the Trinity but unlike them included anathemas; formerly attributed to Athanasius but probably developed in southern Gaul in the early fifth century

augustus title, meaning "revered," given to the first Roman emperor and later to a senior emperor of the Eastern or Western Roman Empire

basilica a rectangular law court or exchange building with a central nave flanked by colonnaded aisles, a style taken over by Christian church builders under the later Roman empire

bishop one of the overseers of a Christian congregation in the earliest church; by the early second century bishops beginning to gain importance as the single heads of the church in a city or region

caesar title of a junior emperor of the Eastern or Western Roman Empire

canon the list of books officially accepted as Scripture; more generally, one of the rulings on matters of faith, morals, or discipline issued by an ecclesiastical authority (the word comes from Greek *kanon* "measuring rod")

catacombs subterranean burial places used by early Christians of Rome

catechumen person undergoing instruction to prepare for Christian baptism

catholic universal, not local or sectarian; by the fifth century, used by most Christians of the Western Empire to describe themselves

Chi-Rho the first two Greek letters of *(CHR)ist*, adopted as an insignia by Constantine the Great

Christology the study of the relationship of the divine and human in the person of Christ

circumcision a Jewish ritual that ceased to be mandatory for Gentile converts to Christianity after the first Jerusalem Council (about A.D. 48); still practiced, however, by Jewish Christians and certain other communities on the fringes of the Roman Empire

confession a declaration or profession of faith made prior to baptism or martyrdom; also, an acknowledgment of sin expressed communally as a part of Christian worship or individually in public or private

confessor an early Christian who was punished for confessing his or her faith but did not suffer martyrdom

consubstantial "sharing the same substance or being," said of the persons of the Trinity; in Latin *consubstantialis* was used as an equivalent of the Greek *homoousios* and expressed the core of the orthodox creed in contrast to Arianism

Coptic the language spoken by native Egyptians from about the 3rd to the 10th centuries; the language of some important surviving Gnostic writings; the liturgical language of the Coptic church of Egypt

council a meeting of church officials that is convened to rule on issues of doctrine or discipline (a regional council is a *synod*)

deacon a "servant," or officer, of an early congregation, subordinate to the bishop and presbyter

Diatessaron a second-century conflation of the four Gospels into a single narrative, used in early congregations in the Syriac-speaking East

Didache the "Teaching of the Twelve Apostles," a manual for early congregations; one of the oldest Christian writings, dating from the late first century

Docetism the teaching that Christ only seemed to be human and only appeared to suffer

Donatism schismatic movement of African Christians who broke from the Western church after 311, insisting on rigorous standards of purity in the church and rejecting all who compromised their faith under persecution

eschatology doctrines concerning the end of the world and mankind's ultimate destiny

Essenes Jewish religious party that included the monastic sect whose sacred writings comprised the Dead Sea Scrolls; may have influenced John the Baptist and possibly Jesus

Filioque Latin for "and [from] the Son," words added to the Nicene Creed to make it say that the Holy Spirit proceeds from the Son as well as from the Father; the earliest known instance in a Spanish council of the sixth century; eventually accepted by Western Christians but rejected by churches of the East

Gnosticism the teaching that matter is evil and salvation achievable only through secret knowledge (*gnosis*), which enables one to ascend to the world of light that was the soul's original home

God-fearers pagans who were attracted to Judaism and worshiped in the synagogues but did not become proselytes; prime candidates for Christian conversion in apostolic times

heresy belief held by a professed Christian that opposes orthodox doctrine, especially a belief denounced by the church

homoiousios "of like substance," said by some Christians to be the Son's relation to the Father; term used to attempt to reconcile the Nicene and Arian parties after the Council of Nicaea (325)

homoousios "of identical substance," or "consubstantial," stated in the Nicene Creed to be the Son's relation to the Father (in other words, the Son is just as divine as the Father); term that won a truce among opposing parties at the Council of Nicaea

Immaculate Conception the doctrine that the Virgin Mary was conceived without the taint of original sin, a concept not explicit in Scripture but in later times linked to the idea of Mary's sinlessness as *Theotokos* ("Mother of God"), a title affirmed at the Council of Ephesus (431)

Incarnation the doctrine that the Second Person of the Trinity took on human flesh as Jesus Christ

Islam the religion founded by Muhammed in the seventh century (the word in Arabic means "absolute submission [to God]")

Judaism the religion of the Jews, who at the time of Christ were spread throughout the world from Spain to Mesopotamia with the Temple in Jerusalem as the center of their religious life; after the destruction of the Temple in A.D. 70, characterized by development of rabbinical Judaism

labarum the military standard adopted by Constantine, bearing the initials Chi-Rho (see *Chi-Rho*)

lapsi "fallen," or "lapsed," Christians who in varying degrees denied their faith during persecutions and subsequently sought readmission into their congregations

Logos Christ as the "Word" of God (a Greek term meaning "Word" or "Reason" used in the Gospel of John and other Christian theology)

Mandaeans a Gnostic group claiming to be spiritual descendants of John the Baptist and surviving to this day in the vicinity of Baghdad

Manichaeism a dualistic religion, founded by the Persian prophet Mani in the third century, which combines elements of Gnosticism, Christianity, Zoroastrianism, and Buddhism

Marcionites followers of the second-century teacher Marcion's doctrine that Christ's gospel was one of grace, not law, and that Christ was sent into the world by the true God in order to undo the work of a putatively evil Creator

Milan, Edict of, in 313 the legal recognition of Christianity by a Roman government, guaranteeing equal toleration of all religions

Mishnah a compilation of the oral law of the Jews, committed to writing around the end of the second century, forming much of the foundation upon which the Talmud came to be based

Mithraism the mystery religion of the Persian sun god Mithras, often represented symbolically slaying a bull; widespread among Roman soldiers in the second and third centuries; exhibited similarities to Christian belief and ritual

Monarchianism a movement in early Christianity to uphold the unity ("monarchy") of the Godhead, leading to the views that either Christ was not divine until "adopted" by the Holy Spirit at the time of his baptism or that he was one manifestation, or mode, of the single divine being

Monophysitism the doctrine that Christ had a single, divine nature after the Incarnation (the orthodox teaching is that he had both divine and human natures), a view held by the Coptic and Jacobite churches

Montanism a second-century prophetic movement, named for Montanus, who taught that Christ would soon return; also known as the New Prophecy

Muratorian Canon the oldest surviving list of the writings that make up the New Testament, reflecting the Christian canon used in Rome at the end of the second century

Muslim an adherent of Islam (Arabic word for "one who submits [to God]")

mysticism direct knowledge of or union with the divine through personal spiritual experience (such experience is described in some passages of Paul's letters, Revelation, and the writings of certain Church Fathers, including Clement of Alexandria, Gregory of Nyssa, and Augustine)

neophyte a recently baptized Christian

Neoplatonism a philosophy based on Plato's teachings, developed into a mystical theology by the third-century philosopher Plotinus and his disciples

Nestorians followers of Nestorius, who held that Christ was composed of two persons, one divine and one human; after Nestorius was condemned by the Council of Ephesus (431), migrated eastward as far as China

New Testament the collection of authoritative writings that form the second of the two grand divisions of the Christian Bible, containing accounts of Jesus and documents of the early church; first became known as the New Testament around A.D. 200

Nicene Creed the confession of faith adopted by the Council of Nicea (325); also, the version of it issued by the Council of Constantinople (381) and accepted in both East and West to this day

Old Testament Christian designation for the Hebrew Scriptures, the first of the two grand divisions of the Christian Bible

original sin the doctrine that sin entered the world through the disobedience of Adam and Eve and has been transmitted at birth to all humans ever since

pagan in the parlance of early Christians, a "rustic" or "civilian," used to mean a polytheist, neither Christian nor Jewish

patriarch starting in the sixth century, a title for the bishops of the five most important cities of Christendom: Rome, Alexandria, Jerusalem, Antioch, and Constantinople

Pelagianism the teachings of Pelagius, asserting man's natural ability to take the first steps toward his own salvation through free will

Pentecost the Feast of Weeks, the Jewish festival held 50 days after Passover; in Christianity, the celebration on the seventh Sunday after Easter of the descent of the Holy Spirit on the Apostles, sometimes called the birthday of the church

pope originally any bishop of the church (Latin *papa* and Greek *papas* both mean "father"); by the 10th century came to refer exclusively to the Roman Catholic bishop of Rome

predestination the doctrine that some persons are providentially guided to salvation, in accord with God's foreordained plan

presbyter a presiding elder of an early congregation, at first the same as a bishop; in later times, a priest

prophets in the Old Testament, those who delivered God's message to Israel; also, a class of Christian ministers mentioned both in the New Testament and the *Didache* (they apparently died out in the second century)

proselytes converts to Judaism who, if male, had undergone circumcision and obtained full admission to the Jewish community, as distinct from the sympathizers and semi-converts known as God-fearers

Q modern name (from German *Quelle*, "source") for the now lost common document from which some parts of the Gospels of Matthew and Luke are believed to have been drawn

sacraments from Latin *sacramentum*, a soldier's oath of allegiance, hence in Christian use, baptism and communion as outward signs and pledges of an inward and spiritual grace; at various times and in different denominations, other rites have been identified as sacraments, including matrimony, confirmation, and anointing of the sick

saints in New Testament usage, members of Christian congregations; also, later, the exceptionally holy persons, many of them martyrs, who came to be venerated starting in the mid-second century

Sanhedrin the high council of the Jews in Jerusalem, having authority in both religious and civil law; abolished about 425 when the Romans dissolved the patriarchate

schism a split from the unity of the church usually based on differences of discipline or practice, as distinct from heresy, which is a doctrine rejected by the orthodox church

Septuagint the Greek version of the Hebrew Scriptures used by the Jews of the Diaspora and by the Christian church

synod a regional meeting of bishops convened to rule on matters of doctrine or discipline

Synoptic Gospels the Gospels of Matthew, Mark, and Luke, so-called because they tell the the story of Jesus' life from similar viewpoints, often using the same words

Talmud the authoritative compilations of Jewish law and tradition, combining the Mishnah (the oral law) and the Gemara (debates on the Mishnah); dates from the fifth century

tetrarchy the system of governing the Eastern and Western halves of the Roman Empire with four emperors (two of them titled "augustus" and two "caesar"), instituted by Diocletian toward the end of the third century

Theotokos "God Bearer," or "Mother of God," a title given to Mary by many Christians, beginning in the third century

Virgin birth the doctrine that Jesus was conceived by Mary by the power of the Holy Spirit and thus had no human father

Vulgate the first comprehensive Latin version of the Bible; prepared by Jerome, starting in 382, to replace older partial translations

Way early term for Christian faith (Christians were sometimes called followers of the Way)

Zealots Jewish patriots resisting Roman rule

Zoroastrianism the religion of Persia founded by Zoroaster (Zarathustra) in the sixth century B.C., featuring the conflict between light and darkness, good and evil, with a predicted final triumph of the good

BIBLICAL CITATIONS

This list provides the chapter and verse of biblical citations used in the text. Boldface numbers indicate the page where the quote appears. If a citation is given in the text, it is not repeated here. All quotes are from the Revised Standard Version of the Bible.

Chapter 1

13 "clothed with power from on high." Luke 24:49. ***14*** "in Jerusalem and in all Judea and Samaria and to the end of the earth." Acts 1:8. ***14–15*** "Peter and John and James and Andrew, Philip and Thomas, Bartholomew and Matthew, James the son of Alphaeus and Simon the Zealot and Judas the son of James." Acts 1:13. ***15*** "Follow me and I will make you become fishers of men." Mark 1:17. ***15*** "But who do you say that I am?" Matthew 16:15. ***15*** "You are the Christ," Matthew 16:16. ***15*** "upper room" Acts 1:13, Mark 14:15. ***16*** "sons of thunder" Mark 3:17. ***16*** "You do not know what you are asking." Mark 10:38. ***16*** "I came not to call the righteous, but sinners." Mark 2:17 and Matthew 9:13. ***16*** "Let us also go, that we may die with him." John 11:16. ***16*** "We have seen the Lord." John 20:25. ***16*** "Unless I see in his hands the print of the nails, and place my finger in the mark of the nails, and place my hand in his side, I will not believe." John 20:25. ***17*** "do not be faithless, but believing." John 20:27. ***17*** "Follow me." John 1:43. ***17*** "We have found him of whom Moses in the law and also the prophets wrote, Jesus of Nazareth, the son of Joseph." John 1:45. ***17*** "Can anything good come out of Nazareth?" John 1:46. ***17*** "Come and see." John 1:46. ***17*** "an Israelite indeed, in whom is no guile!" John 1:47. ***17*** "Rabbi, you are the Son of God! You are the King of Israel!" John 1:49. ***17*** "Truly, truly, I say to you, one of you will betray me." John 13:21. ***17*** "Lord, who is it?" John 13:25. ***17*** "It is he to whom I shall give this morsel." John 13:26. ***17*** "Take; this is my body. . . . This is my blood . . . , which is poured out for many." Mark 14:22–24. ***17*** "You have said so." Matthew 27:11. ***18*** "mighty works and wonders and signs" Acts 2:22. ***21*** "I am innocent of this man's blood"; Matthew 27:24. ***21*** "Jesus of Nazareth, the King of the Jews" John 19:19. ***22*** "Truly this was the Son of God!" Matthew 27:54. ***23*** "dazzling apparel" Luke 24:4. ***23*** "Why do you seek the living among the dead? Remember how he told you . . . that the Son of man must be . . . crucified, and on the third day rise." Luke 24:5–7. ***23*** "Rabboni!" John 20:16. ***23*** "His disciples came by night and stole him away while we were asleep." Matthew 28:13. ***23*** "This story has been spread among the Jews to this day." Matthew 28:15. ***24*** "they recognized him; and he vanished out of their sight." Luke 24:31. ***24*** "hearts burn" Luke 24:32. ***24*** "he was known to them in the breaking of the bread." Luke 24:35. ***24*** "Why do questionings rise in your hearts? . . . a spirit has not flesh and bones as you see that I have." Luke 24:38–39. ***24*** "Have you believed because you have seen me? Blessed are those who have not seen and yet believe." John 20:29. ***24*** "opened" Luke 24:32. ***25*** "lo, I am with you always, to the close of the age." Matthew 28:20. ***25*** "as the Spirit gave them utterance." Acts 2:4. ***26*** "They are filled with new wine." Acts 2:13. ***26*** "the third hour of the day" Acts 2:15. ***26*** "the last days" Acts 2:17. ***26*** "upon all flesh," Acts 2:17. ***26*** "I will pour out my Spirit; and they shall prophesy." Acts 2:18 ***26*** "according to the definite plan and foreknowledge of God," Acts 2:23. ***27*** "This Jesus God raised up, and of that we are all witnesses." Acts 2:32. ***27*** "God has made him both Lord and Christ, this Jesus whom you crucified." Acts 2:36. ***27*** "what shall we do?" Acts 2:37. ***27*** "last days" Acts 2:17. ***28*** "city of David." 2 Samuel 5:7. ***31*** "It is more blessed to give than to receive." Acts 20:35. ***33*** "Son of encouragement" Acts 4:36. ***33*** "to lie to the Holy Spirit" Acts 5:3. ***36*** "full of the Spirit and of wisdom," Acts 6:3. ***36*** "did great wonders and signs among the people." Acts 6:8. ***36*** "you are Peter, and on this rock I will build my church," Matthew 16:18. ***36*** "Christ is the head of the church," Ephesians 5:23. ***37*** "he took him by the right hand and raised him up; and immediately his feet and ankles were made strong." Acts 3:7. ***38*** "by faith in his [Jesus'] name." Acts 3:16. ***38*** "We must obey God rather than men." Acts 5:29. ***38*** "wanted to kill them." Acts 5:33. ***38*** "keep away from these men and let them alone; for if this plan or this undertaking is of men, it will fail; but if it is of God, you will not be able to overthrow them. You might even be found opposing God!" Acts 5:38–39. ***38*** "this Jesus of Nazareth will destroy this place, and will change the customs which Moses delivered to us." Acts 6:14. ***38*** "made with hands." Acts 7:48. ***38*** "tent of witness" Acts 7:44. ***38*** "Heaven is my throne, and earth my footstool." Acts 7:49. ***38*** "the Righteous One," Acts 7:52. ***38*** "betrayed and murdered," Acts 7:52. ***38*** "ground their teeth against him." Acts 7:54. ***38–39*** "I see the heavens opened, and the Son of man standing at the right hand of God." Acts 7:56. ***39*** "stopped their ears" Acts 7:57. ***39*** "Lord, do not hold this sin against them." Acts 7:60. ***39*** "Lord Jesus, receive my spirit." Acts 7:59. ***41*** "Saul, Saul, why do you persecute me?" Acts 9:4. ***41*** "Who are you, Lord?" Acts 9:5. ***41*** "I am Jesus, whom you are persecuting;" Acts 9:5. ***41*** "something like scales fell from his eyes and he regained his sight." Acts 9:18. ***41*** "went away into Arabia"; Galatians 1:17.

Chapter 2

44 "He fell into a trance and saw the heaven opened, and something descending, like a great sheet, let down by four corners upon the earth. In it were all kinds of animals and reptiles and birds of the air. And there came a voice to him, 'Rise, Peter; kill and eat.' But Peter said, 'No, Lord; for I have never eaten anything that is common or unclean.' And the voice came to him again a second time, 'What God has cleansed, you must not call common.' This happened three times, and the thing was taken up at once to heaven." Acts

10:10–16. ***44*** "accompany them without hesitation;" Acts 10:20. ***44*** "an upright and God-fearing man, who is well spoken of by the whole Jewish nation," Acts 10:22. ***46*** "Stand up; I too am a man." Acts 10:26. ***46*** "You yourselves know how unlawful it is for a Jew to associate with or to visit any one of another nation; but God has shown me that I should not call any man common or unclean. So when I was sent for, I came without objection. I ask then why you sent for me." Acts 10:28–29. ***46*** "Truly I perceive that God shows no partiality, but in every nation any one who fears him and does what is right is acceptable to him." Acts 10:34–35. ***46*** "the Holy Spirit fell on all who heard the word." Acts 10:44. ***46*** "amazed, because the gift of the Holy Spirit had been poured out even on the Gentiles." Acts 10:45. ***46*** "they were silenced. . . . Then to the Gentiles also God has granted repentance unto life." Acts 11:18. ***47*** "In his humiliation justice was denied him. Who can desribe his generation? For his life is taken up from the earth." Acts 8:33. ***47*** "How can I, unless some one guides me?" Acts 8:31. ***48*** "Truly, truly, I say to you, he who believes in me will also do the works that I do; and greater works than these will he do," John 14:12. ***49*** "And God did extraordinary miracles by the hands of Paul, so that handkerchiefs or aprons were carried away from his body to the sick, and diseases left them and the evil spirits came out of them." Acts 19:11–12. ***49*** "Jesus I know, and Paul I know; but who are you?" Acts 19:15. ***49*** "I did baptize also the household of Stephanas." 1 Corinthians 1:16. ***49*** "she [Lydia] . . . was baptized, with her household," Acts 16:15. ***49*** "When you come together, each one has a hymn, a lesson, a revelation, a tongue, or an interpretation. Let all things be done for edification." 1 Corinthians 14:26. ***50*** "For one who speaks in a tongue speaks not to men but to God; for no one understands him. . . . On the other hand, he who prophesies speaks to men for their upbuilding and encouragement and consolation." 1 Corinthians 14:2–3. ***53*** "false brethren . . . slipped in to spy out our freedom which we have in Christ Jesus, that they might bring us into bondage" Galatians 2:4. ***53*** "no small dissension and debate" Acts 15:2. ***53*** "the apostles and the elders" Acts 15:2. ***53*** "the church and the apostles and the elders," Acts 15:4. ***53*** "It is necessary to circumcise them, and to charge them to keep the law of Moses." Acts 15:5. ***53*** "did not yield submission even for a moment, that the truth of the gospel might be preserved" Galatians 2:5. ***53*** "had been entrusted with the gospel to the uncircumcised, just as Peter had been entrusted with the gospel to the circumcised" Galatians 2:7. ***53*** "faith apart from works is dead." James 2:26. ***54*** "There is neither Jew nor Greek . . . you are all one in Jesus Christ." Galatians 3:28. ***54*** "For neither circumcision counts for anything, nor uncircumcision, but a new creation." Galatians 6:15. ***54*** "For it has seemed good to the Holy Spirit and to us to lay upon you no greater burden than these necessary things": Acts 15:28. ***55*** "I have made myself a slave to all, that I might win the more. . . . I have become all things to all men, that I might by all means save some. I do it all for the sake of the gospel, that I may share in its blessings." 1 Corinthians 9:19, 22–23. ***55*** "For I will not venture to speak of anything except what Christ has wrought through me to win obedience from the Gentiles . . . so that from Jerusalem and as far round as Illyricum I have fully preached the gospel of Christ." Romans 15:18–19. ***55*** "the appointed time has grown very short. . . . the form of this world is passing away." 1 Corinthians 7:29, 31. ***56*** "have not repented of the impurity, immorality, and licentiousness which they have practiced." 2 Corinthians 12:21. ***56*** "not many of you were wise according to worldly standards, not many were powerful, not many were of noble birth." 1 Corinthians 1:26. ***56–57*** "I appeal to you, brethren, by the name of our Lord Jesus Christ, that . . . there be no dissensions among you, but that you be united in the same mind and the same judgment." 1 Corinthians 1:10. ***57*** "For no other foundation can any one lay than that which is laid, which is Jesus Christ." 1 Corinthians 3:11. ***57*** "If I speak in the tongues of men and of angels, but have not love, I am a noisy gong or a clanging cymbal. . . . Love is patient and kind; love is not jealous or boastful; it is not arrogant or rude. Love does not insist on its own way. . . . When I was a child, I spoke like a child, I thought like a child, I reasoned like a child; when I became a man, I gave up childish ways." 1 Corinthians 13:1, 4, 11. ***57*** "sick with fever and dysentery; and Paul visited him and prayed, and putting his hands on him healed him." Acts 28:8. ***58*** "Five times I have received at the hands of the Jews the forty lashes less one. Three times I have been beaten with rods; once I was stoned. Three times I have been shipwrecked; a night and a day I have been adrift at sea; on frequent journeys, in danger from rivers, danger from robbers, danger from my own people, danger from Gentiles, danger in the city, danger in the wilderness, danger at sea, danger from false brethren; in toil and hardship, through many a sleepless night, in hunger and thirst, often without food, in cold and exposure. And, apart from other things, there is the daily pressure upon me of my anxiety for all the churches." 2 Corinthians 11:24–28. ***58*** "we have this treasure in earthen vessels, to show that the transcendent power belongs to God and not to us." 2 Corinthians 4:7. ***59*** "I do not account my life of any value . . . if only I may accomplish my course and the ministry which I received from the Lord Jesus, to testify to the gospel of the grace of God." Acts 20:24. ***60*** "I mention you always in my prayers, asking that somehow by God's will I may now at last succeed in coming to you. . . . that we may be mutually encouraged by each other's faith," Romans 1:9–10, 12. ***60*** "that I may be delivered from the unbelievers in Judea," Romans 15:31. ***60*** "I am ready not only to be imprisoned but even to die at Jerusalem for the name of the Lord Jesus." Acts 21:13. ***60*** "God had done among the Gentiles through his ministry." Acts 21:19. ***60*** "Men of Israel, help! This is the man who is teaching men everywhere against the people and the law and this place; moreover he also brought Greeks into the temple, and he has defiled this holy place." Acts 21:28. ***60*** "If then I am a wrongdoer, and have committed anything for which I deserve to die, I do not seek to escape death; but if there is nothing in their charges against me, no one can give me up to them. I appeal to Caesar." Acts 25:11. ***60*** "And he lived there two whole years . . . and welcomed all who came to him, preaching the kingdom of God and teaching about the Lord Jesus Christ quite openly and unhindered." Acts 28:30–31. ***61*** "In a short time you think to make me a Christian!" Acts 26:28. ***64*** "And so we came to Rome." Acts 28:14. ***64*** "I have longed for many years to come to you, I hope to see you . . . as I go to Spain," Romans 15:23–24. ***64*** "commanded all the Jews to leave Rome." Acts 18:2. ***66*** "he departed and went to another place." Acts 12:17. ***67*** "To the exiles of the Dispersion in Pontus, Galatia, Cappadocia, Asia, and Bithynia," 1 Peter 1:1. ***67*** "Babylon," 1 Peter 5:13. ***68*** "These men who have turned the world upside down have come here also . . . and they are all acting against the decrees of Caesar, saying that there is another king, Jesus." Acts 17:6–7. ***74*** "So when you see the desolating sacrilege spoken of by the prophet Daniel, standing in the holy place . . . then let those who are in Judea flee to the mountains. . . . Pray that your flight may not be in winter or on a sabbath. For then there will be great tribulation, such as has not been from the beginning of the world, . . . and never will be." Matthew 24:15–21.

Chapter 3

77 "most excellent Theophilus," Luke 1:3. ***78*** "the beloved physician" Colossians 4:14. ***78*** "fellow workers." Philemon 1:24. ***78*** "many have undertaken to compile a narrative of the things which have been accomplished among us," Luke 1:1. ***78–79*** "by those who from the beginning were eyewitnesses and ministers of the word," Luke 1:2. ***79*** "truth" Luke 1:4. ***79*** "the definite plan and foreknowledge of God," Acts 2:23. ***79*** " 'for it cannot be that a prophet should perish away from Jerusalem.' " Luke 13:33. ***81*** "the genealogy of Jesus Christ, the son of David, the son of Abraham." Matthew 1:1. ***81*** "And the Word became flesh and dwelt among us, full of grace and truth; we have beheld his glory, glory as of the only Son from the Father." John 1:14. ***81*** "signs" John 20:30. ***81*** "that you may believe that Jesus is the Christ, the Son of God, and that believing you may have life in his name." John 20:31. ***83*** "I, Paul, write this greeting with my own hand." 1 Corinthians 16:21. ***85*** "Let the lowly brother boast in his exaltation, and the rich in his humiliation, because like the flower of the grass he will pass away. . . . Let every man be quick to hear, slow to speak, slow to anger, for the anger of man does not work the righteousness of God." James 1:9–10, 19–20. ***85–86*** "faith by itself, if it has no works, is dead. . . . For as the body apart from the spirit is dead, so faith apart from works is dead." James 2:17, 26. ***86*** "John," Revelation 1:1. ***87*** "Out of his mouth go flaming torches; sparks of fire leap forth." Job 41:19. ***90*** "the holy city Jerusalem coming down out of heaven from God, having the glory of God, its radiance like a most rare jewel," Revelation 21:10–11. ***91*** "In the beginning was the Word, and the Word was with God, and the Word was God." John 1:1. ***92*** "be prepared to make a defense to any one who calls you to account for the hope that is in you . . . and keep your conscience clear, so that, when you are abused, those who revile your good behavior in Christ may be put to shame." 1 Peter 3:15–16. ***92*** "with regard to this sect we know that everywhere it is spoken against." Acts 28:22. ***92*** "Greet Prisca and Aquila, my fellow workers in Christ Jesus . . . greet also the church in their house." Romans 16:3, 5. ***96*** "a Jew named Apollos, a native of Alexandria," Acts 18:24. ***96*** "had been instructed in the way of the Lord"; Acts18:25. ***96*** "the churches of Asia" 1 Corinthians 16:19. ***96*** "wide door for effective work" 1 Corinthians 16:9. ***96*** "Write what you see in a book and send it to the seven churches," Revelation 1:11. ***96*** "Behold, the devil is about to throw some of you into prison, that you may be tested, and for ten days you will have tribulation. Be faithful unto death, and I will give you the crown of life." Revelation 2:10. ***96*** "Repent" Revelation 2:16. ***96*** "where Satan's throne is"; Revelation 2:13. ***96*** "eat foods sacrificed to the idols and practice immorality." Revelation 2:14. ***97*** "I know your works; you have the name of being alive, and you are dead. Awake, and strengthen what remains and is on the point of death, for I have not found your works perfect in the sight of my God." Revelation 3:1–2. ***97*** "I know your works: you are neither cold nor hot. Would that you were cold or hot!" Revelation 3:15. ***100*** "Maintain good conduct among the Gentiles, so that in case they speak against you as wrongdoers, they may see your good deeds and glorify God." 1 Peter 2:12. ***100*** "Father, hallowed be thy name. Thy kingdom come." Luke 11:2. ***100*** "Rejoice in the Lord always; again I will say, Rejoice." Philippians 4:4. ***101*** "holy and beloved," Colossians 3:12. ***102*** "Let the word of Christ dwell in you richly, teach and admonish one another in all wisdom, and sing psalms and hymns and spiritual songs" Colossians 3:16. ***103*** "kinsmen" Romans 16:7. ***103*** "fellow workers in Christ Jesus," Romans 16:3. ***103*** "led by the Spirit of God" Romans 8:14. ***104*** "must be above reproach, the husband of one wife, temperate, sensible, dignified, hospitable, an apt teacher, no drunkard, not violent but gentle, not quarrelsome, and no lover of money. He must manage his own household well . . . for if a man does not know how to manage his own household, how can he care for God's church?" 1 Timothy 3:2–6. ***104*** "men of good repute, full of the Spirit and of wisdom," Acts 6:3. ***104*** "hold firm to the sure word as taught, so that he may be able to give instruction in sound doctrine and also to confute those who contradict it." Titus 1:9. ***104*** "serious, not double-tongued, not addicted to much wine, not greedy for gain; they must hold the mystery of the faith with a clear conscience." 1 Timothy 3:8–9. ***105*** "there is neither male nor female; for you are all one in Christ Jesus." Galatians 3:28. ***105*** "(For man was not made from woman, but woman from man. Neither was man created for woman, but woman for man.)" 1 Corinthians 11:8–9. ***105–106*** "(Nevertheless, in the Lord woman is not independent of man nor man of woman; for as woman was made from man, so man is now born of woman. And all things are from God.)" 1 Corinthians 11:11–12. ***106*** "the women should keep silence in the churches. For they are not permitted to speak, but should be subordinate, as even the law says. If there is anything they desire to know, let them ask their husbands at home. For it is shameful for a woman to speak in church." 1 Corinthians 14:34–35. ***106*** "Let a woman learn in silence with all submissiveness. I permit no woman to teach or to have authority over men; she is to keep silent." 1 Timothy 2:11–12. ***106*** "Render to Caesar" Mark 12:17. ***106*** "Be subject for the Lord's sake to every human institution, whether it be to the emperor as supreme, or to the governors as sent by him to punish those who do wrong and to praise those who do right. For it is God's will that by doing right you should put to silence the ignorance of foolish men. Live as free men, yet without using your freedom as a pretext for evil; but live as servants of God. Honor all men. Love the brotherhood. Fear God. Honor the emperor." 1 Peter 2:13–17. ***107*** "Render to Caesar the things that are Caesar's," Mark 12:17. ***107*** "let none of you suffer as a murderer, or a thief, or a wrongdoer, or a mischief-maker; yet if one suffers as a Christian, let him not be ashamed, but under that name let him glorify God." 1 Peter 4:15–16. ***107*** "their synagogues" Matthew 4:23. ***107*** "my church," Matthew 16:18. ***108*** "Let not yours be the outward adorning with braiding of hair, decoration of gold, and wearing of fine clothing, but let it be the hidden person of the heart with the imperishable jewel of a gentle and quiet spirit," 1 Peter 3:3–4. ***108*** "Be sober, be watchful. Your adversary the devil prowls around like a roaring lion, seeking some one to devour." 1 Peter 5:8. ***109*** "I will keep you from the hour of trial which is coming on the whole world, to try those who dwell upon the earth." Revelation 3:10. ***109*** "I am coming soon; hold fast what you have, so that no one may seize your crown." Revelation 3:11. ***109*** "Fallen . . . Babylon . . . a dwelling place of demons," Revelation 18:2. ***109*** "a great multitude which no man could number," Revelation 7:9. ***109*** "a beast rising out of the sea, with ten horns and seven heads," Revelation 13:1. ***109*** "out of the earth"; Revelation 13:11. ***109*** "cause those who would not worship the image of the beast to be slain." Revelation 13:15. ***109*** "the holy city, new Jerusalem, coming down out of heaven from God," Revelation 21:2. ***109*** "The end of all things is at hand; therefore keep sane and sober for your prayers." 1 Peter 4:7. ***109*** "He who testifies to these things says, 'Surely I am coming soon.' Amen. Come, Lord Jesus!" Revelation 22:20. ***109*** "Be faithful unto death, and I will give you the crown of life." Revelation 2:10.

Chapter 4

129 "many false prophets will arise and lead many astray." Matthew 24:11. ***131*** "Avoid the godless chatter and contradictions of what is falsely called knowledge, for by professing it some have missed the mark as regards the faith." 1 Timothy 6:20–21. ***141*** "Greet one another with a holy kiss." Romans 16:16.

Chapter 5

161 "In the beginning God created the heavens and the earth." Genesis 1:1. ***175*** "whoever denies me before men, I also will deny before my Father who is in heaven." Matthew 10:33.

Chapter 6

179 "If you would be perfect, go, sell what you possess and give to the poor, . . . come, follow me." Matthew 19:21. ***179*** "do not be anxious about tomorrow," Matthew 6:34. ***182*** " 'you shall love the Lord your God with all your heart,' " Mark 12:30. ***182*** " 'You shall love your neighbor as yourself.' " Mark 12:31. ***183*** "he who humbles himself will be exalted." Luke 14:11.

Chapter 8

254 "the Word became flesh and dwelt among us," John 1:14. ***254*** "Jesus increased in wisdom and in stature, and in favor with God and man." Luke 2:52. ***269*** "the father of a multitude of nations." Genesis 17:4. ***269*** " 'Go out . . . and compel people to come in, that my house may be filled.' " Luke 14:23.

BIBLIOGRAPHY

GENERAL

AUNE, DAVID. *Prophecy in Early Christianity and the Ancient Mediterranean World.* Grand Rapids: William B. Eerdmans Publishing Co., 1983.

BARRACLOUGH, GEOFFREY, ed. *The Christian World: A Social and Cultural History.* New York: Harry N. Abrams Inc., 1981.

BENKO, STEPHEN. *Pagan Rome and the Early Christians.* Bloomington, Ind.: Indiana University Press, 1984.

BENKO, STEPHEN, and JOHN J. O'ROURKE. *The Catacombs and the Colosseum: The Roman Empire as the Setting of Primitive Christianity.* Valley Forge, Pa.: Judson Press, 1971.

BORNKAMM, GÜNTHER. *Paul.* Translated by D.M.G. Stalker. New York: Harper & Row, Publishers, Inc., 1971.

BROWN, PETER. *Augustine of Hippo.* Berkeley and Los Angeles: University of California Press, 1969.

BROWN, PETER. *The World of Late Antiquity, A.D. 150–750.* New York: Harcourt Brace Jovanovich, Inc., 1971.

BROWNING, ROBERT. *Justinian and Theodora.* Rev. ed. London: Thames and Hudson Ltd., 1987.

BROWNRIGG, RONALD. *Who's Who in the New Testament.* New York: Holt, Rinehart and Winston, 1971.

BURY, J.B. *History of the Later Roman Empire.* New York: Dover Publications, Inc., 1958.

CAMPENHAUSEN, HANS VON. *Men Who Shaped the Western Church.* Translated by Manfred Hoffmann. New York: Harper & Row, Publishers, Inc., 1964.

CARRINGTON, PHILIP. *The Early Christian Church.* Cambridge: The University Press, 1957.

CASSON, LIONEL. *The Horizon Book of Daily Life in Ancient Rome.* New York: American Heritage Publishing Co., Inc., 1975.

CHADWICK, HENRY. *The Early Church.* Baltimore: Penguin Books Inc., 1967.

CONNICK, MILO C. *The New Testament: An Introduction to Its History, Literature, and Thought.* 2nd ed. Belmont, Calif.: Wadsworth Publishing Co., 1978.

COOK, S.A., and others, eds. *The Cambridge Ancient History.* Vols. 9–12. Cambridge: The University Press, 1932–39.

CORNELL, TIM, and JOHN MATTHEWS. *Atlas of the Roman World.* New York: Facts on File, Inc., 1982.

CROSS, F.L., and E.A. LIVINGSTONE, eds. *The Oxford Dictionary of the Christian Church.* 2nd ed. Oxford: Oxford University Press, 1983.

DANIELOU, JEAN, and HENRI MARROU. *The Christian Centuries.* Vol. 1, *The First Six Hundred Years.* London: Darton, Longman and Todd, 1964.

DAVIES, J.G. *The Early Christian Church: A History of Its First Five Centuries.* Grand Rapids: Baker Book House, 1965.

DODDS, E.R. *Pagan and Christian in an Age of Anxiety.* New York: W.W. Norton & Co., Inc., 1970.

DOWNEY, GLANVILLE. *Constantinople in the Age of Justinian.* Norman, Okla.: University of Oklahoma Press, 1960.

DRANE, JOHN. *Introducing the New Testament.* San Francisco: Harper & Row, Publishers, Inc., 1986.

DURANT, WILL. *Caesar and Christ: A History of Roman Civilization and of Christianity from Their Beginnings to A.D. 325.* New York: Simon & Schuster, Inc., 1944.

DURANT, WILL. *The Age of Faith: A History of Medieval Civilization—Christian, Islamic, and Judaic—from Constantine to Dante: A.D. 325–1300.* New York: Simon & Schuster, Inc., 1950.

Eerdmans' Handbook to the History of Christianity. Grand Rapids: William B. Eerdmans Publishing Co., 1977.

ELIADE, MIRCEA, ed. *The Encyclopedia of Religion.* New York: Macmillan Publishing Co., 1987.

ENO, ROBERT. *The Rise of the Papacy.* Wilmington: Michael Glazier, Inc., 1990.

FERGUSON, EVERETT. *Backgrounds of Early Christianity.* Grand Rapids: William B. Eerdmans Publishing Co., 1987.

FOAKES JACKSON, F.J. *The History of the Christian Church from the Earliest Times to A.D. 461.* 6th ed. London: George Allen and Unwin Ltd., 1914.

FRANZ, MARIE-LOUISE VON. *The Passion of Perpetua.* Irving, Tex.: Spring Publications, Inc., 1979.

FREND, W.H.C. *The Early Church.* Philadelphia: Fortress Press, 1982.

FREND, W.H.C. *Martyrdom and Persecution in the Early Church.* Grand Rapids: Baker Book House, 1981.

FREND, W.H.C. *The Rise of Christianity*. Philadelphia: Fortress Press, 1984.

FREYNE, SÉAN. *The World of the New Testament*. Wilmington: Michael Glazier, Inc., 1980.

FRYE, RICHARD N. *The Heritage of Persia*. New York: New American Library, 1963.

GEFFCKEN, JOHANNES. *The Last Days of Greco-Roman Paganism*. Translated by Sabine MacCormack. Amsterdam: The North-Holland Publishing Company, 1978.

GENTZ, WILLIAM H., ed. *The Dictionary of Bible and Religion*. Nashville: Abingdon Press, 1986.

GIBBON, EDWARD. *The Decline and Fall of the Roman Empire*. (First published in 1776–88.) 3 vols. New York: Random House, The Modern Library, 1932.

GOODSPEED, EDGAR J. *Paul*. Nashville: Abingdon Press, 1947.

GOUGH, MICHAEL. *The Early Christians*. New York: Frederick A. Praeger, Inc., Publishers, 1961.

GRANT, MICHAEL. *Dawn of the Middle Ages*. New York: Bonanza Books, 1986.

GRANT, MICHAEL, ed. *Greece and Rome: The Birth of Western Civilization*. New York: Bonanza Books, 1986.

GRANT, MICHAEL. *The Jews in the Roman World*. New York: Dorset Press, 1984.

GRANT, MICHAEL. *The Roman Emperors: A Biographical Guide to the Rulers of Ancient Rome: 31 B.C.–A.D. 476*. London: George Weidenfeld & Nicolson Ltd., 1985.

GRANT, ROBERT M. *Augustus to Constantine: The Thrust of the Christian Movement into the Roman World*. New York: Harper & Row, Publishers, Inc., 1970.

GRANT, ROBERT M. *Early Christianity and Society: Seven Studies*. San Francisco: Harper & Row, Publishers, Inc., 1977.

GREER, ROWAN A. *Broken Lights and Mended Lives: Theology and Common Life in the Early Church*. University Park, Pa.: The Pennsylvania State University Press, 1986.

GREGORY OF TOURS. *History of the Franks*. Translated by Lewis Thorpe. New York: Penguin Books, 1983.

GWATKIN, H.M., and J.P. WHITNEY, eds. *The Cambridge Medieval History*. 2nd ed. Cambridge: The University Press, 1924.

HAMMOND, N.G.L., and H.H. SCULLARD, eds. *The Oxford Classical Dictionary*. 2nd ed. Oxford: Clarendon Press, 1970.

HARNACK, ADOLF. *Militia Christi: The Christian Religion and the Military in the First Three Centuries*. Translated by David McInnes Gracie. Philadelphia: Fortress Press, 1981.

HUTTON, EDWARD. *Attila and the Huns*. New York: E.P. Dutton & Company Publishers, 1915.

The Interpreter's Bible, Vols. 9–12. New York: Abingdon Press, 1951–57.

The Jerome Biblical Commentary. 2 vols. Englewood Cliffs, N.J.: Prentice-Hall, Inc., 1968.

JOHNSON, PAUL. *A History of Christianity*. New York: Atheneum, 1976.

JONES, A.H.M. *Constantine and the Conversion of Europe*. London: The English Universities Press Ltd., 1949.

KINROSS, LORD. *Hagia Sophia*. New York: Newsweek, 1972.

KOESTER, HELMUT. *Introduction to the New Testament*. 2 vols. New York: Walter de Gruyter, 1982.

LANE FOX, ROBIN. *Pagans and Christians*. New York: Alfred A. Knopf, Inc., 1987.

LIETZMANN, HANS. *A History of the Early Church*. Translated by Bertram Lee Woolf. London: Lutterworth Press, 1961.

MACMULLEN, RAMSAY. *Crosscurrents in World History: Christianizing the Roman Empire, A.D. 100–400*. New Haven: Yale University Press, 1984.

MACMULLEN, RAMSAY. *Crosscurrents in World History: Constantine*. New York: The Dial Press, Inc., 1969.

MEEKS, WAYNE A. *The First Urban Christians: The Social World of the Apostle Paul*. New Haven: Yale University Press, 1983.

MEEKS, WAYNE A. *The Moral World of the First Christians*. Philadelphia: The Westminster Press, 1986.

MEEKS, WAYNE A., and ROBERT L. WILKEN. *Jews and Christians in Antioch in the First Four Centuries of the Common Era*. Ann Arbor, Mich.: Scholars Press for The Society of Biblical Literature, 1978.

MOMIGLIANO, ARNOLD. *On Pagans, Jews, and Christians*. Middletown, Conn.: Wesleyan University Press, 1987.

New Catholic Encyclopedia. New York: McGraw-Hill Book Co., 1967.

PELIKAN, JAROSLAV. *The Christian Tradition: A History of the Development of Doctrine*. Vol. 1, *The Emergence of the Catholic Tradition (100–600)*. Chicago: The University of Chicago Press, 1971.

PELIKAN, JAROSLAV. *Jesus Through the Centuries: His Place in the History of Culture*. New York: Harper & Row, Publishers, Inc., 1987.

PETERS, F.E. *The Harvest of Hellenism*. New York: Simon & Schuster, Inc., 1970.

RICHARDS, JEFFREY. *Consul of God: The Life and Times of Gregory the Great*. London: Routledge & Kegan Paul Ltd., 1980.

ROSTOVTZEFF, M. *The Social and Economic History of the Roman Empire*. 2nd ed. Oxford: Clarendon Press, 1957.

RUDOLPH, KURT. *Gnosis: The Nature & History of Gnosticism*. San Francisco: Harper & Row, Publishers, Inc., 1987.

SCHÖPS, HANS-JOACHIM. *Jewish Christianity: Factional Disputes in the Early Church*. Translated by Douglas R. A. Hare. Philadelphia: Fortress Press, 1969.

SMITH, JOHN HOLLAND. *Constantine the Great*. New York: Charles Scribner's Sons, 1971.

SNYDER, GRAYDON F. *Ante Pacem: Archaeological Evidence of Church Life Before Constantine*. Macon, Ga.: Mercer University Press, 1985.

STRAYER, JOSEPH R., ed. *Dictionary of the Middle Ages*. New York: Charles Scribner's Sons, 1984.

THURSTON, HERBERT J., and DONALD ATTWATER. *Butler's Lives of the Saints*. Rev. ed. Westminster, Md.: Christian Classics, Inc., 1956.

TOYNBEE, ARNOLD, ed. *The Crucible of Christianity*. New York: World Publishing Co., 1969.

TYSON, JOSEPH B. *The New Testament and Early Christianity*. New York: Macmillan Publishing Co., 1984.

TYSON, JOSEPH B. *A Study of Early Christianity*. New York: The Macmillan Company, 1973.

WADDELL, HELEN, trans. *The Desert Fathers*. Ann Arbor, Mich.: University of Michigan Press, 1957.

WALKER, WILLISTON. *A History of the Christian Church*. Rev. ed. New York: Charles Scribner's Sons, 1959.

WALSH, MICHAEL. *The Triumph of the Meek: Why Early Christianity Succeeded*. San Francisco: Harper & Row, Publishers, Inc., 1986.

WARD, BENEDICTA, S.L.G. *Harlots of the Desert: A Study of Repentance in Early Monastic Sources*. Kalamazoo, Mich.: Cistercian Publications Inc., 1987.

WARE, TIMOTHY. *The Orthodox Church*. Baltimore: Penguin Books Inc., 1963.

WILKEN, ROBERT L. *The Christians as the Romans Saw Them*. New Haven: Yale University Press, 1984.

ANCIENT SOURCES

The Ante-Nicene Fathers. Grand Rapids: William B. Eerdmans Publishing Co., 1951.

ATHANASIUS. *The Life of Saint Antony*. Translated by Robert T. Meyer. Westminster, Md.: The Newman Press, 1950.

AUGUSTINE. *Confessions*. Translated by R.S. Pine-Coffin. Harmondsworth, England: Penguin Books Ltd., 1961.

BEDE. *A History of the English Church and People*. Rev. ed. Translated by Leo Sherley-Price. Baltimore: Penguin Books Inc., 1968.

Beowulf. Translated by Michael Alexander. New York: Penguin Books, 1973.

BETTENSON, HENRY, ed. *Documents of the Christian Church*. 2nd ed. London: Oxford University Press, 1963.

BOETHIUS. *The Theological Tractates*. Loeb Classical Library. Translated by H.F. Stewart and E.K. Rand. *The Consolation of Philosophy*. Revised translation by H.F. Stewart. New York: G.P. Putnam's Sons, 1926.

CAMERON, RON, ed. *The Other Gospels: Non-Canonical Gospel Texts*. Philadelphia: The Westminster Press, 1982.

CLEMENT OF ALEXANDRIA. *The Exhortation to the Greeks and Other Writings*. Loeb Classical Library. Translated by G.W. Butterworth. New York: G.P. Putnam's Sons, 1919.

CURLEY, MICHAEL J., trans. *Physiologus*. Austin, Tex.: University of Texas Press, 1979.

DAGWOOD, N.J., trans. The Koran. Baltimore: Penguin Books Inc., 1956.

DIO CASSIUS. *Roman History*. Loeb Classical Library. Translated by Earnest Cary. Cambridge, Mass.: Harvard University Press, 1927.

EUSEBIUS. *The History of the Church from Christ to Constantine*. Translated by G.A. Williamson. New York: Dorset Press, 1984.

JAMES, MONTAGUE RHODES, trans. *The Apocryphal New Testament*. Oxford: Clarendon Press, 1986.

JAY, PETER, ed. *The Greek Anthology and Other Ancient Epigrams*. Rev. ed. New York: Penguin Books, 1981.

JOSEPHUS. *Jewish Antiquities*. Loeb Classical Library. Translated by H.St.J. Thackeray and others. Cambridge, Mass.: Harvard University Press, 1930–65.

JOSEPHUS. *The Jewish War*. Loeb Classical Library. Translated by H.St.J. Thackeray. Cambridge, Mass.: Harvard University Press, 1927–28.

LAYTON, BENTLEY, trans. *The Gnostic Scriptures*. Garden City, N.Y.: Doubleday & Company, Inc., 1987.

MAGIE, DAVID, trans. *The Scriptores Historiae Augustae*. 3 vols. Loeb Classical Library. Cambridge, Mass.: Harvard University Press, 1979.

MCCLURE, M.L., and C.L. FELTOE, trans. *The Pilgrimage of Etheria*. New York: The Macmillan Co., 1919.

MEYER, MARVIN W., ed. *The Ancient Mysteries, a Sourcebook: Sacred Texts of the Mystery Religions of the Ancient Mediterranean World*. San Francisco: Harper & Row, Publishers, Inc., 1987.

MEYER, MARVIN W., trans. *The Secret Teachings of Jesus: Four Gnostic Gospels*. New York: Vintage Books, 1986.

MUNCK, JOHANNES, trans. The Anchor Bible, The Acts of the Apostles. Garden City, N.Y.: Doubleday & Co., Inc., 1967.

ORIGEN. *An Exhortation to Martyrdom . . . and Selected Works*. Translated by Rowan A. Greer. New York: Paulist Press, 1979.

PHILOSTRATUS. *The Life of Apollonius of Tyana*. 2 vols. Loeb Classical Library. Translated by F.C. Conybeare. Cambridge, Mass.: Harvard University Press, 1912.

PROCOPIUS. *The Secret History*. Translated by G.A. Williamson. Baltimore: Penguin Books Inc., 1966.

ROBINSON, J.M., ed. *The Nag Hammadi Library*. San Francisco: Harper & Row, Publishers, Inc., 1977.

STANIFORTH, MAXWELL, trans. *Early Christian Writings: The Apostolic Fathers*. Harmondsworth, England: Penguin Books Ltd., 1968.

STEVENSON, J., ed. *A New Eusebius: Documents Illustrative of the History of the Church to A.D. 337*. London: S.P.C.K., 1963.

SUETONIUS. *The Twelve Caesars*. Translated by Robert Graves. Baltimore: Penguin Books Inc., 1957.

SWANTON, MICHAEL, ed. *The Dream of the Rood*. New York: Barnes & Noble, 1970.

TACITUS. *The Annals of Imperial Rome*. Translated by Michael Grant. Baltimore: Penguin Books Inc., 1956.

TACITUS. *The Complete Works of Tacitus*. Translated by A.J. Church and W.J. Brodribb. New York: The Modern Library, 1942.

WARD, BENEDICTA, S.L.G., trans. *The Sayings of the Desert Fathers*. Kalamazoo, Mich.: Cistercian Publications Inc., 1975.

ART BOOKS

BANDINELLI, RANUCCIO BIANCHI. *Rome: The Late Empire, Roman Art A.D. 200–400*. Translated by Peter Green. New York: George Braziller, Inc., 1971.

CASSON, LIONEL. *The Barbarian Kings*. Chicago: Stonehenge Press Inc., 1982.

DELL'ORTO, LUISA FRANCHI. *Ancient Rome: Life and Art*. Florence: Scala Books, 1982.

THE EDITORS OF TIME-LIFE BOOKS. *Empires Ascendant: Time Frame 400 B.C.–A.D. 200*. Alexandria, Va.: Time-Life Books, 1987.

THE EDITORS OF TIME-LIFE BOOKS. *Empires Besieged: Time Frame A.D. 200–600*. Alexandria, Va.: Time-Life Books, 1988.

FORMAN, WERNER, ed. *Echoes of the Ancient World: Byzantium*. London: Orbis Publishing Limited, 1983.

FRAZER, MARGARET ENGLISH. *Age of Spirituality*. New York: The Metropolitan Museum of Art, 1977.

FRAZER, MARGARET ENGLISH. *Medieval Church Treasuries.* New York: The Metropolitan Museum of Art, 1986.

Gibbon's Decline and Fall of the Roman Empire. Greenwich, Conn.: Brompton Books Corp., 1979.

HADAS, MOSES, and THE EDITORS OF TIME-LIFE BOOKS. *Great Ages of Man: Imperial Rome.* New York: Time Inc., 1965.

Handbook of the Byzantine Collection. Washington D.C.: Dumbarton Oaks, Trustees for Harvard University, 1967.

HAYWARD, JANE, WALTER CAHN, and others. *Radiance and Reflection: Medieval Art from the Raymond Pitcairn Collection.* New York: The Metropolitan Museum of Art, 1982.

The Horizon History of Christianity. New York: American Heritage Publishing Co., Inc., 1964.

HUTTER, IRMGARD. *The Universe History of Art and Architecture: Early Christian and Byzantine.* New York: Universe Books, 1971.

LASSUS, JEAN. *Landmarks of the World's Art: The Early Christian and Byzantine World.* New York: McGraw-Hill Book Company, 1967.

LYTTELTON, MARGARET, and WERNER FORMAN. *The Romans: Their Gods and Their Beliefs.* London: Orbis Publishing Limited, 1984.

MAIURI, AMEDEO. *The Great Centuries of Painting: Roman Painting.* Geneva: Editions Albert Skira, 1953.

MANCINELLI, FABRIZIO. *Catacombs and Basilicas: The Early Christians in Rome.* Florence: Scala Books, 1981.

NORDENFALD, CARL. *Celtic and Anglo-Saxon Painting.* New York: George Braziller, Inc., 1977.

PAPAFAVA, FRANCESCO, ed.. *The Vatican.* Florence: Scala Books, 1984.

Ravenna Felix. 4th ed. Ravenna: A. Longo Editore, 1971.

RICE, DAVID TALBOT. *Art of the Byzantine Era.* New York: Frederick A. Praeger, Inc., Publishers, 1963.

RICE, DAVID TALBOT, ed. *The Dawn of European Civilization: The Dark Ages.* New York: McGraw-Hill Book Company, 1965.

SHERRARD, PHILIP, and THE EDITORS OF TIME-LIFE BOOKS. *Great Ages of Man: Byzantium.* New York: Time Inc., 1966.

Treasures of Early Irish Art. New York: The Metropolitan Museum of Art, 1977.

WEITZMANN, KURT. *Late Antique and Early Christian Book Illumination.* New York: George Braziller, Inc., 1977.

ACKNOWLEDGMENTS

The editors are grateful to the following individuals and organizations for their help in the preparation of this book.

Jessica Allan, Art Resource, New York
The Ancient Art and Architecture Collection
Lionel Casson
Deanna Cross, The Metropolitan Museum of Art
C.M. Dixon
Prof. Norman Doenges, Dartmouth College
Col. John R. Elting, U.S. Army (Ret.)
Werner Forman Archive
Madeline Grimoldi Archive
Ara Güler
Sonia Halliday Photographs
Robert Harding Picture Library
André Held
Michael Holford
Prof. Thomas F. Mathews, New York University
Zev Radovan
Prof. Gerald Sheppard, University of Toronto
Roger Wood

CREDITS

ART

Dan Brown 100–101, 237.
Joe LeMonnier 47, 128, 277.
Chris Magadini 12–13, 40, 72–73, 110–111, 284–285.
Walter Rane 61, 178–179.
Ray Skibinski 80, 206, 319.
Jeffrey Terrenson 34.
John Thompson 76–77, 144–145.
Richard Williams Cover, 42–43, 57, 114, 154–155, 242–243, 266.
Mary Wilshire 29, 33, 105, 121, 188–189, 210–211, 256.

Background textures in the art portfolio pages courtesy of Champion International Corp.

TEXT

Grateful acknowledgment is made for permission to excerpt featured material from the following works: ***Augsburg Fortress.*** *The Early Church* by W.H.C. Frend. Copyright © 1965, 1982, Fortress Press. ***Augsburg Fortress and Darton Longman & Todd Ltd.*** *The Rise of Christianity* by W.H.C. Frend. Copyright © 1984 by W.H.C. Frend. Used by permission. ***Baker Book House.*** *The Ecclesiastical History of Eusebius Pamphilus.* First printing, September 1955, Baker Book House. ***Penguin Books Ltd.*** *The Twelve Caesars* translated by Robert Graves. Copyright © 1957 by Robert Graves. Reprinted by permission of A P Watt Ltd. and The Trustees of the Robert Graves Copyright Trust. ***Random House, Inc.*** *The Secret Teachings of Jesus* by Marvin W. Meyer. Copyright © 1984 by Marvin W. Meyer. ***University of Texas Press.*** *Physiologus* translated by Michael J. Curley. Copyright © 1979 by the University of Texas Press. ***Westminster Press.*** *The Other Gospels: Non-Canonical Gospel Texts* edited by Ron Cameron. Copyright © 1982 by Ron Cameron.

PHOTOGRAPHS

Listed below in parentheses are the collections and/or museums where the art and artifacts are located.

2 & 3 Scala/Art Resource, N.Y. (Rome, St. Costanza). ***6*** Scala/Art Resource, N.Y. (Musei Vaticani, Rome/Museo Pio Cristiano). ***9*** *left* Scala/Art Resource, N.Y. (Museo Arcivescovile, Ravenna, Italy); *right* Scala/Art Resource, N.Y. (St. Apollinare Nuovo, Ravenna, Italy). ***15*** *top* Sonia Halliday Photographs; *bottom* Laura Lushington/Sonia Halliday Photographs (Israel Museum, Jerusalem). ***16*** *top* Zev Radovan; *bottom* The Ancient Art and Architecture Collection (Landesmuseum, Trier, Germany). ***17*** The Metropolitan Museum of Art, Rogers Fund, 63.206. ***18*** *left* Laura Lushington/Sonia Halliday Photographs (St. John's Church, Gouda, Netherlands); *right* Sonia Halliday Photographs. ***19*** Giraudon/Art Resource, N.Y. (Musée du Louvre, Paris). ***20*** *left* Scala/Art Resource, N.Y. (Galleria Sabauda, Turin); *right* The Pierpont Morgan Library, New York, M.97 f.20v. ***21*** *left* Scala/Art Resource, N.Y. (Biblioteca Laurenziana, Florence). ***22*** *top* David Darom; *bottom* Sonia Halliday Photographs (Langport Church, England). ***23*** Laura Lushington/Sonia Halliday Photographs. ***24*** The Metropolitan Museum of Art, The Cloisters Collection, Purchase, 1970.324.1. ***25*** Scala/Art Resource, N.Y. (Museo dell'Opera del Duomo, Siena). ***26*** Scala/Art Resource, N.Y. (Galleria dell'Accademia, Florence). ***31*** Scala/Art Resource, N.Y. (St. Angelo, Formis, Italy). ***32*** Scala/Art Resource, N.Y. (Museo Archeologico, Venice). ***33*** *right* Scala/Art Resource, N.Y. (Museo Ostiense, Ostia, Italy). ***35*** David Harris (Israel Museum, Jerusalem). ***36*** C.M. Dixon. ***37*** *left* Israel Department of Antiquities, Jerusalem; *right* Syndication International (Zemaljski Museum, Sarajevo, Yugoslavia). ***39*** Sonia Halliday Photographs (Norwich Cathedral, England). ***41*** The Granger Collection, New York. ***44*** Richard Nowitz. ***45*** Reproduced by permission of the British Library, Oriental Collection, Add.14761 f.19v. ***46*** Reproduced by permission of the British Library. ***47*** *bottom* Sonia Halliday Photographs (Archaeological Museum, Istanbul). ***48*** *right* Nikos Kontos (National Museum, Athens); *remainder* Michael Holford (British Museum, London). ***49*** The Ancient Art and Architecture Collection. ***50*** *top* Werner Forman Archive; *bottom* Gerry Clyde/Michael Holford. ***51*** Giraudon/Art Resource, N.Y. (Museo della Civiltà Romana, Rome). ***52*** The Ancient Art and Architecture Collection (Museo Nazionale, Naples). ***53*** Bodleian Library, Oxford, M. Con. Gr.110 f.106v. ***54*** *left* Zev Radovan; *right* V. Gilbert Beers. ***55*** Erich Lessing/Magnum (Victoria and Albert Museum, London). ***58*** Sonia Halliday Photographs (St. Apollinare Nuovo, Ravenna, Italy). ***59*** Bibliothèque Nationale, Paris, M. Lat.1 f.386v. ***62*** *top left* Art Resource, N.Y. (Museo Nazionale del Bargello, Florence); *top right* Sonia Halliday Photographs (St. Anselm's Chapel, Canterbury, England); *bottom* C.M. Dixon (British Museum, London). ***63*** *left* Scala/Art Resource, N.Y. (St. Mary del Carmine, Florence); *right* Laura Lushington/Sonia Halliday Photographs. ***64*** *top* Lee Boltin (Numismatic Department, National Museum of American History, Smithsonian Institution, Washington, D.C.); *bottom* Scala/Art Resource, N.Y. (Musei Vaticani, Rome). ***65*** The Metropolitan Museum of Art, Rogers Fund, 1903.03.14.13. ***66*** C.M. Dixon (Biblioteca Apostolica Vaticana, Rome). ***67*** *left* Werner Forman Archive; *right* C.M. Dixon (Victoria and Albert Museum, London). ***69*** Enrico Polidori/Madeline Grimoldi Archives (Galleria Nazionale, Genoa). ***70*** Alinari/Art Resource, N.Y. (Galleria degli Uffizi, Florence). ***71*** *top* Werner Forman Archive; *bottom* Scala/Art Resource, N.Y. ***73*** *top right* The Ancient Art and Architecture Collection. ***74*** David Harris. ***75*** C.M. Dixon (British Museum, London, Harley M.2788 f.716). ***78*** The Ancient Art and Architecture Collection (Archeological Museum, Athens). ***79*** Courtesy of the Freer Gallery of Art, Smithsonian Institution, Washington, D.C., Coptic painting 55.11. ***81*** John Rylands University Library of Manchester, England, Greek papyrus 457. ***82*** *left* The Ancient Art and Architecture Collection; *right* Landesmuseum für Kärnten, Klagenfurt, Austria/Photography by Ulrich P. Schwarz. ***85*** *left* Photograph courtesy of the Institute for Antiquity and Christianity, The Claremount Graduate School (Coptic Museum, Cairo); *right* The Brooklyn Museum, Museum Collection Fund, 05.14. ***87*** Giraudon/Art Resource, N.Y. (Musée Condé, Chantilly, France, M.65/1284 f.108v). ***88*** C.M. Dixon (Victoria and Albert Museum, London). ***89*** *top left* C.M. Dixon (Victoria and Albert Museum, London); *remainder* Sonia Halliday Photographs. ***90*** The Granger Collection, New York. ***91*** The Master and Fellows of Trinity College Cambridge, England, M.R.16.2 f.30v. ***92*** Scala/Art Resource, N.Y. (Musée du Louvre, Paris). ***93*** *left* Rainer Gaertner, DGPh (Römisch-Germanisches Museum, Cologne); *center* Michael Holford (British Museum, London); *right* Alinari/Art Resource, N.Y. (Musée d'Art et d'Histoire, Geneva). ***94*** *left* Dr. Maxwell L. Anderson; *right* C.M. Dixon. ***95*** O. Louis Mazzatenta © 1984 National Geographic Society. ***96*** Scala/Art Resource, N.Y. (St. Mark's, Venice). ***97*** C.M. Dixon (Bardo National Museum, Tunis, Tunisia). ***98*** Scala/Art Resource, N.Y. (Musei Vaticani, Rome). ***99*** André Held (Museo Nazionale, Naples). ***102*** Stefano Rissone/Madeline Grimoldi Archives (Museo Capitolino, Rome). ***103*** Scala/Art Resource, N.Y. (Museo Nazionale, Naples). ***106*** Scala/Art Resource, N.Y. (Catacomb of Vigna Massima, Rome). ***107*** Zev Radovan. ***108*** Giraudon/Art Resource, N.Y. (Musée des Tapisseries, Angers, France). ***109*** Zev Radovan. ***112*** Scala/Art Resource, N.Y. (Museo Nazionale, Naples). ***113*** *left* The Pierpont Morgan

Library, New York, M.462 f.2v.; *right* M. Mandel/Madeline Grimoldi Archives (Duomo, Como, Italy). ***117*** *left* Erich Lessing/Magnum (National Museum, Bucharest, Romania); *top right* (coins) Zev Radovan; *bottom right* F.H.C. Birch/Sonia Halliday Photographs. ***118*** *top* C.M. Dixon; *bottom* Michael Holford (British Museum, London). ***119*** F.H.C. Birch/Sonia Halliday Photographs. ***122*** *left* André Held (Musée Romain de Vidy, Lausanne, Switzerland); *right* Alinari/Art Resource, N.Y. (Musei Vaticani, Rome). ***123*** Scala/Art Resource, N.Y. (Museo Palatino, Rome). ***124*** *top left & right* Scala/Art Resource, N.Y. (Museo Nazionale, Naples); *bottom left & right* Erich Lessing/Magnum (Museo Nazionale, Naples). ***125*** *left* Scala/Art Resource, N.Y. (Museo Nazionale, Naples); *center* Scala/Art Resource, N.Y. (Antiquarium del Palatino, Rome); *top right* Scala/Art Resource, N.Y. (Museo de Santa Cruz, Toledo, Spain); *bottom right* The Corning Museum of Glass, Corning, New York. ***126*** Alinari/Art Resource, N.Y. (Arch of Constantine, Rome). ***127*** Erich Lessing/Magnum (Musée du Louvre, Paris). ***128*** *bottom* The Granger Collection, New York. ***130*** Roman Villa, Brading, Isle of Wight, England. ***131*** *left* The Bodleian Library, Oxford, M. Drower 8 (R); *right* Zev Radovan. ***132*** Institute for Antiquity and Christianity, Claremont, California (Coptic Museum, Cairo). ***133*** J.B. Segal. ***134*** The Metropolitan Museum of Art, The Cloisters Collection, 1957.57.126 detail. ***135*** *left* The Bodleian Library, Oxford, M. Douce 237 f.50r.; *right* The Bodleian Library, Oxford, M. Canon, Misc.476 f.50r. ***136*** *bottom* Egypt Exploration Society, London, Oxyrhynchus papyrus 1786. ***139*** *left* SEF/Art Resource, N.Y. (Museo Nazionale delle Terme, Rome); *right* Michael Holford (British Museum, London). ***140*** C.M. Dixon (Museo Nazionale, Naples). ***142*** *left* Peter Connolly; *right* C.M. Dixon (Museo di Archeologia Sacra e Profana, Rome). ***143*** Scala/Art Resource, N.Y. (Museo della Civiltà Romana, Rome). ***146 & 147*** Fred Anderegg (National Museum, Damascus, Syria). ***148*** *left* Antikenmuseum, Staatliche Museen Preussischer Kulturbesitz, Berlin/Photography by Jürgen Liepe; *right* Nimataliah/Art Resource, N.Y. (Museo Capitolino, Rome). ***149*** *left* Sonia Halliday Photographs; *right* Scala/Art Resource, N.Y. (Museo Capitolino, Rome). ***150*** Deutsches Archaologisches Institut, Rome. ***151*** *left* Scala/Art Resource, N.Y. (Antiquarium del Palatino, Rome); *right* Drawing by Jeanine Wine from "Ante Pacem," published by Mercer University Press. ***152*** Bibliothèque Nationale, Paris, M.01 Hebrew 418 f.198. ***156*** *left* Josephine Powell/Madeline Grimoldi Archives (Kabul Museum, Kabul, Afghanistan); *right* Sonia Halliday Photographs (Bibliothèque Nationale, Paris). ***157*** Sonia Halliday Photographs (Bibliothèque Nationale, Paris). ***158*** The Granger Collection, New York. ***159*** Burgerbibliothek Bern, Switzerland, Physiologus Cod.318 f.17r detail. ***161*** Alinari/Art Resource, N.Y. (Museo Lateranense, Rome). ***163*** *right* The Bettmann Archive; *remainder* C.M. Dixon (Bardo Museum, Tunis, Tunisia). ***164*** The Ancient Art and Architecture Collection. ***165*** *left* Sonia Halliday Photographs; *right* Werner Forman Archive (Museo Nazionale Romano, Rome). ***166*** Michael Holford (British Museum, London). ***167*** Museum für Indische Kunst, Berlin, Staatliche Museen Preussischer Kulturbesitz, Mik. III 6368. ***168*** *left* Sonia Halliday Photographs (Paphos District Museum, Paphos, Cyprus); *right* C.M. Dixon (Archaeological Museum, Sousse, Tunisia). ***169*** Michael Holford (British Museum, London). ***170*** *top* Kunsthistorisches Museum, Vienna; *bottom* Scala/Art Resource, N.Y. ***171*** Zev Radovan. ***172*** *top* Scala/Art Resource, N.Y. (Museo Teatrale alla Scala, Milan); *bottom* Roger Wood (Tripoli Museum, Tripoli, Libya). ***173*** *top left* Scala/Art Resource, N.Y.; *top right* Sonia Halliday Photographs; *bottom* Roger Wood (Tripoli Museum, Tripoli, Libya). ***174*** *top left* Werner Forman Archive (J. Paul Getty Museum, Malibu, California); *top center* © Brian Brake/Photo Researchers (Bardo Museum, Tunis, Tunisia); *top right* Giraudon/Art Resource, N.Y. (Museo Nazionale, Naples); *bottom left* Scala/Art Resource, N.Y. (Palazzo Vecchio, Florence); *bottom right* Giraudon/Art Resource, N.Y. (Museo della Civiltà Romana, Rome). ***175*** *top* © Berenholtz/The Stock Market; *bottom* Scala/Art Resource, N.Y. (Museo dei Conservatori, Rome). ***176*** *top left* The Ancient Art and Architecture Collection; *lower left* Sonia Halliday Photographs; *right* Roger Wood. ***177*** The Ancient Art and Architecture Collection. ***180*** Scala/Art Resource, N.Y. (Pinacoteca Nazionale di Siena, Siena). ***181*** Giraudon/Art Resource, N.Y. (Musée d'Unterlinden, Colmar, France). ***182*** Scala/Art Resource, N.Y. (Galleria degli Uffizi, Florence). ***183*** Sonia Halliday Photographs. ***184*** Giraudon/Art Resource, N.Y. (La Collégiale Church, Ecouis, France). ***185*** Richard Nowitz. ***186*** *left* Sonia Halliday Photographs (Qallat Seman, Syria); *right* Réunion des Musées Nationaux (Musée du Louvre, Paris). ***190*** Aargauische Denkmalpflege, Aargau (Klosterkirche Königsfelden, Switzerland). ***191*** Erich Lessing/Magnum. ***192*** The Ancient Art and Architecture Collection. ***193*** Alinari/Art Resource, N.Y. (Museo Nazionale Romano, Rome). ***194*** *top* C.M. Dixon (Archaelological Museum, Istanbul); *bottom* Gian Berto Vanni/Art Resource, N.Y. ***195*** Michael Holford. ***196*** *left* Walters Art Gallery, Baltimore, Armenian M. W.537 f.114v; *right* John Rylands University Library, Manchester, England, Armenian M.10 f.258r. ***197*** Ara Güler. ***198*** Michael Holford (Museum of Antiquities of the University, Newcastle on Tyne, England). ***199*** Deutsches Archaologisches Institut, Rome/Madeline Grimoldi Archives. ***201*** Stefano Rissone/Madeline Grimoldi Archives. ***202*** *all* Scala/Art Resource, N.Y. ***203*** *top* André Held/Sonia Halliday Photographs; *bottom* Scala/Art Resource, N.Y. ***204*** André Held/Sonia Halliday Photographs (Cemetery of St. Paul and St. Marcellius, Rome). ***208*** *top* Sonia Halliday Photographs (Bibliothèque Nationale, Paris); *bottom* Simone Branzi/Madeline Grimoldi Archives. ***209*** C.M. Dixon (Musei Vaticani, Rome). ***212*** Sonia Halliday Photographs (Church of the Holy Cross, Platanistasa, Cyprus). ***213*** *left* Robert Harding Picture Library; *right* Sonia Halliday Photographs. ***214*** Robert Harding Picture Library. ***215*** *left* André Held (Hameaux de Boscéaz, Orbe, Switzerland); *right* André Held/Sonia Halliday Photographs. ***216*** Bibliothèque Nationale, Paris, M. GR.510 f.367v. ***217 & 218*** Ara Güler. ***219*** Sonia Halliday Photographs. ***220*** The Pierpont Morgan Library, N.Y., M.828 7v. ***224*** *left* Sonia Halliday Photographs (Bibliothèque Nationale, Paris, Codex Coislin, f.387); *right* The Pierpont Morgan Library, N.Y., M.945 77v. ***227*** *left* By permission of the British Library, Add. M.511 f.11, The Canon Tables; *right* The Bettmann Archive. ***228*** *left* Werner Forman Archive/Prof. Elbern's Collection, Berlin; *middle* Madeline Grimoldi Archives/P.C.A.S. (Catacomb of Domitilla, Rome); *top right* Scala/Art Resource, N.Y. (Catacomb of Pamphilus, Rome). ***228–229*** *bottom* The Metropolitan Museum of Art, Rogers Fund, 1924, 24.240. ***229*** *top* Michael Holford. ***230*** *top left* Scala/Art Resource, N.Y.; *bottom left* The Ancient Art and Architecture Collection; *bottom middle* Werner Forman Archive (British Museum, London); *top right* Zev Radovan; *bottom right* C.M. Dixon (Coptic Museum, Cairo). ***231*** *top* Scala/Art Resource, N.Y. (St. Sabina, Rome); *bottom left* The Ancient Art and Architecture Collection; *bottom right* The Corning Museum of Glass, Corning, New York. ***232*** The Granger Collection, New York. ***233*** *left* Giraudon/Art Resource, N.Y. (Museo Cristiano, Brescia, Italy); *right* Reproduced by courtesy of the Trustees of the British Museum. ***234*** Ara Güler. ***235*** *left* Scala/Art Resource, New York (Basilica di San Pietro Tesoro, Vatican, Rome); *right* The Metropolitan Museum of Art, Gift of J. Pierpont Morgan, 1917, 17.190.715 Lid. ***238*** *left* Werner Braun; *top right* Library of Congress, LC-M361-

1022; *bottom right* Angelo Hornak (British Museum, London). ***241*** Bibliothèque Nationale, Paris, M. GR.510 f.409v. ***244*** *left* The Ancient Art and Architecture Collection; *right* Alinari/Art Resource, N.Y. (Villa Albani, Rome). ***245*** André Held (Musée Cantonal d'Archéologie et d'Histoire, Lausanne, Switzerland). ***246*** Scala/Art Resource, N.Y. (Colección de la Real Académia de la Historia, Madrid). ***247*** Bibliothèque Nationale, Paris. ***248*** *top & lower left* Sonia Halliday Photographs (Eski Gumus Monastery, Cappadocia, Turkey); *right* Bibliothèque Nationale, Paris, M. GR.510 f.452. ***249*** Courtesy of The Byzantine Collection © 1990 Dumbarton Oaks, Trustees of Harvard University, Washington, D.C., D.O.47.24. ***250*** The Granger Collection, New York. ***251*** Malcolm S. Kirk/Peter Arnold, Inc. ***252*** Archivo Oronoz (El Escorial, Spain, Conciliar Codex of Albelda f.142r). ***253*** André Held (Museo de Arte de Cataluña, Barcelona). ***255*** C.M. Dixon. ***258*** Sonia Halliday Photographs. ***259*** Sonia Halliday Photographs (Church of St. Sozomenus, Galata, Cyprus). ***260*** *left* The Metropolitan Museum of Art, The Cloisters Collection, 1947, 47.101.11/Photography by Malcolm Varon; *right* The Cleveland Museum of Art, Purchase, Leonard C. Hanna Jr. Bequest, 67.144. ***261*** Römisch Germanisches Museum, Cologne. ***262*** Hirmer Fotoarchiv. ***263*** By permission of the British Library, Add. 10049 f.64v. ***264*** Robert Harding Picture Library. ***265*** *left* Scala/Art Resource, N.Y. (St. Ambrogio, Milan); *right* Scala/Art Resource, N.Y. ***267*** Scala/Art Resource, N.Y. (La Cava Bible, f.220v). ***268*** The Granger Collection, New York. ***269*** C.M. Dixon (Bardo National Museum, Tunis, Tunisia). ***270*** André Held (St. Agostino, Gubbio, Italy). ***272*** Simone Branzi/Madeline Grimoldi Archives (Museo Nazionale Romano, Rome). ***273*** *top* Erich Lessing/Magnum (Magyar Nemzeti Museum, Budapest); *bottom* The Ancient Art and Architecture Collection. ***275*** Michael Holford (British Museum, London). ***278*** *left* Alinari/Art Resource, N.Y.; *right* Universitetsbiblioteket, Uppsala Universitet, Codex Argenteus, f.30r Mark 4:21-28. ***279*** The Ancient Art and Architecture Collection; ***280*** *top left & top right* Michael Holford (British Museum, London); *middle left* Walters Art Gallery, Baltimore; *bottom left* Faillet/Artephot (Musée Antiquités Historiques, Paris); *bottom center* Art Resource, N.Y. (Musée du Louvre, Paris); *bottom right* Courtesy of the Trustees of the British Museum. ***281*** *top left* SEF/Art Resource, N.Y. (Museo del Duomo di Monza, Monza, Italy); *top right* Courtesy of the Trustees of the British Museum; *center* Courtesy of The Byzantine Collection © 1990 Dumbarton Oaks, Trustees of Harvard University, Washington, D.C.; *bottom left* Lee Boltin (National Museum of Ireland, Dublin); *bottom right* Scala/Art Resource, N.Y. (Museo del Duomo di Monza, Monza, Italy). ***282*** *top left* Pierre Belzeaux/Rapho (Badisches Landesmuseum, Karlsruhe, Germany); *top right* Giraudon/Art Resource, N.Y.; *bottom left & middle right* Erich Lessing/Magnum (National Museum, Copenhagen); *bottom right* Art Resource, N.Y. (Museo Lazaro Galdiano, Madrid). ***283*** *left* Courtesy of the Trustees of the British Museum; *top middle* Michael Holford (British Museum, London); *top right* Giraudon/Art Resource, N.Y. (Musée des Beaux-Arts, Troyes, France); *bottom* Scala/Art Resource, N.Y. (Museo Nazionale del Bargello, Florence). ***286*** Ara Güler. ***287*** Sonia Halliday Photographs. ***288*** André Held. ***289*** Scala/Art Resource, N.Y. ***290*** Michael Holford (British Museum, London). ***291*** C.M. Dixon. ***292*** Victoria and Albert Museum, London/Art Resource, N.Y. ***293*** Borromeo/Art Resource, N.Y. (Coptic Museum, Cairo). ***295*** Archivo Fotografico Oronozo (El Escorial, Spain). ***296*** *left* Madeline Grimoldi Archives (Biblioteca Vaticana, Rome, Cod. Vat. Lat. 1202); *right* F.H.C. Birch/Sonia Halliday Photographs. ***298*** *top left* Courtesy of The Byzantine Collection © 1990 Dumbarton Oaks, Trustees of Harvard University, Washington, D.C., D.O. 24.5; *bottom left* The Metropolitan Museum of Art, The Cloisters Collection, Purchase, 1950; *right* Hirmer Fotoarchiv (Musei Vaticani, Rome). ***299*** *top left* Scala/Art Resource, N.Y. (Musei Civico Cristiano, Brescia, Italy); *bottom left* Antikenmuseum, Staatliche Museen Preussicher Kulturbesitz, Berlin/Photo by Ingrid Geske-Heiden; *top right* Courtesy of The Byzantine Collection © 1990 Dumbarton Oaks, Trustees of Harvard University, Washington, D.C., D.O. 63.36.9-10; *bottom right* Giraudon/Art Resource, New York. (Musée du Louvre, Paris). ***301*** Madeline Grimoldi Archives (Biblioteca Vaticana, Rome; Cod. Vat. Gr. 699, f.43r). ***302*** *left* Lee Boltin; *right* C.M. Dixon. ***303*** Universitätsbibliothek Heidelberg, Cod. Pal. Germ. 60, f. 179v. ***304*** *left* Rheinisches Landesmuseum Bonn; *right* Bibliothèque Nationale, Paris. ***306*** The Pierpont Morgan Library, New York, M.736-7. ***307*** The Ancient Art and Architecture Collection. ***308*** *top* C.M. Dixon (British Museum, London); *bottom* Michael Holford (British Museum, London). ***309*** *left* Michael Holford; *right* The Ancient Art and Architecture Collection. ***310*** The Granger Collection, New York. ***311*** C.M. Dixon. ***312*** Giraudon/Art Resource, N.Y. ***313*** Kunsthistorisches Museum, Vienna. ***314*** *left* Simon Branzi/Madeline Grimoldi Archives (Museo Nazionale Romano, Rome); *right* Scala/Art Resource, N.Y. ***316–317*** Giraudon/Art Resource, N.Y. (Musée Condé, Chantilly, France). ***320*** Werner Forman Archives/Mrs. Bashir Mohamed Collection. ***321*** The Granger Collection, New York. ***322*** *left* The Granger Collection, New York; *right* The Bridgeman Art Library. ***323*** The Bridgeman Art Library. ***324*** *left* The Bridgeman Art Library; *right* Michael Holford. ***325*** *left* The Bridgeman Art Library; *right* The Granger Collection, New York.

Efforts have been made to reach the holder of the copyright for each picture. In several cases these have been untraceable, for which we offer our apologies.

INDEX

Page numbers in **bold** *type refer to captions.*

D

E

F

K

L

M

N

Q

R

S

T

U

V

W

Y

Z